Clipper® Developer's Library

The Lance A. Leventhal

Microtrend® Series

Lance A. Leventhal, Ph.D., Series Editor

Clipper Developer's Library

James Occhiogrosso

Microtrend® Books

Copyright © 1992 James Occhiogrosso

All rights reserved. No part of this book may be reproduced or transmitted in any form or by any means, electronic or mechanical, including photocopying, recording or by any information storage and retrieval system without written permission from the copyright holder, except for the inclusion of brief quotes in a review.

Library of Congress Cataloging-in-Publication Data
James Occhiogrosso
Clipper Developer's Library, 2nd Edition
p. cm. – (The Lance A. Leventhal Microtrend™ series)
ISBN 0-915391-69-4 (pbk.) : $44.95
1. Clipper (Computer programming language)   I. Title.   II. Series.
QA76.73.C23028   1991
0075'65 – dc20   90-28917
CIP

Library of Congress Card Catalog Number: 90-28917

Microtrend™ Books
Slawson Communications, Inc.
165 Vallecitos de Oro
San Marcos, CA 92069

Edited by Lance A. Leventhal, Ph.D., San Marcos, CA
Front cover design by John Odam Design Associates
Produced by Bill McLaughlin, Slawson Communications

Printed in the United States
1   2   3   4   5   6   7   8   9   10

Table of Contents

List of Demonstration Programs, Databases, & Miscellaneous Files xi

Foreword xiii

Preface xv

Acknowledgments xvii

About the Series Editor xix

About the Author xx

Introduction xxi

Technical Support xxviii

ADDRECORD	Recycles a record previously deleted by DELRECORD . . .	1
AEDBAR	Provides a single line Quit, Add, Edit, Find, Delete menu bar with a message window	7
AEDMSG	Displays a message in the add, edit, delete (AEDBAR) message window	21
ALLTRUE	Always returns a logic true value	27
ARREAD	Reads a text file into an array	31
ARRESTORE	Restores a one-dimensional array from a disk file created by ARSAVE	35
ARSAVE	Saves a one-dimensional array in a disk file	39
ARTYPE	Tests a one-dimensional array to see if all elements are of a specified type	43
ARVIEW	Development utility for viewing an array	47

ARWRITE	Saves an array in a text file	51
BACKCHAR	Fills a screen area with a background character	55
CAPFIRST	Capitalizes the first letter of each word in a string	59
CENTERON	Displays a centered one-line message in a selected color	65
CHKKEY	Locates key data in another file and optionally displays or processes it	69
CHKSTATE	Verifies two-letter state code abbreviations	75
CHKZIP	Verifies first five characters of U.S. Zip Codes to match standard two-letter state abbreviations	79
CLRSHADOW	Removes a shadow placed on the screen by SHADOW . .	87
CLRVARS	Clears the set of field variables created by the INITVARS function	91
COMPUTE	Displays the result of a computation	95
CSRINSERT	Controls cursor size during data entry	101
DAYNUM	Determines day number from start of year (day 1 is January 1st)	105
DBNAMES	Extracts database file names and associated text descriptions from a data dictionary	109
DBVIEW	Provides operator messages and simple database views using DBEDIT	115
DECODE	Restores a character string previously encoded by ENCODE to its original value	121
DEFDRIVE	Determines the default DOS disk drive	123
DELRECORD	Deletes a record and marks it for recycling	127
DEVELOP	Initializes and links library functions used for application development	131
DIAL	Dials a telephone number	133
DIALCLR	Disconnects modem from communications port	143
DISKSIZE	Determines formatted capacity of specified disk	145

Clipper Developer's Library

DISKTEST	Tests a disk drive	151
DONEBEEP	Produces a two-tone sound generally used to indicate that an operation is complete	155
DTOF	Determines first day of month	159
DTOL	Determines last day of month	163
ENCODE	Converts a character string to an unreadable form for security purposes	167
EQUVARS	Loads memory variables created by INITVARS from the current database record	171
ERRORBEEP	Produces a slightly unpleasant short error tone	175
FILEDATE	Gets or sets the date on a DOS file	179
FILESIZE	Determines the size of a file in bytes	185
FILETIME	Gets or sets the time on a DOS file	189
FILETOUCH	Updates the date/time stamp of a file to the system date and time	195
FREADLINE	Reads successive lines from a text file	199
FREEVARS	Releases public field variables	203
FULLKEY	Determines ASCII value and scan code for any key	207
GETINT24	Returns the error code stored by the Developer's Library internal INT24 handler	211
GRAPHCHAR	Provides popup graphics symbols for entry as data from the numeric keypad	215
GRID	Displays a calibrated ruler grid	227
HRULER	Displays a horizontal ruler line	231
INITGLOBAL	Creates a set of global memory variables for an application	235
INITVARS	Creates a set of public memory variables corresponding to fields in the currently selected database	239

ISLASTDAY	Determines if the passed date is the last day of the month	243
ISMEMO	Determines whether a database contains memo fields	247
KEYCODE	Development function used to view the scan code and ASCII value of a key	251
LASTDAY	Determines the last day of a month	255
LASTDRIVE	Determines the highest lettered valid DOS disk drive	259
MAKEDBF	Creates or recreates application database files from the definitions in a data dictionary text file	263
MAKEID	Creates a unique alphanumeric identification (ID) code from a string	279
MAKENDX	Creates or recreates application index files from the definitions in a data dictionary text file	285
MEMOCTRL	Generic control function for MEMOEDIT and MEMOVIEW	295
MEMOFIND	Finds text in a memo field	303
MEMOGET	Controls data entered in a memo area using a one-character trigger variable	309
MEMOPACK	Removes unused memo data from a DBT file	315
MEMOVIEW	Generic function for viewing and editing memos	321
NDXCOUNT	Counts active index files associated with a database	327
NDXKEY	Reads the key expression of an index file	331
NDXVIEW	Displays key expressions of indexes	335
NODUPL	Tests for duplicate key field entry	341
OPCONFIRM	Waits for an operator response consisting of a single Y/N or y/n character	347
PARSE	Extracts a word delimited by spaces from a character string	351
PASSWORD	Gets a string and compares it to an encoded password	355
PAUSE	Pauses unconditionally for a specified length of time	361

Clipper Developer's Library

PICKIT	Displays and allows selection of elements from an array	365
PRNCHECK	Tests the printer; displays a message and waits if it is not ready	371
PRNTDATE	Converts a date value to a printable string	375
PRNTTIME	Converts a time string from 24-hour format to 12-hour format	379
READABORT	Displays a message and waits for operator confirmation before aborting a READ operation	383
READTEXT	Displays text files of any size	387
REPLVARS	Replaces database fields in the current record with values from public field variables	395
REQDDATA	Warns the operator with a tone and a message if a required entry is left blank	399
RESTGETS	Restores last set of GETs saved on internal stack by SAVEGETS	403
SAVEGETS	Saves currently active GETs on an internal stack	405
SCANKEY	Determines the ASCII value and scan code for any key	411
SCRNATTR	Gets or sets screen attributes at passed coordinates	415
SCRNCLR	Clears the screen stack used by the Developer's Library screen functions	421
SCRNLOAD	Loads screens onto the Developer's Library screen stack from a disk file	427
SCRNPOP	Restores a screen and removes it from the Developer's Library screen stack	431
SCRNPUSH	Pushes a screen onto the Developer's Library screen stack	435
SCRNREST	Restores a screen to its previous position	439
SCRNSAVE	Saves a screen area and its coordinates in a memory variable	443

SCRNWRIT	Saves the Developer's Library screen stack in a disk file	447
SELVALUE	Permits entry of low and high data selection values and indexes before running a report. Creates a temporary database containing only records matching operator selections.	451
SETINT24	Sets or resets the Developer's Library critical interrupt handler (INT24)	467
SHADOW	Displays a shadow below and to the right of a specified screen area	473
SIGNON	Displays an imploding/exploding application sign-on screen	477
STATENAME	Determines a state name from a standard two-letter abbreviation	481
STREXPAND	Expands a string with spaces	485
SWAPCOLOR	Reverses standard and enhanced colors in a color string	489
SYSHELP	Displays help and other messages from a database	493
SYSSAVE	Backs up or restores data files from Clipper	503
SYSVERSION	Determines if an application has changed by comparing its date and time to a stored value	527
TEMPFILE	Creates a unique temporary file on the selected disk drive	533
VRULER	Displays a vertical ruler line	537
Appendix A	Introduction to Library Concepts	541
Appendix B	Customizing the Developer's Library	548
Appendix C	File and Function Tables	565
Bibliography		575
Trademarks		576
Index by General Category		577
Index by Keyword		583

List of Demonstration Programs, Databases, and Miscellaneous Files

CUSTOMER.DBF 71	T_DISKS.PRG 152
DEVELOP.MAC 555	T_FILES.PRG 186
DEVELOP.RMK 558	T_GETS.PRG 408
DL_KEYS.CH 561	T_MAKEND.PRG 288
ITFILE.DBF 454	T_MMOFND.PRG 305
MAKELIB.BAT 562	T_MMOGET.PRG 311
ORDERS.DBF 71	T_SCRNS.PRG 422
T_AEDBAR.PRG 9	T_SELVAL.PRG 455
T_CHKKEY.PRG 71	T_SYSSAV.PRG 509
T_COMPUT.PRG 97	TESTDICT.DAT 267
T_DBVIEW.PRG 117	ZIPS.DBF 82
T_DIAL.PRG 135	

Foreword

Readers of this book probably belong to one of the following categories:

- Those who use Clipper but do not use any libraries

- Those who use external libraries without source code

- Those who have their own libraries

- Those who thought it was about shipbuilding and are wondering if they can still get a refund

Regardless of where you fit (except for the last category), this book is a treasure chest. Jim Occhiogrosso's expertise in writing Clipper and assembly language functions comes from years of supporting applications in the field. His Developer's Library will save you many hours of programming time.

Even after you have been using the book for a while, I recommend you look through it every few months. Chances are that you will suddenly discover another function you need or a programming technique you never considered.

A unique feature of the book is that it includes source code for the functions as well as the tools needed to regenerate the library.

Appendix A explains the basic concepts of library theory and management. Appendix B provides clear, concise instructions for recreating the library. You thus have everything you need to modify functions or add your own.

Among my primary responsibilities at Dean Witter, the Wall Street firm I work for, is to maintain and improve in-house library functions. I have seen first hand how a well-designed library raises the quality of our work and speeds software development. I cannot imagine being without one.

This book shows the kind of functions that are most valuable in a library. Jim Occhiogrosso's functions are useful, modular, well structured, and well documented. You can use them as examples for writing your own library routines.

Take the time to read the introduction and the appendixes. You will then be ready to start taking advantage of the flexibility and power a well-developed library offers. You won't look back.

Frank Imburgio
Dean Witter, New York City
November 1990

Preface

Background

With the introduction of the Clipper dBASE compiler in 1985, PC database programming took a new direction. Serious developers started using Clipper to make dBASE applications run much faster.

As the number of Clipper developers increased, add-on libraries began appearing. They provided programmers with pre-written and pre-tested User Defined Functions (UDF's).

Clipper's current success is the result of its unique combination of powerful development features, along with the availability of sophisticated add-on products.

Contents of this Book

This book provides an extensive library of general purpose UDF's. Detailed instructions, along with commented source code and typical examples, help you use it immediately.

The library consists of functions drawn from working Clipper applications. The introduction shows how to link it to your own programs.

Where possible, library functions are written entirely in Clipper. Assembly language is used for ones that require low-level features not otherwise accessible. You will need Microsoft's Macro Assembler (MASM) or Borland's Turbo Assembler to modify assembly language functions.

All library functions are based on Clipper Version 5. Users of the Summer '87 version must modify them to eliminate Version 5 specific features.

The library contains complete source code for each function along with a standardized description. Demonstration programs and coding examples are included for more complex functions. Many examples come from actual applications. Together with the source code, they also illustrate programming techniques.

Organization of the Book

The library is arranged alphabetically by function name. Each description is followed by coding examples and source code.

The book has three appendixes. Appendix A introduces library concepts and management. If this is your first exposure to library use with Clipper, it will help you understand the basic concepts.

For more advanced users who want to add new functions or customize existing ones, Appendix B provides instructions and source files for regenerating the library.

Finally, Appendix C is a complete cross reference of the library. It contains a list of functions and associated file names along with cross-dependency information.

Who the Book Is For

This book is for the Clipper user at any level. It assumes a basic familiarity with the dBASE language and the Clipper compiler. It does not assume an extensive programming or computer science background. The standard documentation, examples, and source programs help explain the library.

How will you, the reader, benefit from the book? It provides beginners with functions needed for a wide variety of applications. The examples in each function description make it easy to incorporate them into your programs.

Advanced users can employ the Developer's Library to supplement another library, or combine it with their own functions to form a custom library. In either case, they can take advantage of many functions immediately. This, of course, will save a tremendous amount of time.

The book is also intended as a programming reference. It has explanations and instructions throughout, and extensive comments in the source code. For ease of understanding, all functions use modular and structured techniques. The library thus serves as a source of examples for learning programming or improving skills.

Support, Source Disks, and Comments

I have tested all functions with Clipper Version 5. However, no testing is perfect, and we may have introduced errors during production. The publisher and I welcome your comments. A form is at the end of the book. If you think you have found a bug in a function, contact me directly (see the support information). Please include a complete description of the problem.

Installation instructions and source code are on the accompanying disk. See the READ.ME file.

I hope you will find the Developer's Library to be a good learning tool as well as a source of functions for application development. I also hope you will find the challenge of using it effectively to be as absorbing as I found the task of creating it.

So then, may Clipper be for you, as in Carryl's poem,

>A capital ship for an ocean trip...
>No gale that blew dismayed her crew, ...
>or troubled the captain's mind.

James Occhiogrosso
Holbrook, NY

Acknowledgments

It is difficult to determine how much effort a book like this will require until it is finished. Had I been aware of how long it would take when I started, I might have given up right then.

Finally, though, it is complete and I am looking forward to the next one. I guess writing is addictive.

Several people deserve thanks for their help, patience, and ideas.

Lance Leventhal, the Series Editor, was instrumental in convincing me to write the Developer's Library. His patience and humorous editing transformed me from someone who thought he could write into a writer. At the onset of the project, I told him I had a "thick skin." He responded, "Good! you'll need it!" It did not take long before I realized how right he was!

Thanks to Bill McLaughlin, the Production Editor, who unformatted the files and coolly ignored my constant stream of changes, letting out only occasional screams and whimpers. Joanne Roth did the revisions for the Second Edition.

Thanks to Ron Tucker and all the others at Slawson Communications who helped keep the project on track in spite of the obstacles.

And last, but certainly not least, thanks to my wife Gerry for her patience, ideas, and unending confidence in me. Without her support and encouragement, I would never have finished this project.

About the Series Editor

Lance A. Leventhal is the author of 25 books, including *80386 Programming Guide, 68000 Assembly Language Programming, Turbo C Quickstart,* and *Microcomputer Experimentation with the IBM PC*. His books have sold over 1,000,000 copies and have been translated into many foreign languages. He has also helped develop microprocessor-based systems and has been a consultant for Disney, Intel, NASA, NCR, and Rockwell.

Dr. Leventhal served as Series Editor on Personal Computing for Prentice-Hall and as Technical Editor for the Society for Computer Simulation. He has lectured on microprocessors and C programming throughout the United States for IEEE, IEEE Computer Society, and other groups.

Dr. Leventhal's background includes affiliations with Linkabit Corporation, Intelcom Rad Tech, Naval Electronics Laboratory Center, and Harry Diamond Laboratories. He received a B.A. degree from Washington University (St. Louis, Missouri) and M.S. and Ph.D degrees from the University of California, San Diego. He is a member of AAAI, ACM, ASEE, IEEE, IEEE Computer Society, and SCS.

About the Author

James Occhiogrosso has been an independent consultant for over 20 years. He specializes in teaching Clipper programming and writing custom software in Clipper. He is the author of several commercial software and programmer productivity products.

As the coordinator of the Suffolk County Clipper Users Group, he regularly contributes articles to its newsletter. He has also written features for national magazines. He received an AAS degree from New York City College in Electrical Engineering and studied Physics at Dowling College (Oakdale, NY).

His fascination with computers and software started many years ago, while writing programs in machine language for a minicomputer with 8K of memory. It has continued ever since!

Mr. Occhiogrosso has many interests besides computers. He is an avid racquetball player, an active scuba diver, and an accomplished musician.

Introduction

The Developer's Library provides reliable general-purpose functions for Clipper developers.

The functions are forgiving. Most validate parameters before acting and return without doing anything if passed incorrect information. Although a run-time error may occur if a function is used improperly, at least you will not have to reboot.

To link the library with your application, specify its name in your link command along with the Clipper library and any others you are using. The result is to link only the functions actually used in your application. Refer to your linker manual for more information on external libraries.

Appendix A contains a complete discussion of library concepts. If you are using a library for the first time, or are unfamiliar with library use, I recommend you read it before continuing.

Programming Conventions

The Developer's Library uses conventions and syntax similar to the Clipper manual. The following summarizes them:

- Clipper commands and functions are all uppercase.
- Developer's Library functions are all uppercase.
- Variables are all lowercase.
- Field names are prefixed with an alias name (i.e., aliasname–> fieldname).
- User defined file names are all lowercase.
- External DOS, Clipper, and library files are all uppercase.

The following symbol definitions indicate the types of user-supplied parameters:

<cName>	Character parameter
<nName>	Numeric parameter
<lName>	Logical parameter
<aName>	Array parameter
<bName>	Code block parameter
[ ]	Optional elements
/	Either element may be used (but not both)

Repeating or continuing elements in example code are indicated by a series of horizontal or vertical dots.

All library programs are coded as functions rather than procedures. This allows a standardized calling convention. Throughout the book, I refer to library units synonymously as functions or procedures. Functions that do not need to return anything (that is, they could have been coded as procedures) return NIL.

Also, throughout the book, values passed to functions are referred to synonymously as arguments or parameters. Both terms are in common use.

If you are unfamiliar with parameter passing or the difference between functions and procedures, detailed discussions appear in Rick Spence's *Clipper Programming Guide*, 2nd ed. (San Marcos, CA: Microtrend Books, 1991).

Using the Developer's Library Disk

The companion disk contains all files needed to use or modify the library. The files are in compressed form. Print and read the READ.ME file. It contains installation instructions and last minute information that is not in the book. READ.ME is paginated for printing directly with:

```
TYPE A:READ.ME > PRN or PRINT A:READ.ME
```

If you are using the library as is, DEVELOP.LIB and ZIPS.DBF are the only files you will need.

To modify functions or add to the library, you must install the other files. Follow the instructions in READ.ME. Source code is included for all functions and test programs. In addition, special files are provided to automate the process of regenerating the library.

Appendix C contains a complete cross-reference of the library and lists the files on the disk. If you intend to change the library, you should also read Appendix B. It contains the detailed information you will need to update and recreate the library.

Test and Demonstration Programs

Several sample programs come with the library. You can use them to understand how functions work or to test modifications. Each illustrates the use of library functions.

All test program names begin with "T_", followed by the first six characters of the name of the main function they demonstrate. For example, T_PICKIT.PRG contains a demonstration program for the PICKIT function. If a group of functions is involved, the name reflects its overall purpose. T_SCRNS.PRG, for example, illustrates several screen functions. To use a demonstration program, compile and link it with DEVELOP.LIB.

Linking the Library to Your Application

You can link functions from the Developer's Library to your application in the same way as any other library. Any function explicitly used in your program is linked automatically. Ones that depend on others for their operation will automatically link all required dependents.

The file DEVELOP.LIB must be present when you try to link. It contains the object code for all functions in the Developer's Library and is the only file needed to link them to your application.

The Developer's Library does not contain any functions that replace or redefine elements of Clipper libraries. To link the library, add DEVELOP.LIB to your link line as shown below.

For example, suppose your previous link line was

```
RTLINK FI yourapp
```

Your new link line should be

```
RTLINK FI yourapp LIB DEVELOP
```

If you are not using RTLINK, see the instructions provided with your linker for third-party libraries. The Developer's Library functions can be used with prelinked libraries (RTLINK PLLs) in the same way as Clipper functions.

Libraries other than ones provided with Clipper may have naming conflicts with functions in the Developer's Library. If so, the linker will list them when you link your application. An EXE file will still be created, and the function used will be the one from the library that appears first. To use the function from the Developer's Library, place DEVELOP ahead of the other library's name.

Using the Library

To use a function from the Developer's Library, simply call it in your program as indicated by its instructions. All functions used in this way are linked to your application.

Several library functions use the screen display. The INITGLOBAL function defines ten global color variables and a global message for them. The following functions depend on it:

AEDBAR	AEDMSG	CENTERON	CHKKEY
DBVIEW	GRAPHCHAR	GRID	HRULER
MEMOCTRL	MEMOVIEW	PICKIT	SELVALUE
SIGNON	SYSHELP	SYSSAVE	VRULER

Before using any of them, you must call INITGLOBAL or a run-time error may occur. To do this, put the line

```
INITGLOBAL( )
```

near the top of your main program file. See INITGLOBAL's description and source code for more information. Except for the global variables defined there, library functions assume default values for undefined variables.

Some library functions are development aids. Link them only during development, using the DEVELOP function to simplify the process. It automatically links all development functions and assigns hot keys to them. You can put it inside a preprocessor conditional block so the functions are linked only when needed. See DEVELOP for more information.

Except for the SELVALUE function, the Library does not use the READ command. This avoids conflicts with active GETs in your application.

SELVALUE uses READ to get a series of operator selections. Since it is designed to be called before a report, it assumes that no GETs are active and does not save or restore them. If your application has active GETs when it calls SELVALUE, use SAVEGETS and RESTGETS before and afterward. See the description of SELVALUE for more information.

The Developer's Library provides a rich set of functions for manipulating screens. You can save them in memory variables or DOS files, "push" or "pop" them onto or from a stack, read or change colors at specified positions, create windows with shadows, and produce other effects. The test program T_SCRNS.PRG demonstrates several screen functions. By using them with a little imagination, you can provide professional-looking, attractive windows in your applications.

Help and Hot Key Processing

Several library functions allow hot key procedures to be called. Since they do not use Clipper wait states, SET KEY commands have no effect. Instead, the functions use the predefined variables *apphelp* and *fkeyset*.

The *apphelp* variable is the application help procedure. It is associated with the F1 key only; *fkeyset* is used for all other hot key procedures.

The name of the help procedure to be called when F1 is pressed must go in *apphelp*. Similarly, the name of a procedure to be activated by any other hot key must go in *fkeyset*. For this purpose, the Developer's Library defines hot keys as the function keys and all others having INKEY values greater than 256 (Alt key combinations).

Note that you must define the variables *apphelp* and *fkeyset*, and load your procedure names into them for this option to work. You may also define other variables for your hot key procedure to use.

When the F1 key is pressed in a function that supports the option, your help procedure is called via the *apphelp* variable. Your procedure is passed the caller's name, a simulated line number, and a variable name, as if it had been called from a wait state on a SET KEY. Thus, your procedure is unaware of the different calling technique, and it proceeds as usual to display the help message.

When a hot key (other than F1) is pressed, the same thing happens except that the procedure in the fkeyset variable is called. In this case, the key's INKEY value is also passed. You can use it to decide what to do.

Your procedure can act on its own, or it can transfer control to procedures normally called through the SET KEY command. Thus, you can include a complete set of hot key procedures in your application. The Developer's Library functions will call them independently of the Clipper wait state. This feature is available in the following functions:

 AEDBAR   DBVIEW   MEMOCTRL   OPCONFIRM

A typical example appears in the T_AEDBAR.PRG demonstration program. An internal function HOTKEYS provides simulated hot key processing while waiting for an operator selection in AEDBAR. No Clipper wait state is active. See AEDBAR for more information.

Unresolved Externals

A few library functions are designed to be called as UDFs from Clipper functions. A typical example is the DBVIEW function used with DBEDIT. Since its name is passed as an argument, you do not call it explicitly in your code. Therefore, it will not be linked to your application. MEMOCTRL is another example. To use either function, declare it external. For instance, the following line forces the linker to link DBVIEW to your application:

    EXTERNAL DBVIEW

MEMOVIEW links MEMOCTRL automatically, so you need not declare it external in this case.

Conventionally, external declarations appear at the beginning of the application's main file.

Calling Conditions

Most functions in the Developer's Library restore any system settings they change. The exceptions are critical functions (such as SYSVERSION, MAKEDBF, and MAKENDX) that return to the operating system if an error occurs. Thus, when you call a function, your application will not see any change in its environment afterward. If you add or modify library functions, be sure to preserve this feature.

If you intend to change the library, I strongly recommend you read both Appendixes A and B carefully beforehand.

Technical Support

The author provides technical support via mail and electronic bulletin board system (BBS) at no charge to registered users.

Registered users also receive periodic mailings concerning changes, corrections, enhancements, and new releases of the library.

To register your copy, simply fill out the card enclosed with the program disk and mail it.

You can also register on the BBS. To do this, you must have a modem and communications software. Simply call the BBS and enter the requested information. After registering, you can move to the files area and download the Developer's Library conference summary files, or any others that may interest you. To save time, all conferences with more than 50 messages in them have summary text files you can download.

The preferred method of support is via the BBS. There is a special area for the Developer's Library. Questions posted are usually answered within a few hours. If you have a problem with a specific function, you should also upload the relevant part of your source code.

The BBS operates 24 hours a day, seven days per week.

> BBS telephone number : 516-472-3129
> Modem settings: no parity, 8-bit data, 1 stop bit.

Norton Guides Database

A standard Guides database is available for the Developer's Library. It contains detailed instructions, syntax, and coding examples for all functions in the book. It also contains sections for book errata, handy charts and tables, new information about the library, and source code for a utility that creates database structure and dictionary files.

The database is fully compatible with the Norton Guides engine shipped with Clipper Version 5. With it, you can instantly pop up information about any Developer's Library function from inside an application or word processor. It is available directly from the author; see below for ordering instructions.

Extended Technical Support

Extended support is available directly from the author on an annual basis. It consists of automatic updates to the library when a new version is released, and bi-monthly issues of the Extended Developer's Library Guides database. This special database contains all items in the standard one described above, as well as sections for new or enhanced library functions, utilities, and support memos.

Each issue of the Extended Guides database contains instructions for using enhancements and new functions. Full source code is provided for all items, along with a complete summary of changes. Each issue also contains new support memos. They are stand-alone articles written by the author containing tips for using both Clipper and the library.

Support memos are provided in popup form (in the Guides database), as well as in disk files formatted for printing. All (like the book) are written without assuming extensive programming background or knowledge of Clipper.

By ordering extended support, you are guaranteed that your version of the Developer's Library will stay up to date. The examples and hints in the support bulletins, along with new functions provided in each issue, will save you hours of programming time.

Ordering Instructions

To order, send a check or money order to: James Occhiogrosso
                                            P.O. Box 637
                                            Holbrook, NY 11741

Standard Norton guides database $25.00
Extended support (6 bi-monthly guides issues) $75.00

To charge your order on Visa or MasterCard, call 516-567-8494. Do not order both items. Extended support includes the standard Guides database. Orders are shipped on 5.25" standard-density disks. Shipping and handling is included. NY residents, please add 8% sales tax.

ADDRECORD

Description:
Recycles a record previously deleted by DELRECORD

Syntax:
ADDRECORD(<cIndexKeyField>)

Returns:
True if a recycled or new record is available; false otherwise

File Name:
F_ADDREC.PRG

Screen Use:
None

Arguments:
<cIndexKeyField> — Name of key field previously used to mark a record with DELRECORD

Typical Use:
To make a deleted record available for reuse. The record must have been deleted and marked by DELRECORD.

Cautions:
Always test the return value to guarantee that a record is available.

See Also:
DELRECORD

Discussion

ADDRECORD makes records previously deleted by DELRECORD available for reuse. Use it together with DELRECORD. If no records are available to recycle, it appends a blank record to the file.

If ADDRECORD finds a record to recycle, or appends a new one successfully, it moves the file pointer to the available record and returns true. In a network environment, it locks the record.

ADDRECORD uses the passed key field to select an index and search for a record to recycle. For this to work, the record must have been marked with a CHR(255) character using DELRECORD and the same key field. When the key field index is in control, the marked record appears at the end of the file. ADDRECORD locates it by using the index and testing the bottom record. Thus, it finds a reusable record quickly without searching the entire file.

ADDRECORD works only on the currently selected database. The passed key field must be of character type, and the file must be indexed on it. If the index is a complex expression, the key field must be the first item. The index must be open for either ADDRECORD or DELRECORD, but need not be the controlling index. If the passed key field does not match the key value for an open index file, ADDRECORD returns false.

Coding Examples

The procedure below uses ADDRECORD to recycle a deleted record or append a new blank one. If successful, it loads the data from previously defined memory variables into the record using REPLVARS.

The example assumes an open index file with an index key expression containing the field *orderno*.

```
* Set flag false initially to start loop
rec_ok = .F.

DO WHILE .NOT. rec_ok

    * Test for recyclable record, or a successful append
```

```
            rec_ok = ADDRECORD('orderno')

         * Let operator try again if unsuccessful
         IF !rec_ok
               CENTERON(24, 'File is not available. Retry Y/N? ')
               IF .NOT. OPCONFIRM()
                    EXIT
               ENDIF
         ENDIF

ENDDO

* If no errors, replace record; otherwise, advise operator
IF rec_ok
     AEDMSG('Record added')
     REPLVARS()
     UNLOCK
ELSE
     ?? CHR(7)
     AEDMSG('Record cannot be added')
ENDIF
```

```
*****************************************************************
FUNCTION ADDRECORD (keyfield)
*****************************************************************

* Locate and recycle a deleted record or append a new one

* Copyright(c) 1991 -- James Occhiogrosso

LOCAL counter, num_ndx, old_delete, old_index, ret_value := .F.

* Make sure field exists and is character type

IF .NOT. EMPTY(keyfield) .AND. TYPE(keyfield) = 'C'

    * Get number of open indexes
    num_ndx = NDXCOUNT()

    * Find index containing key field
    FOR counter = 1 TO num_ndx
        IF UPPER(INDEXKEY(counter)) = UPPER(keyfield)
            EXIT
        ENDIF
    NEXT

    * Test counter. If greater than number of
    * open indexes, key field is incorrect

    IF counter <= num_ndx

        * Save current index position
        old_index = INDEXORD()

        * Save current delete status and turn DELETED off
        old_delete = SET(_SET_DELETED, .F.)

        * Set controlling index to key field passed
        SET ORDER TO counter
        GO BOTTOM

        * Look for a recyclable record
        DO WHILE ASC(EVAL(FIELDBLOCK(keyfield))) == 255

            * Found one. If it is deleted and lockable,
            * recall it and return true to caller.

            IF RLOCK() .AND. DELETED()
                * If we can lock it, we can use it
```

```
                    RECALL
                    ret_value = .T.
                    EXIT
                ENDIF
                SKIP -1

            ENDDO

            IF .NOT. ret_value

                * No record available for recycling, add one
                APPEND BLANK

                * In a network environment, NETERR returns false
                * if we cannot append a blank record. Otherwise,
                * return is true and record is locked.
                ret_value = !NETERR()

            ENDIF

            * Restore entry conditions
            SET ORDER TO old_index
            SET(_SET_DELETED, old_delete)

        ENDIF
ENDIF

* Return value is true if a record was recycled
* or a blank record appended without error

RETURN ret_value
```

AEDBAR

Description:
Provides a single line Quit, Add, Edit, Find, Delete menu bar with a message window

Syntax:
AEDBAR([@<Position>])

Returns:
Numeric value of key pressed to leave the menu bar

File Name:
F_AEDBAR.PRG

Screen Use:
Single row defined by the global memory variable aed_row

Arguments:
<nPosition> – Starting or current position of highlighted option on menu bar. Should be passed by reference.

Typical Use:
To provide an operator interface for maintaining data files

Defaults:
Uses the bottom screen row if the global variable aed_row is undefined

Global Variables:
If aedbar is undefined when AEDBAR is called, it is defined as a public logical variable and initialized true. Other library functions use it to determine if AEDBAR is in use.

See Also:
AEDMSG

Discussion

AEDBAR provides a single-line, horizontal menu bar with five options labeled QUIT, ADD, EDIT, FIND, and DELETE, and a 32 character message window. It uses AEDMSG to display messages in the window.

If you prefer a Lotus-style menu with QUIT at the far right (out of the way), simply change the prompt message. Be sure to interpret the output properly. To learn about menu design, see J. Powell, *Designing User Interfaces* (San Marcos, CA: Microtrend Books, 1990).

The row on which the bar appears depends on the global variable aed_row. If it is undefined, MAXROW( ) is the default.

AEDBAR is usually called from a control loop during file maintenance. When called in this way, the position is passed by reference, and AEDBAR changes it as the user moves the cursor highlight.

When the user selects an item, AEDBAR returns to the caller with the ASCII value of the pressed key. The operator selects an item by moving the cursor to it and pressing Enter, or by typing its first letter.

After AEDBAR returns, the caller uses the key and position variables to decide what to do.

Besides item selection, AEDBAR also provides record by record browsing. It returns to the caller when the user presses the up or down arrow key. However, before returning, it moves the database pointer up or down one record, and sets the logic variable *browsing* to true.

The caller predefines the browsing variable and uses it to initiate a browse. This is simply a matter of displaying the fields from the current record, resetting browsing to false, and recalling AEDBAR (see the example below).

If the user presses either the up or down arrow key, AEDBAR also checks for the beginning or end of file condition on the database in use. If either holds, a blinking message appears in the window area. AEDBAR then moves the database pointer to the top or bottom of the file, and returns with browsing set true. On either condition, the message remains visible until the record pointer moves.

Clipper Developer's Library

AEDBAR also processes special keys (hot keys) for help or other functions. If the global variable fkeyset contains a procedure name, it is called whenever the user presses a function or Alt key combination. The procedure receives the three arguments normally passed with a SET KEY call (procedure name, line number, and input variable), and the value of the special key as a fourth argument. The first three arguments are fixed as AEDBAR, 0, and a null string. Thus, all hot keys can be processed by the same procedures used during wait states.

Coding Examples

The example below displays a simple data entry screen using the sample ORDERS database (see CHKKEY for its structure). AEDBAR is used inside the main loop to display a menu bar, process keys, and view database records. When the operator selects a menu option, the appropriate function is called.

Hot keys are processed in AEDBAR by a call to HOTKEYS through the variable fkeyset. The sample program T_AEDBAR.PRG and the ORDERS database are on the companion disk.

```
******************************************************************
* Test program for AEDBAR function - FILE T_AEDBAR.PRG
******************************************************************
* Copyright(c) 1991 - James Occhiogrosso

#include "inkey.ch"

* Menu bar key definitions
#define KEY_A    65
#define KEY_a    97
#define KEY_D    68
#define KEY_d    100
#define KEY_E    69
#define KEY_e    101
#define KEY_F    70
#define KEY_f    102
#define KEY_Q    81
#define KEY_q    113

* Initialize global variables and overall conditions
LOCAL keyhit, position
INITGLOBAL()
DEVELOP()
SETCOLOR(colstd)
CLEAR SCREEN
SET DELETED ON
```

```
SET SOFTSEEK ON
PRIVATE apphelp := 'SYSHELP', fkeyset := 'HOTKEYS'

SET KEY K_F1 TO &apphelp
SET KEY K_F2 TO HOTKEY_2
SET KEY K_F3 TO HOTKEY_3

* Display screen text
@  4, 20 to 15, 60 DOUBLE
@  6, 23 SAY 'Enter order number: '
@  8, 24 SAY 'Customer account : '
@ 10, 30 SAY 'Part Number: '
@ 12, 31 say 'Price Each: '
CENTERON(18, 'Press F1, F2, F3 for simulated hot key functions')
CENTERON(19, 'Press Alt-G, Alt-H, or Alt-V for grid and rulers')

* Open database, initialize field variables, display first record
USE orders INDEX orders NEW
INITVARS()
EQUVARS()
GET_FUNC()
CLEAR GETS

* Set initial position to ADD option
position = 2

DO WHILE .T.

      * Call AEDBAR with predefined browsing & position variables
      browsing = .F.
      keyhit = AEDBAR(@position)

      * AEDBAR sets browsing = true on up or down arrow
      IF browsing
           * Equate memory variables to fields
           EQUVARS()
           * Display record and return
           GET_FUNC()
           CLEAR GETS
           LOOP
      ELSE

           * Test operator selection and call appropriate functions
           DO CASE

                * Operator selected "QUIT"
                CASE (position = 1 .AND. keyhit = K_ENTER) .OR. ;
                     keyhit = KEY_Q .OR. keyhit = KEY_q .OR. ;
                     keyhit = K_ESC
                   EXIT

                * Operator selected "ADD"
                CASE (position = 2 .AND. keyhit = K_ENTER) .OR. ;
                     keyhit = KEY_A .OR. keyhit = KEY_a
```

Clipper Developer's Library

```
                    AEDMSG('mw_pgdn')
                    mw_update = .T.
                    helpcode = 'ADD'
                    EDIT_FUNC()
                    helpcode = ''

            * Operator selected "EDIT"
            CASE (position = 3 .AND. keyhit = K_ENTER) .OR. ;
                  keyhit = KEY_E .OR. keyhit = KEY_e

                    AEDMSG('mw_pgdn')
                    mw_update = .T.
                    helpcode = 'EDIT'
                    EDIT_FUNC()
                    helpcode = ''

            * Operator selected "FIND"
            CASE (position = 4 .AND. keyhit = K_ENTER) .OR. ;
                  keyhit = KEY_F .OR. keyhit = KEY_f

                    helpcode = 'FIND'
                    FIND_FUNC()
                    helpcode = ''

            * Operator selected "DELETE"
            CASE (position = 5 .AND. keyhit = K_ENTER) .OR. ;
                  keyhit = KEY_D .OR. keyhit = KEY_d

                    mw_update = .T.
                    DELE_FUNC()
            ENDCASE
      ENDIF
ENDDO WHILE .T.

* Release field memory variables before returning
FREEVARS()
RETURN


********************* Internal functions *********************
*                                                             *
* Note: The procedures below demonstrate concept only.        *
*                                                             *
*       In practice, they would be much more comprehensive.   *
*                                                             *
***************************************************************
STATIC FUNCTION GET_FUNC
***************************************************************

* Issues GETs for field variables

@  6, 43 GET morderno PICTURE '@Z 999999' VALID ;
           REQDDATA(morderno) .AND. NODUPL(morderno, 1, orderno)
```

```
@  8, 43 GET mcustid VALID REQDDATA(mcustid)
@ 10, 43 GET mpartno VALID REQDDATA(mpartno)
@ 10, 43 GET mprice PICTURE '@Z 99.99'

RETURN NIL


*****************************************************************
STATIC FUNCTION EDIT_FUNC
*****************************************************************
* Adds or edits a record

LOCAL add_flag := IF(helpcode == 'ADD', .T., .F.)
IF add_flag
    * If adding records, clear field variables
    CLRVARS()
ELSE
    * Otherwise, we are editing, equate them to fields
    EQUVARS()
ENDIF

* Load data into field variables
GET_FUNC()
READ

IF LASTKEY() != K_ESC

    * If in add mode, add a record
    IF add_flag
       APPEND BLANK
    ENDIF

    * Replace record with field variables
    DONEBEEP()
    REPLVARS()

ENDIF
RETURN NIL


*****************************************************************
STATIC FUNCTION FIND_FUNC
*****************************************************************

* Locates and displays a record
local find_var := 0

SETCOLOR(colhelp1)
@ 21, 20 SAY " Enter number of order to find: " ;
            GET find_var PICTURE '@Z 999999'
READ
SETCOLOR(colstd)
* Locate record
SEEK find_var
```

```
    IF EOF()
        * If record does not exist, reset pointer
        SKIP -1
    ELSE
        AEDMSG('mw_pgdn')
    ENDIF

    * Display next logical record (SOFTSEEK is on)
    EQUVARS()
    GET_FUNC()
    CLEAR GETS

    @ 21, 0
    RETURN NIL



*****************************************************************
STATIC FUNCTION DELE_FUNC
*****************************************************************

* Deletes a record

AEDMSG('Delete this record? ')
IF OPCONFIRM()

    * Delete and move pointer to next logical record
    DELETE
    * Display message and wait for 1 second
    AEDMSG('Record deleted')
    DONEBEEP()
    PAUSE(1)
    * Move to next or bottom record
    IF !EOF()
        SKIP -1
    ELSE
        GO BOTTOM
    ENDIF
    AEDMSG('mw_pgdn')
ENDIF

* Display record

EQUVARS()
GET_FUNC()
CLEAR GETS
RETURN NIL
```

```
****************************************************************
FUNCTION HOTKEYS (callproc, linenum, inputvar, keypress)
****************************************************************

* Process function key (hot key) calls for non-wait states

* HOTKEYS is called by all Developer's Library functions that
* simulate wait states. It calls the procedure named in the
* variable "apphelp" if the F1 key is pressed. For all other
* special keys, you can call your own "hot key" procedure from
* HOTKEYS. Your procedure can be passed additional parameters.

* The code below calls dummy functions contained in this
* file.
IF keypress = K_F1
     &apphelp(callproc, linenum, inputvar)

ELSEIF keypress = K_F2
     HOTKEY_2()

ELSEIF keypress = K_F3
     HOTKEY_3()

ELSEIF TYPE('DEVELOP()') == 'UI'

     * DEVELOP function is linked, set its hot keys

     IF keypress = 290          && —- Alt-G key
         GRID()
     ELSEIF keypress = 291      && —- Alt-H key
         HRULER()
     ELSEIF keypress = 303      && —- Alt-V key
         VRULER()
     ENDIF

ENDIF

RETURN NIL


****************************************************************
FUNCTION SYSHELP
****************************************************************

* Note: This function is called by F1 instead of the library
*       SYSHELP function for demonstration only.

LOCAL old_screen := SCRNSAVE(21,0,21,79)

CENTERON(21, 'This is a simulated call to SYSHELP from key .F1')
ERRORBEEP(1)
PAUSE(2)
SCRNREST(old_screen)
RETURN NIL
```

```
*****************************************************************
FUNCTION HOTKEY_2
*****************************************************************

* Dummy hot key function called from F2
LOCAL old_screen := SCRNSAVE(21,0,21,79)
CENTERON(21, 'This is the hot key function called by F2')
ERRORBEEP(2)
PAUSE(1.5)
SCRNREST(old_screen)
RETURN NIL

*****************************************************************
FUNCTION HOTKEY_3
*****************************************************************

* Dummy hot key function called from F3
LOCAL old_screen := SCRNSAVE(21,0,21,79)
CENTERON(21, 'This is the hot key function called by F3')
ERRORBEEP(3)
PAUSE(1.5)
SCRNREST(old_screen)
RETURN NIL
```

```
*******************************************************************
FUNCTION AEDBAR (aed_item)
*******************************************************************

* Single line — Quit, Add, Edit, Find, Delete — bar menu

* Copyright(c) 1991 - James Occhiogrosso

#include "inkey.ch"
#include "set.ch"
#include "setcurs.ch"

LOCAL  aed_col  :=1, init_col := 1, keypress := 0, prev_item :=1,;
       old_col  :=1, old_color := '', old_cursor := '',           ;
       spacing  := 9

* Menu bar prompt messages
LOCAL prompts := {' Quit ',' Add ',' Edit ',' Find ',' Delete '}

MEMVAR browsing, colbarhi, colbarlo, colblink, fkeyset

old_cursor = SET(_SET_CURSOR,SC_NONE)
old_color  = SETCOLOR(colbarlo)

* If aedbar variable is undefined or wrong type, define it.
IF TYPE('m->aedbar') != 'L'
    * Set aedbar public for use by AEDMSG
    PUBLIC aedbar
    aedbar = .T.
ENDIF

* If starting row not defined, default to bottom screen row
IF TYPE('m->aedrow') != 'N'
    * Set aed_row public for use by AEDMSG
    PUBLIC aed_row
    aed_row = MAXROW()
ENDIF

* If starting item is not defined, default to item 1
aed_item = IF(aed_item = NIL, 1, aed_item)

* Display menu bar
SETCOLOR(colbarlo)
@ aed_row, init_col                  SAY  prompts[1]
@ aed_row, init_col + (spacing)      SAY  prompts[2]
@ aed_row, init_col + (spacing*2)    SAY  prompts[3]
@ aed_row, init_col + (spacing*3)    SAY  prompts[4]
@ aed_row, init_col + (spacing*4)    SAY  prompts[5]

* If message window update variable is undefined, define it
IF TYPE('m->mw_update') = 'U'
    PUBLIC mw_update
    mw_update = .T.
ENDIF
```

Clipper Developer's Library

```
* Update message window unless mw_update is false.
* BOF or EOF sets it to .F. so messages remain on view.
IF mw_update
    AEDMSG('mw_init')
ENDIF

* Set loop exit for first letter of each prompt,
* or Return (Enter) or Esc key.

DO WHILE .NOT. CHR(keypress) $ 'QAEFDqaefd' .AND. ;
             keypress != K_RETURN .AND. keypress != K_ESC

    * Highlight current menu bar option
    SETCOLOR(colbarhi)
    aed_col = init_col + (spacing * (aed_item - 1))
    @ aed_row, aed_col SAY prompts[aed_item]

    * Position normal size cursor at end of current prompt
    SETCURSOR(SC_NORMAL)
    IF aed_item = 5
        @ aed_row, aed_col + 7 say ''
    ELSEIF aed_item = 2
        @ aed_row, aed_col + 4 say ''
    ELSE
        @ aed_row, aed_col + 5 say ''
    ENDIF

    * Save current settings
    prev_item = aed_item
    old_col = aed_col

    * Wait for operator to press a key
    keypress = INKEY(0)
    SETCURSOR(SC_NONE)

    IF keypress = K_RIGHT

        * Move prompt 1 position right
        aed_item++
        old_col = aed_col
        aed_col = aed_col + spacing

        IF aed_item > 5
            * Wrap around back to item 1
            aed_item = 1
            aed_col = init_col
        ENDIF

    ELSEIF keypress = K_LEFT

        * Move prompt 1 position to left
        aed_item--
        old_col = aed_col
        aed_col = aed_col - spacing
```

```
            IF aed_item < 1
                aed_item = 5
                aed_col = init_col + (spacing * 4)
            ENDIF

        ELSEIF keypress = K_UP

            * Move database pointer up 1 and exit
            SKIP -1
            IF .NOT. BOF()
                mw_update = .T.
            ELSE
                * Display "Top of file" message
                mw_update = .F.
                GO TOP
                AEDMSG('mw_bof', colblink)
            ENDIF
            browsing = .T.
            EXIT

        ELSEIF keypress = K_DOWN

            * Move database pointer down 1 and exit
            SKIP
            IF .NOT. EOF()
                mw_update = .T.
            ELSE
                * Display "Bottom of file" message
                mw_update = .F.
                GO BOTTOM
                AEDMSG('mw_eof', colblink)
            ENDIF
            browsing = .T.
            EXIT

        * Reset menu bar position if option letter key was pressed

        ELSEIF CHR(keypress) $ 'Aa'      // Add mode
            aed_item = 2
        ELSEIF CHR(keypress) $ 'Ee'      // Edit mode
            aed_item = 3
        ELSEIF CHR(keypress) $ 'Ff'      // Find mode
            aed_item = 4
        ELSEIF CHR(keypress) $ 'Dd'      // Delete mode
            aed_item = 5
        ELSEIF CHR(keypress) $ 'Qq' .OR. keypress = K_ESC    // Quit
            aed_item = 1

        ELSEIF (keypress <= K_F2 .OR. keypress > 256 ;
            .OR. keypress = K_F1) .AND. TYPE('fkeyset') != 'U'

            * Call special keys procedure if any function key or
            * alternate key combination is pressed. The variable
            * fkeyset must contain the procedure name
```

```
        IF .NOT. EMPTY(fkeyset)
            SETCOLOR(old_color)
            DO &fkeyset WITH 'AEDBAR', 0, '', keypress
        ENDIF

    ELSE
        LOOP

    ENDIF

    * Key is left or right arrow. Reposition menu bar.

    SETCOLOR(colbarlo)
    @ aed_row, old_col SAY prompts[prev_item]
    SETCOLOR(colbarhi)
    aed_col = init_col + (spacing * (aed_item-1))
    @ aed_row, aed_col SAY prompts[aed_item]
    old_col = aed_col

ENDDO

* Reset entry conditions and return key pressed

SETCURSOR(old_cursor)
SETCOLOR(old_color)
RETURN(keypress)
```

AEDMSG

Description:
Displays a message in the add, edit, delete (AEDBAR) message window

Syntax:
AEDMSG(<cMessage>, [<cMessageColor>])

Returns:
True if the message is displayed in the AEDBAR window, false otherwise

File Name:
F_AEDMSG.PRG

Screen Use:
Row defined by the variable aed_row, from column 48 to 79

Arguments:
<cMessage> – string containing a message name, or a literal message to display

<cMessageColor> – determines the color setting to use when displaying the message

Typical Use:
To display short operator messages while using the AEDBAR (menu bar) function

Defaults:
If <cMessageColor> is not passed, the message appears in the color defined by the global variable colwindow. If aed_row is undefined, the display uses the bottom row.

Error Handling:
The global variable aedbar must be true for AEDMSG to place a message in the AEDBAR window. If aedbar is undefined or set false, AEDMSG returns with no action. The aedbar variable is preset true when AEDBAR is used.

Cautions:
Message cannot exceed 32 characters.

See Also:
AEDBAR

Discussion

AEDMSG provides a consistent display of messages during data maintenance using the AEDBAR function.

All messages are centered in the window area. To use AEDMSG with a row other than the default (the bottom row), predefine variable aed_row with its number.

Twelve standard messages can be displayed by passing their names. The table below lists them.

To display any other message (up to 32 characters), pass it literally.

Message Name	Displayed in Window
mw_bof	' ──────── Start of file ──────── '
mw_dupkey	' Duplicate key - reenter? Y/N '
mw_entval	' Enter value (or blank to exit) '
mw_eof	' ──────── End of file ──────── '
mw_init	' L/R to select, Up/Dn to browse '
mw_memo	' Ctrl-Enter to Save, F2 for keys '
mw_nosave	' Insufficient data - aborted '
mw_pgdn	' PgDn=Save, Esc=Quit, F1=Help '
mw_recrepl	' Replacing record '
mw_recadd	' Adding record '
mw_reqd	' Data is required. Please redo. '
mw_view	' Up/Dn to browse, or Esc to exit '

Coding Examples

```
* Display literal message (not defined in list above)
AEDMSG('Enter data in one area only')

* Display mw_memo message defined above
AEDMSG('mw_memo')

* Display blinking end of file message.
* (See INITGLOBAL for definition of colblink variable.)
AEDMSG('mw_eof', colblink)
```

See AEDBAR and sample program T_AEDBAR.PRG for more examples.

```
*********************************************************************
FUNCTION AEDMSG (msg_id, new_color)
*********************************************************************

* Display message in AEDBAR menu window

* Copyright(c) 1991 -- James Occhiogrosso

#define UPARROW CHR(24)
#define DNARROW CHR(25)
#define RARROW  CHR(26)
#define LARROW  CHR(27)
LOCAL message, old_color
MEMVAR aedbar, aed_row, colwindow

* Check that AEDBAR is in use before displaying message
IF TYPE("aedbar") != 'L'
    RETURN(.F.)
ELSEIF .NOT. aedbar
    RETURN(.F.)
ENDIF

* If color string passed, use it. Otherwise, default
* to window color.

old_color = IF(new_color = NIL, SETCOLOR(colwindow),  ;
               SETCOLOR(new_color))

IF TYPE('aed_row') != 'N'
    * AEDBAR row variable undefined. Default to bottom row.
    aed_row = MAXROW()
ENDIF

* If prefixed by 'mw_', it is a message identifier. Set it to
* lowercase for processing. Otherwise, display passed string
* without changes.

IF LOWER(SUBSTR(msg_id,1,3)) = 'mw_'
    msg_id = LOWER(msg_id)
ENDIF

* Determine choice and save in message variable

IF msg_id = 'mw_bof'
    message = ' ═══════ Start of file ═══════ '
ELSEIF msg_id = 'mw_dupkey'
    message = ' Duplicate key - reenter? Y/N '
ELSEIF msg_id = 'mw_entval'
    message = ' Enter value (or blank to exit) '
ELSEIF msg_id = 'mw_eof'
    message = ' ═══════ End of file ═══════ '
ELSEIF msg_id = 'mw_init'
    message = ' ' + LARROW + ' ' + RARROW + ' to select, '  ;
            + ' ' + UPARROW + ' ' + DNARROW + ' to browse '
ELSEIF msg_id = 'mw_memo'
```

```
      message =   ' Ctrl-Enter to Save, F2 for keys'
ELSEIF msg_id = 'mw_nosave'
      message =   ' Insufficient data - aborted '
ELSEIF msg_id = 'mw_pgdn'
      message =   ' PgDn=Save,  Esc=Quit,   F1=Help '
ELSEIF msg_id = 'mw_recadd'
      message =   ' Adding record '
ELSEIF msg_id = 'mw_recrepl'
      message =   ' Replacing record '
ELSEIF msg_id = 'mw_reqd'
      message =   ' Data is required. Please redo.'
ELSEIF msg_id = 'mw_view'
      message =   ' ' + UPARROW + ' ' + DNARROW + ;
                  ' to browse, or Esc to exit '
ELSEIF .NOT. EMPTY(msg_id)
      * If message is undefined, display first 32 characters
      message =   SUBSTR(msg_id, 1, 32)
ELSE
      * Otherwise, clear window
      message = SPACE(32)
ENDIF

* Display message and return

@ aed_row, 48 CLEAR TO aed_row, 79
@ aed_row, 48 + (31-LEN(message))/2 SAY message

SETCOLOR(old_color)
RETURN .T.
```

ALLTRUE

Description:
Always returns a logic true value

Syntax:
ALLTRUE( )

Returns:
True

File Name:
F_ALLTRU.PRG

Screen Use:
None

Arguments:
None (see discussion below)

Typical Use:
To use library functions that do not return logical values in WHEN or VALID clauses

Discussion

Before discussing ALLTRUE, I want to credit Rick Spence for the idea. He published a similar function in *Data Based Advisor*. I have changed its name to avoid conflict with preprocessor statements, but the idea is his.

ALLTRUE is a simple but powerful one-line function whose only purpose is to return a logic true value. It thus lets you use functions with non-logical return values in WHEN and VALID clauses.

Sometimes during data entry, we must execute a function when the cursor passes through a field. If it does not return a logical value, use ALLTRUE ahead of it to guarantee a true result. Thus, you can call the function, and ALLTRUE returns true to the WHEN or VALID. Unless the function alters the screen, the operation is transparent to the operator, and the cursor moves onto and through the field normally. The function's return value is ignored.

Thus, by using ALLTRUE, you can call almost any function when the cursor enters or leaves a field (using WHEN or VALID, respectively).

Coding Examples

The example uses ALLTRUE to let CAPFIRST capitalize the GET variable M->company properly after entry. Since CAPFIRST returns a string, you cannot use it directly.

```
* Get company name in proper case
@ 10, 10 SAY 'Enter Company Name: ' GET M->company ;
            VALID ALLTRUE(CAPFIRST(M->company))
  .
  . * Other GETs
  .
READ
```

```
*****************************************************************
FUNCTION ALLTRUE
*****************************************************************

* Returns a logical true. Use in WHEN or VALID statements

* Copyright(c) 1991 -- James Occhiogrosso

RETURN .T.
```

ARREAD

Description:
Reads a text file into an array

Syntax:
ARREAD(<cTextFile>)

Returns:
Array reference

File Name:
F_ARREAD.PRG

Screen Use:
None

Arguments:
<cTextFile> – Text file to read

Typical Use:
To load an array with menu or other items stored as lines in a text file

Error Handling:
Returns a reference to an empty array if specified text file cannot be opened

Cautions:
Each line of the file must end with a carriage return/line feed combination. Lines must not exceed 512 characters. Longer ones cause ARREAD to stop reading the text file and return.

See Also:
ARWRITE

Discussion

ARREAD loads a text file line by line into an array. Each line goes into a separate element. The file can be of any length (limited only by available memory) and can contain any kind of information.

A typical use is a large application with many databases. A data dictionary file contains database names, descriptions, index names, and key expressions for maintenance (see SYSVERSION). However, to use the dictionary information elsewhere, you must read the file each time you need it. This is time consuming because the file is large. Instead, when you update the application, use DBNAMES and ARWRITE to save subsets of the dictionary to smaller files. Later operations can then use ARREAD to recover the information quickly.

Coding Examples

The example below assumes that we have saved the names of database files and associated text descriptions in dbnames.txt and dbdesc.txt during each updating of an application. We then use ARREAD to load them into arrays. We pass the arrays to PICKIT for the operator to view and make selections. SYSSAVE, finally, receives an array of selected databases for copying.

```
* Read database names into an array
dbf_array = ARREAD("dbnames.txt")

* Read database descriptions into an array
text_array = ARREAD("dbdesc.txt")

* Use PICKIT to display text array and fill
* return array with operator selections

CENTERON(24, 'Use up/dn arrow keys to move highlight.';
         + ' Press return to select, Esc when done.')

choices = PICKIT(5, 8, 18, 62, text_array, dbf_array)
```

```
IF choices > 0

    * Call SYSSAVE with array of selected database
    * files to copy to drive A

    SYSSAVE(1, 'A', dbnames)

ENDIF
```

```
*******************************************************************
FUNCTION ARREAD (text_file)
*******************************************************************

* Reads text file into array

* Copyright(c) 1991 -- James Occhiogrosso

#include "fileio.ch"
#translate F_LEN(<n>)  => FSEEK(<n>, FS_SET, FS_END)
#translate F_BOF(<n>)  => FSEEK(<n>, FS_SET)
#translate F_MOVE(<n>) => FSEEK(handle, FS_SET, FS_RELATIVE)

LOCAL filelength := 0,handle := 0,pointer := 0,text_array := {}

* Open file in read-only mode
IF (handle := FOPEN(text_file, FO_READ)) != -1

    * If successful, save its length and reset pointer
    filelength := F_LEN(handle) ; F_BOF(handle)

    DO WHILE pointer < filelength

        * Read next line and add to array
        AADD(text_array, FREADLINE(handle))

        * Update file pointer to current position
        pointer := F_MOVE(handle)

    ENDDO

    * Close file
    FCLOSE(handle)

ENDIF

* Return text array. If any error, array length is zero.
RETURN text_array
```

ARRESTORE

Description:
Restores a one-dimensional array from a disk file created by ARSAVE

Syntax:
ARRESTORE(<aArrayName>, <cFileName>)

Returns:
True if the operation succeeds; false otherwise

File Name:
F_ARREST.PRG

Screen Use:
None

Arguments:
<aArrayName> – Array to save

<cFileName> – File to save it in

Typical Use:
To restore an array previously saved in a disk file by ARSAVE

Defaults:
Uses ARR if <cFileName> has no extension defined.

Error Handling:
Both parameters are required. Returns false if either is missing or of incorrect type. Also returns false if the specified disk file was not created by ARSAVE.

Cautions:
Check free memory before restoring large arrays. For a rough estimate of how much memory is needed, use FILESIZE to determine the size of the file.

See Also:
ARSAVE

Discussion

Use ARRESTORE to restore an array from a disk file created by ARSAVE. The array must be initialized when ARRESTORE is called but can be of any length. ARRESTORE sets the array to the size of the file.

All elements (including undefined ones) are restored to the size and type saved by ARSAVE. Use ARRESTORE only on files created by ARSAVE.

Coding Examples

The following code fragment is from the SCRNLOAD function in this library. It uses ARRESTORE to add screens stored in a disk file to an array used by SCRNPUSH and SCRNPOP. The caller passes the file name to SCRNLOAD. The screens array and counter are static variables defined in F_SCRNS.PRG.

```
LOCAL = temp_array := {}

   * Load temporary array from disk file
   IF ARRESTORE(temp_array, filename)

      * Expand screen array to make room for disk file
      ASIZE(screens, LEN(screens) + LEN(temp_array))

      * Add temporary array to screen array
      ACOPY(temp_array, screens, , , counter + 1)

      * Set screen counter and return its value
      counter := LEN(screens)
      RETURN counter

   ENDIF
```

```
*******************************************************************
FUNCTION ARRESTORE (arr_name, arr_file)
*******************************************************************

* Restores an array from a disk file created by ARSAVE

* Copyright(c) 1991 -- James Occhiogrosso

LOCAL arr_string, counter, data_end, dec_pos, elem_delim, ;
      elem_type, num_dec, num_len, str_num

* Define element delimiter as null byte
elem_delim = CHR(255)

* Return error if any problem with parameters
IF PCOUNT() != 2 .OR. VALTYPE(arr_file) != 'C' .OR. ;
                     VALTYPE(arr_name) != 'A'
    RETURN .F.
ENDIF

* If extension not passed, default to ARR
IF AT('.', arr_file) = 0
    arr_file = arr_file + '.ARR'
ENDIF

IF FILE(arr_file)

    * Load file into string
    arr_string = MEMOREAD(arr_file)

    * Test first five bytes. If file was created by ARSAVE,
    * bytes 1-4 are array length and VAL will return
    * a number. Byte 5 must be element delimiter.

    IF .NOT. VAL(SUBSTR(arr_string,1,4)) > 0 .AND. ;
            elem_delim = SUBSTR(arr_string,5,1)
        * Return false if text file not created by ARSAVE
        RETURN(.F.)
    ENDIF
ELSE
    * Return false if text file does not exist
    RETURN(.F.)
ENDIF

* Set size of array to match stored element count
ASIZE(arr_name, VAL(SUBSTR(arr_string,1,4)) )

* Each iteration of FOR/NEXT loop below gets
* element from string and puts it in array.

arr_string = SUBSTR(arr_string, 6)

FOR counter = 1 TO LEN(arr_name)

    * Get element type (first byte) and null position
```

```
        elem_type = LEFT(arr_string,1)
        data_end = AT(elem_delim, arr_string)

        IF elem_type = 'C'
            * Character element. No conversion required.
            arr_name[counter] = SUBSTR(arr_string, 2, data_end-2)

        ELSEIF elem_type = 'D'
            * Date element. Convert to a date value.
            arr_name[counter] = CTOD(SUBSTR(arr_string,2,data_end-2))

        ELSEIF elem_type = 'L'
            * Logic element. Convert to a logical value.
            arr_name[counter] = IF(SUBSTR(arr_string, 2, 1) = 'T', ;
                .T., .F.)
        ELSEIF elem_type = 'N'
            * Numeric element. Initialize length and decimal places.
            num_len = VAL(SUBSTR(arr_string, 2, 3))
            num_dec = VAL(SUBSTR(arr_string, 5, 3))
            arr_name[counter] = REPLICATE('0', (num_len-1)-num_dec) ;
                + '.' + REPLICATE('0', num_dec)
            arr_name[counter] = VAL(SUBSTR(arr_string,8,data_end-8))

        ENDIF
        arr_string = SUBSTR(arr_string, data_end+1)
NEXT

* Return true if array length is greater than zero,
* and the original string is empty

RETURN ( LEN(arr_name) > 0 .AND. EMPTY(arr_string) )
```

ARSAVE

Description:
Saves a one-dimensional array in a disk file

Syntax:
ARSAVE(<aArrayName>, <cFileName>)

Returns:
True if the operation succeeds; false otherwise

File Name:
F_ARSAVE.PRG

Screen Use:
None

Arguments:
<aArrayName> – Array to save

<cFileName> – File to save it in

Typical Use:
Save an array in a disk file for later use

Defaults:
Uses ARR if <cFileName> has no extension defined

Error Handling:
Both parameters are required. Returns false if either is missing or of incorrect type. Also returns false if the specified file cannot be created, or if all elements of the array were not saved in the file.

Cautions:
ARSAVE overwrites <cFileName> without warning if it already exists.

See Also:
ARREST

Discussion

ARSAVE writes the array length in the first four bytes of the file. The fifth byte is a null (ASCII 0). Element data begins in the sixth byte.

Each element of the array is stored as a string preceded by a character indicating its type. For date, character, and logical elements, the data follows immediately. Logical elements are stored as single T or F characters. For numeric elements, a right-justified, 6 byte field is used for the length and decimal places. It is followed by the string representation of the data. Undefined elements are stored with type letter U, followed immediately by a null byte.

The companion function ARREST restores the array.

Coding Examples

The following code fragment is from the SCRNWRIT function in this library. It uses ARSAVE to save the screen array (used by SCRNPUSH and SCRNPOP) in a disk file. The caller passes it the file name. Note that *screens* is a static array defined in F_SCRNS.PRG.

```
IF filename != NIL .AND. ARSAVE(screens, filename)
   * Successful save
   RETURN LEN(screens)
ELSE
   * Unsuccessful save, return -1 as error indicator
   RETURN -1
ENDIF
```

Clipper Developer's Library

```
****************************************************************
FUNCTION ARSAVE (arr_name, arr_file)
****************************************************************

* Saves an array in a disk file

* Copyright(c) 1991 -- James Occhiogrosso

LOCAL arr_string, cntr, str_num, dec_pos, elem_delim, elem_type

* Define element delimiter
elem_delim = CHR(255)

* Return error if any problem with parameters
IF PCOUNT() != 2 .OR. VALTYPE(arr_file) != 'C' .OR. ;
                     VALTYPE(arr_name) != 'A'
     RETURN .F.
ENDIF

* If extension not passed, default to ARR
IF AT('.', arr_file) = 0
    arr_file = arr_file + '.ARR'
ENDIF

* Put length of array at start of array string
arr_string = PADL(LEN(arr_name),4) + elem_delim

* Add each element and delimiter to string
FOR cntr = 1 TO LEN(arr_name)
   elem_type = VALTYPE(arr_name[cntr])

   IF elem_type = 'U'
      * Element is undefined
      arr_string = arr_string + 'U' + elem_delim
   ELSEIF elem_type = 'C'
      * Element is character - no adjustment required
      arr_string = arr_string + 'C' + arr_name[cntr] + elem_delim
   ELSEIF elem_type = 'D'
      * Element is a date - convert to a character string
      arr_string = arr_string + 'D' + DTOC(arr_name[cntr]) + ;
                   elem_delim
   ELSEIF elem_type = 'L'
      * Element is logical - convert to T or F character
      arr_string = arr_string + 'L' + IF(arr_name[cntr], ;
                   'T', 'F') + elem_delim
   ELSEIF elem_type = 'N'

      * Element is a number - convert to left-justified string
      str_num = LTRIM(STR(arr_name[cntr]))
      dec_pos = AT('.', str_num)

      IF dec_pos = 0
         * No decimal position, put zero in last 3 bytes
         arr_string = arr_string + 'N' + PADL(LEN(str_num),3) ;
                    + '  0' + str_num + elem_delim
```

```
            ELSE
                * Decimal positions exist, save them in last 3 bytes
                arr_string = arr_string + 'N' +   ;
                        PADL(LEN(str_num),3) + ;
                        PADL(LEN(str_num)-dec_pos,3) + ;
                        str_num + elem_delim
            ENDIF
        ENDIF
NEXT

* Write file and return .T. if successful
RETURN( MEMOWRIT(arr_file, arr_string) )
```

ARTYPE

Description:
Tests a one-dimensional array to see if all elements are of a specified type

Syntax:
ARTYPE(<aArrayName>, <cElementType>)

Returns:
True if all elements in the array are of the specified type; false otherwise

File Name:
F_ARTYPE.PRG

Screen Use:
None

Arguments:
<aArrayName> – Array to be tested

<cElementType> – Single letter denoting data type to use for comparison (A, B, C, D, L, M, N, O, or U)

Typical Use:
To avoid type mismatch errors caused by array elements of different types

Error Handling:
Returns false if the first argument is not an array

Discussion

ARTYPE compares the type of each element in a one-dimensional array to the passed type. If all elements are of the specified type, it returns true. It tests undefined elements just like defined ones. To determine if an array contains only undefined or NIL elements, pass U for the element type.

ARTYPE is useful for testing an array before performing an operation that requires a particular data type. For example, you could use it before performing numeric or string operations. Without the test, an element of a different type will cause a run time error. ARTYPE prevents this by checking element types beforehand.

Coding Examples

The example below uses ARTYPE to ensure that all elements in the itemcosts array are numeric before summing them.

```
IF ARTYPE(itemcosts, 'N')
   array_len = LEN(itemcosts)
   FOR counter = 1 TO array_len
       total = total + itemcosts[counter]
   NEXT
ELSE
   ? 'Cannot total. All elements are not numeric.'
ENDIF
```

```
*****************************************************************
FUNCTION ARTYPE (arr_name, elem_type)
*****************************************************************

* Test each element of array for match to specified type

* Copyright(c) 1991 -- James Occhiogrosso

LOCAL ret_value := .T.

IF VALTYPE(arr_name) != 'A' .OR. LEN(arr_name) < 1
    * Incorrect array argument passed
    ret_value := .F.

ELSE
    * Check type of each element
    AEVAL(arr_name, { | element | ret_value :=     ;
        IF(VALTYPE(element) != UPPER(elem_type),  ;
           .F., ret_value) } )
ENDIF

RETURN ret_value
```

ARVIEW

Description:
Development utility for viewing an array

Syntax:
ARVIEW(<aArrayName>)

Returns:
Nothing

File Name:
F_ARVIEW.PRG

Screen Use:
Entire screen

Arguments:
<aArrayName> – Array to view

Typical Use:
To inspect arrays during development

Error Handling:
Returns with no action if the passed argument is not an array

See Also:
DEVELOP

Discussion

We often want to view an array during application development. You can use ARVIEW to observe arrays containing elements of any data type. It clears the screen, displays the specified array, and then waits for a key.

The elements appear in a full-screen window with columns for element number, types and contents. If the array is larger than the window, the up/down arrow keys are used to scroll the display vertically. ARVIEW does not provide horizontal scrolling. Pressing Enter, Esc, or the left/right arrow keys cause ARVIEW to restore the screen and return. All other keys are ignored. Elements that are too long for the window area are truncated. You can use ARVIEW to view one-dimensional arrays, or parts of multi-dimensional arrays.

Call ARVIEW from your program by placing it in a preprocessor control structure (see the example below). Thus, it is only linked to your application during debugging.

Coding Examples

This example uses ARVIEW inside a preprocessor control structure for debugging. If the manifest constant DEBUG is undefined, the code for ARVIEW is not included in the application.

```
#ifdef DEBUG
    ARVIEW("ArrayName")
#endif
```

Alternately, you can use the Developer's Library DEVELOP function as shown below to make external declarations that link ARVIEW and other functions needed for debugging.

```
#ifdef DEBUG
    DEVELOP()    // Load Developer's Library debugging functions
#endif
```

```
****************************************************************
FUNCTION ARVIEW (arr_name)
****************************************************************

* Development utility for viewing an array

* Copyright(c) 1991 -- James Occhiogrosso

#include "box.ch"
LOCAL old_screen := SCRNSAVE(1, 1, MAXROW()-1, MAXCOL()-1), ;
      new_array := {}

IF VALTYPE(arr_name) = 'A'

    * Display box and heading area
    @ 1, 1, MAXROW()-1, MAXCOL()-1 BOX B_SINGLE + SPACE(1)
    @ 2, 3  SAY ' Element/Type '
    @ 2, 38 SAY ' Contents '
    @ 3, 4  SAY REPLICATE('-', MAXCOL() - 7)

    * Declare new array and traverse it
    ASIZE(new_array, LEN(arr-name))
    AEVAL(arr_name, { | element | LOADNEW(element, new_array) } )

ENDIF

* Use ACHOICE to view new array
choice = ACHOICE(4, 4, MAXROW()-2, MAXCOL()-4, new_array)

* Restore screen and return
SCRNREST(old_screen)
RETURN NIL

****************************************************************
STATIC FUNCTION LOADNEW (element, new_array)
****************************************************************

* Load new array with character strings formatted for viewing

LOCAL elem_type, elem_num
STATIC counter := 0

counter  := IF(counter >= LEN(new_array), 1, ++counter)
elem_num := PADL(counter,4) + SPACE(5)
elem_type := VALTYPE(element)

IF elem_type == 'A'
    new_array[counter] = elem_num + 'A         ' + ;
        'Array of length = ' + LTRIM(STR(LEN(element)))
```

```
ELSEIF elem_type == 'B'
    new_array[counter] = elem_num + 'B    ' + ;
        'Code block'

ELSEIF elem_type == 'C'
    new_array[counter] = elem_num + 'C    ' + ;
        SUBSTR(element, 1, MAXCOL()-4)

ELSEIF elem_type == 'D'
    new_array[counter] = elem_num + 'D    ' + ;
        DTOC(element)

ELSEIF elem_type == 'L'
    new_array[counter] = elem_num + 'L    ' + ;
        IF(element = .T., '.T.', '.F.')

ELSEIF elem_type == 'N'
    new_array[counter] = elem_num + 'N    ' + ;
        LTRIM(STR(element))

ELSEIF elem_type == 'U'
    new_array[counter] = elem_num + 'U    ' + ;
        'Undefined'

ENDIF

RETURN NIL
```

ARWRITE

Description:
Saves an array in a text file

Syntax:
ARWRITE(<cTextArray>, <cTextFile>)

Returns:
True if the operation succeeds; false otherwise

File Name:
F_ARWRIT.PRG

Screen Use:
None

Arguments:
<cTextArray> – Array containing text information to save

<cTextFile> – Text file in which to save the array contents

Typical Use:
Save text information in a file for later use by other functions

Error Handling:
Returns false if passed incorrect arguments or the array cannot be written to the specified file

Cautions:
All array elements must be of character type. Other types cause ARWRITE to return false without further action.

See Also:
ARREAD

Discussion

ARWRITE saves each element of an array as a line in a text file. Other functions can then use the file. ARWRITE puts a carriage return/line feed pair after each element. It will write an element of any length (up to the Clipper maximum). However, when using ARREAD or FREADLINE, the length should not exceed 512 characters. See ARREAD for more information.

Coding Examples

The example uses ARWRITE to create text files containing information from a system data dictionary (arsystem.def) file. DBNAMES reads the dictionary and puts database names and associated descriptions in arrays. ARWRITE then saves the arrays in dbnames.txt and dbdesc.txt.

```
* Load database names and descriptions into arrays

LOCAL db_names := {}, db_desc := {}
DBNAMES("arsystem.def", db_names, db_desc)

* Save each array in a text file

ret_value = IF (ARWRITE(db_names, "dbnames.txt") .AND. ;
                ARWRITE(db_desc,  "db_desc.txt"), .T., .F.)

* Display message if errors occur
IF !ret_value
    ? 'Error writing text file'
ENDIF
```

```
*********************************************************************
FUNCTION ARWRITE (text_array, text_file)
*********************************************************************

* Saves array in text file

* Copyright(c) 1991 -- James Occhiogrosso

LOCAL array_bytes := 0, file_bytes := 0, handle := 0, ;
      ret_value := .F.

* Test array argument and create text file
IF LEN(text_array) > 0 .AND. ARTYPE(text_array, 'C') ;
   .AND. (handle := FCREATE(text_file)) != -1

   * If successful, add each line of array to file
   AEVAL(text_array, { | element | ( file_bytes := file_bytes + ;
      FWRITE(handle, element + CHR(13)+CHR(10),              ;
      LEN(element)+2) ) , (array_bytes := array_bytes +      ;
      LEN(element)+2) })

   * Test bytes written versus array size and close file
   ret_value := IF(file_bytes=array_bytes .AND. array_bytes != 0;
      .AND. FCLOSE(handle), .T., .F.)

ENDIF

RETURN ret_value
```

BACKCHAR

Description:
Fills a screen area with a background character

Syntax:
BACKCHAR([<nTopRow>], [<nLeftColumn>], [<nBottomRow>], [<nBottomColumn>], [<nAsciiVal>] | [<cCharVal>] , [<cColor>])

Returns:
Nothing

File Name:
F_BACKCH.PRG

Screen Use:
Defined in calling parameters

Arguments:
<nTopRow>, <nLeftColumn>, <nBottomRow>, <nRightColumn> – Coordinates of screen area to fill

[<nAsciiVal>] | [<cCharVal>] Background character to display. Passed inside quotation marks or as an ASCII value.

<cColor> – Color string for displaying background character. Only a foreground argument is needed. The rest of the string is ignored.

Typical Use:
To enhance screen displays with a fill character

Defaults:
All parameters are optional. If any are omitted, the following defaults are used:

- Screen corners for missing screen coordinate values
- CHR(176) for background character
- Current color setting

Discussion

BACKCHAR quickly fills a screen area with a single graphics character. This forms an attractive display like that used by many software vendors as a background for menus or windows. All parameters are optional. Pass a comma to skip any of them. BACKCHAR fills the entire screen with the default character if no arguments are passed.

The background character is specified inside quotation marks or by passing its ASCII value as a numeric. In most cases, the default [CHR (176)] is acceptable.

Coding Examples

```
* Fill screen with default character in current color
BACKCHAR()

* To use a different character
BACKCHAR(,,,,177)

* To use a different character and a passed color
BACKCHAR(,,,, 178, "W/B")

* To fill the screen from row 10, column 20 down
BACKCHAR(10,20)

* To fill a partial screen area with red dashes
BACKCHAR(5, 15, 20, 75, '-', 'n/r')
```

NOTE: You can obtain interesting, attractive combinations using SETBLINK to enable high intensity background colors. The example below uses SETBLINK and BACKCHAR to display the standard fill character on a bright yellow background. More examples are in the test program T_SCRNS.PRG on the disk.

```
* Turn high intensity background color on
SETBLINK(.F.)

* Fill screen
BACKCHAR(,,,,,"n/gr*")

* Turn high intensity background color off
SETBLINK(.T.)
```

```
*******************************************************************
FUNCTION BACKCHAR (top, left, bottom, right, back_char, color)
*******************************************************************

* Fills screen area with specified background character

* Copyright(c) 1991 -- James Occhiogrosso

LOCAL back_line, counter, old_color

* Convert numeric value to character
IF VALTYPE(back_char) == 'N'
    back_char = CHR(back_char)

* Default to shading character (176) if value not passed
ELSEIF back_char == NIL .OR. VALTYPE(back_char) != 'C'
    back_char = CHR(176)
ENDIF

* Use current color if none passed
old_color = IF(VALTYPE(color) == 'C', ;
               SETCOLOR(color), SETCOLOR())

* Set defaults for coordinates not passed
top    = IF(VALTYPE(top)    ) == 'N', top   , 0)
left   = IF(VALTYPE(left)   ) == 'N', left  , 0)
bottom = IF(VALTYPE(bottom) ) == 'N', bottom, MAXROW())
right  = IF(VALTYPE(right)  ) == 'N', right , MAXCOL())

* Fill display with background character
FOR counter = top TO bottom
    @ counter, left SAY REPLICATE(back_char, (right-left) + 1)
NEXT

* Restore original color and return
SETCOLOR(old_color)
RETURN NIL
```

CAPFIRST

Description:
Capitalizes the first letter of each word in a string

Syntax:
CAPFIRST(<cString>)

Returns:
String value

File Name:
F_CAPFIR.PRG

Screen Use:
None

Arguments:
<cString> – String to be processed

Typical Use:
Change a string to proper case before display or during data entry

See Also:
ALLTRUE

Discussion

Use CAPFIRST to convert strings to proper case (i.e., capitalize the first letter of each word). You can use it to format strings before display or printing. Its most common use, however, is to ensure proper entry of names.

For example, using CAPFIRST in a VALID clause on a company name corrects obvious entry errors such as A. b. smith automatically to A. B. Smith.

CAPFIRST assumes a space separates each word in the string from other words. It extracts each one and capitalizes its first letter. It changes all other letters to lowercase. It then searches the word for commas, periods, dashes, and double quotation marks, and capitalizes the first letter after each one.

Finally, if the word contains an apostrophe, CAPFIRST checks the previous character. If it is the beginning of the word, CAPFIRST changes the character after the apostrophe to uppercase. This ensures correct entry of names like O'Brien. CAPFIRST does not correct all capitalization errors, but it eliminates many of them.

Below are some examples:

String passed to CAPFIRST	Returned from CAPFIRST
o'brien's place	O'Brien's Place
JOHN SMITH	John Smith
abbe-nabler co.,inc.	Abbe-Nabler Co.,Inc.
TONY "THE TIGER" JONES	Tony "The Tiger" Jones
James Macdonald	James Macdonald (possibly wrong, but CAPFIRST has no way of knowing if it should be James MacDonald)

You can use CAPFIRST's return value directly in @ SAY statements as shown below. To alter data immediately, use it in a VALID clause. To do this, pass the string to CAPFIRST by reference. However, since CAPFIRST returns a string, you must use it with ALLTRUE to allow the user to leave the VALID (see the last example below).

Coding Examples

```
* Trim and print names in proper case
@ 10,10 SAY TRIM(CAPFIRST(first_name)) + ' ' +
             CAPFIRST(last_name)

* Or,
@ 10,10 SAY CAPFIRST (TRIM(first_name) + ' ' + last_name)

* To use CAPFIRST in a VALID to alter data immediately

* Open a customer database
USE customer NEW

* Get company name in proper case
mcompany := customer->company
@ 10, 10 SAY 'Enter Company Name: ' GET mcompany ;
             VALID ALLTRUE(CAPFIRST(@mcompany))
READ

* Replace company name in database
customer->company := mcompany
```

```
*******************************************************************
FUNCTION CAPFIRST (string)
*******************************************************************

* Capitalize first letter of each word in a string

* Copyright(c) 1991 -- James Occhiogrosso

LOCAL counter, position := 0, punct_mark := '.,-"',;
      ret_string := '', temp_word := '', word := ''

DO WHILE LEN(string) > 0
   * Extract word from passed string
   word = PARSE(@string)

   * Capitalize first letter of word
   word = UPPER(SUBSTR(word,1,1)) + LOWER(SUBSTR(word,2))

   * Test for period, comma, dash, or double quotation mark
   FOR counter = 1 TO 4
       temp_word = ''

       * If any exist, get position in word
       position = AT(SUBSTR(punct_mark, counter, 1), word)

       DO WHILE position > 0

          * Capitalize first letter after punctuation mark
          temp_word = temp_word + SUBSTR(word, 1, position) +;
                      UPPER(SUBSTR(word, position + 1, 1))

          * And trim original word
          word = SUBSTR(word, position + 2)

          * Look for more of that mark in string
          position = AT(SUBSTR(punct_mark, counter, 1), word)

          IF position = 0
             * If no more, done. Otherwise, loop
             word = temp_word + word
             EXIT
          ENDIF

       ENDDO
   NEXT
```

```
* Test for apostrophe
position = AT("'", word)

IF position > 0

    * If found, capitalize first letter afterward if
    * it follows a capital letter (names like "O'Brien")

    IF ISUPPER(SUBSTR(word, position-1))
            word = SUBSTR(word, 1, position)          + ;
                   UPPER(SUBSTR(word, position + 1, 1)) + ;
                   SUBSTR(word, position + 2)
        ENDIF
    ENDIF

    * Add word to return string
    ret_string = ret_string + word + ' '

ENDDO

* Set local string to return string
string = ret_string

RETURN ret_string
```

CENTERON

Description:
Displays a centered one-line message in a selected color

Syntax:
CENTERON(<nRow>, <cMessage>, [<cColor>])

Returns:
Nothing

File Name:
F_CENTON.PRG

Screen Use:
Defined by passed parameters

Arguments:
<nRow> – Row on which message appears

<cMessage> – Message

<cColor> – Optional color specification

Typical Use:
To display a message in a different color to attract the operator's attention

Defaults:
If <cColor> is not passed, CENTERON uses the color definition string in the global variable colwindow.

If <cColor> is a null string, CENTERON uses the current color setting.

Cautions:
Moves the cursor to the end of the displayed string to allow a wait condition afterward

Discussion

To provide an attractive display, CENTERON pads messages with spaces at both ends. The number added varies from 1 to 5 depending on message length. The number increases as the length decreases.

Since CENTERON (by default) displays the message in a different color, the padding creates borders.

Coding Examples

```
* Display a message on line 24 in the color in the global
* variable colwindow
CENTERON(24, 'Press any key to begin printing.')

* Display as above, but in a specific color
CENTERON(24, 'Press any key to begin printing.', 'BG+/W')

* Display as above, but use current color setting
CENTERON(24, 'Press any key to begin printing.', '')

* Display as above, but use colbarhi color variable
CENTERON(24, 'Press any key to begin printing.', 'colbarhi')
```

```
*******************************************************************
FUNCTION CENTERON (line_num, string, new_color)
*******************************************************************

* Center a string on selected line in selected color

* Copyright(c) 1991 - James Occhiogrosso

LOCAL end_col := MAXCOL(), horz_pos, old_color, string_len
MEMVAR colwindow

* Get length of passed string
string_len = LEN(string)

* If window color is undefined, initialize it.
colwindow := IF (TYPE('colwindow') != 'C', SETCOLOR(), colwindow)

DO CASE

   * Invalid length, abort
   CASE string_len > end_col .OR. string_len < 1
      RETURN NIL

   * The CASEs below pad the displayed string with up to 10
   * spaces. The number of spaces increases as the length of
   * the passed string decreases. This produces an attractive
   * display for all strings.

   CASE string_len > end_col-10 .AND. string_len <= end_col-2
      string = ' ' + string + ' '
      horz_pos = INT((end_col - LEN(string))/2)

   CASE string_len > end_col-20 .AND. string_len <= end_col-10
      string = '  ' + string + '  '
      horz_pos = INT((end_col - LEN(string))/2)

   CASE string_len > end_col-30 .AND. string_len <= end_col-20
      string = '   ' + string + '   '
      horz_pos = INT((end_col - LEN(string))/2)

   CASE string_len > end_col-40 .AND. string_len <= end_col-30
      string = '    ' + string + '    '
      horz_pos = INT((end_col - LEN(string))/2)

   CASE string_len <= 40
      string = '     ' + string + '     '
      horz_pos = INT((end_col - LEN(string))/2)

   OTHERWISE
      * String is almost width of screen, do not pad
      horz_pos = 0
ENDCASE
```

```
* Clear line using current color setting
@ line_num, 0
* Save old color and set message color
old_color = IF(new_color == NIL, SETCOLOR(colwindow),  ;
                                 SETCOLOR(new_color) )

* Display padded string
@ line_num, horz_pos SAY string

* Restore entry color
SETCOLOR(old_color)
RETURN NIL
```

CHKKEY

Description:
Locates key data in another file and optionally displays or processes it

Syntax:
CHKKEY(<cSearchFile>, <cSearchKey>, [<cUserProc>], [<nRow>], [<nStartColumm>], [<nEndColumn>], [<cDisplay1>], [<cDisplay2>], [<cSpaceString>])

Returns:
True if key exists in specified file; false otherwise

File Name:
F_CHKKEY.PRG

Screen Use:
Defined by calling parameters

Arguments:
<cSearchFile> – File to search for the key value

<cSearchKey> – Variable containing the key data

<cUserFunc> – Function to execute before leaving CHKKEY

<nRow>, <nStartColumm> – Row and column coordinates for display

<nEndColumn> – Ending column for the displayed data

<cDisplay1>, <cDisplay2> – Fields to display from the file

<cSpaceString> – String to place between the fields

Typical Use:
To locate, verify, and optionally display key data from another file

Defaults:
None. Requires arguments for the file and the key. All others are optional; CHKKEY does not use them if they are not passed.

Cautions:

The file to be searched must be open and indexed on the key data. Pass the display fields (if used) inside quotation marks with an alias (for example, "customer->custid").

Discussion

You usually call CHKKEY from a VALID while entering data. It returns true if the passed key appears in the file. If passed a user function, CHKKEY executes it. If passed more than three arguments, it displays up to two fields from the file or "Not Found" if it does not find the key. It separates the displayed fields with [<cSpaceString>].

In the simplest case, you use CHKKEY to verify a key field in another file. To do this, pass only the first two arguments. CHKKEY returns the logical result of the search with no further action. However, it is more useful and powerful when passed more parameters.

If passed a user function, CHKKEY executes it after searching for the key field. The function can display related data (as in the example below) or perform other tasks. It can also alter CHKKEY's return value to force data reentry based on a test or computation.

If passed more than three arguments, CHKKEY displays one or two named fields from the file. To avoid interference with other displays, specify a maximum display column. CHKKEY truncates the data appropriately.

Coding Examples

The example below uses CHKKEY to look for data in an order file, using the order number as a key. On finding the order, it displays the associated company name and account ID from a related customer file. The user function (ORDER_INFO) then displays part and price information from the order file. The source code for T_CHKKEY.PRG and the sample data files are on the companion disk. Also see DBVIEW and the file T_DBVIEW.PRG for an example that uses CHKKEY to display a window of selections.

Sample data file structures:

```
Structure for ORDERS.DBF
INDEX ON orderno TO orders
----------------------------------------------------
    Field Name         Type       Width      Decimals
----------------------------------------------------
    ORDERNO            N            6           0
    CUSTID             C            6           0
    PARTNO             C           15           0
    PRICE              N            5           2


Structure for CUSTOMER.DBF
INDEX ON custid TO customer
----------------------------------------------------
    Field Name         Type       Width      Decimals
----------------------------------------------------
    CUSTID             C            6           0
    COMPANY            C           30           0
```

```
**********************************************************************
* Test program for CHKKEY functions -   FILE T_CHKKEY.PRG
**********************************************************************

* Copyright(c) 1991 -- James Occhiogrosso

#include "inkey.ch"

LOCAL morderno := 0

* Initialize global colors and clear screen
INITGLOBAL()
SETCOLOR(colstd)
CLEAR

* Open test files and set relationship

USE customer INDEX customer NEW
USE orders INDEX orders NEW
SET RELATION TO orders->custid INTO customer

DO WHILE LASTKEY() != K_ESC    // Exit on Esc key

    * If the order number exists, CHKKEY displays the company
    * from customer. Uses ORDER_INFO optionally to display
    * other related items or perform computations.
```

```
     @ 5, 3 SAY 'Order No: ' GET morderno PICTURE "999999" ;
            VALID CHKKEY("orders", morderno, "order_info", ;
                      5, 30, 70, "customer->company",    ;
                   "customer->custid", ' - ,)
     READ

ENDDO

RETURN

*******************************************************************
FUNCTION ORDER_INFO
*******************************************************************
*
* This is a simple UDF for CHKKEY. If it finds the order number,
* it displays corresponding data from the order file. Otherwise,
* it clears the associated screen area.

LOCAL oldcolor := SETCOLOR(colhelp1)

IF FOUND()
   @ 6, 30 SAY 'Part number: ' + orders->partno
   @ 7, 30 SAY 'Price: $ ' + LTRIM(STR(orders->price))
ELSE
   @ 6, 30 CLEAR TO 7, 70
ENDIF

* Note that CHKKEY's return value can be altered if desired
SETCOLOR(oldcolor)

RETURN FOUND()
```

```
*********************************************************************
FUNCTION CHKKEY(lookfile, lookdata, udf_name, showrow, startcol,;
                donecol, showfld1, showfld2, spac_char)
*********************************************************************

* Verify key data in specified file and optionally display it

* Copyright(c) 1991 -- James Occhiogrosso

LOCAL num_args   := PCOUNT(),                                        ;
      old_color  := SETCOLOR(colhelp1),                              ;
      old_file   := ALIAS(),                                         ;
      ret_value  := .F., showarea1, showarea2, showdata


MEMVAR colblink, colhelp1

* Check for valid parameters
IF num_args=2 .OR. num_args=3 .OR. num_args=7 .OR. num_args=9

    IF num_args > 3

        * Display external data. Check passed row and column
        * for validity. Error message needs 12 characters
        IF startcol > MAXCOL() - 12 .OR. showrow > MAXROW()
            RETURN(.F.)
        ELSE
            @ showrow, startcol CLEAR TO showrow, donecol
        ENDIF
    ENDIF

ELSE
    * Incorrect number of arguments passed
    RETURN(.F.)
ENDIF

* Verify data exists in selected file
SELECT(lookfile)
IF (ret_value := DBSEEK(lookdata))

    DO CASE

        CASE num_args = 2
            * No screen display. Return.
            SETCOLOR(old_color)
            SELECT(old_file)
            RETURN ret_value
```

```
            CASE num_args >= 7
               * Separate work areas and field names
               showarea1 = SELECT(SUBSTR(showfld1, 1,    ;
                           (AT('->', showfld1)-1)))
               showfld1 = SUBSTR(showfld1, AT('->',showfld1)+2)
               showdata = ALLTRIM(EVAL(FIELDBLOCK(showfld1,   ;
                           showarea1)))

               IF showfld2 != NIL
                  showarea2 = SELECT(SUBSTR(showfld2, 1,       ;
                              (AT('->',showfld2)-1)))
                  showfld2 = SUBSTR(showfld2, AT('->',showfld2)+2)
                  showdata = showdata + spac_char +            ;
                             ALLTRIM(EVAL(FIELDWBLOCK(         ;
                             showfld2,showarea2)))
               ENDIF

               * Trim data to display coordinates and display it
               @ showrow, startcol SAY SUBSTR(showdata, 1,  ;
                                   donecol - startcol)  ;


         ENDCASE

   ELSE
      * Data not found, display message
      SETCOLOR(colblink)
      ?? CHR(7)
      IF num_args > 3
         @ showrow, startcol SAY ' Not found! '
      ENDIF
   ENDIF

   * Call user defined procedure if passed and linked
   IF (udf_name != NIL) .AND. (TYPE(udf_name + '()') == 'UI')
      ret_value = &udf_name()
   ENDIF

   SETCOLOR(old_color)
   SELECT(old_file)

   * Called function can alter return value if desired
   RETURN ret_value
```

CHKSTATE

Description:
Verifies two-letter state code abbreviations

Syntax:
CHKSTATE(<cStateAbbrev>)

Returns:
True if the passed string is a valid two-letter state code, or longer than two characters; false otherwise

File Name:
F_CHKSTA.PRG

Screen Use:
If the AEDBAR function is in use, invalid codes cause a message to appear in its window.

Arguments:
<cStateAbbrev> – String containing the state code abbreviation

Typical Use:
To validate data entries

Global File:
ZIPS.DBF – Database containing state abbreviations, state names, and Zip Code ranges (see CHKZIP for structure and listing).

Cautions:
To avoid halting an application, CHKSTATE returns true if the ZIPS database is unavailable.

Defaults:
If <cStateAbbrev> is passed by reference, it is converted to uppercase.

See Also:
AEDMSG, CHKZIP, STATENAME

Discussion

CHKSTATE searches the ZIPS.DBF file for the abbreviated state code. It is designed for use in a VALID clause. If it finds the code, CHKSTATE returns true, permitting the user to leave the field. To allow for province or country names, CHKSTATE always returns true if <cStateAbbrev> has more than two characters. You can customize the ZIPS database to include country or province codes.

If the ZIPS database is not open when CHKSTATE is called, it is opened in the next available area. It is not closed upon exit. See CHKZIP for the structure of ZIPS.DBF.

Coding Examples

```
* Get and verify a 2 letter state code

GET state PICTURE  '!!' VALID CHKSTATE(state)

* Get and verify a 2 letter state code in a field where mixed
* data may be entered.
GET state PICTURE '!!!!!!!!!!' VALID CHKSTATE(@state)
```

Here CHKSTATE changes two-letter state abbreviations to all capital letters. It does not alter longer entries.

```
*******************************************************************
FUNCTION CHKSTATE (statecode)
*******************************************************************

* Verifies a two character state code

* Copyright(c) 1991 -- James Occhiogrosso

LOCAL old_area := SELECT()

* If passed state code exceeds 2 characters, exit
IF LEN(TRIM(statecode)) > 2
   RETURN(.T.)
ENDIF

* Make sure Zip Code database is available
IF EMPTY(SELECT("zips"))
   IF FILE('zips.dbf')
      * If zips file exists, open it
      USE zips NEW
   ELSE
      * Otherwise, exit
      RETURN(.T.)
   ENDIF
ENDIF
SELECT zips

* Check Zip Code database for state code
statecode = UPPER(statecode)
LOCATE FOR TRIM(statecode) $ zips->state
IF FOUND()
   AEDMSG('mw_pgdn')
   SELECT(old_area)
   RETURN(.T.)
ELSE
   ERRORBEEP()
   AEDMSG('Invalid state - Please reenter')
   SELECT(old_area)
   RETURN(.F.)
ENDIF
```

CHKZIP

Description:
Verifies first five characters of U.S. Zip Codes to match standard two-letter state abbreviations

Syntax:
CHKZIP(<cStateCode>, <cZipCode>)

Returns:
True if <cZipCode> is a valid five-digit U.S. Zip Code within the allowed range of the state abbreviation (<cStateCode>); false otherwise

File Name:
F_CHKZIP.PRG

Screen Use:
If AEDBAR is active, its window is used to display a message for invalid Zip Codes. The message indicates the correct range.

Arguments:
<cStateCode> – String containing the standard state abbreviation

<cZipCode> – String with its first five characters containing the Zip Code to be verified

Typical Use:
To validate data entries

Global File:
ZIPS.DBF – Database containing state abbreviations, state names, and Zip Code ranges (see below for structure and listing)

Cautions:
To avoid halting an application, CHKZIP returns true if the ZIPS database is unavailable.

See Also:
AEDMSG, CHKSTATE, STATENAME

Discussion

CHKZIP uses the ZIPS.DBF file to verify the range of the passed Zip Code. It locates the passed state abbreviation and compares its low and high Zip Code values to the passed code. It returns true if the Zip Code is in the range, and false if it is not.

A copy of ZIPS.DBF is on the Developer's Library program disk (and at the end of this discussion). Since the number of states is small, the file is not indexed and only the database is needed.

If the ZIPS database is not open when CHKZIP is called, it is opened in the next available area. It is not closed on exit. ZIPS has the following structure:

Zip Codes (ZIPS.DBF)

Field Name	Type	Width	Decimals
STATE	C	2	0
STATENAME	C	20	0
LOZIP	C	5	0
HIZIP	C	5	0

Coding Examples

```
* Verify that a Zip Code is in correct range
zipcode_ok = CHKZIP(state, zipcode)

* Validation during data entry
@ 5, 10 GET zipcode VALID CHKZIP(state, zipcode)

* Typical data entry sequence

@ 8, 45 GET state PICTURE "!!" ;
   VALID CHKSTATE (state)
@ 8, 57 GET zipcode PICTURE "!!!!!!!!!!" ;
   VALID CHKZIP (state, zipcode)

READ
```

Zip Codes (ZIPS.DBF)

STATE	STATENAME	LOZIP	HIZIP
AK	Alaska	99500	99999
AL	Alabama	35000	36999
AR	Arkansas	71500	72899
AS	American Samoa	96799	96799
AZ	Arizona	85000	86599
CA	California	90000	96699
CO	Colorado	80000	81699
CT	Connecticut	06000	06999
DC	District of Columbia	20000	20599
DE	Delaware	19700	19999
FL	Florida	32000	34699
GA	Georgia	30000	31999
GU	Guam	96910	96919
HI	Hawaii	96700	96899
IA	Iowa	50000	52699
ID	Idaho	83200	83899
IL	Illinois	60000	62999
IN	Indiana	46000	47999
KS	Kansas	66000	67999
KY	Kentucky	40000	42799
LA	Louisiana	70000	71499
MA	Massachusetts	01000	02799
MD	Maryland	20600	21999
ME	Maine	03900	04999
MI	Michigan	48000	49999
MN	Minnesota	55000	56799
MO	Missouri	63000	65899
MS	Mississippi	38600	39799
MT	Montana	59000	59999

STATE	STATENAME	LOZIP	HIZIP
NC	North Carolina	27000	28999
ND	North Dakota	58000	58899
NE	Nebraska	68000	69399
NH	New Hampshire	03000	03899
NJ	New Jersey	07000	08999
NM	New Mexico	87000	88499
NV	Nevada	88900	89899
NY	New York	09000	14999
OH	Ohio	43000	45899
OK	Oklahoma	73000	74999
OR	Oregon	97000	97999
PA	Pennsylvania	15000	19699
PR	Puerto Rico	00600	00999
RI	Rhode Island	02800	02999
SC	South Carolina	29000	29999
SD	South Dakota	57000	57799
TN	Tennessee	37000	38599
TT	Caroline Islands	96940	96949
TT	Mariana Islands	96950	96959
TT	Marshall Islands	96960	96970
TX	Texas	75000	79999
UT	Utah	84000	84799
VA	Virginia	22000	24699
VI	Virgin Islands	00800	00899
VT	Vermont	05000	05999
WA	Washington	98000	99499
WI	Wisconsin	53000	54999
WV	West Virginia	24700	26899
WY	Wyoming	82000	83199

```
*********************************************************************
FUNCTION CHKZIP (statecode, zipcode)
*********************************************************************

* Verify range of first five characters of U.S. Zip Codes

* Copyright(c) 1991 -- James Occhiogrosso

LOCAL old_area := SELECT()

* If passed state code exceeds 2 characters, exit
IF LEN(TRIM(statecode)) > 2
    RETURN(.T.)
ENDIF

* Make sure Zip Code database is available
IF EMPTY(SELECT("zips"))
    IF FILE('zips.dbf')
        * If ZIPS file exists, open it
        USE zips NEW
    ELSE
        * Otherwise, exit
        RETURN(.T.)
    ENDIF
ENDIF
SELECT zips

* If ZIPS pointer is not on correct state, move it
IF UPPER(SUBSTR(statecode,1,2)) != zips->state
    LOCATE FOR UPPER(TRIM(statecode)) $ zips->state
ENDIF

* Validate first 5 digits of passed Zip Code
IF LEN(TRIM(SUBSTR(zipcode,1,5))) > 4 ;
    .AND. zipcode >= zips->lozip .AND. zipcode <= zips->hizip

    * Restore normal add/edit message and return
    AEDMSG('mw_pgdn')
    * Reselect original area and return
    SELECT(old_area)
    RETURN(.T.)

ELSE
    * Sound error beep
    ERRORBEEP()
    IF .NOT. FOUND()
        AEDMSG('State not in database')
    ELSE
        * Otherwise, display correct range
        AEDMSG('Range for ' + SUBSTR(statecode,1,2) + ' is ' + ;
            zips->lozip + ' to ' + zips->hizip)
```

```
   ENDIF

   * Reselect original area and return
   SELECT(old_area)
   RETURN(.F.)

ENDIF
```

CLRSHADOW

Description:
Removes a shadow placed on the screen by SHADOW

Syntax:
CLRSHADOW( )

Returns:
Nothing

File Name:
F_SHADOW.PRG

Screen Use:
Areas previously placed on the SHADOW stack

Arguments:
None

Typical Use:
To restore shadowed areas of the screen sequentially to their original states

Error Handling:
Does nothing if the shadow counter is zero

See Also:
SHADOW

Discussion

Use CLRSHADOW only with SHADOW. It restores screen areas SHADOW has overwritten. It uses SHADOW's internal counter and screen stack to permit sequential clearing of shadows without keeping track of their coordinates. For more information and an example of its use, see SHADOW and the example in T_SCRNS.PRG.

CAUTION: Source code for CLRSHADOW (shown on the next page) is extracted from F_SHADOW.PRG and shown for reference only. You cannot use CLRSHADOW without SHADOW.

```
****************************************************************
FUNCTION CLRSHADOW
****************************************************************

* Restore shadowed screen areas

IF COUNTER > 0

    SCRNREST(screens[1, counter])
    SCRNREST(screens[2, counter])

    * Decrement screen counter
    counter--
ENDIF
RETURN NIL
```

CLRVARS

Description:
Clears the set of field variables created by the INITVARS function

Syntax:
CLRVARS( )

Returns:
Nothing

File Name:
F_MVARS.PRG

Screen Use:
None

Arguments:
None

Typical Use:
To clear field memory variables before issuing GETs for new data

Global Variables:
Uses the current set of public variables created by INITVARS

See Also:
EQUVARS, FREEVARS, INITVARS, REPLVARS

Discussion

CLRVARS fills the public memory variables created by INITVARS with empty values. It is usually used to clear the variables before adding new data. Each variable is set according to its type. Character variables are filled with spaces, numerics are set to zero, and dates are set to empty date values. Logicals are set false, and memo fields are initialized to null strings.

Coding Examples

```
* Open database
USE DataFile NEW

* Initialize public field variables
INITVARS()

* DO WHILE <adding records>
    * Clear field variables
    CLRVARS()

    * Add a record. Issue GETs for desired variables
        .
        .
        .
    * End of add routine. Replace record.

    REPLVARS()

* End of loop
```

See sample program T_AEDBAR.PRG on the companion disk for a typical example.

```
****************************************************************
FUNCTION CLRVARS
****************************************************************

* Clears field variables created by INITVARS

* Copyright(c) 1991 -- James Occhiogrosso

LOCAL counter := 0, field_cnt := FCOUNT(), old_record := RECNO()
PRIVATE field_name

* Move file pointer to end of file (dummy) record
GO BOTTOM
SKIP

* Equate fields to memory variables. Since this is the
* end of file record, all fields are blank.

FOR counter = 1 TO field_cnt
    field_name = LOWER(FIELD(counter))
    m&field_name = &field_name
NEXT

* Restore record pointer and return
GO old_record

RETURN NIL
```

COMPUTE

Description:
Displays the result of a computation

Syntax:
COMPUTE(<Expression>, <nRow>, <nColumn>, <cPictureExp>, [<cUser Function>], [<cColor>])

Returns:
True unless the user specified function changes it (see discussion below)

File Name:
F_COMPUT.PRG

Screen Use:
Defined in calling parameters

Arguments:
<nExpression> – Expression to be evaluated. Must evaluate to a numeric.

<nRow>, <nColumn> – Row and column coordinates for displaying the evaluated expression

<cPictureExp> – Picture expression for formatting the result

[<cUserFunction>] – Optional name of a user defined function called when COMPUTE is executed

[<cColor>] – Optional color string used to display results

Typical Use:
To display and validate computed results as data is entered into interrelated fields

Cautions:
The user defined function must be declared EXTERNAL to link it.

Discussion

You can call COMPUTE from a VALID during data entry. It requires the first four parameters to work correctly. Use it to display the result of calculations while data is being entered into related fields.

The passed expression is evaluated and its result is displayed at the specified coordinates. Pass it without delimiting quotation marks. It must evaluate to a numeric value.

COMPUTE calls a user defined function (UDF) if it is passed one. The function can validate or display results that involve interrelated data items. Thus, you can use COMPUTE to validate fields involved in a total. In each case, call the same UDF. It must return a logical value that then serves as COMPUTE's return value.

You can use COMPUTE to display a calculated result as data is entered into related fields, or to keep the results of interdependent fields within a desired range. In the example below, the UDF displays a message if the total exceeds an arbitrary limit. It also returns false to COMPUTE which in turn returns false to the pending GET. The operator cannot leave the GET until he or she enters data that has all results within the desired range.

You can pass an optional color specification to COMPUTE. If passed, it is used to display all computed values. To pass a color without a user function, pass NIL (comma) for the UDF name.

Coding Examples

The example below uses COMPUTE to display a subtotal for each of two items, while validating a total for all entries. It calls the sample UDF CHKTOTAL for each entry to display the total order value. The example is on the companion disk in the file T_COMPUT.PRG.

To demonstrate validation of a total, I have set an arbitrary upper limit. Note that the user function returns false to COMPUTE if the total exceeds the limit. The previously displayed computation (for the line item) is cleared, and control returns to the GET field that caused the limit to be exceeded. To leave the field, the operator must reenter the data.

```
*******************************************************************
* Test program for COMPUTE function -   FILE T_COMPUT.PRG
*******************************************************************

* Copyright(c) 1991 -- James Occhiogrosso

* Computes, displays, and validates totals for line items.
#include 'inkey.ch'

LOCAL price1 := 0, price2 := 0, quantity1 := 0, quantity2 := 0

#ifdef DEBUG
   DEVELOP()
#endif

INITGLOBAL()
SETCOLOR(colstd)
CLEAR

DO WHILE LASTKEY() != K_ESC

   * Get quantity and price of each item. Update and
   * validate total with each entry.

   @ 5, 15 GET quantity1 PICTURE '999' VALID       ;
             COMPUTE(quantity1 * price1, 5, 30, ;
             "99999.99", "CHKTOTAL", colhelp1)

   @ 5, 22 GET price1 PICTURE '99.99' VALID        ;
             COMPUTE(quantity1 * price1, 5, 30, ;
             "99999.99", "CHKTOTAL", colhelp1)

   @ 6, 15 GET quantity2 PICTURE '999' VALID       ;
             COMPUTE(quantity2 * price2, 6, 30, ;
             "99999.99", "CHKTOTAL", colhelp1)

   @ 6, 22 GET price2 PICTURE '99.99' VALID        ;
             COMPUTE(quantity2 * price2, 6, 30, ;
             "99999.99", "CHKTOTAL", colhelp1)

   @ 7, 15 TO 7, 37 DOUBLE
   READ

ENDDO
RETURN
```

```
****************************************************************
FUNCTION CHKTOTAL (ret_value)
****************************************************************
* Sample user defined function called by COMPUTE

* Displays and validates total each time data is
* entered into one of four quantity and price fields

LOCAL old_color := ''

LOCAL tot_amt := (quantity1 * price1) + (quantity2 * price2)

IF tot_amt > 99999.99

    * Amount exceeds specified limit
    ERRORBEEP()
    CENTERON(MAXROW(), 'Entry too large. ' + hitanykey)

    * Display asterisks in total field
    old_color = SETCOLOR(colbarhi)
    @ 8, 30 SAY '*****.**'
    SETCOLOR(old_color)

    * Wait for operator
    INKEY(0)

    * Clear totals area and return to pending GET
    @ 8, 30 SAY SPACE(8)
    @ MAXROW(), 0
    ret_value = .F.

ELSE
    * Total is within defined limits
    @ 8, 30 SAY tot_amt PICTURE '99999.99'

ENDIF

RETURN ret_value
```

```
****************************************************************
FUNCTION COMPUTE (compexpr, line, col, pictexpr, userfunc, ;
               new_color)
****************************************************************

* Displays on-screen computations during data entry

* Copyright(c) 1991 -- James Occhiogrosso

LOCAL old_color := IF(PCOUNT()=6,SETCOLOR(new_color),SETCOLOR())
LOCAL ret_logic := .T.

* Display data with passed picture expression
@ line, col SAY compexpr PICTURE pictexpr

* If user function passed, execute it

IF PCOUNT() > 4 .AND. .NOT. EMPTY(userfunc)
    ret_logic := &userfunc(ret_logic)
ENDIF

* If UDF returns with error, clear computation area
IF .NOT. ret_logic
    @ line, col SAY 0 PICTURE pictexpr
ENDIF

SETCOLOR(old_color)
RETURN ret_logic
```

CSRINSERT

Description:
Controls cursor size during data entry

Syntax:
CSRINSERT( )

Returns:
Nothing

File Name:
F_CSRINS.PRG

Screen Use:
None

Arguments:
See discussion below

Typical Use:
To change cursor size when the user presses the insert (Ins) key during data entry

Discussion

Application programs do not normally call CSRINSERT directly. It is usually called through a SET KEY on the Ins key (key 22). When used in this way, CSRINSERT toggles the insert status with each press of the Ins key. It also sets the cursor to an underscore if insert is off, and to a block if it is on. The cursor does not move.

CSRINSERT can also set the cursor size to match the current insert mode. To do this, use

    `CSRINSERT(,,, .f.)`

For an example, see the MEMOVIEW source code.

Coding Examples

```
* Set Ins key to call CSRINSERT from any wait state
SET KEY 22 TO CSRINSERT

* Put your data entry procedure here
DO DATA_ENTRY

* On exit, clear hot key
SET KEY 22 TO
```

```
*******************************************************************
FUNCTION CSRINSERT (proc_name, proc_line, input_var, toggle_csr)
*******************************************************************

* Sets cursor form based on current insert state

* Copyright(c) 1991 -- James Occhiogrosso

#include "setcurs.ch"

LOCAL ins_mode

toggle_csr = IF( toggle_csr == NIL, .T., toggle_csr )

* Get entry insert state
ins_mode = READINSERT()

* Toggle setting unless toggle parameter passed false
ins_mode = IF( toggle_csr, !ins_mode, ins_mode )
READINSERT(ins_mode)

IF ins_mode
   * Set block cursor
   SETCURSOR(SC_INSERT)
ELSE
   * Set normal underscore cursor
   SETCURSOR(SC_NORMAL)
ENDIF

RETURN NIL
```

DAYNUM

Description:
Determines day number from start of year (day 1 is January 1st)

Syntax:
DAYNUM(<dDate>)

Returns:
Integer

File Name:
F_DAYNUM.PRG

Screen Use:
None

Arguments:
<dDate> – Date value

Typical Use:
To perform interest calculations and other processes that require day numbers referenced to the beginning of a year

Defaults:
Uses current date if no argument is passed

Error handling:
Returns zero if the passed argument is not of date type

See Also:
DTOF, DTOL, ISLASTDAY, LASTDAY

Discussion

Use DAYNUM to get the value of a date as a numeric referenced to the beginning of the year. It respects all Clipper date formats and compensates for leap years.

Coding Examples

```
* Find number of days from beginning of year to current date
days_num = DAYNUM()

* Find number of days from beginning of year to date variable
days_num = DAYNUM(dDateVar)

* Find number of days in a year, assuming American date format
year_days = DAYNUM(CTOD('12/31/' + LTRIM(STR(YEAR
            (dDateVar)))))
```

```
*******************************************************************
FUNCTION DAYNUM (date_val)
*******************************************************************

* Returns day number of year (day 1 = January 1st)

* Copyright(c) 1991 -- James Occhiogrosso

LOCAL counter := 0, limit := 0, num_days := 0, old_date := ''

IF date_val = NIL
    * Default to current date if no value passed
    date_val = DATE()

ELSEIF VALTYPE(date_val) != 'D'
    * Return zero if argument is wrong type
    RETURN 0

ELSEIF MONTH(date_val) = 1
    * Return actual day if date is in January
    RETURN DAY(date_val)

ENDIF

* Save current date setting and set date to American
old_date = SET(_SET_DATEFORMAT, 'mm/dd/yyyy')

* Limit loop iterations
limit = MONTH(date_val) - 1

FOR counter = 1 TO limit

    * Count number of days in each month from start
    * of year to one month before passed date

    num_days = num_days + LASTDAY(CTOD(          ;
            LTRIM(STR(counter)) + '/01/' +       ;
            LTRIM(STR(YEAR(date_val)))))

NEXT

* Restore old date setting
SET(_SET_DATEFORMAT, old_date)

* Add number of days for current month and return
RETURN num_days + DAY(date_val)
```

DBNAMES

Description:
Extracts database file names and associated text descriptions from a data dictionary

Syntax:
DBNAMES(<cDataDictFile>, <aTextDescriptions>, <aDataBaseNames>)

Returns:
Empty string if no errors occur

File Name:
F_DBNAME.PRG

Screen Use:
None

Arguments:
<cDataDictFile> – Data dictionary file. See MAKEDBF for its structure.

<aTextDescriptions> – Array to be filled with text descriptions from the data dictionary

<aDataBaseNames> – Array to be filled with database names from the data dictionary

Typical Uses:
To create arrays of application database names and associated text descriptions for display or use by other functions, or to test for the presence of all databases named in a data dictionary

Error Handling:
If passed incorrect arguments, DBNAMES returns the character P.

If the data dictionary file is missing or cannot be opened, it returns the character D.

If a database named in the data dictionary is missing, its associated memo file is missing, or it is not a valid dBASE database, DBNAMES returns the file name.

See Also:
MAKENDX, PICKIT

Discussion

DBNAMES reads database names and associated text descriptions from an application data dictionary. It is passed the names of the dictionary and two empty arrays. It fills the arrays with the extracted database names and text descriptions. Other functions can then use them.

The data dictionary is a text file containing at least one line for each database in the following form:

        DBFDEF dbfname text ... text

DBFDEF indicates a database definition line. After DBNAMES finds the line, it loads the name of the database (dbfname) and the rest of the line (text ... text) into the arrays. Usually, the same data dictionary file is used for all operations. Besides the DBFDEF lines, it also contains detailed field and index information. Refer to MAKEDBF for a complete description of its format.

DBNAMES tests all databases defined in the dictionary for memo fields using the Developer's Library function ISMEMO. If a database contains a memo field, DBNAMES checks for an associated memo (DBT) file. If a named database or memo file is missing, or the file is not a valid database, DBNAMES aborts and returns the file's name.

Thus, you can use DBNAMES to ensure that all databases named in the data dictionary are valid and their associated memo files exist.

Coding Examples

The example uses DBNAMES to verify that all application databases and associated memo files exist. The database names are in the data dictionary file arsystem.def. See MAKENDX for a typical example using DBNAMES and PICKIT to allow operator selection of application databases for reindexing.

```
* Declare empty arrays
LOCAL text_array := {}, dbf_array := {}, db_error := ''

* Load arrays with database names and descriptions
db_error = DBNAMES('arsystem.def', text_array, dbf_array)

IF EMPTY(db_error)
   CENTERON(24, 'All files located')

ELSEIF db_error = 'D'
   CENTERON(24, ' Data dictionary file missing.')

ELSEIF db_error = 'P'
   CENTERON(24, ' Incorrect parameter passed. ')

ELSE
   CENTERON(24, ' Error with file ' + db_error)

ENDIF
```

```
*******************************************************************
FUNCTION DBNAMES (app_def, dbf_text, dbf_names)
*******************************************************************

* Reads a data dictionary and tests for existence of databases
* named in it. Extracts database names and text descriptions.

* Copyright(c) 1991 -- James Occhiogrosso

LOCAL dbf_name := '', dbf_type := 0, handle := 0, ;
      ret_value := '', textline := ''

* Check passed parameters

* Return P if number of parameters is wrong
IF PCOUNT() != 3
    RETURN 'P'

* Return P if parameters are wrong type
ELSEIF VALTYPE(app_def) != 'C' .OR. VALTYPE(dbf_names) != 'A' ;
                          .OR. VALTYPE(dbf_texts) != 'A'
    RETURN 'P'
ELSE
    * Open data dictionary file
    IF (handle = FOPEN(app_def)) <= 0
        * File cannot be opened--return D
        RETURN 'D'
    ENDIF
ENDIF

* Get first database definition line from data dictionary
dbf_name = GETDBFDEF(@textline, dbf_name, handle)

DO WHILE .NOT. EMPTY(dbf_name)

    * Check database name. If database exists, test for
    * associated memo file. If either is missing, exit
    * loop and return missing file name.

    IF FILE(dbf_name + '.dbf')

        dbf_type = ISMEMO(dbf_name)
        IF dbf_type = 1
            * Memo file missing, return its name
            IF .NOT. FILE(dbf_name + '.dbt')
                ret_value = dbf_name + '.dbt'
                EXIT
            ENDIF
        ELSEIF dbf_type = -1
            * Memo file error
            ret_value = dbf_name
            EXIT
        ENDIF
```

```
    ELSE
       * Database missing, return its name
       ret_value = dbf_name
       EXIT
    ENDIF

    * Add database name and associated text to arrays
    IF EMPTY(ret_value)
       AADD(dbf_names, dbf_name)
       AADD(dbf_texts, SUBSTR(textline, 1, 60))
    ENDIF

    * Get next database definition line from data dictionary
    dbf_name = GETDBFDEF(@textline, dbf_name, handle)

ENDDO WHILE .NOT. EMPTY(dbf_name)

RETURN ret_value


*******************************************************************
STATIC FUNCTION GETDBFDEF(textline, dbf_name, handle)
*******************************************************************

* Read data dictionary file line by line, looking for a database
* definition line (DBFDEF) or end of file marker.

textline = '*'
DO WHILE (UPPER(SUBSTR(textline, 1, 7)) != 'ENDFILE' .AND.   ;
          UPPER(SUBSTR(textline, 1, 6)) != 'DBFDEF') .OR.    ;
         (SUBSTR(textline, 1, 1) $ '*#' .OR. EMPTY(textline))
   textline = LTRIM(FREADLINE(handle))
ENDDO

IF UPPER(SUBSTR(textline, 1, 7)) = 'ENDFILE'
   * Done, close data dictionary file and return
   FCLOSE(handle)
   RETURN ''
ELSE
   * Strip "DBFDEF" code identifier and return filename
   textline = LTRIM(SUBSTR(textline, 7))
   dbf_name = PARSE(@textline)
ENDIF

RETURN dbf_name
```

DBVIEW

Description:
Provides operator messages and simple database views using DBEDIT

Syntax:
Pass DBVIEW as the user function's name when calling DBEDIT

Returns:
Zero to force DBEDIT to terminate on any key other than a cursor movement key

File Name:
F_DBVIEW.PRG

Screen Use:
Defined in the DBEDIT call

Arguments:
Uses a numeric mode from DBEDIT

Typical Use:
To display a pick list from a database while using the AEDBAR menu

Cautions:
DBVIEW is not linked if it is used only as the user function for DBEDIT. Declare it EXTERNAL at the top of your program.

See Also:
AEDBAR, AEDMSG, CHKKEY

Discussion

DBVIEW provides a quick way to display a list of items from another database. It does not allow any editing. You typically call it from a procedure that has itself been called from a VALID function. The up and down arrow keys scroll items if there are too many for the window.

Pressing any other key ends the view and returns control to the caller. If AEDBAR is in use, informative messages appear in its window.

Coding Examples

The procedure below shows a typical use of DBVIEW. Its source code is in the file T_DBVIEW.PRG on the companion disk, along with sample CUSTOMER and ORDERS databases. See CHKKEY for the database structures.

The example assumes that we must verify a customer account number before allowing further data entry. If the number is not located, a window of valid choices appears.

To verify the account number (custid), use CHKKEY in a VALID on it. Pass CUSTVIEW to CHKKEY as its user defined function. CUSTVIEW uses DBVIEW to control DBEDIT and provide messages in the AEDBAR window.

When the operator enters data for a customer, the VALID calls CHKKEY to locate the account number. Before CHKKEY returns, it calls CUSTVIEW. If the entry is valid (the customer was found), CUSTVIEW simply returns. CHKKEY then returns true to the VALID, and the cursor moves to the next field. Otherwise, DBEDIT and DBVIEW display a popup window of customer account numbers and names. The operator then views the window, moves the cursor to the desired selection, and presses any key to return to the main data entry screen. CUSTVIEW returns the operator selection to the account number, and places the code for the Enter key in the keyboard buffer. CHKKEY is called again, and since the account number is now valid, it simply displays the customer name and returns.

```
*******************************************************************
* Test program for DBVIEW function - FILE T_DBVIEW.PRG
*******************************************************************

* Copyright(c) 1991 -- James Occhiogrosso

* Displays a window of customer records if entered
* account ID is not found in customer database

#include "inkey.ch"
#include "box.ch"

* Force linking of DBVIEW function
EXTERNAL DBVIEW

PRIVATE mcustid := SPACE(6), address1 := SPACE(30)

INITGLOBAL()
SETCOLOR(colstd)
CLEAR

* Set SOFTSEEK on to prevent the window from starting
* at the end of the file
SET SOFTSEEK ON

* Open test files and set relationship

USE customer INDEX customer NEW
USE orders INDEX orders NEW
SET RELATION TO custid INTO customer

DO WHILE LASTKEY() <> K_ESC

   @ 5, 12 GET mcustid PICTURE "!!!999" ;
           VALID CHKKEY("customer", mcustid, "custview", ;
                       5, 20, 50, "customer->company")
   @ 7, 12 GET address1
   READ
ENDDO

CLEAR

RETURN
```

```
*******************************************************************
FUNCTION CUSTVIEW
*******************************************************************

* Note that on entry to this procedure from CHKKEY, the FOUND()
* status is not altered. We use it here to determine if we must
* display the customer window.
*
MEMVAR colwindow, mcustid

LOCAL dbe_view := ARRAY(1), headings := '', old_color := '', ;
      old_screen := '', old_record := RECNO()

IF .NOT. FOUND()

   * Save screen values
   old_color  := SETCOLOR(colwindow)
   old_screen := SCRNSAVE(7, 29, 19, 75)

   * Box window and set up DBEDIT view
   @ 7, 29, 19, 75 BOX B_SINGLE + ' '
   dbe_view[1] = '" " + custid + "      | " + company + " "'
   headings := 'Cust. ID          Company Name'

   * Call DBEDIT using DBVIEW to handle messages
   DBEDIT(8, 31, 18, 73, dbe_view, 'dbview', '', headings)

   * Return selection to mcustid variable
   mcustid = customer->custid

   * Restore screen
   SETCOLOR(old_color)
   SCRNREST(old_screen)

   * Return to original customer record. The cursor is on
   * custid GET as if this procedure never executed. An Enter
   * is placed in the keyboard so that when CUSTVIEW returns,
   * CHKKEY is called again. The cycle repeats, and since the
   * customer ID is now valid, CHKKEY displays the customer
   * name. When CUSTVIEW is called for the second time, it
   * simply returns immediately. Thus, both an account number
   * and a name are displayed.

   GOTO old_record
   KEYBOARD CHR(K_ENTER)
ENDIF

RETURN FOUND()
```

```
*******************************************************************
FUNCTION DBVIEW (dbe_mode)
*******************************************************************

* DBEDIT view control used when AEDBAR is active

* Copyright(c) 1991 -- James Occhiogrosso

#include "inkey.ch"
LOCAL keypress := LASTKEY(), ret_value := 1

DO CASE
    * Mode is idle, put general message in window
    CASE dbe_mode = 0
       AEDMSG('mw_view')

    * Top of file, beep and blink "bof" message
    CASE dbe_mode = 1
       ERRORBEEP()
       AEDMSG('mw_bof', colblink)

    * Bottom of file, beep and blink "eof" message
    CASE dbe_mode = 2
       ERRORBEEP()
       AEDMSG('mw_eof', colblink)

    * Empty file, display message
    CASE dbe_mode = 3
       AEDMSG('File is empty')

    * Any other key
    CASE dbe_mode = 4
       IF (keypress <= K_F2 .OR. keypress > 256 ;
          .OR. keypress = K_F1) .AND. TYPE('fkeyset') != 'U'

          * Call special keys procedure if any function key or
          * Alt key combination is pressed. The variable
          * "fkeyset" must contain the procedure's name.

          IF .NOT. EMPTY(fkeyset)
             SETCOLOR(old_color)
             DO &fkeyset WITH 'AEDBAR', 0, '', keypress
          ENDIF
       * End view and return
       ELSE
          AEDMSG('mw_pgdn')
          ret_value = 0
       ENDIF
ENDCASE

RETURN ret_value
```

DECODE

Description:
Restores a character string previously encoded by ENCODE to its original value

Syntax:
DECODE(<cString>)

Returns:
Decoded character string

File Name:
F_DECODE.PRG

Screen Use:
None

Arguments:
<cString> – Character string to be decoded

Typical Use:
To restore encoded data for comparison to entered data

Cautions:
Only decodes strings encoded by ENCODE

See Also:
ENCODE, PASSWORD

Discussion

Use DECODE to restore a string encoded by ENCODE to its original value.

For more discussion and examples, see ENCODE and PASSWORD.

```
****************************************************************
FUNCTION DECODE (in_string)
****************************************************************

* Decodes a string encoded by ENCODE

* Copyright(c) 1991 -- James Occhiogrosso

#define ADJVAL 30

LOCAL counter := 0, in_len := 0, out_string := ''

IF in_string != NIL

    * Trim passed string
    in_string := ALLTRIM(in_string)
    in_len := LEN(in_string)

    * Get ASCII value of each position and restore original value
    FOR counter = 1 TO in_len
       out_string := out_string +  ;
          CHR((ASC(SUBSTR(in_string, ;
               counter * -1, 1)) /2) - ADJVAL)
    NEXT

ENDIF

RETURN out_string
```

DEFDRIVE

Description:
Determines the default DOS disk drive

Syntax:
DEFDRIVE( )

Returns:
Single uppercase character

File Name:
DEFDRIVE.ASM

Screen Use:
None

Arguments:
None

Typical Use:
To determine current DOS default drive before changing it

See Also:
DISKTEST, LASTDRIVE

Discussion

Use DEFDRIVE to get the current default drive letter before operations that might change it. You can use the saved value later to restore the original drive.

DEFDRIVE returns a single uppercase character for the drive letter.

Coding Examples

The example below assumes that a process must run on default drive M.

```
* Save default disk drive letter
old_drive = DEFDRIVE() + ':'

* Change default drive to M
RUN M:

* Run a process that requires default drive M
DO M_PROCESS

* Reset default to original drive
RUN (old_drive)
```

```
; -----------------------------------------------------------------
; FUNCTION NAME: DEFDRIVE - Returns letter for default DOS drive
; -----------------------------------------------------------------
; Copyright(c)              1991 -- James Occhiogrosso

        INCLUDE DEVELOP.MAC         ; Developer's Library macro file

        PUBLIC  DEFDRIVE            ; Declare function name
                                    ; Declare Clipper EXTERNALS


        EXTRN   __RETC:FAR          ; Return string to Clipper

        CODESEG SEGMENT 'CODE'
                ASSUME CS:CODESEG


DEFDRIVE PROC   FAR

        JMP BEGIN                   ; Jump around data area
DEF_DRIVE DB    'A', 0              ; Last drive letter

BEGIN:
        PUSH_REGS                   ; Save Clipper registers
        MOV AH, 19h                 ; Default drive function
        INT 21h
        ADD AL, 'A'                 ; Convert result to ASCII

        PUSH CS                     ; Set up our data segment
        POP DS
        MOV BX, OFFSET DEF_DRIVE    ; Get drive letter address
        MOV [BX], AL                ; Move our value to it
        POP_REGS                    ; Restore Clipper registers
        RET_STRING CS BX            ; Return drive to Clipper

DEFDRIVE ENDP                       ; End of procedure

        CODESEG ENDS                ; End of code segment
                END                 ; End of assembly
```

DELRECORD

Description:
Deletes a record and marks it for recycling

Syntax:
DELRECORD(<cIndexKeyField>)

Returns:
True if the operation succeeds; false otherwise

File Name:
F_DELREC.PRG

Screen Use:
None

Arguments:
<cIndexKeyField> – Key field in any open index

Typical Use:
To place deleted records at the end of a file for later recycling by ADDRECORD

Cautions:
Always test the return value to guarantee that the record was deleted and marked.

The index containing the desired key field must be open when DELRECORD is called.

See Also:
ADDRECORD

Discussion

DELRECORD deletes records and marks them for recycling. Its companion function, ADDRECORD, recycles the records. A large application is constantly adding and deleting records. As time passes, the number of deleted records increases, and the database must be packed to restore efficiency.

DELRECORD can eliminate the need for packing. Of course, this assumes that the application deletes about as many records as it adds.

DELRECORD works only on the currently selected database. The passed key field must be of character type, and the file must be indexed on it. For a complex index expression, the key field must be the first item. The index must be open for either DELRECORD or ADDRECORD, but it need not be the controlling index.

To prevent a run time error, DELRECORD tests whether the key field exists. If so, it sets the record's DELETED flag, and replaces the value with a CHR(255) character. Thus, when the key field index is in control, the marked record appears at the end of the file. If the key field does not exist, or is not of character type, DELRECORD returns false.

In networked applications, use the Clipper RLOCK function to lock the record before calling DELRECORD.

Coding Example

In the example below, the selected database is indexed on the *orderno* field. The index expression may be complex as long as the key field is the first item in it.

```
* Delete record and mark orderno field with CHR(255)
IF DELRECORD('orderno')
   AEDMSG('Record deleted')
ELSE
   AEDMSG('Cannot delete this record')
ENDIF
```

```
*******************************************************************
FUNCTION DELRECORD (keyfield)
*******************************************************************

* Mark current record in active database for recycling

* Copyright(c) 1991 -- James Occhiogrosso

* Make sure field exists and is character type
IF .NOT. EMPTY(keyfield) .AND. TYPE(keyfield) = 'C'
    DELETE
    * Replace key field with null byte
    EVAL(FIELDBLOCK(keyfield),CHR(255))
    RETURN .T.
ENDIF

* Invalid key field
RETURN .F.
```

DEVELOP

Description:
Initializes and links library functions used for application development

Syntax:
DEVELOP( )

Returns:
Nothing

File Name:
F_DEVEL.PRG

Screen Use:
None

Arguments:
None

Typical Use:
To set hot keys and force linking of development functions

Cautions:
DEVELOP links functions that an application may not use. Always compile it conditionally.

See Also:
ARVIEW, GRID, HRULER, KEYCODE, NDXKEY, NDXVIEW, VRULER

Discussion

You generally use DEVELOP only during application development. It links the Developer's Library functions ARVIEW, GRID, HRULER, KEYCODE, NDXKEY, NDXVIEW, and VRULER, and sets default hot keys of Alt-G,

Alt-H, and Alt-V for GRID, HRULER, and VRULER, respectively. It also links Clipper's low-level file functions FCLOSE, FCREATE, FERROR, FOPEN, FREAD, FREADSTR, FSEEK, and FWRITE. The functions are then available for use from your program or the debugger.

Coding Examples

To use DEVELOP, put it in a preprocessor control structure as shown below. This causes the development functions to be compiled and linked only if the manifest constant DEBUG is defined. The constant can be defined at the top of your main program, in an include file, or by using the /D option with the compiler.

```
#ifdef DEBUG
    DEVELOP()
#enddef
```

For more information on using manifest constants and conditional compilation, see R. Spence, *Clipper Programming Guide*, 3rd ed., San Marcos, CA: Microtrend Books, 1992.

```
*****************************************************************
FUNCTION DEVELOP
*****************************************************************

* Utility to link external routines during testing

* Copyright(c) 1991 -- James Occhiogrosso

#include "inkey.ch"

* Link Developer's Library functions
EXTERNAL ARVIEW, GRID, HRULER, KEYCODE, NDXKEY, NDXVIEW, VRULER

* Link Clipper's low-level file functions
EXTERNAL FCLOSE, FCREATE, FERROR, FOPEN, FREAD, ;
         FREADSTR, FSEEK, FWRITE

* Set up the keys
SET KEY K_ALT_H TO HRULER
SET KEY K_ALT_V TO VRULER
SET KEY K_ALT_G TO GRID

RETURN NIL
```

DIAL

Description:
Dials a telephone number

Syntax:
DIAL(<cTelephoneNum>, [<nCommPort>], [<lTone>])

Returns:
Logical value

File Name:
DIAL.ASM

Screen Use:
None

Arguments:
<cTelephoneNum> – Telephone number to be dialed. May contain embedded formatting or modem control characters.

<nCommPort> – Optional communications port number. (COM1 to COM4 = 1 to 4, see discussion below).

<lTone> – Optional dialing method flag. True for tone dialing, false for pulse dialing.

Typical Use:
To dial a telephone number from a hot key during data entry or review

Defaults:
Does not control the baud rate. The dialing default is 1200 baud.

If <nCommPort> or <lTone> is not passed, the defaults are:
- Communications port = COM1
- Dialing code = TONE

Error Handling:
Returns false if any of the following conditions occur:

- Specified port does not respond.
- Modem does not respond.
- Incorrect parameter type is passed.

Cautions:
Does not check the validity of the passed telephone number string

See Also:
DIALCLR

Discussion

Many third-party libraries contain extensive communications functions. If your application must provide communications capabilities, I recommend you buy one of them.

Quite often, however, we simply need to dial a known telephone number. In this case, DIAL does the job nicely.

Typically, DIAL is called from a hot key during data entry or browsing. The telephone number of the current record is passed to it (usually via a UDF, as shown in example 2 below). After dialing the number, DIAL instructs the user to pick up the handset, and uses DIALCLR to disconnect the modem from the telephone line.

DIAL supports communications ports COM1 and COM2 on 8086/8088 based computers, and COM1 through COM4 on 80286/80386/80486-based computers. It returns false if the port value is outside this range.

DIAL initializes the port with default values of 1200 baud, no parity, 8-bit data, and 1 stop bit. These values permit dialing with almost all modems.

By setting the dialing method flag to false, you can enable pulse dialing for use with older telephone lines.

Coding Examples

Example 1 below is a test program you can compile and link to see how DIAL works. The code for it is in the file T_DIAL.PRG on the companion disk.

```
*******************************************************************
* Test program for DIAL, DIALCLR functions --- FILE T_DIAL.PRG
*******************************************************************
* Copyright(c) 1991 -- James Occhiogrosso
#include "inkey.ch"
LOCAL dial_ok := .F., keypress := 0, phone := SPACE(12), ;
      port := 1, tone   := .T.
INITGLOBAL()
SETCOLOR(colstd)
CLEAR

DO WHILE keypress != K_ESC

   dial_ok := .F.
   * Get dialing values

   @ 8, 15 SAY 'Enter desired values below,  ' + ;
               'or press Esc to exit.'
   @ 11, 18 SAY 'Telephone number to dial .... ' ;
         GET phone PICTURE '999-999-9999'
   @ 12, 18 SAY 'Communications port number .. ' ;
         GET port PICTURE '9'
   @ 13, 18 SAY 'Tone Dial? Y/N.............. ' ;
         GET tone PICTURE 'Y'

   READ

   IF LASTKEY() = K_ESC
       QUIT
   ENDIF

   * Test for telephone number entry

   IF EMPTY(STRTRAN(phone,'-'))
       ERRORBEEP()
       CENTERON(16, 'Please enter telephone number!')
   ELSE
       dial_ok = DIAL(phone, port, tone)

   ENDIF

   * If DIAL returns true, wait 20 seconds for connection

   IF dial_ok
```

```
        CENTERON(16, 'Dialing ... ' +           ;
           IF(SUBSTR(LTRIM(phone),1,1) = '-',   ;
              SUBSTR(LTRIM(phone),2), phone) + ;
           '. Press any key when connection is made.')
        keypress = INKEY(20)
        DIALCLR()
        @ 16, 0

   * Otherwise, if telephone number entered, display
   * error message for port or modem

   ELSEIF .NOT. EMPTY(STRTRAN(phone,'-'))
        CENTERON(16, 'Communications port or modem' + ;
                     ' not responding. Press any'    + ;
                     ' key to try again.')
        keypress = INKEY(0)
        @ 16, 0
   ENDIF

ENDDO

RETURN
```

Example 2 below shows the use of DIAL with a hot key in a typical application. This example assumes the user is browsing through records in a database. The telephone number field is equated to the variable mphone as each record is displayed. On pressing the hot key (F4 here), DIAL is called to dial the number.

```
* Set up hot key on entry to application

SET KEY -3 TO DIALER
CENTERON(21, 'Press F4 to dial telephone number ' + ;
             'of current record')

* Your application editing/browsing routine goes here.
* The DIALER function below is called when F4 is pressed.


******************************************************************
FUNCTION DIALER
******************************************************************

* DIALER is a typical example of a hot key function to display
* screen messages while dialing. The variables mphone, mport,
* and mtone are initialized before DIALER is called.

LOCAL dial_ok, old_screen

* Save message on screen line 21
old_screen = SCRNSAVE(21,0,21,79)
IF EMPTY(STRTRAN(mphone,'-'))
   ERRORBEEP()
```

```
         CENTERON(21, 'Cannot dial. Record has no telephone' + ;
                     'number entry!')
         PAUSE(2)
   ELSE
         dial_ok = DIAL(mphone, mport, mtone)
   ENDIF

   * If DIAL returned true, wait for connection

   IF dial_ok
         CENTERON(21, 'Dialing ... ' +                          ;
               IF(SUBSTR(LTRIM(mphone),1,1) = '-',              ;
                  SUBSTR(LTRIM(mphone),2), mphone) +            ;
                  '. Press any key when connection is made.')

         * Wait for a maximum of 20 seconds, or clear modem
         * and disconnect immediately on any key press

         INKEY(20)
         DIALCLR()

   * Otherwise, display error message

   ELSEIF .NOT. EMPTY(STRTRAN(mphone,'-'))
         ERRORBEEP()
         CENTERON(21, 'Communications port or modem' + ;
                      ' not responding.' )
         PAUSE(2)
   ENDIF

   * Restore screen line 21 and return

   SCRNREST(old_screen)
   RETURN NIL
```

```
;----------------------------------------------------------------
; FILENAME:   DIAL.ASM
;
; FUNCTIONS:
;
; DIAL   ---- Transmits passed phone number to modem for dialing
; DIALCLR -- Clears and resets communications port
;----------------------------------------------------------------
; Copyright(c)  1991 - James Occhiogrosso

        INCLUDE     DEVELOP.MAC     ; Include Developer's Library Macrofile

        PUBLIC      DIAL            ; Declare dialer function
        PUBLIC      DIALCLR         ; Declare dialer clear function

        EXTRN       __PARINFO:FAR   ; Get parameter information
        EXTRN       __PARNI:FAR     ; Get numeric integer parameter
        EXTRN       __PARL:FAR      ; Get logical parameter
        EXTRN       __PARC:FAR      ; Get string parameter
        EXTRN       __RETL:FAR      ; Return logic value to Clipper
        EXTRN       __RET:FAR       ; Return logic value to Clipper
        DGROUP      GROUP   DATASEG ; Clipper's data segment
        DATASEG     SEGMENT    PUBLIC '_DATA'

DIAL_STRING     DB      'AT S7=30 D'        ; Dial string
PULSE_TONE      DB      'T', 0              ; Default to tone dial
PORT_WORD       DB      83h                 ; Default to 1200,N,8,1
PORT_NUM        DB      0                   ; Default port is COM1
CR_STRING       DB      0Dh, 0              ; End modem command

HANG_UP         DB      '~~~+++~~~ATH0', 0Dh, 0  ; Hang-up string

DATASEG  ENDS

CODESEG  SEGMENT    PUBLIC 'CODE'
         ASSUME CS:CODESEG,DS:DGROUP,ES:DGROUP

;----------------------------------------------------------------
DIAL PROC FAR                           ; Dial passed telephone number
;----------------------------------------------------------------

START:
        PUSH_REGS                       ; Save Clipper registers

        P_COUNT                         ; Get number of parameters
        CMP     AX, 0                   ; Any parameters passed?
        JE      ERROR                   ; No! Return to Clipper
        CMP     AX, 3                   ; Yes! Jump to parameter
        JE      SETUP3                  ; handler based on PCOUNT

        CMP     AX, 2
        JE      SETUP2
        JMP     SETUP1                  ; Minimum is 1 parameter

ERROR:  SUB     AX, AX                  ; Clear AX (Return false)
```

Clipper Developer's Library

```
                JMP     DONE                    ;   and return to Clipper
SETUP3:                                         ; Parameter 3 - Tone/Pulse
        P_TYPE  3                               ; Get its type
        CMP     AX, 4                           ; Is it logical?
        JNE     ERROR                           ; No!  Return to Clipper
        GET_PARL 3                              ; Yes! Get its value
        CMP     AX, 1                           ; Is it true?
        MOV     PULSE_TONE, 54h ; Yes! Set for tone dial
        JE      SETUP2                          ;   and continue
        MOV     PULSE_TONE, 50h ; No! Set for pulse dial

SETUP2:                                         ; Parameter 2 - COM port
        P_TYPE  2                               ; Get its type
        CMP     AX, 2                           ; Is it numeric?
        JNE     ERROR                           ; No!  Return to Clipper
        GET_PARNI 2                             ; Yes! Get its value
        CMP     AX, 5                           ; Is it greater than 5?
        JGE     ERROR                           ; Yes! DOS only supports
                                                ;   COM1-4. Return error
        DECL    LL LAX                          ; DOS port is biased to zero
        MOV     PORT_NUM, AL                    ; Save port number

SETUP1:                                         ; Parameter 1 - Telephone no.
        P_TYPE  1                               ; Get its type
        CMP     AX, 1                           ; Is it a string?
        JE      NEXT1                           ; Yes! Continue
        JMP     ERROR                           ; No! Return to Clipper

NEXT1:
        CALL    INIT_COMM                       ; Initialize COM port
        TEST    AL, AL                          ; Did modem respond?
        JE      ERROR                           ; No! Return to Clipper
        TEST    AH, AH                          ; Does port exist?
        JE      ERROR                           ; No! Return to Clipper

        MOV DI, OFFSET DS:DIAL_STRING ; Get dial string address
        CALL    COMM_OUT        ;   and send to modem
        CALL    WRIT_CHAR

        GET_PARC 1                              ; Get telephone number
        PUSH    DS                              ; Save data segment
        PUSH    DX                              ; Save passed data address
        PUSH    AX
        CALL    COMM_OUT                        ; Set up COM port
        POP     DI                              ; Get telephone number
        POP     DS                              ;   address to DS:DI
        CALL    WRIT_CHAR                       ; Send it to modem
        POP     DS                              ; Restore data segment

        MOV DI,OFFSET DS:CR_STRING  ; Get modem end string

        CALL    COMM_OUT
        CALL    WRIT_CHAR                       ; Send modem CR command string
        MOV     AX, 1                           ; Set AX to 1 (Return true)
```

```
DONE:
        POP_REGS                        ; Restore Clipper registers
        RET_LOGIC                       ; Return logical to Clipper

DIAL    ENDP                            ; End of procedure

; ----------------------------------------------------------------
DIALCLR PROC   FAR                      ; Clears modem and disconnects
; ----------------------------------------------------------------
        PUSH_REGS                       ; Save Clipper registers
        CALL       INIT_COMM            ; Test COM port
        TEST       AL, AL               ; Did modem respond?
        JE         CLRERROR             ; No! Return error to Clipper
        TEST       AH, AH               ; Does port exist?
        JE         CLRERROR             ; No! Return error to Clipper

        MOV DI,    OFFSET DS:HANG_UP    ; Get hang-up string address
        CALL       COMM_OUT             ; Set up COM port
        CALL       WRIT_CHAR            ; Disconnect modem
        MOV        AX, 1                ; Set return value to true
        JMP        DONE2                ;    and return to Clipper

CLRERROR:
        MOV        AX, 0                ; Error! Set return to false
DONE2:
        POP_REGS                        ; Restore Clipper registers
        RET_LOGIC                       ; Return logical to Clipper
DIALCLR ENDP

; ----------------------------------------------------------------
; ---------------- Begin subroutines below. ----------------------
; ----------------------------------------------------------------
COMM_OUT PROC NEAR                      ; Get COM port
        SUB DH, DH
        MOV DL, PORT_NUM                ; Move port number to DL
        SUB CL, CL
        RET
COMM_OUT ENDP


WRIT_CHAR PROC NEAR
WRIT_IT:
        MOV AH, 01                      ; Output character request
        MOV AL, [DI]                    ; Get byte to transmit
        INT 14h
        INC DI                          ; Increment to next address
        CMP [DI], CL                    ; Is byte 0?
        JNE WRIT_IT                     ; No! Write next character
        RET                             ; Return to caller
WRIT_CHAR ENDP
```

```
INIT_COMM PROC NEAR              ; Initialize COM port
        SUB AH, AH
        MOV AL, PORT_WORD        ; Get initialization word
        SUB DH, DH
        MOV DL, PORT_NUM         ; Get port number
        INT 14h                  ; Initialize port
        RET                      ; Return to caller
INIT_COMM ENDP

CODESEG  ENDS                    ; End of code segment
         END                     ; End of assembly
```

DIALCLR

Description:
Disconnects modem from communications port

Syntax:
DIALCLR( )

Returns:
Logic value

File Name:
DIAL.ASM

Screen Use:
None

Arguments:
None

Typical Use:
To clear and disconnect modem from telephone line after operator picks up the handset

Defaults:
Clears the last communications port addressed by DIAL

Error Handling:
Returns false if the modem or communications port does not respond

Cautions:
Resets only the communications port previously used by DIAL. Provides no way to clear other ports.

See Also:
DIAL

Discussion

Use DIALCLR only after a successful call to DIAL. Typically, a message is displayed, instructing the operator to pick up the telephone handset and press a key. After a preset wait time, or if the operator presses a key, DIALCLR is called to disconnect the modem from the telephone line. Refer to DIAL for an example and the source code for DIALCLR.

DISKSIZE

Description:
Determines formatted capacity of specified disk

Syntax:
DISKSIZE(<nDriveSpec>)

Returns:
Integer

File Name:
DISKSIZE.ASM

Screen Use:
None

Arguments:
<nDriveSpec> – Integer identifying a disk drive

Typical values are:
        0 = Default drive
        1 = Drive A
        2 = Drive B
        3 = Drive C, etc.

Note: Since DISKSIZE is usually used with Clipper DISKSPACE, <nDriveSpec> takes the same values.

Typical Use:
To determine the number of disks required for a backup operation

Defaults:
Returns the size of the default drive if no parameter is passed

Error Handling:
Returns -1 if the drive is invalid, not ready, or contains an unformatted disk

Cautions:
Returns the formatted capacity of the disk actually in the selected drive. It does not return any information about the drive type.

See Also:
DISKTEST, GETINT24, SETINT24

Discussion

DISKSIZE returns the formatted capacity in bytes of the disk in the specified drive. A typical application is to determine the number of disks required for a copy procedure. By using FILESIZE and DISKSIZE, you can compute the number of a given type needed for a given set of files.

Coding Examples

```
* Get size of disk currently in drive A (in KB)

Drive_A = DISKSIZE(1)

* Display message based on disk size. The first three sizes
* shown are no longer sold with new equipment but are still
* in use on older computers.
IF Drive_A = 160256
    ? 'Disk in drive A is 5.25" SSSD 8 sector disk.'
ELSEIF Drive_A = 179712
    ? 'Disk in drive A is 5.25" SSDD 9 sector disk.'
ELSEIF Drive_A = 322560
    ? 'Disk in drive A is 5.25" DSDD 8 sector disk.'
ELSEIF Drive_A = 362496
      * From here on are disk sizes commonly
      * used today
    ? 'Disk in drive A is 5.25" DSDD (360K) disk.'
ELSEIF Drive_A = 1213952
    ? 'Disk in drive A is 5.25" DSHD (1.2M) disk.'
ELSEIF Drive_A = 730112
    ? 'Disk in drive A is 3.5" DSDD (720K) disk.'
ELSEIF Drive_A = 1457667
    ? 'Disk in drive A is 3.5" DSHD (1.4M) disk.'
ENDIF
```

For more examples, see the file T_DISKS.PRG on the companion disk and the DISKTEST function in this library.

```
; ----------------------------------------------------------------
; FILENAME: DISKSIZE.ASM
;
; FUNCTION: DISKSIZE -- Returns formatted size of disk in drive
;
; ----------------------------------------------------------------
; Copyright(c)  1991 -- James Occhiogrosso

        INCLUDE DEVELOP.MAC         ; Include Developer's Library macro file

        PUBLIC   DISKSIZE           ; Declare function and
                                    ;   Clipper externals
        EXTRN    __RETNL:FAR        ; Return long number to Clipper
        EXTRN    __PARINFO:FAR      ; Get parameter information
        EXTRN    __PARNI:FAR        ; Get numeric integer parameter

        CODESEG  SEGMENT 'CODE'
                 ASSUME CS:CODESEG  ; Define code segment

DISKSIZE PROC    FAR

        PUSH_REGS                   ; Save Clipper registers
        P_COUNT                     ; Get number of parameters in AX
        MOV DL, 0                   ; Default drive for Int 36h
        CMP AX, 0                   ; Was any parameter passed?
        JE  DISK_INFO               ; No! Get information for default
        P_TYPE 1                    ; Yes! Check parameter type
        CMP AX, 2                   ; Is it numeric?
        JE  GET_DRIVE               ; Yes! Get selected drive number
        MOV DX, 0FFFFh              ; No! Set DX:AX to -1 (error),
        MOV AX, 0FFFFh              ;    and return to Clipper
        JMP EXIT

GET_DRIVE:
        GET_PARNI 1                 ; Get value of parameter 1 and
        MOV DX, AX                  ;    put in DX (DL = Drive code)

DISK_INFO:
        MOV AH, 36h                 ; DOS - disk free space function
        INT 21h

        ; Return is:
        ; AX = sectors per cluster, BX = unused clusters
        ; CX = bytes per sector, DX = clusters per drive

        CMP AX, 0FFFFh              ; Did an error occur?
        JNE CALC_SIZE               ; No! Calculate size
        MOV DX, 0FFFFh              ; Yes! Set DX:AX to -1 (error)
        JMP EXIT                    ;    and return to Clipper

CALC_SIZE:                          ; Calculate disk size
        MOV BX, DX                  ; Temporarily save DX
        MUL CX                      ; Total space = AX * BX * CX
        MUL BX                      ; DX:AX is formatted size of disk
```

```
EXIT:
        POP_REGS                ; Restore Clipper registers
        RET_LONG                ; Return DX:AX long integer

DISKSIZE ENDP                   ; End of procedure
CODESEG  ENDS                   ; End of code segment
         END                    ; End of assembly
```

DISKTEST

Description:
Tests a disk drive

Syntax:
DISKTEST(<cDriveLetter>)

Returns:
Numeric value

File Name:
F_DSKTST.PRG

Screen Use:
None

Arguments:
<cDriveLetter> – Single-character drive letter

Typical Use:
To test the validity and readiness of the selected drive before performing disk operations

Error Handling:
Returns a number corresponding to the error encountered (see discussion below)

See Also:
DISKSIZE, GETINT24, SETINT24

Discussion

Use DISKTEST before disk operations if you are unsure of a drive's status. It is particularly useful when your application depends on an operator inserting or formatting floppy disks.

DISKTEST detects almost all physical disk errors, including write protected and unformatted disks. It works by trying to create a temporary file on the selected disk. If it can do so, no error occurs, and it returns zero. DISKTEST uses the Developer's Library INT24 function set (GETINT24 and SETINT24) to trap disk errors. It returns error numbers corresponding to those shown for GETINT24. In addition, it returns -1 if the passed drive letter is invalid.

Coding Examples

The example below uses DISKTEST to determine if the selected disk drive is ready. If it is, the program uses the Developer's Library DISKSIZE and Clipper DISKSPACE functions to display the formatted size and free space on the disk. If it encounters an error, it displays a message. The source code for the example is in the file T_DISKS.PRG on the companion disk.

```
***********************************************************
* TEST program for ----- DISKSIZE, DISKTEST, SETINT24, GETINT24
***********************************************************
* FILE = T_DISKS.PRG
*
#include "inkey.ch"
#include "setcurs.ch"
LOCAL disk_drive := ' ', disk_error := 0, disk_num := 0,  ;
      keypress := 0, old_cursor := SETCURSOR()

INITGLOBAL()
SETCOLOR(colstd)
CLEAR

DO WHILE keypress != K_ESC

    @ 10, 20 SAY 'Enter letter for disk drive to test ...... ' ;
         GET disk_drive PICTURE '!' VALID !EMPTY(disk_drive)

    READ
```

```
* Turn off cursor
SETCURSOR(SC_NONE)

* Test disk
disk_error = DISKTEST(disk_drive)

IF disk_error != 0
    * Error occurred, display error message
    DO CASE
        CASE disk_error = 1
            @ 12, 20 SAY 'Disk in drive ' + disk_drive + ;
                    ' is write protected.'

        CASE disk_error = 3
            @ 12, 20 SAY 'Drive ' + disk_drive + ;
                    ' is not ready.'

        CASE disk_error = 13
            @ 12, 20 SAY 'Disk in drive ' + disk_drive + ;
                    ' is not formatted.'

        CASE disk_error = -1
            @ 12, 20 SAY 'Drive ' + disk_drive +  ;
                    ' is not a valid drive.'
    ENDCASE
ELSE
    @ 12, 20 SAY 'Drive ' + disk_drive + ' is ready. '

    * Note that Clipper DISKSPACE and Developer's Library
    * DISKSIZE use numeric values for the disk argument.
    * The drive letter is translated into a number (A = 1,
    * B = 2, etc.) before calling either function. This
    * is done by subtracting 64 from its ASCII equivalent.

    disk_num = ASC(disk_drive) - ASC('A') + 1

    * Display total disk size and free space

    @ 13, 20 SAY 'Formatted size of this disk is = ' + ;
            LTRIM(STR(DISKSIZE(disk_num))) + ' bytes.'

    @ 14, 20 SAY 'It has ' + LTRIM(STR(DISKSPACE(disk_num))); 
            + ' bytes free.'
ENDIF

* Reset cursor and display message
SETCURSOR(old_cursor)
@ 17, 20 SAY 'Press any key to loop or Esc to exit.'
keypress = INKEY(0)
@ 12, 20 CLEAR TO 17, 70

ENDDO

RETURN
```

```
*******************************************************************
FUNCTION DISKTEST (drive)
*******************************************************************

* Tests a disk drive for validity (or readiness)

* Copyright(c) 1991 -- James Occhiogrosso

* Activate INT 24 handler and initialize local variables
LOCAL old_int24 := SETINT24(.T.), ;
      ret_value := 0, temp_file := ' '

* Make sure drive letter was passed
IF VALTYPE(drive) != 'C'
    RETURN(-1)
ENDIF

* Get first character of passed drive and add a colon
drive = SUBSTR(drive,1,1) + ':'

* Try to create a unique file on selected drive
temp_file = TEMPFILE('', drive)

IF EMPTY(temp_file)
    * Attempt failed, return INT24 error code
    ret_value = GETINT24()

    * If GETINT24 returns zero, disk drive is invalid
    ret_value = IF(ret_value = 0, -1, ret_value)

ELSE
    * Attempt succeeded, erase temporary file
    ERASE(temp_file)
ENDIF

* Reset INT 24 handler to entry condition
SETINT24(old_int24)

RETURN ret_value
```

DONEBEEP

Description:
Produces a two-tone sound generally used to indicate that an operation is complete

Syntax:
DONEBEEP([<nNumberBeeps>])

Returns:
Nothing

File Name:
F_DONBEP.PRG

Screen Use:
None

Arguments:
<nNumberBeeps> – Optional number of times to sound the tone

Typical Use:
To inform the operator that an operation has been completed successfully

Defaults:
Produces a single two-tone beep if <nNumberBeeps> is not passed

See Also:
ERRORBEEP

Discussion

Use DONEBEEP to provide an audible indication that a process is completed. Use ERRORBEEP to indicate that an entry error has occurred or further input is required. If you use them consistently, the operator is less dependent on screen messages and can do tasks more efficiently.

I usually use DONEBEEP in my applications to indicate when a record has been added or replaced in a file, and to confirm successful selection of an item from a list.

Coding Examples

```
* Advise operator that an operation is completed

IF add_ok

    * Display a message
    @ 22, 10 SAY 'Record added'

    * And sound a single two-tone beep
    DONEBEEP()

ENDIF

* To wake up a sleeping operator.  Beeping continues until
* the operator presses a key.

DO WHILE INKEY(.5) = 0
    DONEBEEP(3)
    ERRORBEEP(1)
ENDDO
```

```
*****************************************************************
FUNCTION DONEBEEP (howmany)
*****************************************************************

* Sounds a dual tone on completion of an operation

* Copyright(c) 1991 -- James Occhiogrosso

* Set number of beeps to one if not passed or not numeric
howmany = IF(VALTYPE(howmany) != 'N', 1, howmany)

* Sound tone
DO WHILE howmany-- > 0
    TONE(650,1)
    TONE(850,1)
ENDDO

RETURN NIL
```

DTOF

Description:
Determines first day of month

Syntax:
DTOF(<dDate>)

Returns:
Date value

File Name:
F_DTOF.PRG

Screen Use:
None

Arguments:
<dDate> – Date to be converted

Typical Use:
To set a lower date limit for records on monthly reports

Defaults:
Returns the date for the first day of the current month if no argument is passed

Error Handling:
Returns an empty date value if the passed date is invalid

See Also:
DTOL, ISLASTDAY, LASTDAY

Discussion

Use DTOF when you need the date of the first day of a month. It is usually used to set a lower limit for a monthly report or process. The current values of the

Clipper CENTURY and DATE settings determine the format of the returned date.

Coding Examples

```
* To get date of first day of current month

DTOF()

* To get date of first day of any date value

DTOF(any_date)
```

The example below uses values returned by DTOF and DTOL to copy the previous month's invoice records to a temporary sales file for printing. It assumes that an invoice file is currently open and indexed on a date field inv_date.

```
* Get dates of first and last day of previous month

prev_month = DATE() - LASTDAY(DATE())
prev_start = DTOF(prev_month)
prev_end   = DTOL(prev_month)

/* Move record pointer to first qualifying record. Note that
SOFTSEEK is turned on before performing the SEEK. This prevents
jumping to the end of the file if there are no records for the
first day of the month. */

old_soft = SET(_SET_SOFTSEEK, .T.)
SEEK prev_start
SET(_SET_SOFTSEEK, old_soft)

* Copy previous month's records to tmpsales

COPY TO tmpsales FOR inv_date >= prev_start .AND. ;
                     inv_date <= prev_end

/* Run prior month's sales report here using data in tmpsales.
Tmpsales is indexed before the report is run.  */
```

```
*****************************************************************
FUNCTION DTOF (date_val)
*****************************************************************

* Determines first day of month

* Copyright(c) 1991 -- James Occhiogrosso

IF date_val = NIL
    * Default to current date if no value passed
    date_val = DATE()

ELSEIF VALTYPE(date_val) != 'D'
    * Return null date if argument is wrong type
    RETURN CTOD("")

ENDIF

RETURN date_val - (DAY(date_val) - 1)
```

DTOL

Description:
Determines last day of month

Syntax:
DTOL(<dDate>)

Returns:
Date value

File Name:
F_DTOL.PRG

Screen Use:
None

Arguments:
<dDate> – Date to be converted

Typical Use:
To set an upper date limit for records on monthly reports

Defaults:
Returns the date for last day of current month if no argument is passed

Error Handling:
Returns an empty date value if passed date is invalid

See Also:
DTOF, ISLASTDAY, LASTDAY

Discussion

Use DTOL to find the date of the last day of a month. The common use is to set an upper limit for a monthly report or process. The current values of the Clipper CENTURY and DATE settings determine the format of the returned date.

Coding Examples

```
* To get date of last day of current month
DTOL()
* To get date of last day of any date value
DTOL(any_date)
```

See DTOF for another example.

```
****************************************************************
FUNCTION DTOL (date_val)
****************************************************************

* Determines last day of month

* Copyright(c) 1991 -- James Occhiogrosso

IF date_val = NIL
    * Default to current date if no value passed
    date_val = DATE()

ELSEIF VALTYPE(date_val) != 'D'
    * Return null date if argument is wrong type
    RETURN CTOD("")

ENDIF

RETURN date_val + (LASTDAY(date_val) - DAY(date_val))
```

ENCODE

Description:
Converts a character string to an unreadable form for security purposes

Syntax:
ENCODE(<cString>)

Returns:
Encoded character string

File Name:
F_ENCODE.PRG

Screen Use:
None

Arguments:
<cString> – Character string to be encoded

Typical Use:
Prevent casual reading of sensitive data

Cautions:
Encodes only the letters A through Z, digits 0 through 9, and the decimal point and underscore characters. It ignores all other characters.

See Also:
DECODE, PASSWORD

Discussion

ENCODE converts a character string to make it unreadable by normal means. A typical use is to protect passwords and other sensitive data from unauthorized viewing. A user browsing through a database with an interpreter or utility program cannot read data encoded by ENCODE.

To use ENCODE, pass it a string of any length. It returns an encoded string. Use DECODE to reverse the process.

ENCODE works only with character strings. However, you can encode numeric values by first converting them to strings with the Clipper STR function. Strings to be encoded must consist only of letters, digits, and the decimal point or underscore characters. ENCODE ignores other values. With user passwords, the developer should ensure they contain only valid characters before passing them to ENCODE. It processes the string character by character, starting at the end. Thus, it reverses the original order. It also converts each character to the extended ASCII set (values 128 to 255). It does this by converting each letter to uppercase, adding 30 to each ASCII value, and doubling the result.

Without knowing the algorithm, you cannot read the encoded data. However, ENCODE does not provide a high degree of security. Anyone with a knowledge of ASCII values and some patience could determine the algorithm. Use it only in applications that do not require maximum security and where potential violators are typically non-technical.

Coding Examples

Encode a password before storing it in a system database. Restrict it to capital letters and digits.

```
LOCAL password := SPACE(10)
@ 10, 10 SAY 'Enter Password ..... ' GET password ;
              PICTURE '@! NNNNNNNNNN'
READ
* Save password in system database
sysdata->pr_passwd := ENCODE(password)

* Restore password's original value
password := DECODE(sysdata->pr_passwd)
```

```
*****************************************************************
FUNCTION ENCODE (in_string)
*****************************************************************

* Encodes passed string. Ignores non-alphanumeric characters

* Copyright(c) 1991 -- James Occhiogrosso

#define ADJVAL 30
LOCAL counter := 0,in_len := 0,next_char := '',out_string := ''

IF in_string != NIL

    * Trim passed string and convert letters to uppercase
    in_string := ALLTRIM(UPPER(in_string))
    in_len := LEN(in_string)

    * Reverse string, add 30 to each character, and double it
    FOR counter = 1 TO in_len

        * Get characters in reverse order
        next_char = SUBSTR(in_string, counter * -1, 1)

        * Add character to return string if numeric,
        * alphabetic, space, or underscore characters

        IF next_char == '.'.OR. next_char == '_'.OR. ;
           ISDIGIT(next_char) .OR. ISALPHA(next_char)
              out_string := out_string + ;
                  CHR((ASC(next_char) + ADJVAL) * 2)
        ENDIF
    NEXT
ENDIF

RETURN out_string
```

EQUVARS

Description:
Loads memory variables created by INITVARS from the current database record

Syntax:
EQUVARS( )

Returns:
NIL

File Name:
F_MVARS.PRG

Screen Use:
None

Arguments:
None

Typical Use:
To fill field memory variables with values from the current database record before editing it

Global Variables:
Uses the current set of public variables created by INITVARS

See Also:
CLRVARS, FREEVARS, INITVARS, REPLVARS

Discussion

EQUVARS loads the public memory variables created by INITVARS from the current database record. It fills each variable with data from the corresponding field. Routines can then operate on the memory variables, leaving the database unchanged. It is thus protected against damage and can be restored in the event of errors or other problems. All the program must do is simply not replace the original record.

Coding Examples

```
* Open database
USE DataFile NEW

* Initialize field variables
INITVARS()

* DO WHILE <editing records>

    * Go to desired record
    * Equate variables to fields
    EQUVARS()
    * Your edit or viewing routine. GET or view data
        .
        .
        .
    * End of routine. Replace record if it was changed

    IF UPDATED()
       REPLVARS()
    ENDIF

* End of loop
```

See sample program T_AEDBAR.PRG on the companion disk for a typical example.

```
*******************************************************************
FUNCTION EQUVARS
*******************************************************************

* Load memory variables created by INITVARS from database fields

* Copyright(c) 1991 -- James Occhiogrosso

LOCAL counter := 0, field_cnt := FCOUNT()
PRIVATE field_name

* Load each variable from corresponding field
FOR counter = 1 TO field_cnt
   field_name = LOWER(FIELD(counter))
   m&field_name = &field_name
NEXT

RETURN NIL
```

ERRORBEEP

Description:
Produces a slightly unpleasant short error tone

Syntax:
ERRORBEEP([<nNumberBeeps>])

Returns:
Nothing

File Name:
F_ERRBEP.PRG

Screen Use:
None

Arguments:
<nNumberBeeps> – Optional number of times to sound the tone

Typical Use:
To warn the operator of an invalid entry

Defaults:
If <nNumberBeeps> is not passed, a single tone is sounded.

See Also:
DONEBEEP, WAKEBEEP

Coding Examples

```
* Beep twice to warn the operator of an invalid entry

IF EMPTY(choice)
    @ 22, 10 SAY 'You must enter at least one choice.'
    ERRORBEEP(2)
```

```
ENDIF

* Beep once to warn the operator of an invalid entry

IF EMPTY(choice)
    @ 22, 10 SAY 'You must enter at least one choice.'
    ERRORBEEP()
ENDIF

* Beep until the operator presses a key

@ 22, 10 SAY 'Incorrect entry. Press any key to reenter'
DO WHILE INKEY() == 0
    ERRORBEEP()
ENDDO
```

```
******************************************************************
FUNCTION ERRORBEEP (howmany)
******************************************************************

* Sounds a slightly unpleasant error tone

* Copyright(c) 1991 -- James Occhiogrosso

* Default is 1 beep if no parameter passed
howmany = IF(howmany = NIL, 1, howmany)

DO WHILE howmany-- > 0
    TONE(100,2)
    TONE(0,1)
ENDDO

RETURN NIL
```

FILEDATE

Description:
Gets or sets the date on a DOS file

Syntax:
FILEDATE(<cFileName>, [<dDateToSet>])

Returns:
Clipper date

File Name:
FILEDATE.ASM

Screen Use:
None

Arguments:
<cFileName> – Name of a file to get or set the date on. Supports full DOS path names.

<dDateToSet> – Optional new date setting

Typical Use:
To determine and optionally set the date on a DOS file

Error Handling:
Returns an empty date value on any error in retrieving or setting the file date

Cautions:
Does not set dates before 01/01/1980 correctly. If an earlier date is passed, the century digits default to 20. For example, passing the date 01/01/1901 stamps the file with the date 01/01/2001.

See Also:
FILESIZE, FILETIME, FILETOUCH

Discussion

Like most functions that use low-level file handling techniques, FILEDATE will operate on hidden or system files. Since date setting does not actually involve writing to the file, it will also operate on read-only files. When using FILEDATE, test for errors by using the Clipper EMPTY function to determine whether the return value is a null date.

You can also use the Clipper DIRECTORY function to return the date of a file as an array element. Use it when you need information about a group of files. Use FILEDATE when you need information about a specific file. FILEDATE and FILETIME are also used to alter date and time values on a file when a process rewrites it. A typical example appears in SYSSAVE. The date and time stamp of each copy is set to be the same as the original.

Coding Examples

```
* Get current date of a system definition file
old_date = FILEDATE('arsystem.def')

* Save current date and set file to system date
old_date = FILEDATE('arsystem.def', DATE())

* To test for an error after either of above
* operations, check for a null date return.

IF EMPTY(old_date)
   * Error occurred
   DO ERROR_PROC
ENDIF
```

See T_FILES.PRG on the companion disk, and the code for SYSSAVE for more examples using FILEDATE. The source code for T_FILES.PRG appears with FILESIZE.

```
; ---------------------------------------------------------------
; FUNCTION NAME: FILEDATE - Gets or sets the DOS date on a file
; ---------------------------------------------------------------
; Copyright(c)              1991 — James Occhiogrosso

        INCLUDE   DEVELOP.MAC         ; Developer's Library macro file

        PUBLIC    FILEDATE            ; Declare function name

                                      ; Declare Clipper EXTERNALs
        EXTRN     __PARINFO:FAR       ; Get Clipper parameter information
        EXTRN     __PARDS:FAR         ; Get Clipper date
        EXTRN     __PARC:FAR          ; Get Clipper string
        EXTRN     __RETDS:FAR         ; Return date string to Clipper
        EXTRN     __RETC:FAR          ; Return string to Clipper

        CODESEG   SEGMENT 'CODE'
                  ASSUME CS:CODESEG

        FILEDATE  PROC  FAR           ; Get or set date on file

                  JMP   BEGIN         ; Jump around data area

        FILE_HANDLE DB 0              ; Store file handle
        GET_DATE    DB 08h DUP(0)     ; Store Clipper return date
        SET_FLAG    DB 0              ; Set to 1 if setting date

        BEGIN:
                  PUSH_REGS           ; Save Clipper registers

                  PUSH  DS            ; Save Clipper data segment
                  PUSH  CS
                  POP   DS            ; Set up our data segment
                  MOV   BX, OFFSET FILE_HANDLE ; Get address of first data
                  MOV   AX, 0
                  MOV   CX, 5         ; Loop five times (10 bytes)
        NEXT:     MOV   [BX], AX      ; Clear date string area
                  ADD   BX, 2         ; Increment address
                  LOOP  NEXT
                  POP   DS            ; Restore Clipper DS

                  P_TYPE 1            ; Get parameter type to AX
                  CMP   AX, 1         ; Character string passed?
                  JNE   RET_NULL_1    ; No! Return null date

                  P_COUNT             ; Yes! Get parameter count
                  CMP   AX, 02        ; If no second parameter,
                  JNE   OPEN_FILE     ;   get file date and return
                  P_TYPE 2            ; Else, get parameter type
                  CMP   AX, 8         ;   Is it a date?
                  JNE   RET_NULL_1    ;   No! Return null date
                  MOV   CS:SET_FLAG, 1 ;  Yes! Set flag
                  PUSH  DS            ;   Save data segment
                  JMP   OPEN_FILE     ; Jump around null return
```

```
RET_NULL_1:
        JMP     EXIT_DATE               ; RET_NULL label for direct
                                        ;   jump to exit point due
RET_NULL_2:                             ;   to an error condition
        JMP     CLOSE_FILE
OPEN_FILE:
        GET_PARC 1                      ; Get address of filename
        MOV     DS, DX                  ; Get filename segment
        MOV     DX, AX                  ; Get filename offset
        SUB     AL, AL                  ; Read only mode
        MOV     AH, 3Dh                 ; Open file request
        INT     21h
        JC      RET_NULL_1              ; On error, return null date
        MOV     CS:FILE_HANDLE, AL      ; Save file handle
GET_THE_DATE:
        PUSH    CS                      ; Move data segment to CS
        POP     DS                      ;   for our data
        SUB     BH, BH                  ; Clear upper handle byte
        MOV     BL, FILE_HANDLE         ; Get DOS handle
        MOV     AH, 57h                 ; DOS date/time function
        SUB     AL, AL                  ; Clear lower byte
        INT     21h
        JC      RET_NULL_2              ; Error! Return null date

        MOV     AL, DL                  ; Move days to AL

        AND     AL, 00011111b           ; Mask out unused bits
        AAM                             ; Adjust MS/LS digits
        ADD     AX, 3030h               ; Convert digits to ASCII
        MOV     BX, OFFSET GET_DATE     ; Get address of return date
        MOV     [BX+6], AH              ; Save days digits (tens)
        MOV     [BX+7], AL              ; Save days digits (ones)

        MOV     AX, DX                  ; Restore original date
        MOV     CL, 5                   ; Get shift count
        SHR     AX, CL                  ; Shift month bits for DOS
        AND     AL, 00001111b           ; Mask out unused bits
        AAM                             ; Adjust MS/LS digits
        ADD     AX, 3030h               ; Convert digits to ASCII
        MOV     [BX+4], AH              ; Save days digits (tens)
        MOV     [BX+5], AL              ; Save days digits (ones)

        MOV     AX, DX                  ; Restore original date
        SHR     AH, 1                   ; Shift year bits
        XCHG    AL, AH                  ;   to correct position
        ADD     AL, 80d                 ; Correct to 1980
        CMP     AL, 100d                ; Are we beyond year 2000?
        MOV     [BX], 3931h             ; No! Default to 19 for MS
        JB      AROUND1                 ;   And skip next 2 lines
        SUB     AL, 100d                ; Yes! Adjust digit
        MOV     [BX], 3032h             ; Save MS digit as 20
```

```
AROUND1:
        AAM                             ; Adjust MS/LS digits
        ADD     AX, 3030h               ; Convert digits to ASCII
        MOV     [BX+2], AH              ; Save year MS digit (tens)
        MOV     [BX+3], AL              ; Save year LS digit (ones)
SET_THE_DATE:
        MOV     AL, CS:SET_FLAG         ; Check flag
        CMP     AL, 0                   ; Is it set?
        JE      CLOSE_FILE              ; No! We are done
        POP     DS                      ; Yes! Recover data segment
        MOV     CS:SET_FLAG, 0          ;   reset flag and
        GET_PARDS 2                     ;   get passed date
        MOV     DS, DX                  ; Get date segment into DS
        MOV     BX, AX                  ;   and offset into BX

        MOV     AX, WORD PTR [BX+2]     ; Get year digits
        XCHG    AH, AL                  ; Put them in correct order
        SUB     AX, 3030h               ; Remove ASCII bias
        AAD                             ; Adjust from ASCII
        CMP     AX, 80                  ; Is year value > 80?
        JAE     YEAR_OK                 ; Yes! Leave it alone
        ADD     AX, 100                 ; No! Adjust for century
YEAR_OK:
        SUB     AX, 80                  ; Subtract 80 for DOS
        MOV     CL, 9                   ; Shift constant
        SHL     AX, CL                  ; Shift year left 9 bytes
        PUSH    AX                      ; Save year value

        MOV     AX, WORD PTR [BX+4]     ; Get month digits
        XCHG    AH, AL                  ; Put them in correct order
        SUB     AX, 3030h               ; Remove ASCII bias
        AAD                             ; Adjust from ASCII
        MOV     CL, 5                   ; Shift constant
        SHL     AX, CL                  ; Shift month left 5 bytes
        PUSH    AX                      ; Save month value

        MOV     AX, WORD PTR [BX+6]     ; Get day digits
        XCHG    AH, AL                  ; Put them in correct order
        SUB     AX, 3030h               ; Remove ASCII bias
        AAD                             ; Adjust from ASCII

        POP     BX                      ; Get back month value
        ADD     AX, BX                  ; Add it in
        POP     BX                      ; Get back year value
        ADD     AX, BX                  ; Add it in

        PUSH    AX                      ; Store new date
        SUB     BH, BH
        MOV     BL, FILE_HANDLE         ; Get DOS handle
        MOV     AH, 57h                 ; DOS file date request
        SUB     AL, AL                  ; Clear lower byte
        INT     21h
        MOV     AL, 1                   ; Set date/time DOS value
        POP     DX                      ; Get new date back
```

```
                INT 21h                     ; Set new date
CLOSE_FILE:
                SUB BH, BH
                MOV BL, FILE_HANDLE         ; Get DOS handle
                MOV AX, 3E00h               ; DOS request to close file
                INT 21h

EXIT_DATE:
                MOV AL, CS:SET_FLAG         ; Get set flag
                CMP AL, 0                   ; Is it zero?
                JE  AROUND2                 ; Yes! Jump around next line
                POP DS                      ; No! Fix stack
AROUND2:
                POP_REGS                    ; Restore all registers
                MOV AX, CS                  ; Segment of return date
                MOV BX, OFFSET CS:GET_DATE  ; Offset of return date
                RET_DATE AX BX              ; Return date to Clipper

FILEDATE ENDP                               ; End of procedure

CODESEG ENDS                                ; End of code segment
                END                         ; End of assembly
```

FILESIZE

Description:
Determines the size of a file in bytes

Syntax:
FILESIZE(<cFileName>)

Returns:
Size of the file in bytes, or -1 on any error

File Name:
F_FISIZE.PRG

Screen Use:
None

Arguments:
<cFileName> – File name

Typical Use:
To determine a file's size before an operation that must allocate memory (or disk space) for it

Discussion

Use FILESIZE to allocate space for a file based on its size. A typical example is when copying files to another disk. Use FILESIZE and DISKSPACE to ensure enough room. Another example is when editing text files with MEMOEDIT. Use FILESIZE and MEMORY(1) to make sure enough memory is available.

You can also use the Clipper DIRECTORY function to return a file's size as an array element. Use it when you need information about a group of files. Use FILESIZE when you need the size of a single file.

Coding Examples

The following test program uses several Developer's Library file functions. Although it serves no purpose by itself, it demonstrates the use of each function. Its source code is in the file T_FILES.PRG on the companion disk.

```
*********************************************************************
* Test program for FILEDATE, FILESIZE, FILETIME, FILETOUCH
*********************************************************************
* FILE = T_FILES.PRG

* Copyright(c) 1991 - James Occhiogrosso

#include "inkey.ch"

LOCAL filename, orig_date, orig_time

INITGLOBAL()
SETCOLOR(colstd)

* Save original date and time of this program file,
* and reset it to system date and time
filename = 't_files.prg'
orig_date = FILEDATE(filename, DATE())
orig_time = FILETIME(filename, TIME())

* Stuff a space in keyboard to start loop
KEYBOARD CHR(32)

DO WHILE INKEY(0) != K_ESC

    CLEAR
    * Display original date and time settings
    @ 6, 10 SAY 'The size of .......... ' + UPPER(filename) + ;
             ' is ' + LTRIM(STR(FILESIZE(filename)))
    @ 8, 10 SAY 'It was dated ......... ' + DTOC(orig_date)
    @ 9, 10 SAY 'And had a time of .... ' + orig_time

    * Set date and time to system date and time
    FILETOUCH(filename)

    * Retrieve its date and time using FILEDATE and FILETIME
    @ 11, 10 SAY 'Its new date is ...... ' + ;
                 DTOC(FILEDATE(filename))
    @ 12, 10 SAY 'And its new time is .. ' + FILETIME(filename)
    @ 15, 10 SAY 'Press any key to set date and time' + ;
                 ' back to original values'
    INKEY(0)

    * Reset file back to original values
    FILEDATE(filename, orig_date)
```

```
    FILETIME(filename, orig_time)


    * And display original values
    @ 17, 10 SAY 'Date setting is now .. ' + ;
              DTOC(FILEDATE(filename))
    @ 18, 10 SAY 'Time setting is now .. ' + ;
              FILETIME(filename)
    @ 24, 10 SAY 'Press any key to begin again or Esc to exit'
ENDDO

CLEAR
RETURN
```

Application Example

```
* The example below checks that at least 10K of free memory
* remains after reading a text file into a variable.

IF MEMORY(1) * 1024 < FILESIZE(file_name) + 10000
   ? 'Not enough memory to read file.'
ELSE
   * Enough memory, load file
   memo_var = MEMOREAD(file_name)
ENDIF
```

```
****************************************************************
FUNCTION FILESIZE (file_name)
****************************************************************

* Returns size of a file in bytes

* Copyright(c) 1991 -- James Occhiogrosso

#include "fileio.ch"
#translate F_LEN(<n>) => FSEEK(<n>, FS_SET, FS_END)

LOCAL file_size := 0, handle := 0

* Open file and get handle
handle = FOPEN(file_name, 0)

* Get file size or -1 on error
file_size = IF(handle != -1, F_LEN(handle), -1)

* Close file and return
FCLOSE(handle)

RETURN file_size
```

FILETIME

Description:
Gets or sets the time on a DOS file

Syntax:
FILETIME(<cFileName>, [<cTimeToSet>])

Returns:
Time string in the format hh:mm:ss

File Name:
FILETIME.ASM

Screen Use:
None

Arguments:
<cFileName> – File to get or set the time on. Supports full DOS path names.

<cTimeToSet> – Optional new time setting as a string in the format hh:mm:ss

Typical Use:
To determine and optionally set the time on a DOS file

Error Handling:
Returns an empty string on any error in retrieving or setting the time

Cautions:
If the time string is formatted improperly, the file time may be set incorrectly.

See Also:
FILEDATE, FILESIZE, FILETOUCH

Discussion

Like most functions that use low-level file handling techniques, FILETIME will operate on hidden or system files. Since time setting does not actually involve writing to the file, it will also operate on read-only files. When using it, test for errors by checking whether its return value is empty (see the last example below).

The Clipper DIRECTORY function also returns the file time as an array element. Use it when you need information about a group of files. When you need information about a specific file, use FILETIME.

FILEDATE and FILETIME are also used to alter date and time values on a file when a process rewrites it. A typical example appears in SYSSAVE. The date and time stamp of each copy is set to be the same as the original.

Coding Examples

```
* Get current time of a system definition file
old_time = FILETIME('arsystem.def')

* Save current time and set file to system time
old_time = FILETIME('arsystem.def', TIME())

* To check for an error after using FILETIME,
* test for a null time string return

IF EMPTY(old_time)
   * Error occurred
   DO ERROR_PROC
ENDIF
```

See T_FILES.PRG on the companion disk, and the code for SYSSAVE for more examples using FILETIME. The source code for T_FILES.PRG appears with FILESIZE.

```
;   ----------------------------------------------------------------
;   FUNCTION NAME: FILETIME - Gets or sets the DOS time on a file
;   ----------------------------------------------------------------
;   Copyright(c)            1991 -- James Occhiogrosso

    INCLUDE DEVELOP.MAC         ; Developer's Library macro file

    PUBLIC    FILETIME          ; Declare function name
                                ; Declare Clipper EXTERNALS
    EXTRN     __PARINFO:FAR     ; Get Clipper parameter information
    EXTRN     __PARC:FAR        ; Get Clipper string
    EXTRN     __RETC:FAR        ; Return string to Clipper

    CODESEG   SEGMENT 'CODE'
              ASSUME CS:CODESEG

    FILETIME  PROC  FAR

              JMP   BEGIN               ; Jump around data area

    FILE_HANDLE DB  0                   ; Store file handle here
    GET_TIME    DB  '00:00:00', 0       ; Store Clipper return time
    SET_FLAG    DB  0                   ; Set to 1 for setting time

    BEGIN:
              PUSH_REGS                 ; Save Clipper registers

              PUSH  DS                  ; Save Clipper data segment
              PUSH  CS
              POP   DS                  ; Set up our data segment
              MOV   BX, OFFSET FILE_HANDLE ; Get address of first data
              SUB   AX, AX
              MOV   CX, 11              ; Set to loop 11 times

    NEXT:     MOV   [BX], AL            ; Clear byte of data area
              INC   BX                  ; Increment address
              LOOP  NEXT
              POP   DS                  ; Restore data segment

              P_TYPE 1                  ; Get parameter type to AX
              CMP   AX, 1               ; Character string passed?
              JNE   RET_NULL_1          ; No! Return null time

              P_COUNT                   ; Yes! Get parameters passed
              CMP   AX, 2               ; If no second parameter,
              JNE   OPEN_FILE           ;   get file time and return
              P_TYPE 2                  ; Else, get its type
              CMP   AX, 1               ;   Is it a string?
              JNE   RET_NULL_1          ;   No! Return null time
              MOV   CS:SET_FLAG, 1      ;   Yes! Set flag
              PUSH  DS                  ;   Save data segment
              JMP   OPEN_FILE           ; Jump around null return
```

```
RET_NULL_1:
        JMP     EXIT_TIME               ; RET_NULL labels used for
                                        ;   direct jump to exit
RET_NULL_2:
        JMP     CLOSE_FILE              ;   due to error condition
OPEN_FILE:
        GET_PARC 1                      ; Address of passed filename
        MOV     DS, DX                  ; Get filename segment
        MOV     DX, AX                  ; Get filename offset
        SUB     AL, AL                  ; Set read only mode
        MOV     AH, 3Dh                 ; Open file request
        INT     21h
        JC      RET_NULL_1              ; On error, return null time
        MOV     CS:FILE_HANDLE, AL      ; Save file handle

GET_THE_TIME:
        PUSH    CS                      ; Move data segment to CS
        POP     DS                      ;   for our data
        SUB     BH, BH                  ; Clear BX for handle
        MOV     BL, FILE_HANDLE         ; Get DOS handle
        MOV     AH, 57h                 ; DOS date/time function
        SUB     AL, AL                  ; Get file date/time
        INT     21h
        JC      RET_NULL_2              ; Return null time

        MOV     AL, CL                  ; Move time to AL (seconds)
        AND     AL, 00011111b           ; Mask unused bits
        ADD     AL, AL                  ; DOS resolves 2 seconds
        AAM                             ; Adjust MS/LS digits
        ADD     AX, 3030h               ; Convert to ASCII
        MOV     BX, OFFSET GET_TIME     ; Get return time address
        MOV     [BX+6], AH              ; Save seconds digit (tens)
        MOV     [BX+7], AL              ; Save seconds digit (ones)

        MOV     AX, CX                  ; Restore original time
        AND     AX, 0000011111100000b   ; Mask unused bits
        MOV     CL, 5                   ; Constant for shift
        SHR     AX, CL                  ; Shift minute bits
        AAM                             ; Adjust MS/LS digits
        ADD     AX, 3030h               ; Convert AX to ASCII
        MOV     [BX+3], AH              ; Save minutes digit (tens)
        MOV     [BX+4], AL              ; Save minutes digits (ones)

        MOV     AL, CH                  ; Restore original time
        AND     AL, 11111000b           ; Mask unused bits
        MOV     CL, 3                   ; Constant for shift
        SHR     AL, CL                  ; Shift hour bits
        AAM                             ; Adjust MS/LS digits
        ADD     AX, 3030h               ; Convert to ASCII
        MOV     [BX], AH                ; Save hour MS digit (tens)
        MOV     [BX+1], AL              ; Save hour LS digit (ones)
        MOV     AL, ':'                 ; Put colons in time string
        MOV     [BX+2], AL
        MOV     [BX+5], AL
```

```
SET_THE_TIME:
        MOV   AL, CS:SET_FLAG        ; Check flag
        CMP   AL, 0                  ; Is it set?
        JE    CLOSE_FILE             ; No! We are done
        POP   DS                     ; Yes! Recover data segment,
        MOV   CS:SET_FLAG, 0         ;   reset flag, and get
        GET_PARC 2                   ;   passed time string
        MOV   DS, DX                 ; Get passed segment into DS
        MOV   BX, AX                 ;   and offset into BX

        MOV   AX, WORD PTR [BX]      ; Get hours digits
        XCHG  AH, AL                 ; Put them in correct order
        SUB   AX, 3030h              ; Remove ASCII bias
        AAD                          ; Adjust from ASCII
        MOV   CL, 11                 ; Shift constant
        SHL   AX, CL                 ; Shift year left 9 bytes
        PUSH  AX                     ; Save hours value

        MOV   AX, WORD PTR [BX+3]    ; Get minutes digits
        XCHG  AH, AL                 ; Put them in correct order
        SUB   AX, 3030h              ; Remove ASCII bias
        AAD                          ; Adjust from ASCII
        MOV   CL, 5                  ; Shift constant
        SHL   AX, CL                 ; Shift month left 5 bytes
        PUSH  AX                     ; Save minutes value

        MOV   AX, WORD PTR [BX+6]    ; Get seconds digits
        XCHG  AH, AL                 ; Put them in correct order
        SUB   AX, 3030h              ; Remove ASCII bias
        AAD                          ; Adjust from ASCII
        SHR   AX, 1                  ; Divide by 2 for DOS

        POP   BX                     ; Get back minutes value
        ADD   AX, BX                 ; Add it in
        POP   BX                     ; Get back hours value
        ADD   AX, BX                 ; Add it in
        PUSH  AX                     ; Store new time

        SUB   BH, BH                 ; Clear upper handle byte
        MOV   BL, FILE_HANDLE        ; Get DOS handle
        MOV   AH, 57h                ; DOS set file date/time
        SUB   AL, AL                 ; Date/time DOS request
        INT   21h
        MOV   AL, 1                  ; Set date/time DOS value
        POP   CX                     ; Get new time back
        INT   21h                    ; Set new time

CLOSE_FILE:
        MOV   BH, 0
        MOV   BL, FILE_HANDLE        ; Get DOS handle
        MOV   AX, 3E00h              ; DOS request to close file
        INT   21h
```

```
EXIT_TIME:
        MOV AL, CS:SET_FLAG             ; Get the set flag
        CMP AL, 0                       ; Is it zero?
        JE  AROUND2                     ; Yes! Jump around next line
        POP DS                          ; Error condition, fix stack
AROUND2:
        POP_REGS                        ; Restore all registers
        MOV AX, CS                      ; Segment of return time
        MOV BX, OFFSET CS:GET_TIME      ; Offset of return time
        RET_STRING AX BX                ; Return time string

FILETIME ENDP                           ; End of procedure

CODESEG ENDS                            ; End of code segment
        END                             ; End of assembly
```

FILETOUCH

Description:
Updates the date/time stamp of a file to the system date and time

Syntax:
FILETOUCH(<cFileName>)

Returns:
True if the operation succeeds; false otherwise

File Name:
F_FITOUC.PRG

Screen Use:
None

Arguments:
<cFileName> – Name of a file to be updated

Typical Use:
To update the date and time stamp on a file without altering it

Cautions:
Allows only single filenames. Does not allow wildcards (? or *).

See Also:
FILEDATE, FILESIZE, FILETIME

Discussion

Some applications (such as MAKE utilities) use the date and time stamp on a file to see if it has been altered. FILETOUCH provides a simple way to update the stamp on a DOS file without altering it. Since it (unlike FILEDATE and

FILETIME) actually reads and writes one byte of the file, it can also test for disk or other errors (see SETINT24 and GETINT24).

Coding Examples

```
* To update date and time stamp of file
* arsystem.def and test for errors

* Turn on Developer's Library INT 24 handler
SETINT24(.T.)

* Update file stamp
IF FILETOUCH("arsystem.def")
    * No error occurred
ELSE
    * Error occurred. Return error number
    RETURN(GETINT24())
ENDIF

* Turn off INT 24 handler
SETINT24(.F.)
```

An example using FILETOUCH is in T_FILES.PRG on the companion disk. The source code for T_FILES.PRG appears in the FILESIZE listing.

```
*****************************************************************
FUNCTION FILETOUCH (file_name)
*****************************************************************

* Update date and time of a file to system date and time

* Copyright(c) 1991 -- James Occhiogrosso

LOCAL handle := 0, buffer := ' '

* Open file for read/write operation
handle = FOPEN(file_name, 2)

* Return false if error in opening file
IF FERROR() != 0
    RETURN(.F.)
ENDIF

* Read first byte of file
FREAD(handle, @buffer, 1)

* Reset file pointer to BOF
FSEEK(handle, 0)

* Write byte back in same position
FWRITE(handle, buffer, 1)

* Return value of FCLOSE in case an error occurred
RETURN (FCLOSE(handle))
```

FREADLINE

Description:
Reads successive lines from a text file

Syntax:
FREADLINE(<nFileHandle>, [<nLineLength>])

Returns:
String containing one line of the file, or an empty string if at end of file

File Name:
F_FREADL.PRG

Screen Use:
None

Arguments:
<nFileHandle> – Numeric file handle for the file to read (obtained from FOPEN)

<nLineLength> – Optional maximum line length

Typical Use:
To successively read and process lines from text files

Defaults:
512 character maximum line length if <nLineLength> is not passed

Error Handling:
Identifies lines by locating carriage return/line feed combinations. Returns a null string if it does not find any.

Cautions:
If passed, the maximum line length must be at least two more than the maximum expected text length. The excess allows for the carriage return/line feed combination.

Calls to FREADLINE after the last line in the file cause it to loop back to the beginning. Detect end of file by looking for a specific return value.

Discussion

FREADLINE reads and returns the contents of a text file. Each call returns the next line until end of file is reached. FREADLINE works by searching for a carriage return/line feed sequence. It can be used only on text files with lines ending in CR/LF.

FREADLINE is useful when you must process information in a text file line-by-line. For example, the Developer's Library function MAKEDBF uses it to read lines from a system data dictionary.

One uses FREADLINE with text files that generally have line lengths of 512 characters or less, and it defaults to 512 if no length is passed. However, by specifying a larger value, you can use FREADLINE with any file, as long as each line ends in a carriage return/line feed sequence.

Coding Examples

The example below uses FREADLINE to read successive text lines of the file dbfdefs.txt. It skips comment lines beginning with an asterisk or a number sign(#). This is typical of processing a data dictionary or similar file.

```
* Open file and test for errors
handle = FOPEN("dbfdefs.txt")
IF handle < 0
    * Error occurred opening file
    DO errorproc
ENDIF

* Initialize textline with asterisk to start loop
textline := '*'

* Read and test each line. Skip comments and blank lines.
* Exit loop on any valid text or keyword ENDFILE

DO WHILE (SUBSTR(textline, 1, 1) $ '*#' .OR. EMPTY(textline))  ;
```

```
            .AND. UPPER(SUBSTR(textline, 1, 7)) != 'ENDFILE'

   * Read next line
   textline := LTRIM(FREADLINE(handle))
ENDDO
```

For more examples, see **DBNAMES**, **MAKEDBF**, or **MAKENDX**.

```
******************************************************************
FUNCTION FREADLINE (handle, line_len)
******************************************************************

* Read a line from a text file (from current pointer position)

* Copyright(c) 1991 -- James Occhiogrosso

#define MAXLINE 512
LOCAL buffer, line_end, num_bytes

* If line length not passed, default to MAXLINE
IF VALTYPE(line_len) != 'N'
    line_len = MAXLINE
ENDIF

* Define temporary buffer to hold specified line length
buffer = SPACE(line_len)

* Read from current position to specified line length
num_bytes = FREAD(handle, @buffer, line_len)

* Find carriage return/line feed combination
line_end = AT(CHR(13)+CHR(10), buffer)

IF line_end = 0
    * No carriage return/line feed. Pointer is at end of
    * file, or line is too long. Rewind pointer and return
    FSEEK(handle, 0)
    RETURN('')

ELSE
    * Move pointer to beginning of next line
    FSEEK(handle, (num_bytes * -1) + line_end + 1, 1)
    * And return current line
    RETURN( SUBSTR(buffer, 1, line_end - 1) )

ENDIF
```

FREEVARS

Description:
Releases public field variables

Syntax:
FREEVARS( )

Returns:
NIL

File Name:
F_MVARS.PRG

Screen Use:
None

Arguments:
None

Typical Use:
To release memory used by field variables that are no longer needed

Global Variables:
Uses the current set of public variables created by INITVARS

See Also:
CLRVARS, EQUVARS, INITVARS, REPLVARS

Discussion

FREEVARS releases the public field variables created by INITVARS. It returns the memory they used to the free pool. Use it when you no longer need the variables, or when you must recover the memory they used for another purpose.

Coding Examples

```
* Open database
USE DataFile NEW

* Initialize field variables
INITVARS()

* Your add/edit routine
    .
    .
    . * End of your routine

* Release field memory variables
FREEVARS()
RETURN
```

See sample program T_AEDBAR.PRG on the companion disk for a typical example.

```
****************************************************************
FUNCTION FREEVARS
****************************************************************

* Release variables created by INITVARS

* Copyright(c) 1991 -- James Occhiogrosso

LOCAL counter := 0, field_cnt := FCOUNT()
PRIVATE field_name

* Release each field variable
FOR counter = 1 TO field_cnt
   field_name = LOWER(FIELD(counter))
   RELEASE m&field_name
NEXT

RETURN NIL
```

FULLKEY

Description:
Determines ASCII value and scan code for any key

Syntax:
FULLKEY( )

Returns:
Numeric value in the range -32,768 to +32,767

File Name:
FULLKEY.ASM

Screen Use:
None

Arguments:
None

Typical Use:
To distinguish keys for which Clipper returns the same INKEY value

See Also:
SCANKEY

Discussion

Use FULLKEY to process keystrokes more precisely than Clipper allows. Each key on a standard keyboard returns a unique number that is a combination of its ASCII value and scan code.

The return value of FULLKEY is a signed integer in the range -32,768 to +32,767. Since this value is difficult to use, applications do not normally call

FULLKEY directly. However, they can if response speed is more critical than ease of use.

To calculate FULLKEY's return value, multiply the scan code by 256 and add the ASCII value. If the result exceeds 32,767, subtract 65,536. The Developer's Library function SCANKEY does the calculations and returns the ASCII value and scan code for any key. Use it unless a specific application needs a faster response.

Coding Examples

The example below uses FULLKEY to differentiate between the numeric keypad 1 key and the alphabetic keyboard 1 key.

```
#define ALPHA_1 561
#define KEYPAD_1 20273
keypress = FULLKEY()

IF keypress = ALPHA_1
    * Alphabetic "1" key was pressed
ELSEIF keypress = KEYPAD_1
    * Numeric keypad "1" key was pressed
ELSEIF
    * Test any other key if desired
ENDIF
```

See SCANKEY for more information and a typical use.

```
; ----------------------------------------------------------------
; FULLKEY --- Returns numeric scan code and ASCII value for a key
; ----------------------------------------------------------------
; Copyright(c)   1991 -- James Occhiogrosso
;

INCLUDE  DEVELOP.MAC         ; Include Developer's Library Macro file

PUBLIC   FULLKEY             ; Declare public function
EXTRN    __RETNI:FAR         ; Return numeric integer

CODESEG  SEGMENT 'CODE'
         ASSUME CS:CODESEG

FULLKEY  PROC FAR

         MOV AX, 0           ; Read Character DOS function
         INT 16h
         RET_INT             ; Return integer key value

FULLKEY  ENDP                ; End of procedure
CODESEG  ENDS                ; End of code segment

         END                 ; End of assembly
```

GETINT24

Description:
Returns the error code stored by the Developer's Library internal INT24 handler

Syntax:
GETINT24( )

Returns:
Numeric error code per table below

File Name:
INT24.ASM

Screen Use:
None

Arguments:
None

Typical Use:
To distinguish disk errors that Clipper groups under a single code (see discussion below and SETINT24)

Cautions:
You must activate the Developer's Library internal critical error handler with SETINT24 before calling GETINT24. Otherwise, the return value will be zero.

See Also:
SETINT24

Discussion

GETINT24 returns an error code from the table below when a DOS critical error occurs, or zero otherwise. Critical errors are usually ones for which DOS displays the familiar "Abort, Retry, Ignore, Fail" message. In Clipper, critical errors usually occur when a program tries to write to a disk. However, DOS (*not* Clipper) calls the Developer's Library internal critical error handler (INT24). Thus, GETINT24 returns zero if DOS does not call INT24 for the particular error.

For example, the following code on a write-protected disk does not cause a critical error. No error is returned by the Clipper FERROR( ) or DOSERROR( ) functions, or by GETINT24.

```
SETINT24(.T.)
handle = FOPEN("A:TEMP.TMP", 2)  // Assumes file exists
FWRITE(handle, 'XXXXX')
```

However, when the line

```
    FCLOSE(handle)
```

is executed, an error is generated. This is because the critical error handler is not called until the program tries to write the file buffer to the disk and close the file. At this point, error recovery is difficult, if not impossible.

To avoid having an edited file in memory that you cannot write to a disk, trap critical errors as soon as they occur. The easiest way to do this is to use DISK-TEST on the selected drive before writing to it. DISKTEST automatically invokes the Developer's Library INT24 function to test the disk.

The error codes returned from GETINT24 correspond to those returned by DOS INT 21h function 59h, codes 19 through 31. In a Clipper program, the Clipper error system intercepts code 10 ("printer out of paper") before the critical error handler is invoked.

The following table lists the codes returned by GETINT24 for various error conditions.

Int 24 Error Codes

Code	Meaning
1	Disk is write protected
2	Unknown unit
3	Drive not ready
4	Unknown command
5	Bad CRC (data error)
6	Bad request (structure length)
7	Seek error
8	Unknown media type
9	Sector not found
10	Printer out of paper
11	Fault while writing disk
12	Fault while reading disk
13	General failure – (unformatted disk)

Coding Examples

See SETINT24 for detailed coding examples and assembly language source code. For other examples, see the file T_DISKS.PRG on the companion disk and the DISKTEST function in this library.

GRAPHCHAR

Description:
Provides popup graphics symbols for entry as data from the numeric keypad

Syntax:
SET KEY keyname TO GRAPHCHAR

Returns:
Nothing. The selected key toggles the GRAPHCHAR display on and off.

File Name:
F_GRCHAR.PRG

Screen Use:
Operator selectable area of 9 rows by 13 columns

Arguments:
None

Typical Use:
To simplify entry of graphics characters as data

Cautions:
GRAPHCHAR dedicates keys 0 through 9, the decimal point, and the plus and minus keys to its own internal use while active.

Some early releases of Clipper Version 5 do not allow keyboard entry of graphics characters in response to a READ. If this occurs, modify the READMODAL function in GETSYS.PRG (default location \CLIPPER5\SOURCE\SYS). Find the line that reads:

```
if (nKey >= 32 .and. nKey <= 127)
```

and change it to read:

```
if (nKey >= 32 .and. nKey <= 255)
```

Recompile GETSYS.PRG and link it as a file with your application.

Discussion

GRAPHCHAR permits entry of graphics characters with ASCII values above 128 as data. It is called by setting a key to it. The selected hot key then toggles GRAPHCHAR on and off. When GRAPHCHAR is on, it displays a 9 row by 13 column popup box as shown in the left figure below. Initially, the box appears at the screen corner farthest from the current cursor position.

The operator can move the box using the cursor (and Ctrl-cursor) keys. Any other key causes the display to change to the first graphics set (shown in the right figure below). GRAPHCHAR then returns to the caller.

```
┌─────────────┐    ┌───┬───┬───┐
│ Cursor keys │    │ ┌ │ ┬ │ ┐ │
│ move box.   │    ├───┼───┼───┤
│ Any key for │    │ ├ │ ┼ │ ┤ │
│ graphics.   │    ├───┼───┼───┤
│ Use +/- to  │    │ └ │ ┴ │ ┘ │
│ change key  │    ├───┼───┼───┤
│ set.        │    │ = │   │ ║ │
└─────────────┘    └───┴───┴───┘
```

The keys displayed in the popup box correspond to positions on a standard numeric keypad. While the popup box is displayed, pressing a number key returns the corresponding graphics character to the area being edited. The plus and minus keys change the graphics character selections. The popup box remains visible until the GRAPHCHAR hot key is pressed again.

GRAPHCHAR provides eight sets of graphics characters. The first four include symbols for drawing single, double, and mixed line boxes, and the rest provide other graphics symbols.

GRAPHCHAR can be used in a READ, a MEMOEDIT, or any other function that generates a Clipper wait state. It also can be used with any Developer's Library functions that simulate a wait state.

Coding Examples

The example below uses the Developer's Library MEMOVIEW function to edit a memo at the passed coordinates. The F10 key is set to GRAPHCHAR.

```
* Include standard inkey values (Clipper header file)
#include "inkey.ch"

* Set F10 to call GRAPHCHAR
SET KEY K_F10 TO GRAPHCHAR
* Display and edit a memo
MEMOVIEW(.T., memo1, 12, 10, 22, 70)
* Clear F10
SET KEY K_F10 TO
```

```
STATIC entry_scr := '', graph_col := 0, graph_row := 0,     ;
       graph_set := 0, graph_on, graphics[11], pointer := 1

MEMVAR colwindow

*****************************************************************
FUNCTION GRAPHCHAR
*****************************************************************
* Allows entry of graphics characters during a read or memoedit
* Copyright(c) 1991 -- James Occhiogrosso

#include "dl_keys.ch"
#include "inkey.ch"
#include "set.ch"
#include "setcurs.ch"

* Last graphic set defined
#define LASTGRSET 7

LOCAL init_row, init_col, init_scr, keypress, old_color,   ;
      old_score, old_cursor

* Save entry conditions
old_color  = SETCOLOR(colwindow)
old_score  = SET(_SET_SCOREBOARD, .F.)
old_cursor = SET(_SET_CURSOR, SC_NONE)
init_row = ROW() ; init_col = COL()

* Test for array initialization
IF graph_on = NIL
    * Load graphics array
    graph_on = .T.
    LOADARRAY()
ELSE
    * Otherwise, toggle it
    graph_on = !graph_on
ENDIF

IF graph_on

   * This is first time, set default graphic box position

   IF init_row < INT(MAXROW()/2) .AND. init_col < INT(MAXCOL()/2)
       graph_row = INT(MAXROW()-8)
       graph_col = INT(MAXCOL()-12)
   ELSEIF init_row < INT(MAXROW()/2) .AND. init_col >=  ;
                     INT(MAXCOL()/2)
       graph_row = INT(MAXROW()-8)
       graph_col = 0
   ELSEIF init_row >= INT(MAXROW()/2) .AND. init_col <  ;
                     INT(MAXCOL()/2)
       graph_row = 0
       graph_col = INT(MAXCOL()-12)
   ELSEIF init_row >= INT(MAXROW()/2) .AND. init_col >= ;
                     INT(MAXCOL()/2)
```

```
        graph_row = 0
        graph_col = 0
ENDIF

* Save screen area we are going to use
entry_scr = SCRNSAVE(graph_row, graph_col, ;
                    graph_row + 8, graph_col + 12)

* Let operator move box
MOVEBLOCK()

* When box is positioned, turn on key definitions

SET KEY K_PLUS   TO PROCESSKEY
SET KEY K_MINUS  TO PROCESSKEY
SET KEY K_ZERO   TO PROCESSKEY
SET KEY K_ONE    TO PROCESSKEY
SET KEY K_TWO    TO PROCESSKEY
SET KEY K_THREE  TO PROCESSKEY
SET KEY K_FOUR   TO PROCESSKEY
SET KEY K_FIVE   TO PROCESSKEY
SET KEY K_SIX    TO PROCESSKEY
SET KEY K_SEVEN  TO PROCESSKEY
SET KEY K_EIGHT  TO PROCESSKEY
SET KEY K_NINE   TO PROCESSKEY
SET KEY K_PERIOD TO PROCESSKEY

* Display graphics key set
SHOWBLOCK()

ELSE
* Restore entry screen
SCRNREST(entry_scr)

* Turn off all key definitions

SET KEY K_PLUS   TO
SET KEY K_MINUS  TO
SET KEY K_ZERO   TO
SET KEY K_ONE    TO
SET KEY K_TWO    TO
SET KEY K_THREE  TO
SET KEY K_FOUR   TO
SET KEY K_FIVE   TO
SET KEY K_SIX    TO
SET KEY K_SEVEN  TO
SET KEY K_EIGHT  TO
SET KEY K_NINE   TO
SET KEY K_PERIOD TO

ENDIF

* Restore entry conditions and return
SETCOLOR(old_color)
SET SCOREBOARD (old_score)
```

```
   SETCURSOR(old_cursor)
   @ init_row, init_col SAY ''

   RETURN NIL


   *********************************************************************
   STATIC FUNCTION PROCESSKEY
   *********************************************************************

   * Process keystrokes

   LOCAL init_row, init_col, keypress, old_color

   init_row = ROW()
   init_col = COL()
   old_color = SETCOLOR(colwindow)
   keypress = LASTKEY()

   IF keypress = K_PLUS .OR. keypress = K_MINUS

      * Change graphics character set
      IF graph_set < LASTGRSET .AND. keypress = K_PLUS
         graph_set--
      ELSEIF graph_set > 0 .AND. keypress = K_MINUS
         graph_set++
      ELSEIF graph_set = 0 .AND. keypress = K_MINUS
         graph_set = LASTGRSET
      ELSE
         graph_set = 0
      ENDIF

      * Load new graphics set
      LOADARRAY()

      * Display new graphics set
      SHOWBLOCK()
   ELSE
      * Generate pointer to graphics array element

      IF keypress >= K_ONE .AND. keypress <= K_NINE
         * Subtract 48 from ASCII value of keys 1 through 9
         pointer = keypress - 48
      ELSEIF keypress = K_ZERO
         * Zero key is 10th element
         pointer = 10
      ELSEIF keypress = K_PERIOD
         * Period key is 11th element
         pointer = 11
      ENDIF

      * Stuff selected character in keyboard buffer
      KEYBOARD graphics[pointer]
   ENDIF
```

```
* Restore color and cursor position and return
SETCOLOR(old_color)

@ init_row, init_col SAY ''

RETURN NIL


*******************************************************************
STATIC FUNCTION LOADARRAY
*******************************************************************

* Load graphics array

IF graph_set = 0
   graphics[1]  = CHR(200)   &&
   graphics[2]  = CHR(202)   &&   Double line
   graphics[3]  = CHR(188)   &&
   graphics[4]  = CHR(204)   &&
   graphics[5]  = CHR(206)   &&
   graphics[6]  = CHR(185)   &&
   graphics[7]  = CHR(201)   &&
   graphics[8]  = CHR(203)   &&
   graphics[9]  = CHR(187)   &&
   graphics[10] = CHR(205)   &&
   graphics[11] = CHR(186)   &&

ELSEIF graph_set = 1

   graphics[1]  = CHR(192)   &&
   graphics[2]  = CHR(193)   &&   Single line
   graphics[3]  = CHR(217)   &&
   graphics[4]  = CHR(195)   &&
   graphics[5]  = CHR(197)   &&
   graphics[6]  = CHR(180)   &&
   graphics[7]  = CHR(218)   &&
   graphics[8]  = CHR(194)   &&
   graphics[9]  = CHR(191)   &&
   graphics[10] = CHR(196)   &&
   graphics[11] = CHR(179)   &&
```

```
ELSEIF graph_set = 2
    graphics[1]  = CHR(211)   &&         Double
    graphics[2]  = CHR(208)   &&        Vertical
    graphics[3]  = CHR(189)   &&
    graphics[4]  = CHR(199)   &&
    graphics[5]  = CHR(215)   &&
    graphics[6]  = CHR(182)   &&
    graphics[7]  = CHR(214)   &&
    graphics[8]  = CHR(210)   &&
    graphics[9]  = CHR(183)   &&
    graphics[10] = CHR(196)   &&
    graphics[11] = CHR(186)   &&

ELSEIF graph_set = 3

    graphics[1]  = CHR(212)   &&         Single
    graphics[2]  = CHR(207)   &&        Vertical
    graphics[3]  = CHR(190)   &&
    graphics[4]  = CHR(198)   &&
    graphics[5]  = CHR(216)   &&
    graphics[6]  = CHR(181)   &&
    graphics[7]  = CHR(213)   &&
    graphics[8]  = CHR(209)   &&
    graphics[9]  = CHR(184)   &&
    graphics[10] = CHR(205)   &&
    graphics[11] = CHR(179)   &&

ELSEIF graph_set = 4

    graphics[1]  = CHR(221)   &&      Miscellaneous
    graphics[2]  = CHR(222)   &&         Symbols
    graphics[3]  = CHR(254)   &&
    graphics[4]  = CHR(219)   &&
    graphics[5]  = CHR(220)   &&
    graphics[6]  = CHR(223)   &&
    graphics[7]  = CHR(176)   &&
    graphics[8]  = CHR(177)   &&
    graphics[9]  = CHR(178)   &&
    graphics[10] = CHR(174)   &&
    graphics[11] = CHR(175)   &&
```

```
ELSEIF graph_set = 5

    graphics[1]  = CHR(252)   && Miscellaneous
    graphics[2]  = CHR(253)   &&   Symbols
    graphics[3]  = CHR(172)   &&
    graphics[4]  = CHR(246)   &&
    graphics[5]  = CHR(251)   &&
    graphics[6]  = CHR(171)   &&
    graphics[7]  = CHR(241)   &&
    graphics[8]  = CHR(242)   &&
    graphics[9]  = CHR(243)   &&
    graphics[10] = CHR(155)   &&
    graphics[11] = CHR(156)   &&

ELSEIF graph_set = 6

    graphics[1]  = CHR(224)   && Miscellaneous
    graphics[2]  = CHR(225)   &&   Symbols
    graphics[3]  = CHR(226)   &&
    graphics[4]  = CHR(227)   &&
    graphics[5]  = CHR(228)   &&
    graphics[6]  = CHR(229)   &&
    graphics[7]  = CHR(230)   &&
    graphics[8]  = CHR(231)   &&
    graphics[9]  = CHR(232)   &&
    graphics[10] = CHR(233)   &&
    graphics[11] = CHR(234)   &&

ELSEIF graph_set = 7

    graphics[1]  = CHR(235)   && Miscellaneous
    graphics[2]  = CHR(236)   &&   Symbols
    graphics[3]  = CHR(237)   &&
    graphics[4]  = CHR(238)   &&
    graphics[5]  = CHR(239)   &&
    graphics[6]  = CHR(247)   &&
    graphics[7]  = CHR(244)   &&
    graphics[8]  = CHR(245)   &&
    graphics[9]  = CHR(248)   &&
    graphics[10] = CHR(249)   &&
    graphics[11] = CHR(127)   &&

ENDIF

RETURN NIL
```

```
*******************************************************************
STATIC FUNCTION SHOWBLOCK
*******************************************************************

* Display selected graphics set

@ graph_row + 1, graph_col + 2  SAY graphics[7]
@ graph_row + 1, graph_col + 6  SAY graphics[8]
@ graph_row + 1, graph_col + 10 SAY graphics[9]
@ graph_row + 3, graph_col + 2  SAY graphics[4]
@ graph_row + 3, graph_col + 6  SAY graphics[5]
@ graph_row + 3, graph_col + 10 SAY graphics[6]
@ graph_row + 5, graph_col + 2  SAY graphics[1]
@ graph_row + 5, graph_col + 6  SAY graphics[2]
@ graph_row + 5, graph_col + 10 SAY graphics[3]
@ graph_row + 7, graph_col + 4  SAY graphics[10]
@ graph_row + 7, graph_col + 10 SAY graphics[11]

RETURN NIL


*******************************************************************
STATIC FUNCTION MOVEBLOCK
*******************************************************************

* Let operator position graph box on initial entry

LOCAL init_scr, keypress

* Display initial box at default area

@ graph_row,     graph_col SAY ''
@ graph_row + 1, graph_col SAY 'Cursor keys'
@ graph_row + 2, graph_col SAY 'move box.  '
@ graph_row + 3, graph_col SAY 'Any key for'
@ graph_row + 4, graph_col SAY 'graphics.  '
@ graph_row + 5, graph_col SAY 'Use +/- to '
@ graph_row + 6, graph_col SAY 'change key '
@ graph_row + 7, graph_col SAY 'set.       '
@ graph_row + 8, graph_col SAY ''

init_scr = SAVESCREEN(graph_row, graph_col, ;
                     graph_row + 8, graph_col + 12)

DO WHILE .T.
  * Wait for key
  keypress = INKEY(0)

  * Restore entry screen before moving box
  SCRNREST(entry_scr)

  IF keypress = K_RIGHT
     graph_col = IF(graph_col < (MAXCOL()-12), graph_col + 1, ;
               (MAXCOL()-12))
  ELSEIF keypress = K_LEFT
```

```
          graph_col = IF(graph_col > 1, graph_col - 1, 0)
     ELSEIF keypress = K_UP
          graph_row = IF(graph_row > 0, graph_row - 1, 0)
     ELSEIF keypress = K_DOWN
          graph_row = IF(graph_row < INT(MAXROW()-8), graph_row ;
                         + 1, INT(MAXROW()-8))
     ELSEIF keypress = K_CTRL_RIGHT
          graph_col = (MAXCOL()-12)
     ELSEIF keypress = K_CTRL_LEFT
          graph_col = 0
     ELSEIF keypress = K_CTRL_UP
          graph_row = 0
     ELSEIF keypress = K_CTRL_DOWN
          graph_row = INT(MAXROW()-8)
     ELSE
          * Any other key, exit and display graphics box
          EXIT
     ENDIF

     * Save new entry screen area
     entry_scr = SCRNSAVE(graph_row, graph_col, ;
                         graph_row + 8, graph_col + 12)
     * And redisplay initial box in new position
     RESTSCREEN(graph_row, graph_col, graph_row + 8,;
                graph_col + 12, init_scr)
ENDDO

* When box is positioned, display graphics outline

@ graph_row,     graph_col SAY '            '
@ graph_row + 1, graph_col SAY '            '
@ graph_row + 2, graph_col SAY '            '
@ graph_row + 3, graph_col SAY '            '
@ graph_row + 4, graph_col SAY '            '
@ graph_row + 5, graph_col SAY '            '
@ graph_row + 6, graph_col SAY '            '
@ graph_row + 7, graph_col SAY '            '
@ graph_row + 8, graph_col SAY '            '

RETURN NIL
```

GRID

Description:
Displays a calibrated ruler grid

Syntax:
Normally called by pressing the Alt-G key combination

Returns:
Nothing

File Name:
F_GRID.PRG

Screen Use:
Entire screen

Arguments:
None

Typical Use:
To simplify screen row and column measurements from an application

Cautions:
If GRID is called using a SET KEY statement, you must declare it external in your application.

See Also:
DEVELOP, HRULER, VRULER

Discussion

Use GRID to quickly determine the coordinates of screen items during development. It displays a grid of calibrated vertical and horizontal ruler lines. The horizontal lines appear on every fifth row, and the vertical ones in every tenth column. To remove the grid and restore the application screen, press any key.

Coding Examples

```
* Include standard inkey header file supplied with Clipper
#include "inkey.ch"

* Declare GRID external to your application to force linking
EXTERNAL GRID

* Set up Alt-G key combination for GRID
SET KEY K_ALT_G TO GRID
```

You can use the DEVELOP function at the top of your application program to set up the Alt-G key combination and link GRID. DEVELOP also links other utility functions (see it for more information).

```
*******************************************************************
FUNCTION GRID
*******************************************************************
* Displays a calibrated screen grid

* Copyright(c) 1991 -- James Occhiogrosso

#include "setcurs.ch"

LOCAL colcount, old_color, old_cursor, old_col := COL(), ;
      old_row := ROW(), old_screen, rowcount
MEMVAR colbarhi

* Save entry screen conditions
old_cursor = SETCURSOR(SC_NONE)
old_color  = SETCOLOR(colbarhi)
old_screen = SCRNSAVE(0, 0, MAXROW(), MAXCOL())

* Display vertical ruler at every 10th column
FOR colcount = 10 TO MAXCOL() STEP 10
    FOR rowcount = 0 TO MAXROW()
        @ rowcount, colcount SAY '┼'
    NEXT
NEXT

* Display horizontal ruler at every 5th row
FOR rowcount = 5 TO MAXROW() STEP 5
    FOR colcount = 0 TO MAXCOL()
        IF colcount % 5 = 0 .AND. colcount % 10 != 0
            * Each fifth column
            @ rowcount, colcount SAY '┼'
        ELSEIF colcount % 10 = 0 .AND. colcount < 100
            * Each 10th column less than 100
            @ rowcount, colcount SAY PAD(colcount, 1)
        ELSEIF colcount % 10 = 0
            * Each 10th column greater than 100
            @ rowcount, colcount SAY PAD(colcount-100, 1)
        ELSEIF colcount = 1
            * Column 1 only
            @ rowcount, colcount SAY 'L'
        ELSEIF colcount = MAXCOL()
            * Last column only
            @ rowcount, colcount SAY 'J'
        ELSE
            * All intermediate columns
            @ rowcount, colcount SAY '┴'
        ENDIF
    NEXT
NEXT
```

```
* Wait for a key
DO WHILE INKEY(0) = 0 ; ENDDO

* Restore entry conditions and return
SCRNREST(old_screen)
SETPOS(old_row, old_col)
SETCOLOR(old_color)
SETCURSOR(old_cursor)
RETURN NIL
```

HRULER

Description:
Displays a horizontal ruler line

Syntax:
Normally called by pressing the Alt-H key combination

Returns:
Nothing

File Name:
F_HRULER.PRG

Screen Use:
One horizontal screen line

Arguments:
None

Typical Use:
To determine horizontal positions or measurements from an application

Cautions:
If HRULER is called using a SET KEY statement, you must declare it external in your application.

See Also:
DEVELOP, GRID, VRULER

Discussion

You generally use HRULER only during development. It places a calibrated horizontal ruler at the center of the screen. To facilitate measurements, you can move the ruler with the arrow keys. To leave HRULER, press the Esc key. If the

Alt-V key combination is pressed from inside HRULER, VRULER is called. Thus, horizontal and vertical ruler lines can appear at the same time (see VRULER for more information).

HRULER can be called recursively. Pressing Alt-H while inside it makes another horizontal line appear. Thus, you can display as many ruler lines as needed. One line is removed and the screen below it restored each time Esc is pressed.

Coding Examples

```
* Include standard inkey header file supplied with Clipper
#include "inkey.ch"

* Declare HRULER external to your application to force linking
EXTERNAL HRULER

* Set up Alt-H key combination for HRULER
SET KEY K_ALT_H TO HRULER
```

You can use the DEVELOP function at the top of your application program to set up the Alt-H key combination and link HRULER. It also links other utility functions (see DEVELOP for more information).

****
FUNCTION HRULER
****
* Display a calibrated horizontal ruler line

* Copyright(c) 1991 -- James Occhiogrosso

```
#include "inkey.ch"
#include "setcurs.ch"
#define RULER    '⌊⌊⌊⌊|⌊⌊⌊⌊'

LOCAL colcount, h_col := 0, h_row := INT(MAXROW()/2), ;
      h_ruler := '', keypress := 0, old_col := COL(), ;
      old_color, old_cursor, old_row := ROW(), old_screen
MEMVAR colbarhi

* Save entry conditions
old_cursor = SETCURSOR(SC_NONE)
old_color  = SETCOLOR(colbarhi)
old_screen = SCRNSAVE(h_row, 0, h_row, MAXCOL())

* Define horizontal ruler
FOR colcount = 0 TO MAXCOL() STEP 10
    IF colcount % 10 = 0 .AND. colcount < 100
        * Each 10th column less than 100
        h_ruler := h_ruler + PAD(colcount, 1)
    ELSEIF colcount % 10 = 0
        * Each 10th column greater than 100
        h_ruler := h_ruler + PAD(colcount-100, 1)
    ENDIF
    h_ruler := h_ruler + RULER
NEXT

* Display horizontal ruler
@ h_row, 0 SAY h_ruler

* Process arrow keys for ruler movement

DO WHILE keypress != K_ESC
    keypress = INKEY(0)
    SCRNREST(old_screen)

    * Adjust row and column for each arrow key pressed
    IF keypress = K_RIGHT
        h_col = IF(h_col < MAXCOL(), h_col+1, MAXCOL())

    ELSEIF keypress = K_LEFT
        h_col = IF(h_col > 0, h_col-1, 0)

    ELSEIF keypress = K_UP
        h_row = IF(h_row > 0, h_row-1, 0)
        old_screen = SCRNSAVE(h_row, 0, h_row, MAXCOL())
```

```
    ELSEIF keypress = K_DOWN
        h_row = IF(h_row < MAXROW(), h_row+1, MAXROW())
        old_screen = SCRNSAVE(h_row, 0, h_row, MAXCOL())
    ENDIF

    * Display ruler in new position
    @ h_row, h_col SAY SUBSTR(h_ruler, 1, MAXCOL() - h_col)

    IF keypress = K_ALT_V
        * Display vertical ruler line
        DO vruler
    ENDIF

    IF keypress = K_ALT_H
        * Display another horizontal ruler
        DO hruler
    ENDIF

ENDDO

SCRNREST(old_screen)
SETPOS(old_row, old_col)
SETCOLOR(old_color)
SETCURSOR(old_cursor)
RETURN NIL
```

INITGLOBAL

Description:
Creates a set of global memory variables for an application

Syntax:
INITGLOBAL([<lColorSetting>])

Returns:
Nothing

File Name:
F_INITGL.PRG

Screen Use:
None

Arguments:
[<lColorSetting>] – If true, initializes the global color variables for a color monitor. If false, uses monochrome values.

Typical Use:
To initialize global variables on entry to an application

Defaults:
If no parameter is passed, the Clipper ISCOLOR function is used to determine the setting of the color variables.

Discussion

Some monochrome monitors have EGA capability. They display colors in varying shades of gray. On such monitors, some settings may produce poor contrast or definition. To avoid this, allow the user to choose between a color or monochrome display and pass the selection to INITGLOBAL.

Coding Examples

```
* Typical code placed at the start of an application
*
answer = .F.
@ 10, 10 SAY 'Do you have a color monitor? (Y/N) ... '
@ 10, 50 GET answer PICTURE 'Y'
READ
INITGLOBAL(answer)

* Or using the OPCONFIRM function in this library
*
@ 10, 10 SAY 'Do you have a color monitor? (Y/N) ... '
INITGLOBAL(OPCONFIRM())
```

```
****************************************************************
FUNCTION INITGLOBAL (syscolor)
****************************************************************

* Initialize global memory variables for Developer's Library

* Copyright(c) 1991 -- James Occhiogrosso

PUBLIC colbarlo, colbarhi, colblink, colhelp1, colhelp2,        ;
       colmemosay, colmemoget, colpword, colstd, colwindow,     ;
       hitanykey

IF syscolor == NIL
      * System color variable is not initialized, use ISCOLOR
      * to determine if color monitor is attached
      syscolor = ISCOLOR()
ENDIF

* Initialize global color variables
IF syscolor
      colstd     = "w+/b, gr+/w,,, w+/w"
      colhelp1   = "gr+/b, w+/rb"
      colhelp2   = "gr+/gr, w+/gr"
      colbarlo   = "gr+/b, gr+/r,,,bg+/r"
      colbarhi   = "gr+/rb, gr+/b"
      colwindow  = "w+/g, gr+/r"
      colpword   = "w+/b, b/b"
      colblink   = "w+*/g, gr+*/r"
      colmemosay = "bg+/w"
      colmemoget = "gr+/w"
ELSE
      colstd     = "W/N, N/W"
      colhelp1   = "N/W, W/N"
      colhelp2   = colhelp1
      colbarlo   = colstd
      colbarhi   = colhelp1
      colwindow  = "N/W, N/W,,,W+/N"
      colpword   = "W/N, N/N"
      colblink   = "N*/W, N/W"
      colmemosay = colhelp1
      colmemoget = colhelp1
ENDIF

hitanykey = " Press any key to proceed. "

RETURN NIL
```

INITVARS

Description:
Creates a set of public memory variables corresponding to fields in the currently selected database

Syntax:
INITVARS( )

Returns:
NIL

File Name:
F_MVARS.PRG

Screen Usage:
None

Arguments:
None

Typical Use:
To buffer data entry to memory variables

Cautions:
Creates the variables as public. When you finish using them, release them with FREEVARS.

See Also:
CLRVARS, EQUVARS, FREEVARS, REPLVARS

Discussion

INITVARS creates a set of public memory variables corresponding to the fields in the current database. Each variable name consists of the field name with an "m" in front of it (e.g., mcity for the field "city"). INITVARS creates each variable as a logical and initializes it to false. Typically, CLRVARS, EQUVARS, and REPLVARS then use the public variables. When they are no longer needed, you can release them with FREEVARS.

Coding Examples

```
* Open database
USE DataFile NEW

* Initialize field variables
INITVARS()

* Do your add or edit routines
    .
    .
    .
* End of your routine

* Replace record
REPLVARS()

* Release memory used by field variables
FREEVARS()

* Return to caller
RETURN
```

See sample program T_AEDBAR.PRG on the companion disk for a typical example.

```
***************************************************************
FUNCTION INITVARS
***************************************************************

* Create memory variables for each fields in active database

* Copyright(c) 1991 -- James Occhiogrosso

* Caution: This procedure declares a PUBLIC memory variable
* for each field in the selected database. Release the
* variables by calling FREEVARS when you no longer need them.

LOCAL field_cnt := FCOUNT(), counter := 0
PRIVATE field_name

* Get number of fields
field_cnt = FCOUNT()

* Declare public variable for each field
FOR counter = 1 TO field_cnt
    field_name = LOWER(FIELD(counter))
    PUBLIC m&field_name
NEXT

RETURN NIL
```

ISLASTDAY

Description:
Determines if a date is the last day of the month

Syntax:
ISLASTDAY(<dDate>)

Returns:
True if passed date is the last day of the month; false otherwise

File Name:
F_ISLAST.PRG

Screen Use:
None

Arguments:
<dDate> – Optional date value

Typical Use:
To determine if the current date is the last day of the month for accounting and other procedures

Defaults:
Checks the current date if no argument is passed

See Also:
DTOF, DTOL, LASTDAY

Discussion

ISLASTDAY is useful to initiate processes that must be done on the last day of the month, or before a new month is started. A typical example is to remind an operator to perform a month-end closing in an accounting system.

Coding Examples

```
/* To remind operator to perform month end closing if it is
the last day of the month or a new month has started. Example
assumes the accounting month number is saved in a system file. */

IF ISLASTDAY(DATE()) .OR. MONTH(DATE()) != sysfile->month

    @ 24, 10 SAY 'Run end of month account aging now? Y/N ' ;
    GET answer
    READ
    IF answer
        * Run report or process
    ENDIF
ENDIF
```

```
*****************************************************************
FUNCTION ISLASTDAY (date_val)
*****************************************************************

* Returns true if current date is last day of month

* Copyright(c) 1991 -- James Occhiogrosso

IF date_val = NIL
   * Default to current date if no value is passed
   date_val = DATE()

ELSEIF VALTYPE(date_val) != 'D' .OR. EMPTY(date_val)
   * Return false if argument is wrong
   RETURN .F.

ENDIF

RETURN ( DAY(date_val) = LASTDAY(date_val) )
```

ISMEMO

Description:
Determines whether a database contains memo fields

Syntax:
ISMEMO(<cFileName>)

Returns:
Numeric value as follows:
        0 – No memo fields
        1 – At least one memo field defined
        -1 – Not a dBASE III database, or a file error has occurred

File Name:
F_ISMEMO.PRG

Screen Use:
None

Arguments:
<cFileName> – Name of a database file to be tested with optional extension

Typical Use:
To determine if a database file has an associated memo file before performing a procedure (such as copying files) that must process both files

Defaults:
DBF extension if <cFileName> lacks one. The memo file extension always defaults to DBT.

Error Handling:
Returns -1 on an error. Use the Clipper FERROR function to determine error type.

Discussion

Use ISMEMO before any operation that must process memo files along with the database. A typical example is copying database files during a backup operation.

You can also use ISMEMO to determine if a database is in dBASE III format. Just combine it with the Clipper FERROR function as shown in the example below. If ISMEMO returns -1 and FERROR returns zero, the file is not a dBASE III database. The FERROR value eliminates the possibility of a file error having occurred.

Coding Examples

```
* Display a message for each possible result
* of testing a database with ISMEMO

file_name = SPACE(12)
@ 10, 10 say 'Enter filename ... ' GET file_name
READ

file_type = ISMEMO(file_name)

IF file_type = 1
   ? 'File is a dBASE III database with memos'

ELSEIF file_type = 0
   ? 'File is a dBASE III database without memos'

ELSEIF FERROR() = 0 .AND. file_type = -1
   ? 'File is not a dBASE III database.'

ELSEIF FERROR() != 0 .AND. file_type = -1
   ? 'A file error occurred. Error code = ' + ;
             LTRIM(STR(FERROR()))
ENDIF
```

```
* Test a file for memo fields before opening it
filename = 'cFileName'
IF ISMEMO(filename) = 1

    IF !FILE( filename + '.DBT' )
       ? 'Memo file ' + filename + '.DBT is missing.'
       RETURN .F.
    ENDIF

ENDIF

USE (filename) NEW
```

```
****************************************************************
FUNCTION ISMEMO (filename)
****************************************************************

* Test whether a database contains memo fields

* Copyright(c) 1991 -- James Occhiogrosso

LOCAL buffer := ' ', handle := 0, ret_value := -1, memofile := ''


* Add DBT extension for memo file

IF AT(".", filename) > 0
    memofile = SUBSTR(filename,1,AT('.',filename) - 1) + '.DBT'
ELSE
    * If no extension passed, default to DBF and DBT
    memofile = TRIM(filename) + ".DBT"
    filename = TRIM(filename) + ".DBF"
ENDIF

* Open database file as read only
handle = FOPEN(filename, 0)

* If no open error, read first byte
IF FERROR() = 0 .AND. FREAD(handle, @buffer, 1) = 1

    * First byte of a dBASE III file is 131 if memo fields
    * are defined, or 3 if not. If neither holds, the file
    * is not a dBASE III database and the default value
    * of -1 is returned.

    * Check for memo code in buffer
    IF buffer = CHR(131)
       * File is dBASE III file with memo fields
       ret_value = 1

    ELSEIF buffer = CHR(03)
       * File is dBASE III file without memo fields
       ret_value = 0

    ENDIF
ENDIF

* Clean up and return
FCLOSE(handle)
RETURN(ret_value)
```

KEYCODE

Description:
Development function used to view the scan code and ASCII value of a key

Syntax:
KEYCODE( )

Returns:
Character string

File Name:
F_KEYCOD.PRG

Screen Use:
None

Arguments:
None

Typical Use:
To determine scan code and ASCII value of a key during application development

See Also:
DEVELOP, FULLKEY, SCANKEY

Discussion

KEYCODE returns a character string in the format:

```
Scan code = nnn    ASCII value = nnn
```

The ASCII value returned represents the actual DOS ASCII equivalent of the key. In most cases, it is the same as the INKEY value returned by Clipper. However, special keys such as the function, alternate (Alt), and cursor pad keys lack ASCII equivalents. For them, KEYCODE returns an ASCII value of zero. You normally use KEYCODE only during application development. It is useful to quickly determine key values when you are using both scan codes and ASCII values.

KEYCODE is linked automatically if you use the DEVELOP function. You call it directly from the debugger command window. It waits for a key to be pressed, and returns a string in the above format to the debugger screen for viewing.

Coding Examples

You can link KEYCODE to your application by declaring it EXTERNAL or by using DEVELOP.

```
* Link keycode function by itself
#ifdef DEBUG
    EXTERNAL KEYCODE
#enddef

* Or link all development functions including KEYCODE
#ifdef DEBUG
    DEVELOP()
#enddef
```

```
*****************************************************************
FUNCTION KEYCODE
*****************************************************************

* Returns scan code and ASCII value for any key as a string

* Copyright(c) 1991 -- James Occhiogrosso

* Initialize variables
LOCAL scancode := 0, ascii_val := 0

ascii_val := LTRIM(STR(SCANKEY(@scancode)))

* Return string to screen or debugger
RETURN ('Scan code = ' +  LTRIM(STR(scancode)) + ;
        '    ASCII value = ' + ascii_val)
```

LASTDAY

Description:
Determines the last day of a month

Syntax:
LASTDAY(<dDate>)

Returns:
Integer

File Name:
F_LASTDA.PRG

Screen Use:
None

Arguments:
<dDate> – Optional date value

Typical Use:
To determine the last day of a month for accounting and other monthly processes

Defaults:
Returns the last day of the current month if no parameter is passed. Returns zero if passed date is invalid.

See Also:
DTOF, DTOL, ISLASTDAY

Discussion

LASTDAY is useful when you need to know the last day of the month for calculations. A typical use is to determine how many days are left in the current month (see example below).

Coding Examples

```
* Get last day of current month
last_day = LASTDAY(DATE())

* Get last day of February 1991
last_day = LASTDAY(CTOD("02/01/91"))

* Get number of days left in current month
days_left = LASTDAY(DATE()) - DAY(DATE())
```

```
*******************************************************************
FUNCTION LASTDAY (date_val)
*******************************************************************

* Returns number of last day of the month for any date

* Copyright(c) 1991 -- James Occhiogrosso

LOCAL last_day, month_num, num_days

IF date_val = NIL
    * Default to current date if no value passed
    date_val = DATE()

ELSEIF VALTYPE(date_val) != 'D' .OR. EMPTY(date_val)
    * Return zero if argument is wrong
    RETURN 0

ENDIF

month_num = MONTH(date_val)

* Default month length is 31 days
num_days = 31

DO CASE
    * Is it a 30 day month? Thirty days hath...
    CASE month_num = 4 .OR. month_num = 6 .OR. ;
         month_num = 9 .OR. month_num = 11

        * Yes, return 30
        num_days = 30

    CASE month_num = 2

        * If it is February, check for leap year
        * and return 28 or 29 accordingly.

        IF YEAR(date_val) % 4 = 0 .AND. ;
           YEAR(date_val) % 100 != 0

            * If year is divisible by four, but not
            * 100, it is a leap year.
            num_days = 29

        ELSEIF YEAR(date_val) % 100 = 0 .AND. ;
               YEAR(date_val) % 400 = 0

            * If year is divisible by 100, it must also be
            * divisible by 400 to be a leap year.
```

```
            num_days = 29

      ELSE

            * Otherwise, it is not a leap year.
            num_days = 28

      ENDIF
ENDCASE

RETURN(num_days)
```

LASTDRIVE

Description:
Determines the highest lettered valid DOS disk drive

Syntax:
LASTDRIVE( )

Returns:
Single uppercase character

File Name:
LASTDRIV.ASM

Screen Use:
None

Arguments:
None

Typical Use:
To determine or verify available drives before performing disk operations

Cautions:
Returns B if only floppy drives are attached (see discussion below)

See Also:
DISKTEST

Discussion

Use LASTDRIVE before disk operations if you are unsure whether a drive exists. It is particularly useful to verify a user's selection. If the selection is invalid, your program can warn the user and let him or her try again. This avoids problems caused by typing errors and misinterpretations.

With DOS version 3.0 or later, LASTDRIVE returns a letter corresponding to the number of logical drives or the last drive value specified in CONFIG.SYS. The minimum value is E.

For DOS versions before 3.0, the minimum value returned is B for a floppy-only system (DOS views a single floppy drive as being logical drives A and B).

By comparing the operator selection to the returned value, you can validate its existence. This, however, does not ensure that the disk is writable. For a complete test, use DISKTEST.

Coding Examples

The example below uses LASTDRIVE to validate the operator's selection. It then uses DISKTEST to test the selected drive. If no error occurs, the process can continue.

```
valid_drive := .F.

DO WHILE !valid_drive

    * Get operator selection
    @ 10, 20 SAY 'Enter drive to copy to ...... : ' ;
             GET disk_drive PICTURE '!' VALID !EMPTY(disk_drive)
    READ

    * See if drive exists
    valid_drive := IF(LASTDRIVE() >= disk_drive, .T., .F.)

ENDDO

* It is valid, see if it is ready

IF DISKTEST(disk_drive) = 0
    * Disk is ready, proceed with copy operation
ELSE
    * Disk is not ready (see DISKTEST for list of errors)
ENDIF
```

```
; ---------------------------------------------------------------
; FUNCTION NAME: LASTDRIVE - Returns last logical DOS drive
; ---------------------------------------------------------------
; Copyright(c) 1991 -- James Occhiogrosso

        INCLUDE   DEVELOP.MAC          ; Developer's Library macro file

        PUBLIC    LASTDRIVE            ; Declare function name
                                       ; Declare Clipper EXTERNALs
        EXTRN     __RETC:FAR           ; Return string to Clipper

        CODESEG   SEGMENT 'CODE'
                  ASSUME CS:CODESEG

LASTDRIVE PROC    FAR

          JMP     BEGIN                ; Jump around data area
LAST_DRV  DB      'A', 0               ; Last drive letter

BEGIN:
          PUSH_REGS                    ; Save Clipper registers
          MOV     AH, 19h              ; Default drive function
          INT     21h
          MOV     DL, AL               ; AL is default drive
          MOV     AH, 0Eh              ; Select disk function
          INT     21h                  ;   (returns last drive)
          ADD     AL, 64               ; Convert it to ASCII
          PUSH    CS                   ; Set up our data segment
          POP     DS
          MOV     BX, OFFSET LAST_DRV  ; Get drive letter address
          MOV     [BX], AL             ; Move our value to it
          POP_REGS                     ; Restore Clipper registers
          RET_STRING CS BX             ; Return drive to Clipper

LASTDRIVE ENDP                         ; End of procedure

        CODESEG   ENDS                 ; End of code segment
                  END                  ; End of assembly
```

MAKEDBF

Description:
Creates or recreates application database files from the definitions in a data dictionary text file

Syntax:
MAKEDBF(<cDataDictName>)

Returns:
True if database files were updated; false otherwise

File Name:
F_MAKEDB.PRG

Screen Use:
Entire screen (see discussion below)

Arguments:
<cDataDictName> – Complete name, including extension, of the data dictionary file (path is optional)

Typical Use:
To update application databases when a new version is released or to create databases for a new application

Defaults:
Assumes data dictionary is in current directory if path is not defined

Error Handling:
Since proper operation of MAKEDBF is usually critical to application integrity, it returns to DOS with a message if a major error occurs. Possible errors are:

- Application data dictionary file is missing or cannot be opened.
- Existing field changed type.

- Existing database has memo fields, and DBT file is missing or cannot be opened.
- Backup files cannot be created for an existing database.
- Incorrect field definition in the data dictionary file.
- A database cannot be opened exclusively in a network environment.

Cautions:
MAKEDBF performs minimal checking of field definitions in the data dictionary. The developer must ensure that field and file names and definitions are valid.

See Also:
MAKENDX, SYSVERSION

Discussion

MAKEDBF is a powerful function that frees the developer from the tedious process of manually updating database files when changing an application. When used with SYSVERSION and MAKENDX, it totally automates system updates.

The caller passes MAKEDBF the name of a text file, including its extension. It serves as a data dictionary containing all information about application database and index files. MAKEDBF reads the database names from the dictionary, opens each file, and compares each field to the dictionary specifications. If they do not match, it recreates the database. The database is created if it does not exist.

This approach has the following advantages:

- Definitions for all multiple database and index files are in a single, easily updated text file.
- The dictionary can contain extensive documentation.
- All application databases are updated simultaneously.
- New applications can be delivered with minimal files (MAKEDBF is used to create database files).

- You can update applications (maintaining existing data) without manual, on-site database updates.

Before using MAKEDBF, you must create a data dictionary containing field definitions for all databases. It is created with a word processor in the nondocument mode. Usually, it also contains index definitions for MAKENDX.

The overall format of the data dictionary is:

```
* Definition for database 1

DBFDEF DBFNAME1 TEXT1
     FIELDNAME   FIELDTYPE   FIELDLEN   FIELDDECS
     FIELDNAME   FIELDTYPE   FIELDLEN   FIELDDECS
                    .
                    .
                    .
ENDDEF

* Definition for database 2

DBFDEF DBFNAME2 TEXT2
     FIELDNAME   FIELDTYPE   FIELDLEN   FIELDDECS
     FIELDNAME   FIELDTYPE   FIELDLEN   FIELDDECS
                    .
                    .
                    .
ENDDEF

* Index definitions for database 1

NDXDEF   DBFNAME1   NDXNAME1   KEYEXPR1   TEXT3
NDXDEF   DBFNAME1   NDXNAME2   KEYEXPR2   TEXT4
NDXDEF   DBFNAME1   NDXNAME3   KEYEXPR3   TEXT5

* Index definitions for database 2

NDXDEF   DBFNAME2   NDXNAME4   KEYEXPR4   TEXT6
NDXDEF   DBFNAME2   NDXNAME5   KEYEXPR5   TEXT7

ENDFILE
```

A database definition starts with the keyword DBFDEF. Immediately afterward comes the name of the database, followed by a displayable text message.

The three areas (DBFDEF, DBFNAME, and TEXT) can be preceded with or separated by spaces as desired. The text field begins with the next non-blank character following the database name, and continues to the end of the line. The text is a message of up to 60 characters that appears when the database is updated. It may contain any characters, including embedded spaces and quotation marks.

Following the database definition is one line for each field, containing its name, type, length, and number of decimal places. Again, you can separate the areas with spaces for formatting purposes.

After all field definition lines, the database definition ends with the keyword ENDDEF.

This format repeats for each database in the application.

Index files are defined similarly, except that each requires only one line, consisting of the following five elements:

1.	NDXDEF	Keyword that begins an index definition
2.	DBFNAME	Associated database
3.	NDXNAME	Index file
4.	KEYEXPR	Clipper expression or field name for the index key. (This area **MUST NOT** contain embedded spaces.)
5.	TEXT	Message of up to 60 characters that appears if the index is updated. (It may contain any printable character.)

Index definition lines are listed successively. Indexes are generated only for databases that are created or updated. (See MAKENDX and the Theory of Operation section below.)

After all index definitions, the dictionary ends with the keyword ENDFILE.

You can include a comment in the data dictionary by starting each line with an asterisk or number (#) sign. MAKEDBF also ignores blank lines and is not case sensitive. All definitions can be uppercase, lowercase, or mixed.

MAKEDBF is sensitive to the order of the fields in the database and the dictionary. If the orders do not match, the database is recreated.

Thus, the data dictionary defines all databases and indexes for an application. It is a text file maintained by a word processor. You can use it to create databases and index files for a new application, and to document updates to existing applications.

A typical data dictionary file for a single database with three indexes is:

```
*   Data Dictionary *

*****************************************************************
*   Structure of SAMPLE.DBF   Last update: 01/26/90    Vers. 1.23
*****************************************************************
*
*   Change History:
*
*       Date                    Item
*     _____                _____
*    12/15/89        Increased size of 'address' field - was 25
*    01/05/90        Added memo field for 'comment'
*    01/26/90        Deleted 'terms' field


DBFDEF   SAMPLE   Updating Customer samples database file

  *
  *                   Field Name      Type      Width       Decimals
  *                  _____

                     COMPANY           C          30           0
                     CUSTID            C           6           0
                     ADDRESS           C          30           0
                     CITY              C          19           0
                     STATE             C           6           0
                     ZIP               C          10           0
                     PHONE             C          12           0
 * 01/26/90          TERMS             C          15           0
                     CREDITLIM         N          10           2
                     REPID             C           6           0
                     SAMPLEPN          C          20           0
                     LASTSALE          D           8           0
                     ACTIVE            L           1           0
                     COMMENT           M          10           0
ENDDEF

NDXDEF  SAMPLE  SAMPLE1  COMPANY   Indexing samples file on Company
NDXDEF  SAMPLE  SAMPLE2  CUSTID    Indexing samples file on Account No.
NDXDEF  SAMPLE  SAMPLE3  SAMPLEPN  Indexing samples file on Part No.

ENDFILE
```

A data dictionary for the sample databases in the Developer's Library is on the companion disk in TESTDICT.DAT.

Theory of Operation

The call to MAKEDBF usually appears at the top of the main file in an application. SYSVERSION is used to detect an update or a new application. It calls MAKEDBF, passing it the name of the application data dictionary. (SYSVERSION detects an update by reading a version file. See it for more information.)

MAKEDBF reads the data dictionary until it encounters a database definition (DBFDEF). If the subject database exists, it is opened, and all fields in it are compared to the definitions in the dictionary. Each field must match the corresponding definition exactly. If differences exist, MAKEDBF sets a flag to recreate the database. The flag is also set if the database does not exist. Thus, fields can be added, deleted, or changed as needed, and MAKEDBF will detect the changes and flag the database to be recreated.

If the DBF file exists and is to be recreated, MAKEDBF renames it with a BAK extension. At the same time, it tests the file for memo fields, and renames any DBT file with a TBK extension. It erases previous versions of the file with these extensions.

MAKEDBF then creates a new file structure and copies the data in the backup files (BAK and TBK) into it. Thus, it recreates the database and saves all existing data. This, of course, applies only to fields that have not been renamed or deleted, i.e., data is copied from the backup file only for fields with the same name.

If the database defined in the dictionary does not exist, MAKEDBF creates it as an empty DBF file. If memo fields are defined, it also creates an empty DBT file.

After creating or recreating all database files according to the data dictionary definitions, MAKEDBF calls MAKENDX, passing it an array of database names. The array contains the name of each database created or recreated.

MAKENDX then creates (or recreates) the indexes for each file according to the data dictionary.

Screen Use

MAKEDBF uses the entire screen. Since it is normally called on entry to an application, it does not save or restore the screen.

When MAKEDBF is called, a boxed area appears with a few lines of operator explanations at the top. The lower part is empty. When a database is created (or recreated), the text associated with its definition appears on successive lines.

Similarly, the associated text in the data dictionary for each index appears on successive lines while the file is being indexed. The messages begin scrolling up after 15 lines have appeared.

The operator thus sees new messages in the window during a process that, if it must recreate many files and indexes, may be quite long. Presumably, the changing display assures the operator that something is happening and there is no need to reboot!

Coding Examples

The example below is from an accounts receivable system in which the executable file is ar.exe, the version update control file is arvers.dat, and the database and index definitions are in the file arsystem.def.

SYSVERSION compares the DOS date/time stamp of ar.exe with the date/time string in arvers.dat. If ar.exe is later (indicating an update), or if arvers.dat does not exist (indicating a new application), SYSVERSION writes the new date and time to arvers.dat, and returns false.

On the other hand, if ar.exe is simultaneous or earlier, SYSVERSION takes no further action and returns true.

```
* Check for correct version

IF .NOT. SYSVERSION( "ar.exe", "arvers.dat" )
```

```
     * Version is incorrect! Check application database and
     * index files using data dictionary arsystem.def.

     MAKEDBF("arsystem.def")

ENDIF

* Continue with application
```

****
FUNCTION MAKEDBF (app_def)
****

* Creates or recreates an application's database files

* Copyright(c) 1991 -- James Occhiogrosso

* Note: Since successful operation of MAKEDBF is usually critical
* to application integrity, it returns to DOS with a message if
* an error prevents proper updating.

```
#include "box.ch"
#define f_names   1
#define f_types   2
#define f_lens    3
#define f_decs    4
#define f_ok      5

LOCAL counter      := 0,    create_dbf := .F.,   dbf_exist  := .F., ;
      dbf_stru     := {},   dbf_name   := '',    dbf_names  := {},  ;
      dbf_text     := '',   handle     := 0,     memo_files[1],     ;
      memoflds     := .F.,  num_fields := 0,     new_stru   := {},  ;
      old_cursor   := .F.,  old_exact  := .F.,   textline   := '',  ;
      text_row     := 7

* Return to DOS if data dictionary file cannot be opened
IF (handle = FOPEN(app_def)) <= 0
   * Critical error - return to DOS
   ?? CHR(7)
   ? 'Application definition file missing'
   SET CURSOR ON
   QUIT
ENDIF

* Save cursor status and turn cursor off
old_cursor = SETCURSOR(.F.)

* Display MAKEDBF installation screen

CLEAR SCREEN
DISPBOX(1, 7, 23, 70, B_DOUBLE + SPACE(1))
DEVPOS(1, 0)
TEXT
```

```
╔═══════════════════════════════════════════════════════════╗
║           S Y S T E M    I N S T A L L A T I O N          ║
╠═══════════════════════════════════════════════════════════╣
║  This is a new or updated system configuration. System files ║
║  will be checked and updated as required. Data will not be   ║
║  lost. The process takes a few minutes. Please be patient    ║
╚═══════════════════════════════════════════════════════════╝

ENDTEXT

* Get first database definition from data dictionary
GETDBFDEF(@dbf_name,@dbf_text,@textline,handle)

* Loop until no more database definition (DBFDEF) lines

DO WHILE .NOT. EMPTY(dbf_name)

   * Reset loop control variables
   create_dbf = .F.
   dbf_exist = .F.

   * Check for existence of database
   IF FILE(dbf_name + '.dbf')
      * Database exists, set flag and open it for exclusive use
      dbf_exist = .T.
      USE &dbf_name EXCLUSIVE NEW
      IF NETERR()
         ?? CHR(7)
         ? 'File ' + UPPER(dbf_name) + ' cannot be opened ' + ;
           'exclusively. '
         SET CURSOR ON
         QUIT
      ENDIF

      * Load field structures to dbf_stru array
      dbf_stru = DBSTRUCT()
      num_fields = LEN(dbf_stru)


      * Add and initialize a logical dimension for field status

      FOR counter = 1 TO num_fields
          ASIZE(dbf_stru[counter], 5)
          dbf_stru[counter][5] = .F.
      NEXT

      * Open and load temporary file with field definitions
      LOADSTRU(@textline,@new_stru,handle)

      * Set EXACT on and verify fields to data dictionary
      old_exact = SET(_SET_EXACT, .T.)
      IF LEN(new_stru) != num_fields
         * Database and dictionary have different number
```

```
            * of fields. Set create flag
            create_dbf = .T.
      ELSE
         * Compare all fields to dictionary definitions
         FOR counter = 1 TO num_fields

            IF dbf_stru[counter][f_names] == ;
                  TRIM(new_stru[counter][f_names])
               * Field names match. Check type and length

               IF new_stru[counter][f_types] != ;
                     dbf_stru[counter][f_types]
                  ?? CHR(7)
                  ? 'Field type ' + ;
                     TRIM(new_stru[counter][f_names]) + ;
                     ' in database ' + dbf_name +         ;
                     ' changed. Cannot continue. '
                  SET CURSOR ON
                  QUIT

               ELSEIF new_stru[counter][f_lens]  !=    ;
                        dbf_stru[counter][f_lens]  .OR. ;
                        new_stru[counter][f_decs]  !=   ;
                        dbf_stru[counter][f_decs]

                  * Dictionary definition is not same
                  * as database. Set create flag
                  create_dbf = .T.

               ELSE
                  * Flag verified field in f_ok array
                  dbf_stru[counter][f_ok] = .T.
               ENDIF

            ELSE
               * Field name changed. Set create flag
               create_dbf = .T.

            ENDIF
         NEXT
      ENDIF

      * Reset EXACT to entry condition
      SET(_SET_EXACT, old_exact)

      * Check flags array. False indicates field exists in
      * database but not in dictionary. (Field was deleted)

      IF !create_dbf
         * Test for deletions unless create flag already set
         FOR counter = 1 TO num_fields
            IF !dbf_stru[counter][f_ok]
               * Field was deleted. Set create flag
               create_dbf = .T.
            ENDIF
```

```
         NEXT
      ENDIF

   ELSE
      * Database does not exist, set flag to recreate it
      LOADSTRU(@textline,@new_stru,handle)
      create_dbf = .T.
   ENDIF

   * Close file
   USE

   * Test flags and recreate database if necessary
   IF dbf_exist .AND. create_dbf

      * Old database exists. Create backup files.
      * Delete old backups

      IF FILE(dbf_name + '.BAK')
         ERASE(dbf_name + '.BAK')
      ENDIF
      IF FILE(dbf_name + '.TBK')
         ERASE(dbf_name + '.TBK')
      ENDIF

      * Test database for defined memo fields
      memoflds = IF(ISMEMO(dbf_name) = 1, .T., .F.)

      * Rename old database files to backups
      IF memoflds .AND. .NOT. FILE(dbf_name + '.DBT')
         ?? CHR(7)
         ? 'Memo file ' + dbf_name + '.DBT missing.'
         SET CURSOR ON
         QUIT
      ELSEIF memoflds .AND. FILE(dbf_name + '.DBT')
         RENAME (dbf_name + '.DBT') TO (dbf_name + '.TBK')
      ENDIF
      RENAME (dbf_name + '.DBF') TO (dbf_name + '.BAK')

      * Make sure both backup files exist before creating
      * new ones. CREATE destroys existing DBT files!

      IF .NOT. FILE(dbf_name + '.BAK') .OR. ;
               (memoflds .AND. !FILE(dbf_name + '.TBK'))
         ?? CHR(7)
         ? 'Backup files cannot be created for ' + dbf_name
         SET CURSOR ON
         QUIT
      ENDIF

   ENDIF
```

```
        IF create_dbf

           * Scroll screen up if at bottom of window
           IF text_row = 22
               SCROLL(8, 9, 22, 68, 1)
           ELSE
               text_row++
           ENDIF

           * Display associated text (balance of textline)
           @ text_row, 7 SAY ':' + ' ' + SUBSTR(dbf_text, 1, 60)
           @ text_row, 70 SAY ':'

           * Recreate database file from structure file
           DBCREATE(dbf_name, new_stru)
           USE

           * Rename DBT file if memo fields exist
           IF memoflds .AND. dbf_exist
               ERASE (dbf_name + '.DBT')
               RENAME (dbf_name + '.TBK') TO (dbf_name + '.DBT')
           ENDIF

           * If database exists, copy all records from backup
           IF dbf_exist
               USE (dbf_name) EXCLUSIVE NEW
               IF NETERR()
                  ?? CHR(7)
                  ? 'File ' + UPPER(dbf_name) + 'cannot open ' + ;
                    'exclusively. '
                  SET CURSOR ON
                  QUIT
               ENDIF

               APPEND FROM (dbf_name + '.BAK')
               IF memoflds
                  * Pack DBT file if memo fields exist
                  memo_files[1] := dbf_name
                  MEMOPACK(memo_files)
               ENDIF
               USE
           ENDIF

           * Add current database file name to array
           AADD(dbf_names, dbf_name)
        ENDIF

        * Get next database definition line from data dictionary
        GETDBFDEF(@dbf_name,@dbf_text,@textline,handle)

ENDDO

* Call MAKENDX to recreate indexes of updated databases
SETCURSOR(old_cursor)
RETURN MAKENDX(dbf_names, textline, text_row)
```

```
*********************************************************************
STATIC FUNCTION GETDBFDEF (dbf_name, dbf_text, textline, handle)
*********************************************************************

* Locate and read next database definition (DBFDEF) line

* Get next defined line from data dictionary
NEXTLINE(@textline, handle)

* Check line for database definition code

IF UPPER(SUBSTR(textline, 1, 6)) = 'DBFDEF'
   * Line is a valid database definition, strip
   * DBFDEF code identifier and return

   textline = LTRIM(SUBSTR(textline, 7))
   dbf_name = PARSE(@textline)
   dbf_text = textline

ELSE
   * Otherwise, set dbf_name to an empty string
   * and return without altering text line
   dbf_name = ''
ENDIF
RETURN ''

*********************************************************************
STATIC FUNCTION NEXTLINE (textline, handle)
*********************************************************************

* Get next non-comment line in definitions file

* Test first character of line
textline = '*'
DO WHILE (SUBSTR(textline, 1, 1) $ '*#' .OR. EMPTY(textline))  ;
      .AND. UPPER(SUBSTR(textline, 1, 7)) != 'ENDFILE'

   * If line is a comment or blank, skip it
   textline = LTRIM(FREADLINE(handle))

ENDDO
RETURN NIL

*********************************************************************
STATIC FUNCTION LOADSTRU (textline, new_stru, handle)
*********************************************************************

* Load database definitions into structure array

LOCAL fld_dec := '', fld_len := '', fld_name := '',;
      fld_type := '', message := ''

* Clear new structure array
new_stru := {}
```

```
* Get next non-comment line of definitions file
NEXTLINE(@textline, handle)

* Stay in loop until we read end of definitions code
DO WHILE UPPER(SUBSTR(textline, 1, 6)) != 'ENDDEF'

   * Get and verify field definitions from data dictionary

   fld_name = UPPER(PARSE(@textline))      && Get field name
   fld_type = UPPER(PARSE(@textline))      && Get field type
   fld_len  = PARSE(@textline)             && Get field length
   fld_dec  = PARSE(@textline)             && Get field decimals

   IF EMPTY(fld_name) .OR. LEN(fld_name) > 10
      message = 'Field name'

   ELSEIF EMPTY(fld_type) .OR. LEN(fld_type) > 1 ;
                          .OR. .NOT. (fld_type) $ 'CDNLM'
      message = 'Field type'

   ELSEIF EMPTY(fld_len) .OR. .NOT. VAL(fld_len) >= 0 ;
                         .OR. VAL(fld_len) > 999
      message = 'Field length'

   ELSEIF EMPTY(fld_dec) .OR. .NOT. VAL(fld_dec) >= 0 ;
                         .OR. VAL(fld_dec) > 999
      message = 'Field decimals'

   ENDIF
   IF .NOT. EMPTY(message)
      * If message loaded, display it and return to DOS
      ?? CHR(7)
      ? message + ' error in data dictionary ..... ' + fld_name
      ? 'Text line = ' + SUBSTR(textline,1,60)
      SET CURSOR ON
      QUIT
   ELSE
      * Load each field definition into structure array
      AADD(new_stru, { fld_name, fld_type,  ;
                       VAL(fld_len), VAL(fld_dec) } )
   ENDIF

   * Get next non-comment line of definitions file
   NEXTLINE(@textline,handle)

ENDDO

* Reset pointer to top of file and return
GO TOP
RETURN NIL
```

MAKEID

Description:
Creates a unique alphanumeric identification (ID) code from a string

Syntax:
MAKEID (<cNameString>, <cIDCode>, [<nIndexNum>], [<nDisplayRow>], [<nDisplayColumn>])

Returns:
True if successful, false if <cNameString> is empty or more than 999 codes were tried without finding a unique one

File Name:
F_MAKEID.PRG

Screen Use:
Defined by calling parameters. If the AEDBAR function is in use, messages appear in its window.

Arguments:
<cNameString> – Literal string or variable from which to create an ID code

<cIDCode> – Variable to receive the generated ID code. Passed by reference.

[<nIndexNum>] – Optional index position in the index order. If passed, MAKEID uses it to ensure that the generated ID code is unique. If not passed, the current open index is used.

[<nDisplayRow>], [<nDisplayColumn>] – Optional display row and column coordinates for the generated ID code. If not passed, the ID code is not displayed.

Typical Use:
To generate unique alphanumeric codes from character strings. Typically used to create suggested account ID codes from the names of companies or people and display them.

Defaults:
Generated ID codes are 6 characters long.

If coordinates are passed, the created ID code appears in the enhanced (GET) color.

Cautions:
Cannot generate more than 999 unique ID codes. If you need more, use a different system.
Returns true if no database is in use when it is called.

Global Variables:
aedbar, helpcode

See Also:
AEDBAR, AEDMSG, NODUPL, REQDDATA

Discussion

MAKEID is generally used in a VALID clause during data entry. Typically, it generates a unique 6 character ID code based on a company's or person's name. It uses the first 3 characters of the name along with a 3 digit number to create a code of the form "XXX999".

After generating the code, MAKEID verifies that it is unique. It does this by SEEKing the code with the index order set as specified. If the ID code is found, its numeric part is incremented by 1 and the process repeats. MAKEID returns up to 999 unique ID codes for passed names with the same first 3 letters. This is generally adequate for small business applications. If row and column arguments are passed, MAKEID displays the generated ID code at the coordinates in the current GET color. Thus, the operator sees the code immediately. If a GET has also been issued for it (usually at the same screen coordinates), the operator can edit the value suggested by MAKEID.

If AEDBAR is in use, MAKEID displays messages in its window. Otherwise (global variable aedbar is undefined), it does not display any messages. MAKEID also uses the helpcode variable. If it is defined, it must contain the string ADD for MAKEID to return an ID code. Any other value causes

MAKEID to do nothing. This lets it generate ID codes only when ADDing records. The name field can be edited later without changing the ID code.

Coding Examples

You can use MAKEID with the NODUPL function to guarantee the generation of unique customer account numbers during data entry. In the example below, MAKEID provides an on-screen suggestion for the ID code when a company name is entered. The operator can accept the suggestion or edit it. NODUPL is then used as a VALID on the customer ID code to prevent duplications.

```
* Get customer name and create a unique code from it. Use
* index 2, and display created ID code at row 5, column 71.

@ 5, 15 GET mcustname VALID MAKEID(mcustname, @mcustid, 2, 5, 71)

* Get returned ID code at same coordinates using NODUPL to
* prevent duplicates

@ 5, 71 GET mcustid PICTURE "@! !!!999" ;
          VALID NODUPL(mcustid, 2, custid)

READ
```

```
*********************************************************************
FUNCTION MAKEID (name_var, id_var, look_ndx, id_row, id_col)
*********************************************************************

* Creates a six character unique ID code from a string
* Copyright(c) 1991 -- James Occhiogrosso

LOCAL old_ndx := 0, old_recd := 0, count1 := 0, count2 := 0,  ;
      id_char := ''
MEMVAR helpcode

* Use REQDDATA to force data entry in name variable
IF .NOT. REQDDATA(name_var)
    RETURN(.F.)
ENDIF

* If help code undefined, define it for use below
IF TYPE('helpcode') != 'C'
    helpcode = 'ADD'
ENDIF

* Generate ID codes in ADD mode
IF UPPER(helpcode) == 'ADD'

    * Clear passed receiving variable
    id_var = SPACE(LEN(id_var))

    * Save current index order and record number
    old_ndx = INDEXORD()
    old_recd = RECNO()
    SET ORDER TO IF(look_ndx = NIL, INDEXORD(), look_ndx)

    * Set for three character positions
    FOR count1 = 1 TO 3
        DO WHILE count2++ <= LEN(TRIM(name_var))

            * Get next character in passed name variable
            id_char = UPPER(SUBSTR(name_var,count2,1))

            * Reject it if not a letter
            IF id_char >= 'A' .AND. id_char <= 'Z'
                id_var = TRIM(id_var) + id_char
                EXIT
            ELSE
                LOOP
            ENDIF
        ENDDO
    NEXT

    * Pad to minimum of three letters
    id_var = PADR(id_var,3,'?') + '001'

    * Test for unique value
    count1 = 1
    DO WHILE count1 < 1000
```

```
            SEEK id_var
            IF FOUND()
               * ID code exists, increment counter and retry
               count1++
               id_var = SUBSTR(id_var,1,3) + PADL(count1,3,'0')

            ELSE
               * No record with this key, exit loop
               EXIT
            ENDIF
         ENDDO WHILE count1 < 1000

         * Display data in GET color if row and column passed
         IF VALTYPE(id_row) = 'N' .AND. VALTYPE(id_col) = 'N'
            SWAPCOLOR(id_row, id_col, id_var)
         ENDIF

         GOTO old_recd
         SET ORDER TO old_ndx
      ENDIF

      * Return true if ID code valid or no database in use
      RETURN IF(count1 < 1000 .OR. EMPTY(ALIAS()), .T., .F.)
```

MAKENDX

Description:
Creates or recreates application index files from the definitions in a data dictionary text file

Syntax:
MAKENDX(<aDataBases>, <cDataDictName>)

Returns:
True if index files were updated; false otherwise

File Name:
F_MAKEND.PRG

Screen Use:
Entire screen

Arguments:
<aDataBases> – Array of database files to be indexed (or reindexed)

<cDataDictName> – Complete name, including extension, of the data dictionary file (path is optional).

Typical Use:
To index or reindex application databases with changes when a new version is released, or to create indexes for a new application

Defaults:
Creates index files with extensions matching the application default (NTX or NDX)

Error Handling:
Since correct indexing is usually critical to application integrity, MAKENDX returns to DOS if the data dictionary file is missing or cannot be opened.

Cautions:
Does not check the integrity of the index expression in the data dictionary. The developer must ensure that index expressions are valid.

See Also:
MAKEDBF, PICKIT, SYSVERSION

Discussion

MAKENDX creates index files for databases using key expressions from the referenced data dictionary. The index files have either an NTX or NDX extension. If the application is compiled with Clipper's NDX.OBJ file, MAKENDX creates dBASE compatible indexes with an NDX extension. Otherwise, the extension is NTX. You can change the default by specifying an extension in the data dictionary.

MAKENDX is a powerful function that frees the developer from the tedious process of manually updating index files after changing an application. When used with SYSVERSION and MAKEDBF, it automates system updates completely. See the discussion of MAKEDBF for detailed information on using MAKENDX for this purpose. You can also use MAKENDX by itself to reindex selected files for an application.

Before using MAKENDX, you must create a data dictionary file containing definitions for recreating the application indexes. The dictionary may also contain detailed field information for recreating application databases (used by MAKEDBF). Create the dictionary using a word processor in the non-document mode without formatting characters.

The convention that I use is to limit database names to 7 characters, and create index names from the database name plus a digit. For example, the database ARCREDS uses indexes ARCREDS1, ARCREDS2, and ARCREDS3.

After the dictionary is created, you can use MAKENDX to reindex the databases. To do this, put their names in an array. Pass it, along with the name and extension of the data dictionary, to MAKENDX.

For indexing only, the format of the data dictionary is:

```
   * Index definitions for database 1
  NDXDEF   DBFNAME1   NDXNAME1   KEYEXPR1   TEXT3
  NDXDEF   DBFNAME1   NDXNAME2   KEYEXPR2   TEXT4
  NDXDEF   DBFNAME1   NDXNAME3   KEYEXPR3   TEXT5

   * Index definitions for database 2
  NDXDEF   DBFNAME2   NDXNAME4   KEYEXPR4   TEXT6
  NDXDEF   DBFNAME2   NDXNAME5   KEYEXPR5   TEXT7
ENDFILE
```

An index definition line consists of the following five elements:

1. NDXDEF   Keyword that starts an index definition
2. DBFNAME   Name of associated database
3. NDXNAME   Name of index file to be created or recreated
4. KEYEXPR   Clipper expression or field name for the index key. (This area must **NOT** contain any embedded spaces.)
5. TEXT   Message of up to 60 characters that appears if the index is updated. (This area may contain any printable character, including embedded spaces.)

Index definition lines are listed successively and cannot exceed 512 characters. The keyword ENDFILE indicates the end of all definitions. There is no limit to the number of databases, fields, or indexes that can be defined (except those imposed by Clipper). Although the definitions for all application index files can be in the data dictionary, MAKENDX creates indexes only for the databases named in the passed array. Thus, you can index selectively by limiting that array (see example below).

You can include comments in the data dictionary by starting lines with an asterisk or number (#) sign. MAKENDX also ignores blank lines and is not case sensitive. All definitions can be uppercase, lowercase, or mixed.

Screen Use

MAKENDX uses the entire screen. If called from any routine other than MAKEDBF, it saves the screen and restores it on return.

When MAKENDX is called, a boxed area appears with a few lines of operator explanations at the top. The rest of the screen is empty. Text associated with an index definition in the data dictionary appears on successive lines as the index is created.

If more than 15 indexes are recreated, or if MAKEDBF has filled the window previously, the messages scroll up.

Coding Examples

The example below uses the Developer's Library functions DBNAMES and PICKIT with MAKENDX to allow the operator to select the databases to reindex. It uses DBNAMES to read the data dictionary and load the database names and associated text descriptions into a set of arrays. It then passes the arrays to PICKIT for the operator to select databases for reindexing. It passes the array returned by PICKIT (containing only selected databases) to MAKENDX to regenerate the index files. The source code for the example is in the file T_MAKEND.PRG on the companion disk.

In the example, the data and index definitions are in a dictionary file arsystem.def, and the application file is ar.exe. To use the test program, change the names to match your application and compile T_MAKEND with the /n option.

```
*****************************************************************
* Test program for MAKENDX, DBNAMES, PICKIT    FILE T_MAKEND.PRG
*****************************************************************

* Copyright(c) 1991 -- James Occhiogrosso

#include "inkey.ch"

LOCAL choices := 0, db_error := '', dbf_array := {}, ;
      index_ok := .F., keypress := 0, text_array := {}


INITGLOBAL()
SETCOLOR(colstd)
```

```
DO WHILE keypress != K_ESC

   * Clear and load arrays with database names/descriptions
   text_array := {} ; dbf_array := {}
   CLEAR
   * Get database names for indexing
   db_error = DBNAMES('arsystem.def', text_array, dbf_array)

   IF EMPTY(db_error)

      * Use PICKIT to display text array and fill
      * return array with operator selections

      CENTERON(24, 'Use up/dn arrow keys to move highlight.';
               + ' Press return to select, Esc when done.')

      choices = PICKIT(5, 12, 15, 64, text_array, dbf_array)
      @ 24, 0
      index_ok = .F.
      IF choices > 0

         * Call MAKENDX with array of selected database names
         * and name of application data dictionary to
         * recreate indexes for selected databases

         index_ok = MAKENDX(dbf_array, "arsystem.def")

      ENDIF

      IF index_ok
         @ 24, 10 SAY 'Indexing complete. '
      ELSE
         @ 24, 10 SAY IF (choices = 0. 'No selections made,' ;
                         'Indexing error')
      ENDIF

   ELSEIF db_error = 'D'
      @ 24, 10 SAY 'Data dictionary file missing.'
   ELSEIF db_error = 'P'
      @ 24, 10 SAY 'Incorrect parameter passed. '
   ELSE
      @@ 24, 10 SAY 'Error with file ' + db_error
   ENDIF

   ?? ' Press any key to loop, or Esc to quit '
   keypress = INKEY(0)
   @ 24, 0

ENDDO

RETURN NIL
```

```
*********************************************************************
FUNCTION MAKENDX (dbf_names, textline, text_row, handle)
*********************************************************************

* Creates or recreates an application's index files

* Copyright(c) 1991 -- James Occhiogrosso

LOCAL counter := 1, dbf_name := '', dbf_count := 0,  ;
      ndx_expr := '', ndx_name := '',                ;
      old_cursor := SETCURSOR(.F.), old_screen := ''
#include 'box.ch'

IF VALTYPE(dbf_names) != 'A' .OR. ;
        (dbf_count := LEN(dbf_names)) = 0
     * Incorrect argument passed or array is empty
     RETURN .F.
ENDIF

dbf_count := LEN(dbf_names)

* Test handle argument. If NIL, MAKENDX was called directly.
* Open data dictionary and read first line. Otherwise, file
* is open, the file handle (obtained in MAKEDBF) is used, and
* the pointer is on the next available line.

IF handle = NIL

     * Not called from MAKEDBF, save screen
     SAVE SCREEN TO old_screen

     * Note: If called by MAKEDBF, second argument
     * passed is current line of data dictionary file.
     * If called by itself, second argument is name of
     * dictionary. The third and fourth arguments
     * exist only if called by MAKEDBF.

     * Open data dictionary file

     handle = FOPEN(textline)
     IF handle <= 0
         * Critical error - return to DOS
         ?? CHR(7)
         ? 'Application definition file missing.'
         SET CURSOR ON
         QUIT
     ENDIF

     * Display default screen and get first valid
     * index definition line
     text_row = 7
```

```
        * Display MAKENDX installation screen
        CLEAR SCREEN
        DISPBOX(2,7,23,70,B_DOUBLE)
        SETPOS(2,0)
        TEXT

                    S Y S T E M    I N D E X I N G

           Files that are being reindexed will be listed below.
           Reindexing takes a few minutes.  Please be patient.

        ENDTEXT
        textline = GETNDXDEF(textline, handle)
ELSE
        * Check line passed by MAKEDBF
        IF UPPER(SUBSTR(textline,1,6)) != 'NDXDEF'
           * Not an index definition, get another line
           textline = GETNDXDEF(textline, handle)
        ELSE
           * Strip NDXDEF code from line
           textline = SUBSTR(textline,7)
        ENDIF

ENDIF

* Get database name from index definition line
dbf_name = UPPER(ALLTRIM(PARSE(@textline)))

FOR counter = 1 TO dbf_count

    * Trim and force file name to uppercase
    dbf_names[counter] = UPPER(TRIM(LTRIM(dbf_names[counter])))

NEXT
* If dictionary NDXDEF line matches a database name in
* passed array, rebuild index per dictionary

DO WHILE .NOT. EMPTY(dbf_name)

    * Execute loop until we reach a blank database name
    * (Indicates a null return reading definition file).

    IF (dbf_count = 1 .AND. dbf_name = dbf_names[1]) .OR. ;
       (dbf_count > 1 .AND. ASCAN(dbf_names, dbf_name) != 0)

        * Get index name and key expression
        ndx_name = PARSE(@textline)
        ndx_expr = PARSE(@textline)

        * Scroll screen up if at bottom of window
        IF text_row = 22
           SCROLL(8, 9, 22, 68, 1)
        ELSE
```

```
            text_row++
        ENDIF

        * Display rest of associated text
        @ text_row, 7 SAY ':' + ' ' + SUBSTR(textline, 1, 60)
        @ text_row, 70 SAY ':'

        * Reindex file
        USE (dbf_name)
        INDEX ON &ndx_expr TO (ndx_name)
        USE

    ENDIF

    * Get next valid index definition line
    textline = GETNDXDEF(textline, handle)

    * Parse database name
    dbf_name = UPPER(ALLTRIM(PARSE(@textline)))

ENDDO

* Restore screen if not called from MAKEDBF
IF TYPE('old_screen') != 'U'
    RESTORE SCREEN FROM old_screen
ENDIF

SETCURSOR(old_cursor)
RETURN .T.
```

```
*******************************************************************
STATIC FUNCTION GETNDXDEF (textline, handle)
*******************************************************************

* Locate and read next index definition (NDXDEF) line
* Get next defined line from data dictionary

NEXTLINE(@textline, handle)

* Check line. If not an index definition or
* end of file, get another.

DO WHILE UPPER(SUBSTR(textline, 1, 6)) != 'NDXDEF' .AND. ;
    UPPER(SUBSTR(textline, 1, 7)) != 'ENDFILE'

    * Get another line from definition file
    NEXTLINE(@textline, handle)
ENDDO

* Check for valid index definition line

IF UPPER(SUBSTR(textline, 1, 6)) != 'NDXDEF' .OR. ;
    UPPER(SUBSTR(textline, 1, 7)) = 'ENDFILE'
    * No INDEX definitions exist, or we are at end of file
    RETURN ''

ELSE
    * Line is valid index definition, strip NDXDEF
    * code identifier and return line

    RETURN LTRIM(SUBSTR(textline, 7))

ENDIF


*******************************************************************
STATIC FUNCTION NEXTLINE (textline, handle)
*******************************************************************

* Get next non-comment line in definition file

* Test first character of line
textline = '*'
DO WHILE (SUBSTR(textline, 1, 1) $ '*#' .OR. EMPTY(textline))  ;
    .AND. UPPER(SUBSTR(textline, 1, 7)) != 'ENDFILE'

    * If it is a comment or blank line, skip it
    textline = LTRIM(FREADLINE(handle))

ENDDO

RETURN NIL
```

MEMOCTRL

Description:
Generic control function for MEMOEDIT and MEMOVIEW

Syntax:
None – called indirectly from MEMOEDIT or MEMOVIEW

Returns:
Numeric to MEMOEDIT

File Name:
F_MMOCTL.PRG

Screen Use:
None

Arguments:
<nMemoMode>, <nMemoLine>, and <nMemoColumn> are passed automatically by MEMOEDIT.

<nMemoMode> – Value of 0 to 3 indicating MEMOEDIT's mode as follows:
- 0 = Idle, all keys processed
- 1 = Key exception, memo is unchanged
- 2 = Key exception, memo is changed
- 3 = Initialization mode

<nMemoLine> – Current text buffer line

<nMemoColumn> – Current text buffer column

Typical Use:
To process keys pressed while editing or viewing long character strings with MEMOEDIT

Defaults:
Message positions and the altered/unaltered state of the memo are determined by the variables *format*, *altered*, and *word_wrap*. (See MEMOVIEW for more information.)

Cautions:
MEMOCTRL is designed to be called from the MEMOVIEW function in this library as a UDF to control MEMOEDIT. It can be used outside this context, but some features will not be available.

Global Variables:
Uses predefined variables that can be global, or defined by the calling procedure at your option. See the discussion below for more information.

See Also:
AEDBAR, MEMOCTRL, MEMOEDIT

Discussion

MEMOCTRL is designed to operate with the MEMOVIEW function in this library. MEMOVIEW calls it through parameters passed to the Clipper MEMOEDIT function.

Since MEMOCTRL is not called directly, MEMOVIEW declares it external. If you use it elsewhere, your program must declare it external.

If the logic variable *altered* is predefined, MEMOCTRL sets it true if the memo was changed, or false if not.

If the logic variable *word_wrap* is predefined, MEMOCTRL sets the initial default word wrapping state in accordance with its contents. If word_wrap is not defined, the MEMOEDIT default (word wrap on) is used.

If the logic variable *format* is predefined, MEMOCTRL places all messages in accordance with its value. If it is true, all messages are placed in the area defined by the parameters passed to MEMOEDIT. If false, the messages are placed on the row defined in the variable aed_row at column 48. If aed_row is undefined, the message area defaults to row 24, column 48.

In addition, if *format* is true, the insert on/off status appears in the top right corner of the display. When the Ins key is pressed, the cursor is set to an underscore if *insert* is off, or a block if it is on. This is independent of the *format* setting, and is done by calling CSRINSERT.

MEMOCTRL also processes special keys (hot keys) for help or other functions. If the global variable fkeyset contains a procedure name, it is called whenever a function or Alt key combination is pressed. The procedure receives the first three arguments normally passed with a SET KEY call (procedure name, line number, and input variable) and the value of the special key as the fourth argument. The first three arguments are fixed as MEMOCTRL, 0, and the memo name. Thus, all hot keys can be processed by the same procedures used during wait states.

MEMOCTRL also provides a popup window of key definitions for memo editing. It appears whenever the user presses the F2 key. It displays on the right side in the color defined in the global variable *colwindow*.

Coding Examples

See the MEMOVIEW function.

```
*******************************************************************
FUNCTION MEMOCTRL (mode, line, col)
*******************************************************************
* Generic control function for MEMOEDIT or MEMOVIEW
* Copyright(c) 1991 -- James Occhiogrosso

#include "dl_keys.ch"
#include "inkey.ch"
#include "set.ch"
#include "setcurs.ch"
#define ABORT    27
#define IGNORE   32
#define SAVEMEMO 23
#define WORDWRAP 34

LOCAL ret_value, keypress, message, spacing, ;
      old_color, old_cursor, memo_scr, line_24

MEMVAR bottom, colstd, colwindow, fkeyset, format, hitanykey, ;
       left, memo_scrn, right, top, word_wrap

STATIC counter := 1

ret_value = 0

* Initialize undefined parameters

format = IF(format == NIL, .T., format)

* If logic variable "altered" is predefined, it is set
* when the memo is changed. Otherwise, it is used locally.

IF TYPE('altered') != 'L'
    PRIVATE altered
ENDIF
altered = .F.

IF mode = 3
    * Initialize MEMOEDIT and test for word_wrap toggle

    IF TYPE("word_wrap") = 'L' .AND. counter = 1
        IF .NOT. word_wrap
            * Return code to toggle word wrap off
            ret_value = WORDWRAP
            counter = 0
        ENDIF
    ENDIF

ELSEIF mode = 0
```

```
            * Idling mode - waiting for next key
         IF format
            * Write current line and column information
            @ top, left + 2 SAY " Line        Col        "
            @ top, left + 8 SAY LTRIM(STR(line))
            @ top, left + 16 SAY LTRIM(STR(col))
         ENDIF
ELSE
      * Keystroke exception, get key value
      keypress = LASTKEY()

      IF keypress = K_CTRL_W .OR. keypress = K_CTRL_ENTER
          * User pressed Ctrl-Enter or Ctrl-W. Save and exit.
          IF mode = 2
              * User made changes. Set altered variable.
              altered = .T.
          ENDIF
          ret_value = SAVEMEMO

      ELSEIF keypress = K_ESC
        * User pressed Esc. Check for changes.

          IF mode = 2
              * User made changes. Confirm that abort is desired.
              message = ' Abandon edits? (Y/N) '

              IF format .OR. TYPE('aed_row') = 'U'

                  * If aed_row is undefined, operator is using
                  * MEMOCTRL without AEDBAR. Place message at
                  * bottom of window.

                  spacing = (((right - left)-2) - LEN(message))/2
                  @ bottom, left + 1 SAY REPLICATE('D',spacing) +;
                      message + ' ' + REPLICATE('D', spacing-2)

                  * Move cursor to end of message
                  @ bottom, left + spacing + LEN(message) + 1 ;
                      SAY ''

              ELSE
                  AEDMSG(message)
              ENDIF

              * Get operator response
              IF OPCONFIRM()
                  * Abandon edit
                  ret_value = ABORT
              ELSE
                  * Operator pressed Esc in error, ignore it
                  altered = .T.
                  ret_value = IGNORE

              ENDIF
          ENDIF
```

```
        ELSEIF keypress = K_INS

            * User pressed Ctrl-V or Ins key. Toggle cursor
            * size and display insert "on/off" status.

            CSRINSERT()
            IF format
                @ top, right-4 SAY IF(READINSERT(), "on ", "off")

            ENDIF

            * Tell MEMOEDIT to ignore this key
            ret_value = IGNORE

        ELSEIF (keypress <= K_F2 .OR. keypress > 256 ;
                .OR. keypress = K_F1) .AND. TYPE('fkeyset') != 'U'

            * Call special keys procedure if any function key or
            * Alt key combination is pressed. The variable
            * "fkeyset" must contain the procedure name.

            IF .NOT. EMPTY(fkeyset)
                DO &fkeyset WITH 'MEMOCTRL', 0, READVAR(), keypress
            ENDIF

        ELSEIF keypress = K_F2

            * Display key definition help for user

            memo_scrn  = SCRNSAVE(3, 50, 20, 79)
            line_24    = SCRNSAVE(24, 0, 24, 79)
            old_color  = SETCOLOR(colstd)
            CENTERON(24, hitanykey)
            SETCOLOR(colwindow)
            old_cursor = SET(_SET_CURSOR, SC_NONE)

            @  3, 50 SAY '┌─────────────────────────────┐'
            @  4, 50 SAY '│     Memo Editing Keys       │'
            @  5, 50 SAY '│                             │'
            @  6, 50 SAY '│Esc ............. Exit memo  │'
            @  7, 50 SAY '│Ctrl-Enter ....... Save memo │'
            @  8, 50 SAY '│Ins........... Insert on/off │'
            @  9, 50 SAY '│Enter(Ins on)... Insert line │'
            @ 10, 50 SAY '│Enter(Ins off).... Next line │'
            @ 11, 50 SAY '│Ctrl-B.......... Reform para │'
            @ 12, 50 SAY '│Del............. Delete char │'
            @ 13, 50 SAY '│BackSpace..... Del char left │'
            @ 14, 50 SAY '│Ctrl-T....... Del word right │'
            @ 15, 50 SAY '│Ctrl-Y.......... Delete line │'
            @ 16, 50 SAY '│Arrow keys ..... Move cursor │'
            @ 17, 50 SAY '│PgUp/PgDn ..... Window up/dn │'
            @ 18, 50 SAY '│Home/End .... Window top/bot │'
            @ 19, 50 SAY '│Crtl-PgUp/PgDn..Memo top/bot │'
            @ 20, 50 SAY '└─────────────────────────────┘'
```

```
        INKEY(0)
        SETCOLOR(old_color)
        SCRNREST(memo_scrn)
        SCRNREST(line_24)
        SETCURSOR(old_cursor)

    ENDIF
ENDIF

RETURN ret_value
```

MEMOFIND

Description:
Finds text in a memo field

Syntax:
MEMOFIND(<cDbfName>, <cMemoField>, <cSearchString>, <aRecordNumbers>, [<lCaseSensitive>])

Returns:
True if the specified text is in at least one record; false otherwise

File Name:
F_MMOFND.PRG

Screen Use:
None

Arguments:
<cDbfName> – Database to search

<cMemoField> – Memo field to search

<cSearchString> – Text to search for

<aRecordNumbers> – Array to return the number of each record where search text is found. Passed by reference (see discussion below).

<lCaseSensitive> – If true, activates case sensitivity during the search

Typical Use:
To locate records containing specified text in a memo field

Defaults:
Case sensitivity is disabled if no value is passed for <lCaseSensitive>.

Cautions:
The database to be searched must be open. To avoid unnecessary overhead, MEMOFIND does not check passed parameters.

See Also:
MEMOCTRL, MEMOVIEW

Discussion

MEMOFIND uses the $ operator to search the memo field. For most applications, its response time is fine, but it may be unacceptable for very large files.

The time required to find text in a DBT file depends on many factors, including the average length of the memos, size of the database, length of the search string, and speed of the computer.

Using a sample database containing 2,000 records, it took less than 10 seconds to locate 100 matches. Approximately 10% of the records contained data in the memo field, and half of them contained the search string. The test was done on a 10 MHz PC/AT clone with a 30 ms hard disk.

The above is only a guide. I have used MEMOFIND in several applications and found its response acceptable. However, you should test it in your situation to determine its suitability.

The array specified as parameter 4 should be passed by reference. An element is added to it for each matching record. You can call MEMOFIND repeatedly using the same array and different search strings.

When <lCaseSensitive> is true, the search string and the memo field must match in case.

The database used with MEMOFIND must be open but need not be in use. To speed the search, MEMOFIND disables open indexes. On return, it reenables all indexes, and moves the record pointer back to its original position. MEMOFIND does not open or close any files.

Coding Examples

The program below demonstrates MEMOFIND. To use it, change the file name, index names, and memo name to match your database. The test program is on the companion disk in the file T_MMOFND.PRG.

```
**********************************************************************
* Test program for MEMOFIND -- FILE = T_MMOFND.PRG
**********************************************************************
* Copyright(c) 1991 -- James Occhiogrosso

LOCAL case_on, counter, elapsed, filename, find_array, index1, ;
      index2, look_for, memoname, rec_found, start
INITGLOBAL()
SETCOLOR(colstd)
CLEAR

filename = "itfile"              && Change the names in quotes
index1   = "itfile1"             && to match your database
index2   = "itfile2"
memoname = "comment"
USE (filename) INDEX (index1), (index2) NEW

look_for = space(25)
case_on = .F.

DO WHILE .T.

    find_array := {}

    CLEAR

    @ 10, 10 SAY 'Enter search text ........ ' ;
             GET look_for pict "@x"
    @ 11, 10 SAY 'Enable case sensitivity .. ' ;
             GET case_on pict 'Y'
    READ

    start = SECONDS()

    rec_found = MEMOFIND(filename,memo_name,ALLTRIM(look_for), ;
             @find_array,case_on)

    elapsed =  SECONDS() - start
    @ 14, 10 SAY 'elapsed time = ' + LTRIM(STR(elapsed))

    IF rec_found
       FOR counter = 1 TO LEN(find_array)
```

```
            @ 18, 0
            GOTO (find_array[counter])
            @ 18, 5 say 'Found at record ' + ;
            LTRIM(STR(find_array[counter])) + ' Press a key.'
            INKEY(0)
         NEXT
      ELSE
         @ 18, 0
         @ 18, 10 say 'Nothing found! Press any key.'
         INKEY(0)
      ENDIF
ENDDO

RETURN
```

The example below shows a typical use of MEMOFIND to locate matching records. The procedure SHOW_ITEM (not shown) is your procedure to sequentially display or print specific items from them.

```
searchtext = SPACE(20)
DO WHILE .T.
    @ 22, 10 Say 'Enter search text string.  ' GET searchtext
    READ

    * Locate matching records
    IF MEMOFIND(dbfname, memoname, searchtext, arrayname, ;
                case_on)

        * Display pertinent information for each record

        FOR counter = 1 TO LEN(arrayname)
            SHOW_ITEM(arrayname[counter])
        NEXT

        CENTERON(24, 'No more records. Search again? Y/N ')

    ELSE
        CENTERON(24, 'No matches. Try again? Y/N ')

    ENDIF

    * Wait for operator answer

    SETPOS(ROW(), COL()-2)
    IF OPCONFIRM()
        LOOP
    ENDIF

ENDDO
```

```
*******************************************************************
FUNCTION MEMOFIND (file_name, memo_field, search_for,      ;
                   recs_array, case_sen)
*******************************************************************

* Finds text in a memo field

* Copyright(c) 1991 - James Occhiogrosso

* Save entry conditions
LOCAL old_area   := SELECT(), old_finds := LEN(recs_array), ;
      old_index, old_rec, field_text

* Create blocks for DBEVAL
LOCAL bMainBlock := {|| AADD(recs_array, RECNO()) }, ;
      bForBlock  := {|| field_text := ;
                        FIELDGET(FIELDPOS(memo_field)),           ;
                        IF(case_sen .AND. search_for $ field_text ;
                        .OR. !case_sen .AND. upper(search_for) $  ;
                        upper(field_text), .T., .F. ) }

* Set case sensitivity off if no value passed
case_sen = IF(case_sen = NIL, .F., case_sen )

* Select file and save entry conditions
SELECT(file_name)
old_index := INDEXORD()
old_rec   := RECNO()
SET ORDER TO 0

* Search for specified text
DBEVAL(bMainBlock, bForBlock)

* Reinstate entry conditions
SELECT(old_area)
SET ORDER TO old_index
GO old_rec

* Return true if at least one record was found
RETURN (LEN(recs_array) > old_finds)
```

MEMOGET

Description:
Controls data entered in a memo area using a one-character trigger variable

Syntax:
MEMOVIEW (<lFormat>, <cString>, <nRowTop>, <nColumnTop>, <nRowBottom>, <nColumnBottom>, [<lEditMode>], [<cUserFunction>], [<nLineLength>], [<nTabSize>], [<nTextBufferRow>], [<nTextBuffer Column>], [<nWindowRow>], [<nWindowColumn>])

Returns:
True if the trigger variable is N or n, blank, or has an ASCII value of 251; false otherwise

File Name:
F_MMOGET.PRG

Screen Use:
Defined in calling parameters

Arguments:
All arguments are passed through MEMOGET to MEMOVIEW and, subsequently, MEMOEDIT. See MEMOEDIT for a detailed description.

Typical Use:
To allow navigation on a data entry GET screen containing memos intermixed with other data

Defaults:
The first six parameters are mandatory. The seventh and eighth ([<lEditMode>] and [<cUserFunction>]) default to .T. and MEMOCTRL, respectively. All other parameters default to the same values as in MEMOVIEW.

Cautions:
The name of the memo to be edited must be passed by reference.

MEMOGET uses free memory of approximately twice the memo's size. Check available memory using MEMORY(1) before calling it.

See Also:
MEMOCTRL, MEMOEDIT, MEMOVIEW

Discussion

Use MEMOGET to enter data into a memo at the same time and on the same screen as other data. To use it, a one-character variable is defined as a *trigger*. It is initialized, displayed, and placed on the GET list along with other data items. MEMOGET is used as a VALID clause on the trigger variable.

Each time the cursor passes through the trigger GET, the VALID calls MEMOGET. If the trigger is blank, or contains the letter N (or n) or the graphic check mark character (ASCII value 251), MEMOGET returns true and the cursor moves to the next GET. If the operator enters Y for the trigger, the memo is displayed and edited at the passed coordinates.

When editing is complete, MEMOGET returns true to the VALID, allowing the cursor to move to the next GET. In addition, if the memo is not empty, the trigger variable is changed to a check mark (ASCII value 251). If the memo is empty, MEMOGET returns N to the trigger field. Thus, the operator can view the trigger variable to determine quickly if the memo contains data.

Since the memo area is defined by the calling parameters to MEMOGET (and subsequently to MEMOVIEW and MEMOEDIT), the screen area can be used for other purposes when the memo is not being edited. By using MEMOGET, memo areas can appear in windows as desired, and memos can be edited anywhere in other GETs. MEMOGET calls the Developer's Library function MEMOVIEW, which in turn uses MEMOCTRL and MEMOEDIT. These functions are linked automatically to your application when MEMOGET is used.

Coding Examples

The example below uses MEMOGET to get a memo field inside the GETs for other fields. Its source code is on the companion disk in T_MMOGET.PRG.

```
*******************************************************************
* Test program for MEMOGET -- FILE = T_MMOGET.PRG
*******************************************************************

* Copyright(c) 1991 -- James Occhiogrosso

#include 'inkey.ch'

* Set format for memo. If using AEDBAR, change to .F.
#define MEMOFORMAT .T.

LOCAL comments, descrip, partno, vendor
PRIVATE trigger

INITGLOBAL()
SETCOLOR(colstd)
CLEAR
SET SCOREBOARD OFF
SET KEY 22 TO CSRINSERT

partno   = SPACE(10)
descrip  = SPACE(20)
trigger  = 'N'              // Trigger variable for MEMOGET
comments = ''               // Memo
vendor   = SPACE(30)

DO WHILE LASTKEY() != K_ESC
     @ 6, 10 SAY 'Part number ................ ' GET partno
     @ 7, 10 SAY 'Description................. ' GET descrip

     @ 8, 10 SAY 'Enter/View comments (Y/N).... ' GET trigger ;
          VALID MEMOGET(MEMOFORMAT, @comments, 12, 10, 21, 70)

     @ 9, 10 SAY 'Vendor Name ................ ' GET vendor

     READ
ENDDO

RETURN
```

```
*******************************************************************
FUNCTION MEMOGET
*******************************************************************

* Initiates data entry in a memo through a trigger variable

* Copyright(c) 1991 -- James Occhiogrosso

LOCAL old_screen, trig_block, trig_value

PARAMETERS format, memo_name, top, left, bottom, right, update, ;
           userfunc, line_len, tab_size, start_line, start_col, ;
           init_row, init_col

* First six arguments are mandatory

IF PCOUNT() < 6
    RETURN .F.

ELSE
    * Create defaults for arguments not passed

    update     = IF(update     == NIL, .T., update)
    userfunc   = IF(userfunc   == NIL, "memoctrl", userfunc)
    line_len   = IF(line_len   == NIL, (right-left)-1, line_len)
    tab_size   = IF(tab_size   == NIL, 4, tab_size)
    start_line = IF(start_line == NIL, 1, start_line)
    start_col  = IF(start_col  == NIL, 0, start_col)
    init_row   = IF(init_row   == NIL, 0, init_row)
    init_col   = IF(init_col   == NIL, 0, init_col)

ENDIF

* Get block for memo trigger variable
trig_block := MEMVARBLOCK(READVAR())

* Get its value and test it
trig_value := UPPER(ALLTRIM(EVAL(trig_block)))

IF ! trig_value $ 'YN√ '
    * Stay in GET if trigger is wrong value
    RETURN(.F.)

* If trigger is 'Y', edit memo
ELSEIF trig_value = 'Y'

    * If AED menu bar is in use, put a message in its window
    AEDMSG('mw_memo')

    * Edit memo by reference
    MEMOVIEW(format, @memo_name, top, left, bottom, right,    ;
             update, userfunc, line_len, tab_size,            ;
             start_line, start_col, init_row, init_col )
```

```
         AEDMSG('mw_pgdn')

      *  Replace trigger variable with a "check" character
      *  to indicate memo has data

         EVAL(trig_block, IF(EMPTY(memo_name), 'N', CHR(251)))

ENDIF

RETURN(.T.)
```

MEMOPACK

Description:
Removes unused memo data from a DBT file

Syntax:
MEMOPACK(<aDbfList>)

Returns:
Null string if all files were packed successfully. Otherwise, a string containing a descriptive error number and the name of the offending file.

File Name:
F_MMOPAC.PRG

Screen Use:
None

Arguments:
<aDbfList> – Array of names of databases to pack, without extensions

Typical Use:
To prevent uncontrolled growth of database memo files

Defaults:
MEMOPACK uses the standard default extensions of DBF and DBT for the database and memo files, respectively.

Error Handling:
MEMOPACK returns an error on any of the following conditions:
1. A database named in the passed array, or its associated memo file, does not exist.
2. Original database or memo files cannot be erased.
3. A temporary memo file could not be created.
4. All records in the specified database were not copied to the temporary file.

The value returned consists of a character string containing an error number (1-4, corresponding to the four errors above), plus the name of the file for which the error occurred.

Cautions:
In a network environment, make sure you close or have exclusive access to all files before using MEMOPACK.

See Also:
ISMEMO

Discussion

Clipper allocates space in memo (DBT) files in 512-byte sectors. When a memo field is edited, Clipper replaces the data in the same area of the DBT file if it fits in the originally allotted number of sectors.

If the new memo does not fit, it is added to the end of the file, and the database pointer to the memo is adjusted. The old memo data remains in the file, even though Clipper will never use it again. For a complete explanation, see R. Spence, *Clipper Programming Guide*, 2nd ed., San Marcos, CA: Microtrend Books, 1991.

MEMOPACK is used to remove unused memos from the DBT file. It verifies that both DBF and DBT files exist, and then copies the data and memo fields to a set of unique temporary files.

MEMOPACK does not pack or reindex the database. It ignores the Clipper DELETED setting and does not remove deleted records. To remove them, pack and reindex the database before calling it.

Coding Examples

```
* Create local array of databases to be packed
LOCAL filelist[3]
filelist[1] = 'customer'
filelist[2] = 'orders'
filelist[3] = 'invoice'

* Pass array name to MEMOPACK to pack files

error_msg = MEMOPACK(filelist)

* Check for errors
IF SUBSTR(error_msg,1,1) = '1'
    ? SUBSTR(error_msg,2) + 'DBF OR DBT file missing'
ELSEIF SUBSTR(error_msg,1,1) = '2'
    ? SUBSTR(error_msg,2) + '.DBF (or .DBT) cannot be erased'
ELSEIF SUBSTR(error_msg,1,1) = '3'
    ? 'Temporary file cannot be created for ' + ;
            SUBSTR(error_msg,2)
ELSEIF SUBSTR(error_msg,1,1) = '4'
    ? 'Database ' + SUBSTR(error_msg,2) + ' cannot be copied'
ELSE
    ? 'All memo files packed successfully'
ENDIF
```

```
*****************************************************************
FUNCTION MEMOPACK (packlist)
*****************************************************************

* Removes unused memo data from a database DBT file

* Copyright(c) 1991 -- James Occhiogrosso

#include "set.ch"

LOCAL counter, old_delete, real_recs, ret_value, temp_file

ret_value = ''

* Get a unique temporary database file name
temp_file = TEMPFILE('DBF')

* Strip its extension
temp_file = SUBSTR(temp_file, 1, AT('.', temp_file) - 1)

FOR counter = 1 TO LEN(packlist)

    * Make sure all files in passed array exist
    IF .NOT. FILE(packlist[counter] + '.DBF') .OR. .NOT. ;
            FILE(packlist[counter] + '.DBT')
        ret_value = '1 - ' + packlist[counter]
        EXIT
    ENDIF

    * Open database and get record count
    USE (packlist[counter])
    real_recs = LASTREC()

    * Save deleted setting and set deleted off
    * (so deleted records are copied)
    old_delete = SET(_SET_DELETED, .F.)

    * Copy to temporary file name and open it
    COPY TO (temp_file)
    USE (temp_file)

    * Restore original deleted setting
    SET(_SET_DELETED, old_delete)

    IF LASTREC() = real_recs
        * Copy succeeded if record count is same
        USE
        IF FILE(temp_file + '.DBT')

            * Erase old files
            ERASE (packlist[counter] + '.dbf')
            ERASE (packlist[counter] + '.dbt')
```

```
                    * Make sure they were erased
                    IF ( FILE(packlist[counter]+'.DBF') .OR. ;
                         FILE(packlist[counter]+'.DBT') )
                         * If they are still present, we cannot rename
                         ret_value = '2 - ' + packlist[counter]
                         EXIT
                    ENDIF

                    * Rename temporary files to passed name
                    RENAME (temp_file + '.DBF') TO ;
                           (packlist[counter] + '.dbf')
                    RENAME (temp_file + '.DBT') TO ;
                           (packlist[counter] + '.dbt')
                ELSE
                    * Temporary DBT file is missing
                    ret_value = '3 - ' + packlist[counter]
                    EXIT
                ENDIF
            ELSE
            * Database was copied incorrectly
            ret_value = '4 - ' + packlist[counter]
            EXIT
        ENDIF
NEXT
RETURN ret_value
```

MEMOVIEW

Description:
Generic function for viewing and editing memos

Syntax:
MEMOVIEW (<lFormat>, <cString>, [<nRowTop>], [<nColumnTop>], [<nRowBottom>], [<nColumnBottom>], [<lEditMode>], [<cUserFunction>], [<nLineLength>], [<nTabSize>], [<nTextBufferRow>], [<nTextBufferColumn>], [<nWindowRow>], [<nWindowColumn>])

Returns:
Character string containing the memo

File Name:
F_MMOVEW.PRG

Screen Use:
Defined by calling parameters

Arguments:
<lFormat> – If true, boxes the data in a window defined by the passed coordinates

All other arguments to MEMOVIEW are passed to MEMOEDIT. See MEMOEDIT in the Clipper manual and the discussion below for more information.

Typical Use:
To edit or view large blocks of text with a standard calling convention

Defaults:
Uses the MEMOCTRL function from this library to process keystrokes unless you explicitly pass the name of another function. MEMOCTRL is automatically linked when you use MEMOVIEW.

Cautions:

Check for sufficient memory before calling MEMOVIEW (see discussion below)

See Also:

AEDBAR, MEMOCTRL, MEMOGET

Discussion

Except for the first argument (<lFormat>), MEMOVIEW takes the same parameters as MEMOEDIT. MEMOVIEW uses <lFormat> to determine the formatting of the memo area. If it is true, the entire memo area is outlined with a single-line box. Also, a row/column counter is displayed at the top left and an insert status indicator at the top right of the boxed area. All other messages appear at the bottom center of the window.

When MEMOVIEW is called with <lFormat> true, the memo is displayed using the color definition in the global variable colhelp2. Also, the memo area is reduced from the calling coordinates by two rows and four columns. The formatted area must be at least 30 columns wide to hold the messages.

If called with <lFormat> false, the memo area is not boxed, and the row/column counter and insert status are not displayed. The memo is displayed using the color definition in the global variable colmemoget. All other messages appear in the AEDBAR window.

By default, MEMOVIEW uses MEMOCTRL to process keys pressed while editing. It also sets the cursor to a large block if *insert* is on.

When you use MEMOVIEW to edit a file (as in the example below), it requires free memory of about twice the size of the file plus 6K bytes. To avoid an error, check available memory before calling it.

Coding Examples

The code below displays and edits a file using the entire screen with all defaults.

```
* Load file into variable for editing

memo_var := MEMOREAD(file_name)

* Define altered variable. This is optional. However, if it
* is predefined, it is set true if the memo is changed.
PRIVATE altered := .F.

* Note that the memo variable is passed to MEMOVIEW by reference
* (prefixed with the "@" symbol). This avoids creating another
* copy of the memo in memory.

MEMOVIEW(.T., @memo_var)

* On return from MEMOVIEW, check for changes to memo

IF altered
    * Operator made changes, rewrite file to disk
    MEMOWRIT(file_name, memo_var)
ENDIF

* Release memo variable

RELEASE memo_var
```

```
*******************************************************************
FUNCTION MEMOVIEW
*******************************************************************

* Display or edit a memo in a predefined window
* Copyright(c) 1991 -- James Occhiogrosso

#include "setcurs.ch"

LOCAL bInsert_key, infoline, message, old_color ;
      old_screen, spacing

MEMVAR colhelp2, colmemoget

PARAMETERS format, memo_name, top, left, bottom, right, update, ;
           userfunc, line_len, tab_size, start_line, start_col, ;
           init_row, init_col

* Link default control function
EXTERNAL MEMOCTRL

IF PCOUNT() < 2
   * Not enough parameters. Give memo back
   RETURN(memo_name)

ELSEIF PCOUNT() >= 2 .AND. PCOUNT() < 6
   * Set up full screen MEMOEDIT with default control function
   top = 0
   left = 0
   bottom = 24
   right = 79
   update = .T.
   userfunc = "MEMOCTRL"

ELSEIF PCOUNT() = 6
   * Use passed coordinates with default control function
   update = .T.
   userfunc = "MEMOCTRL"

ELSEIF PCOUNT() = 7
   * Use passed coordinates with default control function
   userfunc = "MEMOCTRL"
ENDIF

* Define defaults for other parameters not passed

line_len   = IF(line_len   == NIL, (right-left)-1, line_len)
tab_size   = IF(tab_size   == NIL, 4, tab_size)
start_line = IF(start_line == NIL, 1, start_line)
start_col  = IF(start_col  == NIL, 0, start_col)
init_row   = IF(init_row   == NIL, 0, init_row)
init_col   = IF(init_col   == NIL, 0, init_col)

* Save old color setting
old_color = SETCOLOR()
```

```
* Save current insert key setting as a block
bInsert_key := SETKEY(22)

* Clear insert key and display cursor in appropriate size
SET KEY 22 TO
CSRINSERT(,,, .F.)

* Set up message variable
message = ' Press F2 for edit keys '

* Save screen area to be used
old_screen = SCRNSAVE(top,left,bottom,right)

IF format

    * Clear memo area, draw box, and display initial message
    SETCOLOR(colhelp2)
    @ top, left, bottom, right BOX '┌─┐│┘─└│ '
    spacing = (((right - left) - 2) - LEN(message)) / 2
    @ bottom, left + 1 SAY REPLICATE('D',spacing) + message + ;
                            REPLICATE('D',spacing)

    * Display insert status
    IF update
        @ top, right-12 SAY " Insert " + IF(READINSERT(),    ;
                    "on ", "off ")
    ENDIF

    * Edit memo inside boxed area
    memo_name = MEMOEDIT(memo_name, top+1, left+2, bottom-1, ;
                right-1, update, userfunc, line_len, ;
                tab_size, start_line, start_col,     ;
                init_row, init_col)

ELSE
    * Edit memo without special formatting
    SETCOLOR(colmemoget)
    memo_name = MEMOEDIT(memo_name, top, left, bottom, right, ;
                        update, userfunc, line_len, tab_size, ;
                        start_line, start_col, init_row,      ;
                        init_col)
ENDIF

* Restore initial conditions

SETCOLOR(old_color)
SCRNREST(old_screen)
SETKEY(22, bInsert_key)
RETURN (memo_name)
```

NDXCOUNT

Description:
Counts active index files associated with a database

Syntax:
NDXCOUNT( )

Returns:
Numeric value

File Name:
F_NDXCNT.PRG

Screen Use:
None

Arguments:
None

Typical Use:
To determine the number of open indexes in a work area

Defaults:
Currently selected work area if not preceded by an alias expression

See Also:
NDXKEY, NDXVIEW

Discussion

Use NDXCOUNT when the number of open indexes may vary. The return value cannot exceed 15, the most indexes Clipper can open in a work area. A typical application is to obtain the number of active indexes for use in a FOR/NEXT loop to search for a particular key.

Coding Examples

```
* Get number of open indexes in current area
num_ndx = NDXCOUNT()

* Get number of open indexes for the "invoice" database
num_ndx = invoice->(NDXCOUNT())
```

See ADDRECORD for another example.

```
*****************************************************************
FUNCTION NDXCOUNT (aliasname)
*****************************************************************

* Determine number of active index files for selected database

* Copyright(c) 1991 -- James Occhiogrosso

#define CMAXINDX 15  // Maximum number of Clipper open indexes
LOCAL counter

* Count active indexes to the Clipper maximum

FOR counter = 1 TO CMAXINDX
      IF EMPTY(INDEXKEY(counter))
EXIT
      ENDIF
NEXT

RETURN (counter - 1)
```

NDXKEY

Description:
Reads the key expression of an index file

Syntax:
NDXKEY(<cIndexName>, <lClipperNTX>)

Returns:
Character string

File Name:
F_NDXKEY.PRG

Screen Use:
None

Arguments:
<cIndexName> – Index file to read

<lClipperNTX> – Logical that is true for Clipper indexes, false for dBASE indexes

Typical Use:
To read the key expression of an index file without opening it

Defaults:
Clipper (NTX) index format if <lClipperNTX> is not passed.

See Also:
DEVELOP, NDXCOUNT, NDXVIEW

Discussion

Use NDXKEY during development to get the key expression of an index file. Unlike the Clipper INDEXKEY function, NDXKEY does not require the index to be open. Use it only during development or in other functions. It returns a character expression for the index key, or an empty string on any error.

You must pass the complete name of the index file including its extension. You can also include a path name. The extension need not be NTX or NDX.

NDXKEY does not determine the type of index file it is reading. Instead, it uses the passed or default value for <lClipperNTX> to decide how to read the key expression. If <lClipperNTX> is true (Clipper indexes), NDXKEY reads the expression beginning at byte 22. Otherwise, it assumes the key begins at byte 24 (dBASE indexes).

Coding Examples

```
* Return key expression for Clipper-compatible index
key_value = NDXKEY("ARCUST1.NTX", .T.)

* or
key_value = NDXKEY("ARCUST1.NTX")

* Return key expression for dBASE-compatible index
key_value = NDXKEY("ARCUST1.NDX", .F.)
```

```
*******************************************************************
FUNCTION NDXKEY (ndx_name, clip_ndx)
*******************************************************************

* Reads key expression of an index file

* Copyright(c) 1991 -- James Occhiogrosso

LOCAL handle := 0, key_start := 0, ret_string := ''

* Default to Clipper NTX extension if nothing passed
clip_ndx = IF(VALTYPE(clip_ndx) != 'L', .T., clip_ndx)
key_start = IF(clip_ndx, 22, 24)

* Open index file in read-only mode
handle = FOPEN(ndx_name,0)
IF FERROR() = 0

    * Move file pointer to beginning of key expression
    FSEEK(handle, key_start, 0)

    * Read index key to first null byte or maximum length of 256
    ret_string = FREADSTR(handle, 256)

ENDIF

* Close file and return index expression
FCLOSE(handle)
RETURN(ret_string)
```

NDXVIEW

Description:
Displays key expressions of indexes

Syntax:
NDXVIEW(<cIndexExt>, <cPath>)

Returns:
Nothing

File Name:
F_NDXVEW.PRG

Screen Use:
Entire screen

Arguments:
<cIndexExt> – A 3-letter string for the extension of the desired index files

<cPath> – DOS path to the index files

Typical Use:
To view the key expressions of index files in a directory

Defaults:
Both arguments are optional. If <cIndexExt> is not passed, NDXVIEW uses NTX for the file extension. If <cPath> is not passed, it uses the current directory.

Cautions:
The index files must be the same type as in the running application (see discussion below).

See Also:
DEVELOP, NDXCOUNT, NDXKEY

Discussion

Use NDXVIEW during application development to view key expressions of the index files in a directory. It provides a full-screen boxed display with the name of each index and its key expression. The selected indexes need not be open.

If there are too many indexes for the window, you can use the up/down arrow keys to scroll vertically. Pressing Enter, Esc, or the left/right arrow keys cause NDXVIEW to restore the screen and return. All other keys are ignored. The function does not provide horizontal scrolling. Instead it truncates long key expressions.

NDXVIEW uses NDXKEY to read the key expression of each index file. If the application was not compiled with the NDX.OBJ file supplied with Clipper, it assumes the index files to be Clipper indexes and displays the key expressions accordingly. If the NDX.OBJ file was used, it treats the index files as dBASE indexes.

Normally, the index files to be viewed are in the same format as the running application. If NDXVIEW is used on different index files, it may not display the key expressions correctly. If this occurs, use NDXKEY to read the files one at a time.

To link NDXVIEW to your application, you must declare it EXTERNAL. Alternately, you can use the preprocessor to link NDXVIEW only during development (see DEVELOP).

For example, to link NDXVIEW, use

```
EXTERNAL NDXVIEW
```

To link all development functions including NDXVIEW, use

```
DEVELOP()
```

Coding Examples

Use the lines below to display index files and their key expressions:

```
Display all indexes in current directory
NDXVIEW()

Display all indexes in \APP1 directory
NDXVIEW('NTX', '\APP1\')

Display all dBASE format indexes in \APP2 directory
NDXVIEW('NDX', '\APP2\')
```

```
*******************************************************************
FUNCTION NDXVIEW (extension, ndx_path)
*******************************************************************

* Display index key expressions during application development
* Copyright(c) 1991 -- James Occhiogrosso

#include "box.ch"

LOCAL counter, files := {}, list := {}

* Save entry screen
LOCAL old_screen := SCRNSAVE(1, 1, MAXROW()-1, MAXCOL()-1)

* Get type of indexes for running application
LOCAL clip_ntx := IF(INDEXEXT() = '.NDX', .F., .T.)

* If path or extension not passed, use defaults

IF VALTYPE(extension) != 'C'
    * Default extension is NTX
    extension = "NTX"
ENDIF

IF ndx_path = NIL
    * Default path is null (current directory)
    ndx_path = ''
ELSEIF VALTYPE(ndx_path) = 'C'
    ndx_path = TRIM(ndx_path)
    IF RIGHT(ndx_path, 1) != '\'
        ndx_path = ndx_path + '\'
    ENDIF
ELSE
    RETURN NIL
ENDIF

* Get number of files and load file names into array

files = DIRECTORY(ndx_path + '*.' + extension)

* If any files found
IF files != NIL
    * Load list array with file name and key expression
    FOR counter = 1 TO LEN(files)
        AADD(list, PADR(files[counter][1], 17) + ;
            NDXKEY(ndx_path + files[counter][1], clip_ntx))
    NEXT

    * Display boxed heading
    @ 1, 1, MAXROW()-1, MAXCOL()-1 BOX B_SINGLE + ' '
    @ 2, 4   SAY ' Index Name '
    @ 2, 31  SAY ' Key Expression '
    @ 3, 4   SAY REPLICATE('D', MAXCOL() - 7)
```

```
    * Display array with ACHOICE
    ACHOICE(4, 4, MAXROW()-2, MAXCOL()-4, list)
ENDIFF

* Restore screen and return
SCRNREST(old_screen)
RETURN NIL
```

NODUPL

Description:
Tests for duplicate key field entry

Syntax:
NODUPL(<cKeyData>, <nSearchIndexNo>, <cKeyField>, [<cUserFunction>])

Returns:
True if the specified key does not exist in currently selected database; false otherwise

File Name:
F_NODUPL.PRG

Screen Use:
If AEDBAR is active, a message appears in its window when a duplicate is found.

Arguments:
<cKeyData> – Key to use to search for a duplicate value

<nSearchIndexNo> – Numeric representing the order of the index file to use for the search

<cKeyField> – Field in active database to compare to key

<cUserFunction> – Optional user function to execute before testing for a duplicate (see discussion below)

Typical Use:
To prevent entry of duplicate keys into a database

Cautions:
NODUPL is designed for use with AEDBAR and AEDMSG. If used without them, no screen messages appear and the only indication of a duplicate entry is an error tone.

Global Variables:
You can use the global variable *helpcode* with NODUPL (see discussion below)

See Also:
AEDBAR, AEDMSG, READABORT

Discussion

NODUPL is designed for use in a VALID clause during data entry. It tests the key against a database field and returns true if it does not find a match or false if it does. Thus, you can use it to prevent the operator from leaving the field if a duplicate key exists.

You should generally use NODUPL with AEDBAR active; it then produces messages in AEDBAR's window. When a duplicate key exists, an error tone sounds and the message "Duplicate key – reenter? Y/N" appears. NODUPL then waits for a response. If the response is Y, it returns false to permit data reentry. An N response places the Esc key in the keyboard buffer, forcing an exit from the READ.

If you use NODUPL with AEDBAR inactive, the only indication of a duplicate entry is the error tone. The message and choice of reentering or abandoning are not available. In this case, you should provide your own messages and a way to exit the VALID.

The first three arguments passed to NODUPL are mandatory. It returns false if any are missing.

A database and appropriate indexes must be open in the current area when NODUPL is called. It changes the index order to the number specified in the argument during the search. It restores the original order before returning.

To use NODUPL with the same VALID clause for both adding and editing records, the global variable *helpcode* is defined.

Helpcode has the value EDIT during editing only. NODUPL then permits a duplicate value, provided that the initial value is not altered. All other values of helpcode are ignored. Thus, during the editing of records, the cursor moves normally over the key field as long as the operator does not change it. If the key field is altered, the database is tested for a duplicate using the new data.

If passed a user function, NODUPL executes it upon entry. The function can handle cases where the passed value is part of a complex key field. For example, suppose the key field combines an account number with another item and we want to test for duplicate account numbers only. The user function adds the item to the account number before testing for a duplicate.

Coding Examples

Use NODUPL as shown below in a DO WHILE loop to get variables for a database. If a duplicate is found and the operator chooses not to reenter the data, the read is aborted. Otherwise, the cursor returns to the field for data reentry. If no duplicate exists, the cursor simply moves to the next field.

The example assumes that a customer file is open and indexed on the field custid. NODUPL prevents customers from having the same identification. If the record is being edited, the variable mcustid is equated to the database field custid before starting.

```
* Get data for desired fields. Set DONE true when finished

DO WHILE .NOT. done

    @ 10, 10 SAY 'Customer Account ID:' GET mcustid ;
             VALID NODUPL(mcustid, 1, custid)

    @ 11, 10 SAY 'Company Name:......' GET mcompany
      .
      . Other SAY and GET statements
      .

    READ

    * If data is valid, set DONE true to exit loop
    done := .T.

ENDDO
```

```
****************************************************************
FUNCTION NODUPL (key_mvar, look_index, key_field, user_func)
****************************************************************

* Tests key field and displays message if duplicate value exists
* Copyright(c) 1991 -- James Occhiogrosso

#include "inkey.ch"

MEMVAR aedbar, helpcode

LOCAL old_help := IF(TYPE('helpcode') = 'C', helpcode, ''), ;
      old_ndx  := INDEXORD(), old_recd := RECNO(),          ;
      ret_value := .T.

IF PCOUNT() < 3
    * Error in calling syntax
    RETURN(.F.)
ENDIF

IF PCOUNT() = 4
    * If user function passed, execute it
    &user_func()
ENDIF

IF TYPE('helpcode') = 'C' .AND. UPPER(helpcode) = 'EDIT'   ;
                      .AND. key_mvar = key_field
    * Allow key variable to remain unchanged when editing
    RETURN(.T.)
ENDIF

* Check for duplicate key value
SET ORDER TO look_index
SEEK key_mvar

IF FOUND()

    * We have duplicate key field
    ret_value = .F.
    ERRORBEEP()
    helpcode = "DUPLICATE"

    * If AEDBAR in use, display "duplicate" message, and
    * ask operator whether reentry of data is desired

    IF TYPE('aedbar') = 'L' .AND. aedbar
       * Display "duplicate" message
       AEDMSG('mw_dupkey')

       IF OPCONFIRM()
           * Operator wants to reenter
           AEDMSG('mw_pgdn')
           ret_value = .F.
       ELSE
```

```
            * Operator wants to abort
            AEDMSG('mw_init')
            * Stuff keyboard with Esc to abort READ
            KEYBOARD CHR(K_ESC)
        ENDIF
    ENDIF
ENDIF

helpcode = old_help
GOTO old_recd
SET ORDER TO old_ndx
RETURN(ret_value)
```

OPCONFIRM

Description:
Waits for an operator response consisting of a single Y/N or y/n character

Syntax:
OPCONFIRM([<lEchoToScreen>])

Returns:
True if the operator presses Y or y, false if he or she presses N or n

File Name:
F_OPCONF.PRG

Screen Use:
Current cursor row and column position

Arguments:
[<lEchoToScreen>] – If true, the key pressed is echoed to the screen. If false, it is not echoed.

Typical Use:
To get a yes/no response from an operator without issuing a READ

Defaults:
If <lEchoToScreen> is omitted, it defaults to true.

Discussion

OPCONFIRM gets a yes/no response from the operator without issuing a READ command. An application can thus get an operator response at any time during data entry (for example, from a VALID) without disturbing the current READ state.

OPCONFIRM does not initiate a Clipper wait state. However, it processes special keys (hot keys) for help or other functions. If the global variable fkeyset contains a procedure name, it is called whenever a function or Alt key combination is pressed. The procedure receives the first three arguments normally passed with a SET KEY call (procedure name, line number, and input variable), and also the value of the special key as the fourth argument. The first three arguments are fixed as OPCONFIRM, 0, and a null string. Thus, all hot keys can be processed by the same procedures used during wait states.

On return from the hot key procedure, OPCONFIRM continues waiting for an operator Y/N response.

Coding Examples

```
* Get response from operator

@ 10, 10 SAY 'Do you want to proceed? (Y/N) - Press F1 for help.'

IF OPCONFIRM()
    * Continue process
    DO PROCESS
ELSE
    RETURN
ENDIF
```

```
*****************************************************************
FUNCTION OPCONFIRM (echo_on)
*****************************************************************

* Wait for operator confirmation in "Y/N" format
* Copyright(c) 1991 - James Occhiogrosso

#include "inkey.ch"
#include "set.ch"
#include "setcurs.ch"

MEMVAR fkeyset

LOCAL keypress, old_cursor

* Save entry cursor setting
old_cursor = SETCURSOR(SC_INSERT)

* If "echo" parameter not passed, default is echo on
IF echo_on = NIL
    echo_on = .T.
ENDIF

* Wait in loop for Y/N operator response
keypress = 0

DO WHILE .T.

    * Get key
    keypress = INKEY(0)

    IF CHR(keypress) $ 'YNyn'
        EXIT

    ELSEIF (keypress <= K_F2 .OR. keypress > 256 .OR.           ;
        keypress = K_F1) .AND. TYPE('fkeyset') != 'U'

        * Call special keys procedure if any function key or
        * Alt key combination is pressed. The variable
        * fkeyset must contain the procedure name.

        IF .NOT. EMPTY(fkeyset)
            &fkeyset('OPCONFIRM', 0, READVAR(), keypress)
        ENDIF

    ELSE
        ERRORBEEP()
    ENDIF
ENDDO
```

```
* Echo key at current position
IF echo_on
     @ ROW(), COL() SAY UPPER(CHR(keypress))
ENDIF

* Reset cursor to entry state
SETCURSOR(old_cursor)

* Return true on answer = "Y" or "y", otherwise, return false.
RETURN (IF (CHR(keypress) $ 'Yy', .T., .F.))
```

PARSE

Description:
Extracts a word delimited by spaces from a character string

Syntax:
PARSE(<@cString>)

Returns:
Extracted substring

File Name:
F_PARSE.PRG

Screen Use:
None

Argument:
<@cString> – Character string from which to extract a space-delimited substring. It should be passed by reference.

Typical Use:
To remove multiple data items from a concatenated text string

Discussion

When handling a set of items of unknown length, you may prefer to save them as a string rather than continually redefine an array or put them in a database. PARSE is used to extract items from such a string. They must be separated by spaces.

Each time PARSE is called, it searches the passed string for a space, and extracts the leftmost word as its return value. It also removes the word from the string before returning.

Successive calls to PARSE return embedded words, and remove them from the string until it has no more spaces. You can thus use PARSE in a loop to extract all space-delimited data items from a text string.

Note that this works only if you pass PARSE's string argument is passed by reference (preceded by an @ symbol). Otherwise, PARSE always returns the first word in the string.

Coding Examples

The example below extracts state abbreviations from a character string, puts them in an array, and then displays it.

```
LOCAL cStateList := 'al ar az ca nj nm ny', aStates := {}

CLEAR SCREEN
SETCOLOR('W+/N')

DO WHILE !EMPTY(cStateList)
    * Extract state abbreviations and put them in array
    AADD(aStates, UPPER(PARSE(@cStateList)))
ENDDO
ARVIEW(aStates)

RETURN
```

Several functions in the Developer's Library use PARSE. For more examples, see MAKEDBF and MAKENDX.

```
*****************************************************************
FUNCTION PARSE (string)
*****************************************************************

* Extract a word delimited by spaces from a string

* Copyright(c) 1991 -- James Occhiogrosso

LOCAL ret_string, space_char

* Remove leading spaces
string = LTRIM(string)

* Get position of first space character
space_char = AT(' ', string)

IF space_char = 0
    * No spaces, return balance of line and clear string
    ret_string = string
    string = ''
ELSE
    * Return all characters to next space character
    ret_string = SUBSTR(string, 1, space_char - 1)
    * Strip removed word from string
    string = LTRIM(SUBSTR(string, space_char))
ENDIF

RETURN ret_string
```

PASSWORD

Description:
Gets a string and compares it to an encoded password

Syntax:
PASSWORD(<nRow>, <nColumn>, <cEncodedPassword>, [<cEchoCharacter>])

Returns:
True if the string matches the password exactly; false otherwise.

File Name:
F_PASSWD.PRG

Screen Use:
Defined by calling arguments

Arguments:
<nRow>, <nColumn> – Row and column coordinates at which to get a password string for validation

<cEncodedPassword> – Previously encoded password to compare with user entry

[<cEchoCharacter>] – Optional character to echo for each one entered

Typical Use:
To prevent operator access to sensitive information

Defaults:
No display during password entry if <cEchoCharacter> is not passed.

See Also:
DECODE, ENCODE

Discussion

Use PASSWORD to get a string entry and compare it to a stored value previously encoded by ENCODE. Usually, a system database holds many encoded passwords. PASSWORD decodes the passed string and compares it to the entered one. If they match, it returns true. Otherwise, it returns false.

PASSWORD gets a string of the same length as the encoded password. This avoids indicating its length on the screen.

If the optional echo character is passed, the length of the untrimmed password appears in enhanced color as if it were a GET field. The echo character appears for each key pressed. If no character is passed, nothing appears during password entry, and its length is not indicated.

No editing keys are provided except BackSpace and Left Arrow. The Return, Esc, PgUp, and PgDn keys all terminate entry. All other keys are taken as part of the password. However, when the comparison is made to the decoded password, only characters, digits, decimal points, and underscores are processed.

By using PASSWORD along with DECODE and ENCODE, you can provide security for sensitive information. However, it is not foolproof. Technical users with a knowledge of ASCII values could determine how to decode a password. Use the functions in applications that do not require maximum security and where potential violators are usually non-technical. See ENCODE for details on the method used.

Coding Examples

The example below assumes that a password encoded using ENCODE is stored in the file sysdata.dbf. It uses PASSWORD before allowing the operator to gain access to employee pay rate information.

```
MEMVAR getlist ; FIELD pr_passwd
LOCAL choice := counter := 1
INITGLOBAL()
SETCOLOR(colstd)
USE SYSDATA NEW        // Database containing encoded passwords
                       // Field name is pr_passwd
```

```
DO WHILE choice > 0
   counter = 1
   CLEAR
   @ 10, 30 SAY     ' Employee Reports   '
   @ 12, 30 PROMPT ' Group affiliations '
   @ 13, 30 PROMPT ' Pay rates          '
   @ 14, 30 PROMPT ' Home addresses     '
   MENU TO choice
   IF choice = 1
        DO groups

   ELSEIF choice = 2     // Sensitive information
        @ 17, 20 SAY 'Password: '
        * Allow three tries at a correct password
        DO WHILE counter++ <= 3

             * Get password
             IF ! PASSWORD(17, 30, pr_passwd, '*')
                 @ 19, 30 SAY 'Incorrect password'
                 LOOP
             ELSE
                 EXIT
             ENDIF

        ENDDO

        IF counter <= 4
             * If we drop out of loop before third try,
             * operator entered valid password
             @ 19, 0
             DO payrates
        ELSE
             * Otherwise, deny access
             @ 19, 30 SAY '   Access denied    '
             ERRORBEEP(2)
             PAUSE(1)
        ENDIF

   ELSEIF choice = 3
        DO address

   ENDIF
ENDDO
```

Note: Groups, Payrates, and Address are names of user procedures not shown here.

```
*****************************************************************
FUNCTION PASSWORD (pw_row, pw_col, encoded_pw, echo_char)
*****************************************************************

 * Gets string at passed coordinates, encodes and
 * tests it against passed, encoded password

 * Copyright(c) 1991 -- James Occhiogrosso

 #include "inkey.ch"

 LOCAL   end_col := pw_col + LEN(encoded_pw) - 1,         ;
         keypress := 0, next_char := '', old_color := '', ;
         old_cursor := '', password := ''

 * Position cursor at start of simulated GET
 SETPOS(pw_row, pw_col)
 old_color = SETCOLOR(SWAPCOLOR())

 IF VALTYPE(echo_char) == 'C'
    * Clear area to password length in GET color
    @ pw_row, pw_col CLEAR TO pw_row, end_col
 ENDIF

 * Stay in loop until exit key is pressed or
 * we reach end of password area

 DO WHILE LEN(password) < LEN(encoded_pw)

    * Wait for a key
    keypress = INKEY(0)

    * Backspace/left arrow. Move cursor and trim last character
    IF keypress = K_BS .OR. keypress = K_LEFT
        IF COL() > pw_col
            SETPOS(ROW(), COL() - 1)
        ENDIF
        password = SUBSTR(password, 1, LEN(password) - 1)

    ELSE

        * All keys except exit keys are added to password
        IF keypress != K_ESC   .AND. keypress != K_ENTER .AND. ;
           keypress != K_PGUP .AND. keypress != K_PGDN

           * Add each valid key to password
           password = password + UPPER(CHR(keypress))

           IF VALTYPE(echo_char) == 'C'
               * Display echo character
               @ ROW(), COL() SAY echo_char
           ENDIF
```

```
      ELSE
         * Exit loop on Esc, Enter, PgUp, or PgDn
         EXIT
      ENDIF
   ENDIF
ENDDO

* Reset color and return true if password matches
SETCOLOR(old_color)

RETURN IF(TRIM(password) == DECODE(encoded_pw), .T., .F.)
```

PAUSE

Description:
Pauses unconditionally for a specified length of time

Syntax:
PAUSE(<nPauseTime>)

Returns:
Nothing

File Name:
F_PAUSE.PRG

Screen Use:
None

Arguments:
<nPauseTime> – Time in seconds

Typical Use:
To wait for slow devices such as printers, or to display popup messages for a fixed time without operator interruption. Typically, <nPauseTime> is an integer but it can have decimal places.

Cautions:
There is no way for the operator to exit this function, except by aborting the program. Do not use it for time delays longer than 10 seconds without displaying a message.

Discussion

Use PAUSE when you must stop an application briefly and do not want the operator to interrupt.

A typical use is to guarantee that a popup warning remains visible for at least a few seconds, even during fast data entry. Since PAUSE does not poll the keyboard, the time delay is unaffected by typing speed.

Coding Examples

```
* Sound warning and display message for 2.5 seconds

@ 22, 10 SAY 'This item must be reordered! '
? ERRORBEEP( )
PAUSE(2.5)
@ 22, 10
```

```
*******************************************************************
FUNCTION PAUSE (timedelay)
*******************************************************************

* Pause unconditionally

* Copyright(c) 1991 -- James Occhiogrosso

#define MAXSECS 86400  // Number of seconds in a day

LOCAL starttime := SECONDS()

IF starttime + timedelay >= MAXSECS

    * Passing through midnight, adjust delay time
    timedelay = timedelay - (MAXSECS - starttime)

    * Wait until past midnight and delay is satisfied
    WHILE SECONDS() >= starttime .OR. SECONDS() <= timedelay ; END

ELSE
    * Not passing midnight, wait for specified time
    WHILE SECONDS() - starttime < timedelay ; END

ENDIF

RETURN NIL
```

PICKIT

Description:
Displays and allows selection of elements from an array

Syntax:
PICKIT(<nTopRow>, <nLeftColumn>, <nBottomRow>, <nRightColumn>, <aTextChoices>, <aReturnChoices>, [<cNewColor>])

Returns:
Number of selections, or -1 on error

File Name:
F_PICKIT.PRG

Screen Use:
Defined by calling parameters

Arguments:
<nTopRow>, <nLeftColumn>, <nBottomRow>, <nBottomColumn> – Screen coordinates for the display

<aTextChoices> – Array of character strings to display for operator selections

<aReturnChoices> – Parallel array of valid data or expressions. Returned with unselected items removed (see discussion below).

<cNewColor> – Optional color variable or literal color specification

Typical Use:
To interactively display, mark, and return a group of operator selections

Defaults:
If a color specification (<cNewColor>) is not passed, PICKIT uses the global color variable colwindow.

Error Handling:
Returns -1 if <aTextChoices> contains data types other than character strings

Cautions:
Does not validate the passed row and column positions

See Also:
DBNAMES

Discussion

PICKIT interactively displays and marks text items from the choice array, and returns with only the operator's selections. The array appears in a boxed area defined by the passed coordinates. When the operator moves the highlight to a desired item and presses Enter, PICKIT displays a check mark [CHR(251)] to its left, indicating selection. Pressing Enter a second time deselects the item and removes the mark.

The process continues until the operator presses the Esc key to end selection. PICKIT then returns the number of selections, and removes unselected items from the return array.

To allow room to box, mark, and display the choices properly, PICKIT's coordinates should provide at least nine columns more than the longest string the array contains.

By default, PICKIT uses the global variable colwindow to display the choice box. You can override this by passing it a valid color string or another color variable name. If passed a null string for the color, PICKIT uses the current setting.

Coding Examples

A typical use of PICKIT is to select specific databases for reindexing. Rather than displaying database filenames, which could be cryptic, PICKIT lets you present meaningful names instead.

In the first example, the arrays to be passed are hard coded with literal values before calling PICKIT. In the second example, DBNAMES reads the application data dictionary and loads database names and associated text into the arrays.

In both examples, the array of operator selections returned from PICKIT is passed to MAKENDX to index the files.

Example 1

```
* Load arrays with selection text and dbf file names
LOCAL pick_array[8], ret_array[8]

pick_array[1] = 'Sales representatives file'
pick_array[2] = 'Customer file'
pick_array[3] = 'Orders file'
pick_array[4] = 'Invoice file'
pick_array[5] = 'Payments file'
pick_array[6] = 'Credit memos file'
pick_array[7] = 'Blanket orders file'
pick_array[8] = 'Shipping addresses file'

ret_array[1]  = 'arreps'
ret_array[2]  = 'arcust'
ret_array[3]  = 'arords'
ret_array[4]  = 'arinvs'
ret_array[5]  = 'arpays'
ret_array[6]  = 'arcred'
ret_array[7]  = 'arblkt'
ret_array[8]  = 'araddr'

* Use PICKIT to get operator selections

choices = PICKIT(5, 10, 15, 70, pick_array, ret_array)

index_ok = .f.
IF choices > 0

    * Reindex databases using array returned from PICKIT
    * and application data dictionary file (arsystem.dbf)

    index_ok = MAKENDX(ret_array, "arsystem.def")

ENDIF
```

Example 2

Similar to Example 1 except that it uses DBNAMES to fill the arrays for PICKIT from the data dictionary. T_MAKEND.PRG on the companion disk also uses this technique.

```
* Load arrays with selection text and DBF file names
LOCAL pick_array[0], ret_array[0]
DBNAMES("arsystem.def", pick_array, ret_array)

* Use PICKIT to get operator selections
choices = PICKIT(5, 10, 15, 70, pick_array, ret_array)

index_ok = .F.
IF choices > 0

    * Call MAKENDX with array of selected database names
    * and application data dictionary file

    index_ok = MAKENDX(ret_array, "arsystem.def")

ENDIF
```

```
*********************************************************************
FUNCTION PICKIT (top, left, bottom, right, in_array, ;
                 out_array, new_color)
*********************************************************************
* Allow selection of elements from array

* Copyright(c) 1991 -- James Occhiogrosso

#include "box.ch"

LOCAL choice := 1, counter := 1, new_array[0],          ;
      num_elems := LEN(in_array), old_screen, old_color, ;
      pad_len := (right-1) - (left+1), viewrow := 1

MEMVAR colwindow

* Check display array for all character elements
IF .NOT. ARTYPE(in_array, 'C')
    RETURN(-1)
ENDIF

* Save old screen
old_screen = SCRNSAVE(top, left, bottom, right)

* Test color argument
IF VALTYPE(new_color) = 'C' .AND. .NOT. EMPTY(new_color)
    * Color was passed, use it
    old_color = SETCOLOR(new_color)

ELSEIF new_color = NIL
    * No argument passed, use default color
    old_color = SETCOLOR(colwindow)
ELSE
    * Use current color
    old_color = SETCOLOR()
ENDIF

* Box display area
DISPBOX(top, left, bottom, right, B_SINGLE + SPACE(1))

FOR counter = 1 TO num_elems

    * Pad selections to same length for viewing
    in_array[counter]   = ;
           PADR('  ' + in_array[counter], pad_len)

    * Pad return array for marking
    out_array[counter] = SPACE(1) + out_array[counter]
NEXT

DO WHILE choice != 0

    * Wait in ACHOICE for operator selection
    choice = ACHOICE(top+1, left+1, bottom-1, right-1,;
                     in_array, , , choice)
```

```
      IF choice > 0

          * Set row for next iteration
          viewrow := ROW()-(top+1)

          * Mark or unmark array elements
          IF SUBSTR(in_array[choice],2,1) = '✓'

              * If element already marked, unmark it
              in_array[choice] = '   ' + ;
                    SUBSTR(in_array[choice],4)
              out_array[choice] = ' ' + ;
                    SUBSTR(out_array[choice],2)
          ELSE

              * Otherwise, mark selected element
              in_array[choice] = ' ✓ ' + ;
                    SUBSTR(in_array[choice],4)
              out_array[choice] = '✓' + ;
                    SUBSTR(out_array[choice],2)
          ENDIF
      ENDIF
ENDDO

FOR counter = 1 TO num_elems

    IF SUBSTR(out_array[counter],1,1) = '✓'

        * If element marked, strip mark
        * and add element to new array

        AADD(new_array, SUBSTR(out_array[counter],2))

    ENDIF

    * Restore input array to original state
    in_array[counter] = SUBSTR(in_array[counter],4)

NEXT

* Copy new array to return array

ASIZE(out_array, LEN(new_array))
ACOPY(new_array, out_array)

* Clean up and return number of selections

SETCOLOR(old_color)
SCRNREST(old_screen)

RETURN LEN(new_array)
```

PRNCHECK

Description:
Tests the printer; displays a message and waits if it is not ready.

Syntax:
PRNCHECK(<nMessageLine>)

Returns:
True if the printer is ready; false otherwise or if the operator presses Esc

File Name:
F_PRNCHK.PRG

Screen Use:
Message appears on <nMessageLine>

Arguments:
<nMessageLine> – Line number on which message appears

Typical Use:
To warn the operator if the printer is not ready

Defaults:
If <nMessageLine> is not passed, the message appears on the bottom line.

Cautions:
Waits for one second before displaying a message. Although this is sufficient for most printers, slow units may need a longer delay.

Discussion

Use PRNCHECK to test the printer before sending it data. If it is off-line or not ready for some other reason, PRNCHECK waits in a loop, continually retesting it. As soon as the operator places the printer on-line or otherwise corrects the problem, PRNCHECK returns true. The operator can terminate the loop at any time by pressing Esc. If this happens, PRNCHECK returns false.

Coding Examples

```
* Check printer
IF .NOT. PRNCHECK()    * Abort print operation
   RETURN
ELSE
   * Run report
   DO report1
ENDIF
```

```
*****************************************************************
FUNCTION PRNCHECK (msg_line)
*****************************************************************

* Displays a message if printer is not ready

* Copyright(c) 1991 -- James Occhiogrosso

#include "inkey.ch"

LOCAL old_screen := '', keypress := 0

* Initialize message line if not passed
msg_line := IF(msg_line = NIL, MAXROW(), msg_line)

IF .NOT. ISPRINTER()
   * Wait 1 second just in case print buffer is full.
   * For slower printers, increase time delay.
   PAUSE(1)
ENDIF

* Try again. If printer still is not ready, display a message.
* Wait for operator to press Esc or make printer ready

IF .NOT. ISPRINTER()

   * Save message line screen
   old_screen = SCRNSAVE(msg_line, 0, msg_line, MAXCOL())

   * Sound bell and display message
   ?? CHR(7)
   CENTERON(msg_line, 'Your printer is not ready! ' + ;
           'Correct or press Esc to abort.')

   * Wait for printer to be ready or Esc key to be pressed
   DO WHILE .NOT. ISPRINTER() .AND. keypress != K_ESC
      keypress = INKEY()
   ENDDO

   * Restore message line screen
   SCRNREST(old_screen)

ENDIF
RETURN( IF(keypress = K_ESC, .F.,.T.) )
```

PRNTDATE

Description:
Converts a date value to a printable string

Syntax:
PRNTDATE([<dDateValue>], [<nFormat>])

Returns:
Character string in the specified format

File Name:
F_PRNDAT.PRG

Screen Use:
None

Arguments:
<dDateValue> – Date for display or printing

<nFormat> – Format desired (from list below)

    1 = month day, year (e.g., January 1, 1991)

    2 = day of week, month day, year (e.g., Saturday, January 1, 1991)

    3 = day month, year (e.g., 1 January 1991)

    4 = day of week, day month year (e.g., Saturday, 1 January 1991)

Typical Use:
To print or display Clipper dates in specific formats

Defaults:
If <dDateValue> is not passed, it defaults to the system date
If <nFormat> is not passed or exceeds 4, it defaults to 1.

See Also:
PRNTTIME

Discussion

Use PRNTDATE to display or print date values in different formats. Select a format by passing its number (as given in the list above). The length of the returned string is format dependent.

You can use PRNTDATE directly in an @ SAY statement, or you can save its return value in a variable for later display or printing.

Coding Examples

```
* Display current date in MonthName dd, yyyy format
? PRNTDATE()

* Print date stored in a database as DayName, MonthName dd, yyyy
@ 10, 10 SAY PRNTDATE(database->field_name, 2)

* Print system date and time at current printer position
@ PROW(), PCOL() SAY PRNTDATE() + ' ' + PRNTTIME()
```

```
*******************************************************************
FUNCTION PRNTDATE (indate, choice)
*******************************************************************

* Returns passed date value as a string in selected format

* Copyright(c) 1991 -- James Occhiogrosso

LOCAL outdate := ''

* If date argument is empty or not a date, default to system date
IF VALTYPE(indate) != 'D' .OR. EMPTY(indate)
   indate = DATE()
ENDIF

* If choice is invalid, default to 1
IF VALTYPE(choice) != 'N' .OR. choice = 0 .OR. choice > 4
   choice = 1
ENDIF

* Create return string in selected format
DO CASE

   CASE choice = 1
      * Return date = MonthName, dd yyyy
      outdate = CMONTH(indate) + ' ' + LTRIM(STR(DAY(indate))) ;
              + ', ' + LTRIM(STR(YEAR(indate)))

   CASE choice = 2
      * Return date = DayName, MonthName, dd yyyy
      outdate = CDOW(indate) + ', ' + CMONTH(indate) + ' ' + ;
                LTRIM(STR(DAY(indate))) + ', ' + ;
                LTRIM(STR(YEAR(indate)))

   CASE choice = 3
      * Return date = dd MonthName yyyy
      outdate = LTRIM(STR(DAY(indate))) + ' ' + CMONTH(indate) ;
              + ' ' + LTRIM(STR(YEAR(indate)))

   CASE choice = 4
      * Return date = DayName, dd MonthName yyyy
      outdate = CDOW(indate) + ', ' + LTRIM(STR(DAY(indate))) ;
              + ' ' +  CMONTH(indate) + ' ' + ;
                LTRIM(STR(YEAR(indate)))

ENDCASE

RETURN outdate
```

PRNTTIME

Description:
Converts a time string from 24-hour format to 12-hour format

Syntax:
PRNTTIME(<cTimeString>)

Returns:
Character time string in format "hh: mm AM" or "hh: mm PM"

File Name:
F_PRNTIM.PRG

Screen Use:
None

Arguments:
<cTimeString> – Time string in format "hh: mm: ss" or "hh: mm"

Typical Use:
To display or print time in 12-hour format

Defaults:
Uses the system time if no argument is passed

Cautions:
Returns an empty string if the passed time string is invalid

See Also:
PRNTDATE

Discussion

Use PRNTTIME to convert time values in 24-hour format to 12-hour format for display or printing. It returns a time string in the format "hh:mm AM" or "hh:mm PM". It does not return the seconds value. The returned string is always 8 characters long, so you can use PRNTTIME in columnar presentations.

Coding Examples

```
* To display system time in 12-hour format
? PRNTTIME()

* To print time stored in a database at current printer position
@ PROW(), PCOL() SAY PRNTTIME(database->field_name)

* To save 12-hour formatted time in a database field
REPLACE database->field_name WITH PRNTTIME()

* To print system date and time at current printer position
@ PROW(), PCOL() SAY PRNTDATE() + ' ' + PRNTTIME()
```

```
****************************************************************
FUNCTION PRNTTIME (intime)
****************************************************************

* Converts a 24-hour time string to hh:mm AM or hh:mm PM format

* Copyright(c) 1991 -- James Occhiogrosso

LOCAL outtime := ''

* If time string not passed or wrong type, default to system time
IF VALTYPE(intime) != 'C' .OR. EMPTY(intime)
   intime = TIME()
ENDIF

* Check first two characters (hours value) of time string
IF VAL(intime) > 12 .AND. VAL (intime) < 24
   * If hours above 12, subtract 12 and set to PM
   outtime = STR(VAL(intime) - 12, 2) + ;
             SUBSTR(intime, 3, 3) + ' PM'

ELSEIF VAL(intime) < 12
   * If hours below 12, test for midnight and set to AM
   outtime = IF(LEFT(intime, 2) = '00', '12' + SUBSTR(intime, ;
             3, 3), IF(LEFT(intime, 1) = '0', + ' ' + ;
             SUBSTR(intime, 2,4), SUBSTR(intime, 1, 5))) + ' AM'

ELSEIF VAL(intime) = 12
   * If hours is 12 (noon), set to PM
   outtime = SUBSTR(intime, 1, 5) + ' PM'

ENDIF

RETURN outtime
```

READABORT

Description:
Displays a message and waits for operator confirmation before aborting a READ operation

Syntax:
READABORT([<nMessageRow>])

Returns:
True if operator confirms the abort, false otherwise

File Name:
F_READAB.PRG

Screen Use:
AEDBAR message window, bottom screen row, or optional passed line number (see discussion below)

Arguments:
<nMessageRow> – Optional line number for the message

Typical Use:
To ask for operator confirmation when the Esc key is pressed to terminate a READ

Defaults:
If <nMessageRow> is not passed and AEDBAR is inactive, the message appears on the bottom screen row.

Global Variable:
aedbar

See Also:
AEDBAR, AEDMSG

Discussion

READABORT gives the operator a second chance if he or she accidentally terminates a READ operation by pressing Esc. It displays the message, "Abandon this record? (Y/N)", and returns a logic value based on the operator's response. Accidental pressing of Esc is particularly common on keyboards where it is located just left of the 1 key.

If the AEDBAR function is active, the message appears in its window. Otherwise, it appears on the passed line number, or the bottom screen line if no number is passed.

Coding Examples

Use READABORT as shown below in a DO WHILE loop to get variables for a database. If the operator presses Esc, a message asks for confirmation before aborting the read cycle.

```
* Get data for desired fields. Set done true when finished
done = .F.
DO WHILE .NOT. done

    DO SCRNGET     // Procedure containing GET statements
    READ

    IF READABORT()

        * Operator pressed Esc deliberately. Clear field
        * variables
        DO CLRVARS
        DO SCRNGET
        CLEAR GETS

        * Display initial window message and exit loop
        AEDMSG('mw_init')
        EXIT
```

```
    ELSE
        * Operator probably pressed Esc accidentally.
        * Redisplay editing message in window,
        * and return to top of loop.

        AEDMSG('mw_pgdn')
        LOOP

    ENDIF
    * Normal end is here if Esc key was not pressed

ENDDO WHILE .T.
```

```
*****************************************************************
FUNCTION READABORT (msg_line)
*****************************************************************

* Asks for operator confirmation before aborting READ

* Copyright(c) 1991 -- James Occhiogrosso

#include "inkey.ch"

LOCAL message := 'Abandon this record?  Y/N  '
LOCAL old_screen := '', ret_value := .F.

* Test for Escape key
IF LASTKEY() = K_ESC

    * If message line not passed, default to bottom screen row
    msg_line := IF(VALTYPE(msg_line) = 'N', msg_line, MAXROW())

    * If AEDBAR is in use, AEDMSG will display message.
    * Otherwise, message is displayed on passed line number.

    IF .NOT. AEDMSG(message)
        * AEDBAR not in use, use message line
        old_screen = SCRNSAVE(msg_line, 0, msg_line, MAXCOL())
        CENTERON(msg_line, message)
    ENDIF

    * Move cursor to end of message text
    @ ROW(), COL() SAY ''
    ?? CHR(7)

    IF OPCONFIRM()
        * Operator confirms abandoning record
        ret_value = .T.
    ENDIF

    * If we saved a screen area, restore it
    IF .NOT. EMPTY(old_screen)
        SCRNREST(old_screen)
    ENDIF

ENDIF

RETURN (ret_value)
```

READTEXT

Description:
Displays text files of any size

Syntax:
READTEXT(<cTextFile>, [<nTopRow>], [<nLeftColumn>], [<nBottomRow>], [<nRightColumn>], [<nStartLine>])

Returns:
Nothing

File Name:
F_READTX.PRG

Screen Use:
Entire screen or specified coordinates

Arguments:
<cTextFile> – Text file to be viewed

[<nTopRow>], [<nLeftColumn>], [<nBottomRow>], [<nRightColumn>] – Optional numeric screen coordinates for displaying the selected file

[<nStartLine>] – Optional line number (in text file) for the initial display

Typical Use:
To view text files of any size from a Clipper application

Defaults:
If no starting line is passed, the display begins with line 1 of the text file.

To pass a starting line only, pass NIL (commas) for the coordinates.

If no coordinates are passed, entire screen is used.

Error Handling:
None. If it cannot open the specified text file, READTEXT returns with no further action.

Discussion

Clipper has many functions for handling memo or text information. Most require that the text be in a single character variable. This is fine for short strings, small files, and applications with lots of free memory (an unlikely situation!). However, if the file (or text string) exceeds 64K, or if your application has limited memory, you cannot use the Clipper functions.

READTEXT is a powerful function that lets you view a text file of any size. It does this by reading only enough lines to fill the screen area. Thus, it uses just the memory needed to save the entry screen and display the window.

Typically, READTEXT can display a file on an entire standard 25 x 80 monitor using less than 8K of memory. Since it processes only the lines that fit in the window, its memory requirements (for a given argument set) are constant. The amount used depends on window size and the length of the text lines, not on the overall size of the file. You can use READTEXT only to view files. It has no provisions for editing.

Window coordinates and a starting line are optional parameters. READTEXT uses the entire screen if coordinates are not passed. The text file appears in a single-line boxed window. If a starting line number is passed, READTEXT displays that line at the top of the window. Otherwise, the window starts with the first line. READTEXT does not affect color settings.

READTEXT provides navigation keys (see following table) for moving through the displayed file. It ignores all other keys. The viewing window is updated only when no keys are pending. If a navigation key is pressed, the text file is read and the viewing array reloaded, but the display update is interrupted. When the key is released, the correct text appears. This permits fast movement through the text in the display window.

READTEXT Navigation Keys

Key	Action
Up arrow	Moves text one line toward top of file
Down arrow	Moves text one line toward bottom of file
PgUp	Scrolls text toward top of file by window size
PgDn	Scrolls text toward bottom of file by window size
Home	Restarts display at top line of text file
End	Places last line of text file at bottom of window
Right arrow	Scrolls text view one column right
Left arrow	Scrolls text view one column left
Ctrl-right arrow	Scrolls text view eight columns right
Ctrl-left arrow	Scrolls text view eight columns left

Coding Examples

```
* Full-screen display
READTEXT("FileName")

* Window area 20 rows by 60 columns
READTEXT("FileName", 2, 10, 21, 70)

* Start window text display at line 550 of "FileName"
READTEXT("FileName", 2, 10, 21, 70, 550)
```

```
*******************************************************************
FUNCTION READTEXT (text_file, top, left, bottom, right, ;
                   start_line)
*******************************************************************

* Display a text file of any size in a window for reading

* Copyright(c) 1991 -- James Occhiogrosso

#include "inkey.ch"
#include "box.ch"
#define  WIND_ROWS   (bottom - top) - 1    // window rows
#define  WIND_COLS   (right - left) - 3    // window columns

LOCAL buffer := SPACE(512), col_offset := 1, counter := 0,;
      handle := 0, keypress := 0, line_end := 0, line_num := 0,;
      old_cursor := SETCURSOR(0), old_screen := '',;
      pointer := 0, text_array := {}, text_eof

* Initialize arguments not passed with defaults

top = IF(top = NIL, 0, top)
left = IF(left = NIL, 0, left)
bottom = IF(bottom = NIL, MAXROW(), bottom)
right = IF(right = NIL, MAXCOL(), right)
start_line = IF(start_line = NIL, 1, start_line)

* If file cannot be opened, return
IF (handle := FOPEN(text_file)) > 0

    * Save old screen and box text area
    old_screen = SCRNSAVE(top, left, bottom, right)
    @ top, left, bottom, right BOX B_SINGLE + SPACE(1)

    * Save end of file value
    text_eof = FSEEK(handle, 0, 2)

    * Declare view array as number of window rows by 2 columns
    * Columns: 1 = file pointer, 2 = line text
    text_array := array(WIND_ROWS,2)

    FOR counter = 1 TO (start_line)
        * Move file pointer to specified line
        FREADLINE(handle)
    NEXT

    * Load array and display initial window of lines
    FILL_ARRAY(WIND_ROWS, text_array, handle, text_eof)
    DISP_ARRAY(top, left, bottom, right, text_array, col_offset)


    * Process keys pressed and redisplay the array
    DO WHILE keypress != K_ESC
```

```
          * If key is valid, process it

        IF keypress = K_UP          .OR. keypress = K_DOWN     .OR. ;
           keypress = K_HOME        .OR. keypress = K_END      .OR. ;
           keypress = K_PGUP        .OR. keypress = K_PGDN     .OR. ;
           keypress = K_LEFT        .OR. keypress = K_RIGHT    .OR. ;
           keypress = K_CTRL_LEFT   .OR. keypress = K_CTRL_RIGHT ;
                                    .OR. keypress = K_ENTER

           * Move up 1 line or 1 screen
           IF keypress = K_UP .OR. keypress = K_PGUP

              IF text_array[1][1] != 0   // Top of file

                 * Move file pointer to top array line
                 pointer = FSEEK(handle, text_array[1][1], 0)

                 * Back up file pointer (row or screen window)
                 pointer = REWIND(handle, IF(keypress = K_UP, ;
                           1, WIND_ROWS), pointer)

                 * And reload array
                 FILL_ARRAY(WIND_ROWS, text_array, handle, ;
                            text_eof)
              ENDIF

           * Move down 1 line or 1 screen
           ELSEIF keypress = K_DOWN .OR. keypress = K_PGDN

              * Test for end of file
              IF text_array[WIND_ROWS][1] != text_eof
                 * If not EOF or BOF, reload array
                 IF keypress = K_DOWN
                    * Move pointer to second array element
                    FSEEK(handle, text_array[2][1], 0)
                 ELSE
                    * Move pointer to last array element
                    FSEEK(handle, text_array[WIND_ROWS][1], 0)
                 ENDIF

                 FILL_ARRAY(WIND_ROWS, text_array, handle, ;
                            text_eof)
              ENDIF

           * Move to top of file
           ELSEIF keypress = K_HOME
              pointer = FSEEK(handle,0,0)
              FILL_ARRAY(WIND_ROWS, text_array, handle, ;
                         text_eof)

           * Move to bottom of file
           ELSEIF keypress = K_END
              pointer = FSEEK(handle,0,2)
              * Move pointer back one screen window
              pointer = REWIND(handle, WIND_ROWS, pointer)
```

```
                    FILL_ARRAY(WIND_ROWS, text_array, handle, ;
                          text_eof)

                * Scroll window 1 column right
                ELSEIF keypress = K_RIGHT
                    col_offset := IF(col_offset < 512,++col_offset,512)

                * Scroll window 1 column left
                ELSEIF keypress = K_LEFT
                    col_offset := IF(col_offset > 1, --col_offset, 1)

                * Scroll window 8 columns right
                ELSEIF keypress = K_CTRL_RIGHT
                    col_offset := IF(col_offset < 512,col_offset+8, 512)

                * Scroll window 8 columns left
                ELSEIF keypress = K_CTRL_LEFT
                    col_offset := IF(col_offset > 8, col_offset-8, 1)

                * Reset window offset to first column
                ELSEIF keypress = K_ENTER
                    col_offset := 1

                ENDIF

                * Redisplay array
                keypress = DISP_ARRAY(top, left, bottom, right,  ;
                               text_array, col_offset)

            ELSE
                * Key is invalid, get another
                keypress = INKEY(0)
            ENDIF
        ENDDO

        * Restore old screen and close file
        SCRNREST(old_screen)
        FCLOSE(handle)

ENDIF

SETCURSOR(old_cursor)
RETURN NIL


*****************************************************************
STATIC FUNCTION FILL_ARRAY (text_rows,text_array,handle,text_eof)
*****************************************************************

* Load viewing array with pointer and text of each line

LOCAL counter := 1
FOR counter = 1 TO text_rows
    text_array[counter][1] := FSEEK(handle, 0, 1)
    text_array[counter][2] := FREADLINE(handle)
```

```
           IF FSEEK(handle, 0, 1) >= text_eof ; EXIT ; ENDIF
NEXT

* If at EOF, fill balance of array with dummy values
IF counter++ < text_rows
    FOR counter = counter TO text_rows
        text_array[counter][1] := text_eof
        text_array[counter][2] := ''
    NEXT
ENDIF

RETURN NIL


*******************************************************************
STATIC FUNCTION DISP_ARRAY (top, left, bottom, right, ;
                            text_array, col_offset)
*******************************************************************

* Display window lines from array

LOCAL counter := 0, disp_string, keypress

* Clear keyboard buffer and window area
CLEAR TYPEAHEAD
CLEAR TO bottom-1, right-2

DO WHILE ++counter <= WIND_ROWS
    * Display string and increment line counter
    @ (top + counter), left + 2 SAY ;
            SUBSTR(text_array[counter][2], col_offset, WIND_COLS)
ENDDO

RETURN keypress


*******************************************************************
STATIC FUNCTION REWIND (handle, num_lines, pointer)
*******************************************************************

* Move file pointer back specified number of lines

LOCAL buffer := SPACE(512), first_line := .F., line_end := 0

DO WHILE num_lines > 0
    * Clear buffer
    buffer := SPACE(512)

    IF pointer >= 514
        * Move pointer back 514 bytes
        FSEEK(handle, -514, 1)

        * Fill buffer without carriage return/line feed (CR/LF)
        FREAD(handle, @buffer, 512)
```

```
    ELSE
        * Move pointer to BOF and read remaining text
        FSEEK(handle, -pointer, 1)
        FREAD(handle, @buffer, pointer-1)

        * Set first line flag if no CR/LF in buffer
        buffer = TRIM(buffer)
        first_line := IF(AT(CHR(13)+CHR(10), buffer) > 0,.F.,.T.)
    ENDIF

    * Look for previous CR/LF
    DO WHILE (line_end := RAT(CHR(13)+CHR(10), buffer)) > 0 ;
             .AND. num_lines > 0

        * Move pointer to end of previous line
        pointer = FSEEK(handle, -(LEN(buffer)-(line_end-1)), 1)

        * Strip line from buffer and decrement number remaining
        buffer = SUBSTR(buffer, 1, line_end - 1)
        num_lines--
    ENDDO

    IF !first_line
        * Move pointer to beginning of next line (skip CR/LF)
        pointer = FSEEK(handle, 2, 1)
    ELSE
        * Reset pointer to BOF and exit
        FSEEK(handle, 0, 0)
        EXIT
    ENDIF
ENDDO

RETURN pointer
```

REPLVARS

Description:
Replaces database fields in the current record with values from public field variables

Syntax:
REPLVARS( )

Returns:
NIL

File Name:
F_MVARS.PRG

Screen Use:
None

Arguments:
None

Typical Use:
To update a database record with new values from field variables

Global Variables:
Uses the current set of public variables created by INITVARS

See Also:
CLRVARS, EQUVARS, FREEVARS, INITVARS

Discussion

REPLVARS replaces each field in the current record with data from the public memory variables created by INITVARS. It is used to save updated values in the database, typically after editing, data entry, or other changes. REPLVARS does not provide record locking for network operation. If you are working in a network environment, lock the record before calling it. See the LOCKS.PRG file supplied with Clipper for examples of locking techniques.

Coding Examples

```
* Open database
USE DataFile NEW

* Initialize and clear field variables
INVITVARS()
CLRVARS()
* Issue your GET statements here
    .
    .
    .
* If adding a record
APPEND BLANK

* Replace record values
REPLVARS()
```

See sample program T_AEDBAR.PRG on the companion disk for a typical example.

```
****************************************************************
FUNCTION REPLVARS
****************************************************************

* Replace record with values from memory variables

* Copyright(c) 1991 -- James Occhiogrosso

LOCAL field_cnt := FCOUNT(), counter := 0
PRIVATE field_name

* Get number of fields
field_cnt = FCOUNT()

* Replace each field from its associated variable
FOR counter = 1 TO field_cnt
    field_name = LOWER(FIELD(counter))
    REPLACE &field_name WITH m&field_name
NEXT

RETURN NIL
```

REQDDATA

Description:
Warns the operator with a tone and a message if a required entry is left blank

Syntax:
REQDDATA(<cVarName>, [<cUDFName>])

Returns:
True if data is entered in the area, false otherwise

File Name:
F_REQDAT.PRG

Screen Use:
If AEDBAR is in use, a message appears in its window; otherwise, no message is displayed.

Arguments:
<cVarName> – Memory variable into which data must be entered

<cUDFName> – Optional UDF to execute before returning to the GET

Typical Use:
To warn the operator when a data item has been left blank inadvertently

See Also:
AEDBAR, AEDMSG

Discussion

Use REQDDATA to keep the operator from leaving an entry blank. It usually appears in a VALID clause on a variable during a GET/READ cycle. If the operator leaves the variable blank, REQDDATA sounds an error tone. It also returns false to the VALID, preventing the operator from proceeding. In an application that uses AEDBAR, REQDDATA places a warning message in its window.

You can pass an optional UDF to REQDDATA. It can perform more data validation, or display a message if AEDBAR is not in use. REQDDATA calls it just before returning control to the VALID. The UDF can change the private variable ret_value to provide more control.

Coding Examples

```
* Sound warning and return cursor to GET if custid is blank
@ 10, 10 GET custid PICTURE "!!!999" VALID REQDDATA(custid)


* Same as above, using a UDF to display a message

@ 10, 10 GET custid PICTURE "!!!999" VALID ;
          REQDDATA(custid, "UDF_NAME")

******************************************************************
FUNCTION UDF_NAME (get_var, ret_value)
******************************************************************

* UDF called by REQDDATA

STATIC cMsgLine

IF EMPTY(get_var)
   * Save current line and display message
   cMsgLine := IF(cMsgLine = NIL, SCRNSAVE(22,0,22,79), cMsgLine)
   @ 22, 10 SAY 'Customer identification code must be entered.'
ELSE
   * Restore message line if one was saved
   cMsgLine := IF(cMsgLine != NIL, SCRNREST(cMsgLine), NIL)
ENDIF

RETURN ret_value
```

```
*******************************************************************
FUNCTION REQDDATA (mvar_name, proc_name)
*******************************************************************

* Warns operator that an entry is required

* Copyright(c) 1991 -- James Occhiogrosso

LOCAL ret_value := .T.

IF EMPTY(mvar_name)
   ERRORBEEP()
   ret_value = .F.
ENDIF

* Display message if AEDBAR in use
IF (ret_value, AEDMSG("mw_pgdn"), AEDMSG("mw_reqd"))

* If UDF name passed, execute it
* Note that UDF can alter return value

IF proc_name != NIL
   ret_val := &proc_name(mvar_name, ret_value)
ENDIF

RETURN(ret_value)
```

RESTGETS

Description:
Restores last set of GETs saved on internal stack by SAVEGETS

Syntax:
RESTGETS( )

Returns:
Nothing

File Name:
F_GETS.PRG

Screen Use:
None

Arguments:
None

Typical Use:
To restore the last set of active GETs after entry of another data set (nested READs)

Defaults:
Assumes current GETs are defined in the array *getlist*

Error Handling:
Returns with no action if there are no pending GETs

Global Variables:
getlist array

See Also:
SAVEGETS

Discussion

RESTGETS reactivates the GETs stored on an internal stack by SAVEGETS. Use it to restore the latest saved set of GETs. RESTGETS decrements an internal counter (incremented by SAVEGETS), and removes one set of GETs from the internal stack. It places them back on the public *getlist*, where the READ system can access them again.

See SAVEGETS for source code and more discussion and examples.

SAVEGETS

Description:
Saves currently active GETs on an internal stack

Syntax:
SAVEGETS( )

Returns:
Nothing

File Name:
F_GETS.PRG

Screen Use:
None

Arguments:
None

Typical Use:
Nested READs for entry of multiple data sets

Defaults:
Assumes current GETs are defined in array *getlist*

Error Handling:
Returns with no action if there are no pending GETs

Cautions:
You must use RESTGETS to remove saved GETs from the internal stack.

Global Variables:
getlist array

See Also:
RESTGETS

Discussion

Use SAVEGETS to temporarily store currently defined GET objects. You do this when you must enter related data. Clipper stores the current GETs in a public array named *getlist*. SAVEGETS maintains an internal stack and counter. During each call, it increments the counter and saves the current GETs (getlist array) on the stack. RESTGETS reinstates the previous set of GETs. Thus, you can use SAVEGETS and RESTGETS to implement nested READs to any level, limited only by available memory.

Coding Examples

The first example uses SAVEGETS and RESTGETS to get a shipping address during data entry for incoming orders. Note that, for clarity, the example shows only block code and procedure names. In practice, you would normally save and restore the original screen area, box or use different colors for the shipping address area, and provide other cosmetic code.

The example assumes that only a few orders need a special shipping address. Thus, we prefer not to clutter the screen with it. Instead, the user can press the F10 hot key to enter the shipping address when necessary (procedure SHIP_ADDR). When SHIP_ADDR is called, SAVEGETS places the current GETs (incoming orders screen) on its internal stack. A window then appears with new GETs for entering the shipping address. When the operator leaves the window, RESTGETS restores the previous GETs.

Clipper Developer's Library   407

```
****************************************************************
PROCEDURE EDIT_ORDERS     // Incoming order data entry
****************************************************************

* SAYs for order entry screen
DO SAY_ORDER_SCREEN

* Use F10 as hot key for shipping address entry
SET KEY K_F10 TO SHIP_ADDR

* GETs for incoming order data
DO GET_ORDER_DATA
READ

* Release F10
SET KEY K_F10 TO

RETURN


****************************************************************
PROCEDURE SHIP_ADDR     // Nested READ for shipping address
****************************************************************

* Turn off F10 hot key to prevent recursive calls
SET KEY K_F10 TO

* Save current GETs
SAVEGETS()

* Display partial screen for shipping address entry
DO SHIP_ADDR_SAYS

* Issue GETs for shipping address
DO SHIP_ADDR_GETS
READ

* Restore previous set of GETs

RESTGETS()

* Reset F10 to this procedure
SET KEY K_F10 TO SHIP_ADDR

RETURN
```

The second example is a demonstration program showing two levels of nested READs. Its source code is in the file T_GETS.PRG on the companion disk.

```
*******************************************************************
* Test program for SAVEGETS and RESTGETS -   FILE T_GETS.PRG
*******************************************************************

* Copyright(c) 1991 -- James Occhiogrosso

#include "inkey.ch"

MEMVAR colstd, getlist
LOCAL nothing1 := space(10), nothing2 := space(10), ;
      nothing3 := space(10)

INITGLOBAL()
SETCOLOR(colstd)
CLEAR
SET KEY K_F10 TO NEST1    // Set F10 to call first nested READ
CENTERON (MAXROW(), 'Press F10 for next level')

DO WHILE LASTKEY() != K_ESC
    @ 10, 10 GET nothing1
    @ 11, 10 GET nothing2
    @ 12, 10 GET nothing3
    READ
ENDDO
RETURN


**************
FUNCTION NEST1
**************

MEMVAR getlist
LOCAL nothing4 := space(10), nothing5 := space(10)

SET KEY K_F10 TO NEST2        // Set F10 to next nesting level
    SAVEGETS()                // Save current GETs
    @ 17, 10 GET nothing4     // Add new variables to get list
    @ 18, 10 GET nothing5
    READ                      // Read them
    RESTGETS()                // Restore previous set of GETs
    @ 17,10 CLEAR TO 18,20
    SET KEY K_ESC TO NEST1    // Reset F10 to first nesting level
RETURN
```

Clipper Developer's Library

```
**************
FUNCTION NEST2
**************

MEMVAR getlist
LOCAL nothing6 := space(10), nothing7 := space(10)

SET KEY K_F10 TO              // Clear hot key F10
SAVEGETS()                    // Save current GETs
@ 17, 40 GET nothing6         // Add new variables to get list
@ 18, 40 GET nothing7
READ                          // Read them
RESTGETS()                    // Restore previous set of GETs
@ 17,40 CLEAR TO 18,50
SET KEY K_F10 TO NEST1        // Reset F10 to first nesting level
RETURN NIL
```

```
*******************************************************************
** File = F_GETS.PRG  ** Functions: SAVEGETS, RESTGETS
*******************************************************************

* Copyright(c) 1991 -- James Occhiogrosso

* Create static array for saving GETs, counter for nesting count
STATIC getstack := {}, counter := 0
MEMVAR getlist

*******************************************************************
FUNCTION SAVEGETS
*******************************************************************

* Saves currently active GETs on getstack

* Return with no action if getlist undefined or empty

IF TYPE('getlist') = 'A' .AND. LEN(getlist) > 0
   * Add public getlist array to stack array (getstack)
   AADD(getstack, getlist)

   * Increment stack counter
   counter++

   * Clear current GETs and return
   getlist := {}
ENDIF

RETURN NIL


*******************************************************************
FUNCTION RESTGETS
*******************************************************************

* Restores and reactivates last set of pending GETs
IF counter > 0

   * Move last set of GETs back to getlist array
   getlist = getstack[counter--]

   * Resize internal stack
   ASIZE(getstack, counter)

ENDIF

RETURN NIL
```

SCANKEY

Description:
Determines the ASCII value and scan code for any key

Syntax:
SCANKEY( )

Returns:
Numeric value

File Name:
F_SCNKEY.PRG

Screen Use:
None

Arguments:
None

Typical Use:
To differentiate between keys for which INKEY returns the same value

Cautions:
Does not return the same codes for Alt key combinations and function keys as the Clipper INKEY function

Global Variables:
Returns scan code of the key pressed in the variable *scancode* if it is passed by reference

See Also:
FULLKEY

Discussion

Use SCANKEY to process keystrokes with more precision than Clipper allows. Each key on a standard keyboard has a unique combination of an ASCII value and a scan code. However, the Clipper INKEY function returns only the ASCII value, and cannot distinguish all keys on the keyboard. For example, the number keys on the numeric keypad and the ones on the alphabetic keyboard return the same INKEY values. With SCANKEY, you can distinguish them.

SCANKEY calls the assembly language function FULLKEY to get the value of the key pressed. FULLKEY waits for a key and returns an integer representing its scan code and ASCII value. SCANKEY then separates the two parts.

If the variable *scancode* is predefined, SCANKEY loads it with the key's scan code, and returns the key's ASCII value. In most cases, this is the same value returned by Clipper's INKEY function.

INKEY returns special codes for function and alternate (Alt) key combinations. They have no ASCII equivalents. SCANKEY returns zero for them, and the scan code must be used for identification. For all other keys, SCANKEY returns the same value as INKEY.

Values for the scan codes and ASCII equivalents for standard keyboards are in most computer manuals.

Coding Examples

The example below is from a screen painter that uses SCANKEY to draw graphic boxes. The user enters graphics characters by pressing keys on the numeric keypad. Number keys on the alphabetic keyboard produce normal values. Since both sets of keys return the same INKEY (ASCII) values, the scan codes must be used to distinguish them. A STD_KEY procedure (not shown) handles all other keys.

The Developer's Library preprocessor header file, DL_KEYS.CH, defines names for the numeric keys.

```
* Display graphics characters for keys on numeric keypad
#include "dl_keys.ch"
#include "inkey.ch"

LOCAL keypress := 0, scancode := 0
CLEAR SCREEN

DO WHILE keypress != K_ESC

   keypress = SCANKEY()
   DO CASE

      CASE keypress = K_ONE
         @ ROW(), COL() SAY IF(scancode = 79, CHR(200), "1")

      CASE keypress = K_TWO
         @ ROW(), COL() SAY IF(scancode = 80, CHR(202), "2")

      CASE keypress = K_THREE
         @ ROW(), COL() SAY IF(scancode = 81, CHR(188), "3")

      CASE keypress = K_FOUR
         @ ROW(), COL() SAY IF(scancode = 75, CHR(204), "4")

      CASE keypress = K_FIVE
         @ ROW(), COL() SAY IF(scancode = 76, CHR(206), "5")

      CASE keypress = K_SIX
         @ ROW(), COL() SAY IF(scancode = 77, CHR(185), "6")

      CASE keypress = K_SEVEN
         @ ROW(), COL() SAY IF(scancode = 71, CHR(201), "7")

      CASE keypress = K_EIGHT
         @ ROW(), COL() SAY IF(scancode = 72, CHR(203), "8")

      CASE keypress = K_NINE
         @ ROW(), COL() SAY IF(scancode = 73, CHR(187), "9")

      CASE keypress = K_ZERO
         @ ROW(), COL() SAY IF(scancode = 82, CHR(205), "0")

      CASE keypress = K_PERIOD
         @ ROW(), COL() SAY IF(scancode = 83, CHR(186), ".")

      OTHERWISE
         DO STD_KEY      // Process all other keys
   ENDCASE

ENDDO

RETURN
```

```
*******************************************************************
FUNCTION SCANKEY (scancode)
*******************************************************************

* Returns numeric ASCII equivalent and SCANCODE value for a key

* Copyright(c) 1991 -- James Occhiogrosso

LOCAL keypress := 0

* Wait for a key and return its value
keypress = FULLKEY()

* Adjust value to a positive number
keypress = IF(keypress < 0, keypress + 65536, keypress)

IF VALTYPE(scancode) = 'N'
   scancode = INT(keypress/256)
ENDIF

* Return ASCII value
RETURN INT(keypress % 256)
```

SCRNATTR

Description:
Gets or sets screen attributes at passed coordinates

Syntax:
SCRNATTR(<nTopRow>, <nLeftColumn>, <nBottomRow>, <nBottomColumn>, <nColorAttribute>)

Returns:
Numeric value of screen attribute at passed <nTopRow>, <nLeftColumn> coordinates

File Name:
F_SCRNAT.PRG

Screen Use:
Defined in calling parameters

Arguments:
<nTopRow>, <nLeftColumn>, <nBottomRow>, <nRightColumn> – Coordinates of the screen area to be changed

<nColorAttribute> – Numeric value of a new screen attribute determined from the table below

Typical Use:
To quickly change the color of a specified screen area without affecting text

Error Handling:
Nothing happens if passed coordinates or screen attribute is invalid

Discussion

SCRNATTR can change the color of a specific screen area without affecting its text. Its common use is to highlight an area temporarily.

The routine first reads the attribute byte at the passed top row and left column. It then compares it to the attribute of each screen position within the passed coordinates and changes all positions with matching bytes to the new value.

Thus, SCRNATTR changes the color of specific items without affecting others. A powerful use of it is to change the color of related items based on a data entry. For example, you can use SCRNATTR inside a VALID to temporarily change the color of related items when an invalid entry occurs. This highlights the dependent areas for the operator's review. When the VALID is satisfied, they are restored to their original color.

The example assumes that dependent areas were originally displayed with the same background, and that data and text in the specified area are displayed using different backgrounds.

Complex menu systems can use SCRNATTR to quickly change the colors of a prompt based on an operator entry without affecting MENU commands or the cursor position.

SCRNATTR uses numeric (DOS) color definitions for the attribute parameter. It defines both foreground and background colors.

Use the following table to determine attribute values. Add the one for the desired standard or high intensity color to the one for the desired background.

Display Attributes

Desired Color	Foreground Standard	Foreground High Intensity	Background
Black/Gray	0	8	0
Blue	1	9	16
Green	2	10	32
Cyan (blue-green)	3	11	48
Red	4	12	64
Magenta	5	13	80
Brown/Yellow	6	14	96
White	7	15	112

For example, the attribute value for high intensity white on brown is:

```
       High intensity white =  15
          Brown background =  96
      Attribute value = 15 + 96 = 111
```

SCRNATTR also supports blinking and high intensity background attributes. Add 128 to the value calculated above to enable either one. Enable high intensity background by using SETBLINK before calling SCRNATTR.

Coding Examples

```
* Get attribute value at screen position 10, 10
* without changing existing setting

attr_val = SCRNATTR(10,10)
* or
attr_val = SCRNATTR(10,10,10,10)


* To set screen area from row 20, column 5 to row 20, column
* 75 to blinking bright white text on red background
SCRNATTR(20, 5, 20, 75, 207)      // bright white    = 15
                                  // red background  = 64
                                  // blink/high      = 128
                                  // --------------------
                                  //          value  = 207

* To set same screen area to bright white
* text on a high intensity red background

SETBLINK(.F.)
SCRNATTR(20, 5, 20, 75, 207)

* To set same screen area to bright white
* text on a normal red background

SCRNATTR(20, 5, 20, 75, 79)       // bright white    = 15
                                  // red background  = 64
                                  // --------------------
                                  //          value  = 79
```

```
*******************************************************************
FUNCTION SCRNATTR (top, left, bottom, right, new_attr)
*******************************************************************

* Get or set screen color attribute at specified coordinates

* Copyright(c) 1991 -- James Occhiogrosso

LOCAL counter, new_screen, old_attr, old_screen, scrn_len

new_screen = ''
old_screen = SAVESCREEN(top, left, bottom, right)
old_attr   = SUBSTR(old_screen, 2, 1)
scrn_len   = LEN(old_screen)

IF VALTYPE(new_attr) = 'N'

   * If new attribute passed, restore screen using it
   FOR counter = 1 TO scrn_len STEP 2
       new_screen = new_screen + SUBSTR(old_screen, counter, 1);
                  + CHR(new_attr)
   NEXT
   RESTSCREEN(top, left, bottom, right, new_screen)

ENDIF

* Return original numeric attribute

RETURN ASC(old_attr)
```

SCRNCLR

Description:
Clears the screen stack used by the Developer's Library screen functions

Syntax:
SCRNCLR( )

Returns:
Numeric value (either zero or the size of the screen stack in bytes)

File Name:
F_SCRNS.PRG

Screen Use:
None

Arguments:
[<Expression>] – Optional expression of any type. See defaults below.

Typical Use:
To clear the screen array used by SCRNLOAD, SCRNPOP, SCRNPUSH, and SCRNWRIT

Defaults:
Returns the current size of the screen stack in bytes if passed any argument. The stack is not cleared and the argument is not used otherwise. Returns zero and clears the stack if no argument is passed.

See Also:
BACKCHAR, CLRSHADOW, SCRNATTR, SCRNLOAD, SCRNPOP, SCRNPUSH, SCRNWRIT, SHADOW

Discussion

SCRNCLR resets the Developer's Library screen stack to zero and clears the stack array. Use it before loading a new set of screens with SCRNLOAD, or to release memory when the current screen set is no longer needed.

You can also use SCRNCLR to determine the size of the screen stack. To do this, pass it an argument of any type. The value returned is the number of bytes used by all screens in the stack. The stack is not cleared in this case.

Coding Examples

```
* To reset screen stack to zero
SCRNCLR()

* To return number of bytes used by screen stack
SCRNCLR('')
```

You can produce interesting combinations with the Developer's Library screen functions. The sample program below displays boxed areas in various colors with shadows, high intensity backgrounds, and other color combinations. It saves the screens in disk files and then restores them to the screen stack. Although the example by itself is not useful, it demonstrates several library functions.

The source code for the example is in T_SCRNS.PRG on the companion disk. It writes the files screens1.arr and screens2.arr to the default directory.

```
*******************************************************************
* Test program for SCRNCLR, SCRNLOAD, SCRNPOP, SCRNPUSH, and
* SCRNWRIT - FILE T_SCRNS.PRG
*******************************************************************

* Copyright(c) 1991 -- James Occhiogrosso

#include "box.ch"
#include "dl_keys.ch"
#include "inkey.ch"

LOCAL old_color := SETCOLOR("w+/b")
CLEAR
SET CURSOR OFF
```

```
* Enable high intensity background colors
SETBLINK(.F.)
* Stuff a space in keyboard to start loop
KEYBOARD CHR(K_SPACE)
DO WHILE INKEY(0) != K_ESC

   * Fill screen with bright white on red background character
   CLEAR
   BACKCHAR(,,,,,'w+/r')
   @ 24, 33 SAY ' Press a key '

   * Display and shadow four boxed areas. High intensity
   * foregrounds and backgrounds are used differently
   * with each box to show possibilities.
   old_color = SETCOLOR('W+/R+')
   @ 1, 10, 10, 70 box B_SINGLE + CHR(2)
   SHADOW(1, 10, 10, 70, 239)
   SCRNPUSH(1, 10, 10, 70)
   SETCOLOR(old_color)
   INKEY(0)
   CLRSHADOW()

   @ 5, 20, 21, 40 box B_SINGLE + CHR(3)
   SHADOW(5, 20, 21, 40, 96)
   SCRNPUSH(5, 20, 21, 40)
   INKEY(0)
   CLRSHADOW()

   SETCOLOR('W+/BG')
   @ 3, 45, 20, 65 box B_SINGLE + CHR(4)
   SHADOW(3, 45, 20, 65, 240)
   SETCOLOR(old_color)
   SCRNPUSH(3, 45, 20, 65)
   INKEY(0)
   CLRSHADOW()

   SETCOLOR('W+/B+')
   @ 13, 10, 18, 75 box B_SINGLE + CHR(5)
   SHADOW(13, 10, 18, 75)
   SETCOLOR(old_color)
   SCRNPUSH(13, 10, 18, 75)

   INKEY(0)
   CLRSHADOW()

   * Write current screen array to a file
   SCRNWRIT('screens1')
   * And clear screen stack
   SCRNCLR()

   CLEAR SCREEN
   @ 24, 18 SAY ' Press any key to restore screens from disk'
   INKEY(0)
```

```
* Create another screen in memory without displaying it
DISPBEGIN()
SETCOLOR('N*/BG')
DISPBOX(15, 2, 17, 49, B_SINGLE + SPACE(1))
@ 16, 4 SAY 'This screen was saved without displaying it!'

* Put new screen on stack, write to screens2, and clear
stack
SCRNPUSH(15, 2, 17, 49)
SCRNWRIT('screens2')
SCRNCLR()

* Display a clear screen
SETCOLOR(old_color)
CLEAR SCREEN
DISPEND()

* Load all screens on stack with latest in position 1
SCRNLOAD('screens2')
SCRNLOAD('screens1')

* Restore screens in reverse order (except last one)
BACKCHAR(,,,,,'w+/r')
@ 24, 33 SAY ' Press a key '
WHILE SCRNPOP() != 0
    INKEY(0)
ENDDO

@ 24, 18 SAY ' Press any key to begin again or Esc to exit '

ENDDO

SET CURSOR ON
CLEAR
RETURN
```

```
*****************************************************************
FUNCTION SCRNCLR (no_clear)
*****************************************************************

* Clears screen stack or returns its size in bytes

LOCAL size := 0, cntr := 0

IF no_clear = NIL
    * Reset screen count and screen stack array and return
    counter := 0 ; screens := {}
    RETURN 0
ELSE
    * Otherwise, return size of screen stack
    FOR cntr = 1 TO counter
        size = size + LEN(screens[counter])
    NEXT
    RETURN size
ENDIF
```

SCRNLOAD

Description:
Loads screens onto the Developer's Library screen stack from a disk file

Syntax:
SCRNLOAD(<cFilename>)

Returns:
Number of screens on the stack after the new screens are loaded, or -1 if an error occurs

File Name:
F_SCRNS.PRG

Screen Use:
None

Arguments:
<cFilename> – File containing an array of screens

Typical Use:
To load screens previously saved in a disk file onto the screen stack

Defaults:
Uses an ARR extension if <cFilename> lacks one

Cautions:
Does not clear the screen stack.

Places screens onto the stack after any that are already there.

See Also:
BACKCHAR, CLRSHADOW, SCRNATTR, SCRNCLR, SCRNPOP, SCRNPUSH, SCRNWRIT, SHADOW

Discussion

SCRNLOAD restores screens previously saved in a disk file to the Developer's Library screen stack. It adds the number restored to the screen stack counter and makes the last screen loaded available for display with SCRNPOP. The disk file is created by SCRNWRIT, and different applications can use it.

Saving screens in a disk file can reduce memory requirements and improve performance. Constant text screens used by many applications can be created externally and shared.

Coding Examples

```
* Write current screen stack (array) to screens1.scr
SCRNWRIT('screens1.scr')

* Clear screen stack
SCRNCLR()

* Load new set of screens onto the stack from screens2.scr
SCRNLOAD('screens2.scr')
```

See the program T_SCRNS.PRG (listed in SCRNCLR) for more examples.

```
*****************************************************************
FUNCTION SCRNLOAD (filename)
*****************************************************************

* Loads a set of screens from a disk file

LOCAL temp_array := {}

* If extension not passed, default to ARR
filename = IF (AT('.', filename) = 0, filename + '.ARR', ;
               filename)

    IF filename != NIL .AND. FILE(filename)

    * If file exists, load temporary array
    ARRESTORE(temp_array, filename)

    * Resize screen array to include new set
    ASIZE(screens, LEN(screens) + LEN(temp_array))

    * Add temporary array to screen array
    ACOPY(temp_array, screens, 1, LEN(temp_array), counter + 1)

    * Set screen counter and return its value
    counter := LEN(screens)
    RETURN counter

ELSE
    * Return -1 as error indicator
    RETURN -1
ENDIF
```

SCRNPOP

Description:
Restores a screen and optionally removes it from the Developer's Library screen stack

Syntax:
SCRNPOP( )

Returns:
Number of screens on the screen stack afterward

File Name:
F_SCRNS.PRG

Screen Use:
Area previously pushed onto the stack

Arguments:
[nScreenNum] - optional position (in stack) of screen to restore

Typical Use:
To restore layered screens in the reverse of the order in which they were displayed

To save and restore frequently used screens

See Also:
BACKCHAR, CLRSHADOW, SCRNATTR, SCRNCLR, SCRNLOAD, SCRNPUSH, SCRNWRIT, SHADOW

Discussion

Use SCRNPOP to redisplay a screen previously pushed onto the screen stack. The screen is displayed using the coordinates and attributes with which it was saved. If no argument is passed, the screen stack counter is decremented by one, and the screen is removed from the array. Otherwise, the selected screen is restored and the stack array remains unchanged.

Coding Examples

```
* Push partial screen onto the stack (screen1)
SCRNPUSH(1, 10, 10, 70)

* Push another partial screen onto the stack (screen2)
SCRNPUSH(20, 5, 22, 75)

* Restore screen2
SCRNPOP()

* Restore screen1 and leave it on the stack
SCRNPOP(1)
```

See the program T_SCRNS.PRG, shown in SCRNCLR, for more examples.

```
*****************************************************************
FUNCTION SCRNPOP (ScreenNum)
*****************************************************************

* Restore screen from screen stack

IF counter >  0
    IF ScreenNum = NIL
        * Restore last screen saved
        SCRNREST(screens[counter])
        * Decrement screen counter and screens array
        ASIZE(screens, --counter)

    ELSEIF ScreenNum >  0 .AND. ScreenNum  <= counter
        * Restore selected screen
        SCRNREST(screens[ScreenNum])
    ENDIF
ENDIF

RETURN counter
```

SCRNPUSH

Description:
Pushes a screen onto the Developer's Library screen stack

Syntax:
SCRNPUSH([<nTopRow>], [<nLeftColumn>], [<nBottomRow>], [<nBottomColumn>])

Returns:
Number of screens on the screen stack afterward

File Name:
F_SCRNS.PRG

Screen Use:
None

Arguments:
<nTopRow>, <nLeftColumn>, <nBottomRow>, <nRightColumn> – Coordinates of the area to be placed on the screen stack

Typical Use:
To create layered screens that are removed in the reverse of the order in which they were displayed

Defaults:
Coordinates default to screen corners if not passed

Cautions:
Screens are saved with attributes. A standard 25 x 80 screen requires 4K of memory. Check free memory before saving many large areas.

See Also:
BACKCHAR, CLRSHADOW, SCRNATTR, SCRNCLR, SCRNLOAD, SCRNPOP, SCRNWRIT, SHADOW

Discussion

The screen stack is a static array. Use SCRNPUSH to save a full or partial screen on it. The specified area is saved with all attributes, and can be restored exactly.

SCRNPOP removes the latest screen placed on the stack and redisplays it. The stack is limited in size only by available memory.

You can clear the screen stack with SCRNCLR, write it to a disk file with SCRNWRIT, or load it from a file with SCRNLOAD. Thus, you can use the stack dynamically for multi-page data entry screens, layered menus, and other last in, first out (LIFO) applications.

Coding Examples

```
* Push partial screen onto the stack (screen1)
SCRNPUSH(1, 10, 10, 70)

* Push another partial screen onto the stack (screen2)
SCRNPUSH(20, 5, 22, 75)

* Restore screen2
SCRNPOP()

* Restore screen1
SCRNPOP()
```

See the program T_SCRNS.PRG, shown with SCRNCLR, for more examples.

```
STATIC counter := 0, screens := {}

**************************************************************
FUNCTION SCRNPUSH (top, left, bottom, right)
**************************************************************

* Push a screen onto screen stack

* Copyright(c) 1991 -- James Occhiogrosso

* Initialize parameters not passed
top    = IF(top = NIL, 0, top)
left   = IF(left = NIL, 0, left)
bottom = IF(bottom = NIL, MAXROW(), bottom)
right  = IF(right = NIL, MAXCOL(), right)

* Increment screen counter and screen array
counter++
ASIZE(screens, counter)

* Push screen onto stack
screens[counter] = SCRNSAVE(top, left, bottom, right)

RETURN counter
```

SCRNREST

Description:
Restores a screen to its previous position

Syntax:
SCRNREST(<cScreenVar>)

Returns:
Nothing

File Name:
F_SCRRES.PRG

Screen Use:
Defined in call

Arguments:
<cScreenVar> – Character variable created by SCRNSAVE( )

Typical Use:
To restore a screen to the position from which it was saved

Cautions:
SCRNREST can only restore a screen saved by SCRNSAVE.

See Also:
SCRNSAVE

Discussion

SCRNREST restores a screen to its position when saved by SCRNSAVE. Use it instead of RESTSCREEN when the screen is always restored to its original position. It can restore full or partial screens. The only requirement is that the screen must have been saved with SCRNSAVE.

SCRNREST uses the first four bytes of the saved screen to determine its coordinates. See SCRNSAVE for a discussion of how screens are saved.

Coding Examples

```
* Save screen area for lines 22 to 24

screen_var = SCRNSAVE(22,0,24,79)

* Overwrite lines 22 through 24 with a message

@ 22, 10 SAY 'A temporary message'
@ 23, 10 SAY 'More message'
@ 24, 10 SAY 'Press any key to continue'
INKEY(0)

* Restore original screen on lines 22 through 24

SCRNREST(screen_var)
```

```
*****************************************************************
FUNCTION SCRNREST (scrname)
*****************************************************************

* Loads screen from character variable created by SCRNSAVE

* Copyright(c) 1991 -- James Occhiogrosso

* Restore screen to original coordinates

RESTSCREEN(ASC(SUBSTR(scrname,1,1)), ASC(SUBSTR(scrname,2,1)), ;
           ASC(SUBSTR(scrname,3,1)), ASC(SUBSTR(scrname,4,1)), ;
           SUBSTR(scrname,5))

RETURN NIL
```

SCRNSAVE

Description:
Saves a screen area and its coordinates in a memory variable

Syntax:
SCRNSAVE(<nTopRow>, <nLeftColumn>, <nBottomRow>, <nRightColumn>)

Returns:
Character string

File Name:
F_SCRSAV.PRG

Screen Use:
None

Arguments:
<nTopRow>, <nLeftColumn>, <nBottomRow>, <nRightColumn> – Coordinates of the screen area to be saved

Typical Use:
To save a screen for restoring to the same position later

Cautions:
Only SCRNREST should use the returned string.

See Also:
SCRNREST

Discussion

SCRNSAVE creates a character variable prefixed with a four byte code representing screen coordinates. The code is created by converting the coordinates to ASCII characters. To restore the screen, use SCRNREST. Since SCRNSAVE saves the screen coordinates in the variable, the original area is restored.

Use SCRNSAVE and SCRNREST when you always save and restore a screen area to the same position. If the area may move, use the Clipper functions SAVESCREEN and RESTSCREEN.

Coding Examples

```
* Save screen area for lines 22 to 24

screen_var = SCRNSAVE(22,0,24,79)

* Overwrite lines 22 through 24 with a message

@ 22, 10 SAY 'A temporary message'
@ 23, 10 SAY 'More message'
@ 24, 10 SAY 'Press any key to continue'
INKEY(0)

* Restore original screen on lines 22 through 24

SCRNREST(screen_var)
```

```
*******************************************************************
FUNCTION SCRNSAVE (top, left, bottom, right)
*******************************************************************

* Save partial screen and its coordinates in character variable

* Copyright(c) 1991 - James Occhiogrosso

* Convert coordinates to a 4 character string and place it
* at the beginning of the screen variable

RETURN(CHR(top) + CHR(left) + CHR(bottom) + CHR(right) + ;
       SAVESCREEN(top, left, bottom, right))
```

SCRNWRIT

Description:
Saves the Developer's Library screen stack in a disk file

Syntax:
SCRNWRIT(<cFilename>)

Returns:
Number of screens on the screen stack, or -1 if an error occurs

File Name:
F_SCRNS.PRG

Screen Use:
None

Arguments:
<cFilename> – File in which to save stack

Typical Use:
To save a group of screens in a disk file for later use

Defaults:
Uses ARR extension if <cFilename> lacks one

Cautions:
Does not clear the screen stack. Use SCRNCLR for that purpose.

See Also:
BACKCHAR, CLRSHADOW, SCRNATTR, SCRNCLR, SCRNLOAD, SCRNPOP, SCRNPUSH, SHADOW

Discussion

SCRNWRIT saves the current screen stack in a disk file. It does not alter the stack. You can use it to create screen files for other applications, or to save screens on disk temporarily to reduce memory requirements.

Coding Examples

```
* Save current screen stack (array) in screens1.scr
SCRNWRIT('screens1.scr')

* Clear screen stack
SCRNCLR()

* Load new set of screens on stack from screens2.scr
SCRNLOAD('screens2.scr')
```

See the program T_SCRNS.PRG (listed in SCRNCLR) for more examples.

```
*****************************************************************
FUNCTION SCRNWRIT (filename)
*****************************************************************

* Saves a set of screens in a disk file

* If extension not passed, default to ARR
filename = IF (AT('.', filename) = 0, filename + '.ARR', ;
               filename)

* Save screens array
If file name != NIL .AND. ARSAVE(screens, filename)
    * Successful save
    RETURN LEN(screens)
ELSE
    * Unsuccessful save, return -1 as error indicator
    RETURN -1
ENDIF
```

SELVALUE

Description:
Permits entry of low and high data selection values and indexes before running a report. Creates a temporary database containing only records matching operator selections.

Syntax:
SELVALUE(<cSayProcName>, <cGetProcName>)

Returns:
Name of the temporary database file

File Name:
F_SELVAL.PRG

Screen Use:
Bottom five rows for messages (see discussion below)

Arguments:
<cSayProcName> – User defined procedure containing code to display a selection screen

<cGetProcName> – User defined procedure containing GETs for fields to be used for selection

Typical Use:
To select and index records from a database before producing a report

Error Handling:
Returns an empty string if an error occurs or the operator aborts the process

Cautions:
Creates temporary files for a report to use. Be sure to erase them when they are no longer needed.

Discussion

You usually call SELVALUE from a menu before producing a report. It requires the names of user defined procedures that display a screen and place data in memory variables. Together, the procedures produce a selection screen that appears three times. The database used for record selection must be open in the current area.

The routine first asks the operator to enter lower selection limits. Then it repaints the screen and asks for upper limits. The values need not fill the fields; SELVALUE uses only the number of characters entered for selection. Up to 10 fields may contain data on each screen. Finally, SELVALUE asks the operator to select index fields for the report. The operator uses the arrow keys to move to a field, and the plus key to mark it. A blinking number appears to the left of each selected field, indicating its position in the selection order. The operator may select up to five index fields.

SELVALUE then creates a temporary database containing only records with values greater than (or equal to) the lower limits, and less than (or equal to) the upper limits. The database is indexed on the marked fields. SELVALUE returns to the caller with the temporary file open, indexed, and selected.

Each call to SELVALUE creates a unique temporary database. The caller may use it immediately for a report or repeat the process on another database to obtain related selections. Thus, a program may call SELVALUE several times on different databases to create a report.

Entry/Exit Conditions

The database from which selections are made must be open in the current work area when you call SELVALUE. It does not need any indexes, and open indexes make it run slower.

You must define memory variables for all fields in the database before calling SELVALUE. Use INITVARS in this library to initialize them.

SELVALUE's caller should test its return value. If there are no errors, it returns the name of the temporary file. The file and its index are open and selected. On any error, or if the operator aborts the process, SELVALUE returns an empty string, and the original database is selected.

User Defined Procedures

To use SELVALUE, you must first create procedures to display and get the fields for operator selection. They are specific to the current database. The display procedure should contain SAY statements for the selection screen. It can also contain code to box the screen or change colors. The similar GET procedure contains GET statements for the selection fields. Neither can use READ commands. SELVALUE controls all data entry; it calls the procedures as needed to obtain operator selections.

To avoid interfering with SELVALUE's messages, the procedures must leave at least five blank lines at the bottom of the screen. For an attractive display, box the selection area.

Special Considerations and Limitations

SELVALUE uses the READ command along with the GET procedure to get the operator's selections. It is thus a "wait state" function. You can use hot keys for help or other procedures by defining them before entering it.

SELVALUE restricts lower and upper limits to ten per category. They need not use the same fields. SELVALUE bases the records copied to the temporary database on the combination of all entries in both lower and upper limit fields. Thus, you can create complex conditions. Of course, the operator may specify values that select no records. SELVALUE handles this situation by asking whether to restart the process.

Coding Examples

The program below demonstrates the use of SELVALUE on a typical database named ITFILE. The user procedures display a screen and allow selections of lower and upper limits from the file.

The structure of ITFILE.DBF and the code for the procedures ITFILE_SAY and ITFILE_GET appear below as examples only. To use SELVALUE, you must design your own procedures to match your database.

The demonstration program T_SELVAL.PRG and sample database files are on the companion disk.

```
Structure for ITFILE.DBF    Last update: 06/03/90
File Size: 137406  Bytes. -- Records in file: 545
```

Field Name	Type	Width	Decimals
ENTRY	D	8	0
FILEID	C	2	0
COMPANY	C	36	0
ADDRES1	C	36	0
ADDRES2	C	36	0
CITY	C	20	0
STATE	C	15	0
ZIP	C	10	0
LNAME	C	15	0
FNAME	C	15	0
PHONE	C	12	0
LSTSALE	D	8	0
INQDATE	D	8	0
FOLDATE	D	8	0
PRNLABL	C	1	0
LSTMAIL	D	8	0
MAILNO	N	2	0
COMMENT	M	10	0

```
***********************************************************************
* Test program for SELVALUE function - FILE T_SELVAL.PRG
***********************************************************************

* Copyright(c) 1991 -- James Occhiogrosso

* Demonstrates use of selection values before running a report
LOCAL temp_file
INITGLOBAL()
SETCOLOR(colstd)

* Open selection database
USE ITFILE NEW

* Initialize memory variables
INITVARS()

DO WHILE .T.
   CLEAR
   CENTERON(12, 'Selection value demonstration. Proceed? Y/N  ')
   @ 12, COL() - 2 say ''
   IF .NOT. OPCONFIRM()
       EXIT
   ENDIF

   * Select database to use before calling SELVALUE
   SELECT ITFILE

   * Let operator enter selection values
   temp_file = SELVALUE("itfile_say", "itfile_get")

   * Check for error condition or operator abort
   IF EMPTY(temp_file)
       CENTERON(24, 'Aborted! ' + hitanykey)
       INKEY(0)
       LOOP
   ELSE
       CENTERON(24, 'The temporary file is ' + temp_file + ;
               '  ' + hitanykey)
       INKEY(0)

       /***********************************************************
       * Code to run your report goes here. It should use the
       * temporary file and index. The file is open and
       * selected in the current area. You can use a standard
       * PRG file or a FRM report.
       ***********************************************************/

       * Close temporary file
       USE

       * Erase temporary DBF and index files
       ERASE (temp_file)
       temp_file = SUBSTR(temp_file, 1, 8) + INDEXEXT()
```

```
            ERASE (temp_file)

            * Erase temporary DBT file
            temp_file = SUBSTR(temp_file, 1, 8) + '.DBT'
            IF FILE(temp_file)
                ERASE (temp_file)
            ENDIF
        ENDIF
ENDDO

FREEVARS()
CLOSE DATABASES
RETURN

/******************************************************************
The procedures below are sample SAY and GET procedures to pass
to SELVALUE. You may include any number of fields. For best
appearance, do not write below line 18. SELVALUE writes messages
from line 20 to line 24.
******************************************************************/


******************************************************************
PROCEDURE ITFILE_SAY
******************************************************************
*
* Typical display procedure to pass to SELVALUE

@  2, 16 SAY 'MAIN INQUIRY FILE -- SELECTION VALUE SCREEN'
@  3, 16 SAY REPLICATE('■', 32)))
@  5,  1 SAY '   Entry Date: '
@  5, 55 SAY 'General Category: '
@  8,  1 SAY '  Company Name: '
@  9,  1 SAY '        Address: '
@ 10,  1 SAY '        Address: '
@ 11,  1 SAY '           City: '
@ 11, 38 SAY 'State: '
@ 11, 61 SAY 'Zip: '
@ 12,  1 SAY '  Contact Last: '
@ 12, 33 SAY 'First '
@ 12, 57 SAY 'Phone: '
@ 14,  1 SAY '  Last mailing: '
@ 14, 27 SAY 'Number of mailings:    '
@ 14, 54 SAY 'Last Contact: '
@ 15,  1 SAY '  Inquiry date: '
@ 15, 27 SAY 'Follow up date: '
@ 15, 54 SAY 'Print Label? Y/N '

@ 1, 0 TO 18, 79 DOUBLE
RETURN
```

```
****************************************************************
PROCEDURE ITFILE_GET
****************************************************************

*   Typical GET procedure to pass to SELVALUE

@  5, 15 GET mentry
@  5, 73 GET mfileid PICTURE "99"
@  8, 17 GET mcompany
@  9, 17 GET maddres1
@ 10, 17 GET maddres2
@ 11, 17 GET mcity
@ 11, 45 GET mstate PICTURE "@! "
@ 11, 66 GET mzip PICTURE "@! "
@ 12, 17 GET mlname
@ 12, 39 GET mfname
@ 12, 64 GET mphone PICTURE "999-999-9999"
@ 14, 17 GET mlstmail
@ 14, 49 GET mmailno PICTURE  '@Z 99'
@ 14, 68 GET mlstsale
@ 15, 17 GET minqdate
@ 15, 43 GET mfoldate
@ 15, 72 GET mprnlabl PICTURE "Y"

RETURN
```

```
*******************************************************************
FUNCTION SELVALUE
*******************************************************************

* Creates a temporary file based on operator selections

* Copyright(c) 1991 -- James Occhiogrosso

#include 'dl_keys.ch'
#include 'inkey.ch'
#include 'setcurs.ch'
#define MAX_NDX 5

LOCAL old_cursor := SETCURSOR(SC_NONE)
LOCAL mvar, selvar

PRIVATE aborted, counter, db_file, fieldcnt, filt_strg,          ;
        filt_word, fldnames, hilow, ndx_file, ndx_strg,          ;
        ndx_word, num_flds, num_sels, pass, temp_file, var_prefix

PARAMETERS say_proc, get_proc
PRIVATE bSayProc := {|| &say_proc() }, ;
        bGetProc := {|| &get_proc()}

* Initialize main variables
db_file = ALIAS()
aborted = .F.

* Create unique temporary DBF file
temp_file = TEMPFILE("DBF")

IF EMPTY(temp_file)
    RETURN('')
ENDIF

* Display screen
CLEAR
EVAL(bSayProc)

* Outer loop restarts only on entry error
DO WHILE .T.
    SELECT (db_file)
    * Initialize inner loop variables
    filt_strg := ndx_strg := hilow := ''
    counter := pass := 1
    num_flds := 0

    DO WHILE pass <= 2
        * Load array with field names
        fieldcnt = FCOUNT()
        fldnames := ARRAY(fieldcnt)
        AFIELDS(fldnames)

        CLRVARS()
        IF pass = 1
            hilow = ' LOW '
```

```
            filt_word = 'lofilt'
            var_prefix = 'lo_'
            filt_strg = ''
        ELSE
            hilow = ' HIGH '
            filt_word = 'hifilt'
            var_prefix = 'hi_'
        ENDIF

        * Get selection values from operator
        TONE(2000,1)
        GETSEL (fldnames)
        * Get number of selection field entries
        num_flds = counter - 1

        IF num_flds != 0
            * Fill array with selections
            num_sels := ARRAY(num_flds)
            ACOPY(fldnames, num_sels, 1, num_flds, 1)

            * Create lower and upper limit variables,
            * each containing 15 parses (4 fields)

            MAKFILT (num_sels)

            * Create lower and upper limit variables
            FOR counter = 1 TO num_flds
                mvar = 'm' + num_sels[counter]
                selvar = var_prefix + num_sels[counter]
                &selvar = &mvar
            NEXT
            filt_strg = IF(pass = 1, filt_strg + ' .AND. ', ;
                           filt_strg)
            RELEASE num_sels
        ELSE
            * No selections entered by operator
            IF pass = 2
                * If second pass, remove ' .AND. '
                filt_strg = SUBSTR(filt_strg, 1, ;
                           LEN(filt_strg) - 7)
            ENDIF
        ENDIF
        pass++
ENDDO

* Get operator's index fields
TONE(2000,1)
MAKNDX (fldnames)
IF aborted
    EXIT
ENDIF
@ 20, 0 CLEAR TO 24, 79
CENTERON(22, 'Creating report file. Please wait. ')
IF LEN(filt_strg) > 0
    COPY TO (temp_file) FOR &filt_strg
```

```
        ELSE
            COPY TO (temp_file)
        ENDIF

        USE (temp_file) NEW

        * No records in temporary file, query operator
        IF LASTREC() = 0
            ?? CHR(7)
            CENTERON(24, 'No records selected. ' + ;
                         'Do you want to try again? Y/N    ')
            ans = .T.
            @ 24, COL() -2 GET ans PICTURE 'Y'
            READ
            IF ans
                * Repaint screen if operator wants to reenter
                EVAL(bSayProc)
                @ 20, 0 CLEAR TO 24, 79

                * Close temporary file and loop to beginning
                USE
                LOOP
            ELSE
                * Otherwise, return with aborted true
                aborted = .T.
                EXIT
            ENDIF
        ELSE
            * Create index
            @ 24, 0
            CENTERON(22, 'Indexing report file. ' + ;
                         LTRIM(STR(LASTREC())) + ' records.')
            ndx_file = SUBSTR(temp_file,1,8)
            INDEX ON &ndx_strg TO (ndx_file)
        ENDIF
        EXIT
ENDDO WHILE .T.

SETCURSOR(old_cursor)

IF aborted
    * If aborted for any reason, erase all temporary files

    IF UPPER(ALIAS()) + '.DBF' = UPPER(temp_file)
        * If temporary file is still open, close it
        USE
        * And reselect original DBF file
        SELECT(db_file)
    ENDIF

    * Erase temporary files
    IF FILE(temp_file)
        ERASE(temp_file)
    ENDIF
```

Clipper Developer's Library

```
        * Erase temporary DBT file
        temp_file = SUBSTR(temp_file, 1, 11) + 'T'
        IF FILE(temp_file)
            ERASE (temp_file)
        ENDIF

        * Erase temporary index file
        temp_file = SUBSTR(temp_file, 1, 8) + INDEXEXT()
        IF FILE(temp_file)
            ERASE (temp_file)
        ENDIF

        * Set return value to null to indicate no report file
        temp_file = ''
ENDIF

RETURN(temp_file)


****************************************************************
STATIC PROCEDURE GETSEL
****************************************************************

* Get low and high selection values

LOCAL varname

PARAMETERS fldnames

CLRVARS()
DO WHILE .T.
    * Get selections for all memory variables
    ans = .F.
    DO WHILE .NOT. ans
        EVAL(bGet_Proc)
        @ 21, 5 SAY 'Enter ' + SPACE(LEN(hilow)) + ;
                    ' selection values.  Press PgDn when done.'
        SETCOLOR(colbarhi)
        @ 21, 11 SAY hilow
        SETCOLOR(colstd)
        @ 23, 5 SAY 'You may enter data in a maximum of ' + ;
                    '10 field areas'
        SETCURSOR(SC_INSERT)
        READ
        ans = .T.
        @ 21, 58 SAY '  Finished? Y/N ' GET ans PICTURE 'Y'
        READ
        @ 21, 58 CLEAR TO 23, 79
    ENDDO
    SETCURSOR(SC_NONE)
    @ 21, 0
    * Remove unused fields from array
    counter = 1
    DO WHILE TYPE("fldnames[counter]") # 'U'
        varname = 'm' + fldnames[counter]
```

```
            IF EMPTY(&varname)
                ADEL(fldnames,counter)
                IF counter = LEN(fldnames)
                    EXIT
                ENDIF
                LOOP
            ENDIF
            counter++
        ENDDO

        * Loop if operator entered too many selection fields.
        * Maximum is 10 high, 10 low.

        IF counter-1 > 10
            ?? CHR(7)
            CENTERON(24,'Too many selection fields.  Maximum is 10.')
            LOOP
        ELSE
            EXIT
        ENDIF

ENDDO WHILE .T.
@ 24, 0

RETURN


******************************************************************
STATIC PROCEDURE MAKNDX
******************************************************************

*
* Create an index expression

* Clear screen and redisplay memory variables
CLRVARS()
EVAL(bGetProc)

@ 20, 0 CLEAR TO 24, 79

@ 20, 7 SAY 'Position cursor on beginning of field(s) you '  + ;
            'want to index on.'
@ 21, 7 SAY 'Press plus key to select.  Up to 5 fields can ' + ;
            'be selected in '
@ 22, 7 SAY 'any order. Selected order will display.  Press ' + ;
            'PgDn when done.'
ans = .F.
DO WHILE .NOT. ans
    counter = 0
    ndx_strg = ''
    ndx_word = ''

    * Set the "+" key to call FINDVAR procedure
    SET KEY K_PLUS TO FINDVAR
```

```
        EVAL(bGetProc)
        SETCURSOR(SC_INSERT)
        READ
        SET KEY K_PLUS TO
        ans = .T.
        TONE(2000,1)
        CENTERON(24, 'To abort, press Esc. -- Otherwise, ' + ;
                    'are index selections correct? Y/N     ')
        @ 24, col()-4 GET ans PICTURE 'Y'
        READ
        @ 24, 0
        SETCURSOR(SC_NONE)
        IF ans .AND. .NOT. EMPTY(ndx_strg) .AND. LASTKEY() != K_ESC
            EXIT
        ELSEIF LASTKEY() = K_ESC
            aborted = .T.
            EXIT
        ELSEIF EMPTY(ndx_strg)
            ?? CHR(7)
            CENTERON(24, 'At least one index must be selected. ' + ;
                        'Please reenter. ')
            ans = .F.
        ENDIF
        EVAL(bSayProc)
ENDDO

RETURN


******************************************************************
STATIC PROCEDURE MAKFILT
******************************************************************

* Create filter statement from selected fields

LOCAL filt_cnt := 1, filt_var := ''

PARAMETERS num_sels

counter := 1
DO WHILE (counter <= num_flds .OR. counter = 1)
    filt_var = filt_word + LTRIM(STR(filt_cnt))
    &filt_var = ''
    FOR counter = counter TO counter + 3
        IF TYPE('num_sels[counter]') = 'C' .AND. pass = 1
            &filt_var = &filt_var + num_sels[counter] + ' >= ' +;
                        var_prefix + num_sels[counter]
        ELSEIF TYPE('num_sels[counter]') = 'C' .AND. pass = 2
            &filt_var = &filt_var + num_sels[counter] + ' <= ' +;
                        var_prefix + num_sels[counter]
        ENDIF
        IF (counter % 4) != 0 .AND. counter < num_flds
            &filt_var = &filt_var + ' .AND. '
        ELSE
            filt_cnt++
```

```
            counter++
            EXIT
        ENDIF
    NEXT
ENDDO

* Create filter string
counter = 1
filt_cnt--
DO WHILE counter <= filt_cnt
    filt_var = filt_word + LTRIM(STR(counter))
    filt_strg = filt_strg + &filt_var
    IF counter # filt_cnt
        filt_strg = filt_strg + ' .AND. '
    ENDIF
    counter++
ENDDO
RETURN
*

*******************************************************************
STATIC PROCEDURE FINDVAR
*******************************************************************

/* Mark field for indexing

Loads the current GET variable into ndxfld, and displays a
number next to the selected GET field (in highlighted color).
The index expression is stored in ndx_word and then added to
ndx_strg in the caller to form an index expression.

To keep index sizes manageable, character fields are indexed
on the first 10 characters only. The number of allowed indexes
is limited to 5 to keep run times reasonable. If more are need-
ed, change the MAX_NDX constant defined at the top of the file.

*/

LOCAL fldlen := 0, fldlens := {}, ndxfld, subscrp
LOCAL old_color := SETCOLOR(colblink)

PARAMETERS callproc, linenum, inputvar

* Clear hot key
SET KEY K_PLUS TO
ndxfld = inputvar

* Determine data type for index expression

IF TYPE(ndxfld) = 'D'
    ndx_word = 'DTOS(' + SUBSTR(ndxfld,2) + ')'
    fldlen = LEN(DTOC(&ndxfld)) + 1

ELSEIF TYPE(ndxfld) = 'C'
    * Index only on first 10 characters
```

Clipper Developer's Library   465

```
        IF LEN(&ndxfld) > 10
            ndx_word = 'SUBSTR(' + SUBSTR(ndxfld,2) + ', 1, 10)'
        ELSE
            ndx_word = SUBSTR(ndxfld,2)
        ENDIF
        fldlen = LEN(&ndxfld) + 1

    ELSEIF TYPE(ndxfld) = 'N'
        ndx_word = 'STR(' + SUBSTR(ndxfld,2) + ')'
        fldnames := ARRAY(fieldcnt)
        fldlens  := ARRAY(fieldcnt)
        AFIELDS(fldnames, '', fldlens)
        subscrp = ASCAN(fldnames, SUBSTR(ndxfld,2))
        fldlen = fldlens[subscrp] + 1

    ELSE
        ndx_word = ''
        fldlen = 0

    ENDIF

    counter++
    IF counter <= MAX_NDX
        * Display index number and force jump to next field
        SWAPCOLOR(ROW(), COL() - 1, LTRIM(STR(counter)))
        KEYBOARD CHR(13)
    ENDIF

    IF counter = 1
        ndx_strg = ndx_word
    ELSEIF counter <= MAX_NDX
        ndx_strg = ndx_strg + ' + ' + ndx_word
    ELSE
        * Stuff PgDn in keyboard to force exit from read
        KEYBOARD CHR(3)
    ENDIF

    SETCOLOR(old_color)
    SET KEY K_PLUS TO FINDVAR
    RETURN
```

SETINT24

Description:
Sets or resets the Developer's Library critical interrupt handler (INT24)

Syntax:
SETINT24([<lOnOff>])

Returns:
Logical value for current setting

File Name:
INT24.ASM

Screen Use:
None

Arguments:
<lOnOff> – Logical value for desired setting. True activates the INT24 handler, false deactivates it.

Typical Use:
To trap disk errors when using low-level file functions (see discussion below)

Cautions:
Redirects the DOS internal critical error handler called by interrupt 24 to the internal Developer's Library function INT24. Loading TSR utilities with the Clipper RUN command while SETINT24 is active could cause a system crash.

SETINT24 directly modifies internal DOS interrupt vectors. To change the source code, you should have a thorough understanding of DOS interrupt handlers and assembly language.

See Also:
DISKTEST, GETINT24

Discussion

Critical errors are ones that usually produce the familiar DOS "Abort, Retry, Ignore, Fail" message. SETINT24 and its companion GETINT24 let you create more precise recovery procedures from critical DOS errors.

When SETINT24 is active and a critical error occurs, DOS calls the Developer's Library internal INT24 function (listed here). INT24 determines and stores the error code and returns control to your Clipper program. You can then retrieve the error code with GETINT24. (See the table of error codes in the description of GETINT24). The internal INT24 function replaces the DOS critical error handler and is not directly accessible to Clipper.

Many Clipper functions and third-party library functions, including several in the Developer's Library, return -1 on failed file and disk functions. Thus, you cannot determine what type of error occurred. For example, the Clipper FCREATE function returns the same value (-1) if the disk is not ready, unformatted, or write protected. Later testing of FERROR( ) and DOSERROR( ) does not always provide enough information to identify the error.

If you activate SETINT24 before using FCREATE (or FOPEN), GETINT24 returns a different error code for each condition.

Coding Examples

The example below tries to create a file on the floppy disk in drive A and displays a message if the attempt fails. For other examples, see T_DISKS.PRG on the companion disk and the DISKTEST function in this library. Source code for T_DISKS.PRG appears with DISKTEST.

```
* Save current INT24 status and turn INT24 handler on
old_int24 = SETINT24(.T.)
* Try to create a file on disk in drive A
IF FCREATE("A:new_file.tmp", 0) < 0
```

```
      * Get cause of error
      crit_error = GETINT24()
      IF crit_error != 0
         DO CASE
            CASE crit_error = 1
                 CENTERON(24, 'Disk is write protected')
            CASE crit_error = 3
                 CENTERON(24, 'Drive A is not ready')
            CASE crit_error = 13
                 CENTERON(24, 'Disk in drive A is not formatted')
         ENDCASE
      ENDIF
ENDIF

* Restore original INT24 state
SETINT24(old_int24)
```

```
;------------------------------------------------------------
; FILENAME:  INT24.ASM  -- Critical error (interrupt 24) handler
;
; FUNCTIONS:
;
; INT24    ---- Internal function. Called by DOS on a critical error
; GETINT24 - Returns critical error number to Clipper
; SETINT24 - Activates critical error (interrupt 24) handler
;------------------------------------------------------------
; Copyright(c)  1991 -- James Occhiogrosso
;
        INCLUDE   DEVELOP.MAC       ; Include Developer's Library macro file

                                    ; Declare function names
        PUBLIC    SETINT24          ; Sets DOS INT24 vector to our function
        PUBLIC    GETINT24          ; Returns INT24 critical error code
        PUBLIC    INT24             ; Our internal INT24 handler

                                    ; Declare Clipper externals
        EXTRN     __RET:FAR         ; Return nothing to Clipper
        EXTRN     __RETNI:FAR       ; Return numeric integer to Clipper
        EXTRN     __RETL:FAR        ; Return logical to Clipper
        EXTRN     __PARINFO:FAR     ; Get Clipper parameter information
        EXTRN     __PARL:FAR        ; Get Clipper logical

        CODESEG   SEGMENT 'CODE'
                  ASSUME CS:CODESEG

;------------------------------------------------------------
SETINT24 PROC    FAR                ; Toggle setting of INT24 handler
;------------------------------------------------------------
        JMP       BEGIN             ; Jump around data storage area

OLD_INT24   DD   ?                  ; Storage for DOS INT24 address
RET_VALUE   DB   0                  ; SETINT24 return value
INT24_STAT  DB   0                  ; Current INT24 handler status
INT24_ERR   DB   0                  ; GETINT24 error number

BEGIN:
        PUSH_REGS                   ; Save Clipper registers

        P_TYPE 1                    ; Get parameter type to AX
        CMP AX, 4                   ; Was a logical value passed?
        MOV AH, 0                   ; No! Set up for current
        MOV AL, CS:INT24_STAT       ;   status byte to be
        JNE SET_RETURN              ;   returned to Clipper

        GET_PARL 1                  ; Yes! Put logical value in AX
        MOV CX, AX                  ; Save passed parameter in CX
        MOV AH, 0
        MOV AL, CS:INT24_STAT       ; Get current handler status
        CMP AX, CX                  ; Is it same as incoming?
        JNE CONTINUE                ; No! Continue

SET_RETURN:
```

Clipper Developer's Library

```
                MOV  CS:RET_VALUE, AL   ; Yes! Set up return value
                JMP  EXIT_SETINT24      ;   and return it to Clipper
CONTINUE:
                PUSH CS                 ; Move code segment address
                POP  DS                 ;   into data segment register
                ASSUME DS:NOTHING       ;   and tell assembler
                MOV  CS:RET_VALUE, AL   ; Set return to current status
                CMP  CX, 1              ; Are we installing interrupt?
                JE   INSTALL_INT24      ; Yes! Set DOS vector address

REMOVE_INT24:                           ; No! Default to removing it
                CMP  CS:INT24_STAT, 0   ; Is it already removed?
                JE   EXIT_SETINT24      ; Yes! Return to Clipper

                MOV  CS:INT24_STAT, 0   ; No! Change handler status byte
                MOV  CS:INT24_ERR, 0    ; Clear error number
                MOV  DI, OFFSET CS:OLD_INT24  ; Get data address for DOS
                                        ; INT24 handler
                MOV  DX, [DI]           ; Move offset to DX
                MOV  DS, [DI+2]         ; Move segment to DS
                JMP  SET_VECTOR         ; Set vector to original value

INSTALL_INT24:
                CMP  CS:INT24_STAT, 1   ; Is it already installed?
                JE   EXIT_SETINT24      ; Yes! Return to Clipper

                MOV  CS:INT24_STAT, 1   ; No! Set handler status byte
                MOV  CS:RET_VALUE, 0    ; Reset return value to zero
                MOV  CS:INT24_ERR, 0    ; Clear error number
                MOV  AL, 24h            ; DOS critical error handler
                MOV  AH, 35h            ; DOS request for vector address
                INT  21h

                MOV  DI, OFFSET CS:OLD_INT24 ; Get address for old vector
                MOV  [DI], BX           ; Save offset
                MOV  [DI+2], ES         ; Save segment

                MOV  DX, OFFSET CS:INT24  ; Get address of our handler
SET_VECTOR:
                MOV  AL, 24h            ; DOS critical error handler
                MOV  AH, 25h            ; DOS request to set vector
                INT  21h

EXIT_SETINT24:
                SUB  AH, AH             ; Put Clipper return value
                MOV  AL, CS:RET_VALUE   ;   in AX
                POP_REGS                ; Restore all registers
                RET_LOGIC               ; Return logic value to Clipper

SETINT24   ENDP                         ; End SETINT24 procedure
```

```
;-----------------------------------------------------------------
GETINT24 PROC   FAR             ; Return INT24 error number to Clipper
;-----------------------------------------------------------------

        SUB AX, AX              ; Clear AX register
        MOV AL, CS:INT24_ERR    ; Get pending error code
        MOV CS:INT24_ERR, 0     ; Reset code to zero
        RET_INT                 ; Return error code to Clipper

GETINT24 ENDP                   ; End Procedure

;-----------------------------------------------------------------
INT24   PROC    FAR             ; Critical error (INT24) handler
;-----------------------------------------------------------------

; This is the actual interrupt handler procedure. It replaces the
; normal DOS INT 24 handler, and stores the critical error in its
; code segment for return to Clipper.

        CMP AH, 128             ; Disk status byte - if < 128,
        JB  SAVE_ERROR          ; error was disk I/O, save it

        JMP DWORD PTR CS:[OLD_INT24] ; Otherwise, let DOS handle
        JMP EXIT_INT24          ; it, and then return.

SAVE_ERROR:
        MOV AX, DI              ; Put error number in AX
        INC AL                  ; Increment for Clipper return
        MOV CS:INT24_ERR, AL    ;   and save it
        MOV AX, 3               ; Tell DOS to return
                                ;   using Int 23h
EXIT_INT24:
        IRET                    ; Return from INT24 handler

INT24   ENDP                    ; End interrupt handler

CODESEG ENDS                    ; End of code segment
        END                     ; End of assembly
```

SHADOW

Description:
Displays a shadow below and to the right of a specified screen area

Syntax:
SHADOW(<nTopRow>, <nLeftColumn>, <nBottomRow>, <nBottomColumn>, [<nColorAttribute>])

Returns:
Nothing

File Name:
F_SHADOW.PRG

Screen Use:
Defined in calling parameters

Arguments:
<nTopRow>, <nLeftColumn>, <nBottomRow>, <nRightColumn> – Screen coordinates of the area to be shadowed

<nColorAttribute> – Numeric value of shadow attribute. Determine it from the table provided with SCRNATTR.

Default
Shadows appear on a black background if no color attribute is passed.

Typical Use:
To enhance menu and other boxes with a simulated shadow

Error Handling:
If the passed coordinates reach the maximum screen row or within one of the maximum column, no shadow is displayed.

See Also:
BACKCHAR, CLRSHADOW, SCRNATTR, SCRNCLR, SCRNLOAD, SCRNPOP, SCRNPUSH, SCRNWRIT

Discussion

Many software vendors use combinations of colors and shadowed boxes to enhance screen presentations. SHADOW brings this capability to the Developer's Library by displaying a simulated shadow one line below and two columns to the right of any screen area (usually boxed).

SHADOW maintains an internal screen stack (and counter) so multiple screens can be shadowed without calculating and saving each area. It uses CLRSHADOW to automatically restore the original screen for each shadowed area in turn.

By using SETBLINK and BACKCHAR with SHADOW, you can obtain interesting combinations. A sample program using SHADOW and other Developer's Library screen functions is in the program file T_SCRNS.PRG on the disk. Its source code appears with SCRNCLR.

Coding Examples

```
* Save current screen
old_screen = SCRNSAVE(5, 20, 21, 40)

* Draw single line box and fill it with diamond character
@ 5, 20, 21, 40 box B_SINGLE + CHR(4)

* Display shadow on box
SHADOW(5, 20, 21, 40, 96)
*
*    .... Do something inside box
*
INKEY(0)

* Clear shadow area and restore boxed area
CLRSHADOW()
RESTSCRN(5, 20, 21, 40, old_screen)
```

```
STATIC counter := 0, screens := { {''}, {''} }

*******************************************************************
FUNCTION SHADOW (top, left, bottom, right, attribute)
*******************************************************************

* Display a shadow (in any color) below and right of boxed area

* Copyright(c) 1991 -- James Occhiogrosso

LOCAL pointer := 0, shad_cnt := 0, shad_len := 0, shadow := ''

* Increment shadow counter, shadow coordinates, and stack array
counter++ ; bottom++ ; right++
ASIZE(screens[1], counter) ; ASIZE(screens[2], counter)

* Use attribute if passed, otherwise default is black background
attribute = IF(VALTYPE(attribute) == 'N', attribute, 7)

* Push shadow area on screen stack for restoring
screens[1, counter] = SCRNSAVE(bottom, left+1, bottom, right+1)
screens[2, counter] = SCRNSAVE(top+1, right, bottom, right+1)

* Display shadow only if coordinates are on screen
IF bottom <= MAXROW() .AND. right <= MAXCOL() - 1

    FOR shad_cnt = 1 TO 2

        * Create vertical and horizontal shadows
        shad_len = LEN(screens[shad_cnt, counter])
        shadow = screens[shad_cnt, counter]

        * Stuff new attribute in shadow variable
        FOR pointer = 6 TO shad_len STEP 2
           shadow = STUFF(shadow, pointer, 1, CHR(attribute))
        NEXT
        * Display shadow screen
        SCRNREST(shadow)
    NEXT
ENDIF

RETURN NIL
```

SIGNON

Description:
Displays an imploding/exploding application sign-on screen

Syntax:
SIGNON([<cAppName1>], [<cAppName2>], [<cDevName1>], [<cDevName2>], [<lCycleScreen>])

Returns:
Nothing

File Name:
F_SIGNON.PRG

Screen Use:
Entire screen

Arguments:
<cAppName1>, <cAppName2> – Strings containing a two-line application name. Each is limited to a maximum of 50 characters.

<cDevName1>, <cDevName2> – Strings containing the developer's name. Each is limited to 44 characters.

<lCycleScreen> – Logical value. If true, the sign-on screen is cycled on and off approximately once every two seconds, or until a key is pressed. If false, the sign-on screen displays and SIGNON terminates.

Typical Use:
To display an introductory and copyright screen for an application

Defaults:
<lCycleScreen> defaults to false if not defined.

Cautions:
To reduce the likelihood of burning the screen on monochrome monitors, pass <lCycleScreen> true if the monitor type is unknown.

Discussion

SIGNON displays a boxed message area in the center of the screen with two lines for the application's title and developer's name. A fixed copyright notice appears just below the name. All arguments are optional. To omit some, pass commas in their places.

After displaying the message, SIGNON draws double-line boxes from the outer screen edge inward. It then pauses, changes the color (if a color monitor is in use), and draws more overlapping boxes from the center outward.

If <lCycleScreen> is true, SIGNON alternates its display with a clear screen until the user presses a key. If <lCycleScreen> is false, SIGNON returns to the caller after a two second pause to give the user time to read the screen. It does not clear the screen on return.

SIGNON is usually called on entry to an application, just before the main menu is displayed.

Coding Examples

```
* Initialize global variables
INITGLOBAL()
SETCOLOR(colstd)

* Display sign-on screen until operator presses a key
SIGNON "S A M S O N ' S    B A R B E R    S H O P S",    ;
       "Accounts Receivable and Order Tracking",          ;
       "A Clipper Developer's Library" ,                  ;
       "by James Occhiogrosso", .T. )

* Wait two seconds
PAUSE(2)

* Display application main menu
MAINMENU()
```

```
*******************************************************************
FUNCTION SIGNON(app_name1, app_name2, dev_name1, dev_name2, hold)
*******************************************************************

* Draws imploding/exploding application "sign-on" screen

* Copyright(c) 1991 -- James Occhiogrosso

#include "setcurs.ch"
MEMVAR colbarlo, colbarhi, colstd, hitanykey
LOCAL top := 1, left := 1, bottom := 22, right := 78,  ;
      keypress := 0, old_color := SETCOLOR(colstd),  ;
      old_cursor := SETCURSOR(SC_NONE)

IF PCOUNT() < 4
    RETURN NIL
ENDIF

* Set hold screen flag to false if undefined
hold = IF(hold == NIL, .F., hold)

CLEAR SCREEN

DO WHILE keypress = 0

    SETCOLOR(colbarlo)

    * Display application name
    @ 8, 15 SAY PADC(IF(app_name1 != NIL, app_name1, ''), 50)
    @ 9, 15 SAY PADC(IF(app_name2 != NIL, app_name2, ''), 50)

    SETCOLOR(colstd)
    * Display innermost boxed area
    @ 10, 17 TO 15, 62

    * Display developer's name
    @ 11, 18 SAY PADC(IF(dev_name1 != NIL, dev_name1, ''), 44)
    @ 12, 18 SAY PADC(IF(dev_name2 != NIL, dev_name2, ''), 44)

    * Display copyright notice
    @ 13, 17 SAY '├──────────────────────────────────┤'
    @ 14, 20 SAY 'Copyright (c) 1991 -- All Rights Reserved'

    * Change colors
    SETCOLOR(colbarlo)

    * Draw double-line boxes inward
    DO WHILE top <  8
       @ top,left TO bottom,right DOUBLE
       top++
       bottom--
       left = left + 2
       right = right - 2
    ENDDO
```

```
* Wait for a second
PAUSE(1)

* Reset row and column
top    = 7
left   = 14
bottom = 16
right  = 65

* Draw double-line boxes outward, overlaying original
* lines at top and bottom of screen

DO WHILE top > 0 .AND. right <= 79
   @ top, left TO bottom, right DOUBLE
   SETCOLOR(colbarhi)
   top--
   bottom++
   left = left - 2
   right = right + 2
ENDDO

* Check "hold" flag. If true, clear screen and redisplay
* signon message every 2 seconds or until a key is pressed

IF hold
   * Put message on screen, and wait for a key
   SETCOLOR(colstd)
   CENTERON(24, hitanykey)
   keypress = INKEY(2)

   IF keypress = 0
      * Wait 2 seconds before looping
      CLEAR SCREEN
      PAUSE(2)
   ENDIF

ELSE
   * No hold, so simulate key closure to end display loop
   keypress = 1
   PAUSE(2)
ENDIF

ENDDO

* Restore entry conditions and return

SETCOLOR(old_color)
SETCURSOR(old_cursor)
RETURN NIL
```

STATENAME

Description:
Determines a state name from a standard two-letter abbreviation

Syntax:
STATENAME(<cStateCode>)

Returns:
Character string

File Name:
F_STATE.PRG

Screen Use:
None

Arguments:
<cStateCode> – String containing a standard two-letter state abbreviation

Typical Use:
To print or display full state names instead of abbreviations

Global File:
ZIPS.DBF – Database containing state abbreviations, state names, and Zip Code ranges (see CHKZIP for its structure and contents)

Defaults:
Returns the original string if the state name is not located or the database is missing

See Also:
CHKSTATE, CHKZIP

Discussion

STATENAME searches the ZIPS.DBF file for a matching two-letter standard state abbreviation. It returns the name of the corresponding state. Use it to display or print unabbreviated state names.

If the ZIPS database is not open when STATENAME is called, it is opened in the next available area. ZIPS is not closed on exit.

Coding Examples

```
* To display full state name instead of its abbreviation
@ 10, 10 SAY STATENAME(StateAbbrev)

* To place string "District of Columbia" in state_name
state_name = STATENAME('DC')
```

```
****************************************************************
FUNCTION STATENAME (statecode)
****************************************************************

* Returns full state name from standard 2 character state code

* Copyright(c) 1991 -- James Occhiogrosso

LOCAL old_area := SELECT()

* If passed state code exceeds 2 characters, exit
IF LEN(TRIM(statecode)) > 2
   RETURN statecode
ENDIF

* Make sure Zip Code database is available

IF EMPTY(SELECT('zips'))
   IF FILE('zips.dbf')
      * If zips file exists, open it
      USE zips NEW
   ELSE
      * Otherwise, exit
      RETURN statecode
   ENDIF
ENDIF
SELECT zips

* Check Zip Code database for state code

LOCATE FOR UPPER(TRIM(statecode)) $ zips->state
IF FOUND()
   SELECT(old_area)
   RETURN zips->statename
ELSE
   SELECT(old_area)
   RETURN statecode
ENDIF
```

STREXPAND

Description:
Expands a string with spaces

Syntax:
STREXPAND(<cString>)

Returns:
Character string

File Name:
F_STREXP.PRG

Screen Use:
None

Arguments:
<cString> – String to expand

Typical Use:
To enhance the display or printing of headings and similar information

Cautions:
Doubles the length of the passed string. Remember this when displaying the result.

Discussion

STREXPAND places a space after each letter of the passed string except the last one. It enhances the appearance of displayed or printed headings.

Coding Examples

```
* Display an expanded report title centered on a line
CENTERON(10, STREXPAND('UNPAID INVOICES'))
```

```
****************************************************************
FUNCTION STREXPAND (string)
****************************************************************

* Expands a string with a space after each character

* Copyright(c) 1991 -- James Occhiogrosso

LOCAL string_len := LEN(string), counter := 0, ret_string := ''

* Expand string with spaces
FOR counter = 1 TO string_len
   ret_string = ret_string + SUBSTR(string,counter,1) + ' '
NEXT

* Return string with trailing space trimmed
RETURN TRIM(ret_string)
```

SWAPCOLOR

Description:
Reverses standard and enhanced colors in a color string

Syntax:
SWAPCOLOR ([<nRow>], [<nColumn>], [<expData>], [<expPicture>])

Returns:
Character string

File Name:
F_SWAPCO.PRG

Screen Use:
Optionally defined in call

Arguments:
[<nRow>], [<nColumn>] – Row and column coordinates for displaying data

[<expData>] – Data of any type for display

[<expPicture>] – Picture expression for formatting data

Typical Uses:
To quickly display a data item in enhanced color, or to temporarily reverse standard and enhanced color settings

Discussion

SWAPCOLOR returns a color definition string with the standard SAY and GET colors reversed. The border, background, and unselected color part of the string are unaffected.

SWAPCOLOR does not change the current color setting. All arguments are optional.

Use SWAPCOLOR to quickly reverse the standard and enhanced color settings by simply using its return value as the argument for SETCOLOR. You can also use it to display a single item in the enhanced color without affecting the current color setting.

Coding Examples

```
* Return a string with standard and enhanced colors reversed
reverse_col = SWAPCOLOR()

* Return a reversed color string and position cursor
reverse_col = SWAPCOLOR(anyrow, anycol)

* Disregard returned value and display data
* in current enhanced (GET) color
reverse_col = SWAPCOLOR(anyrow, anycol, anydata)

* Display data in enhanced color with a PICTURE clause
reverse_col = SWAPCOLOR(anyrow, anycol, anydata, anypicture)

* Reverse standard and enhanced colors
old_color = SETCOLOR(SWAPCOLOR())
    .
    . Display items in reversed color
    . and restore original color
    .
SETCOLOR(old_color)
```

```
***************************************************************
FUNCTION SWAPCOLOR (swaprow, swapcol, swapdata, swappict)
***************************************************************

* Reverses standard and enhanced colors in a color string

* Copyright(c) 1991 -- James Occhiogrosso

LOCAL comma1, comma2, new_color, old_color

* Save current color
old_color = SETCOLOR()

* Locate comma positions for SAY/GET colors
comma1 = AT(',', old_color)
comma2 = comma1 + AT(',', SUBSTR(old_color, comma1+1))
new_color = (SUBSTR(old_color, comma1+1, comma2-comma1) + ;
             SUBSTR(old_color, 1, comma1) + SUBSTR(old_color, ;
             comma2+1))

IF PCOUNT() >= 2
    * Set reversed colors and display data
    SETCOLOR(new_color)

    IF PCOUNT() = 4
        * Format passed, use it to display data
        @ swaprow, swapcol SAY swapdata PICTURE swappict

    ELSEIF PCOUNT() = 2
        * No data passed, position cursor and return
        SETPOS(swaprow, swapcol)

    ELSE
        * Display data without formatting
        @ swaprow, swapcol SAY swapdata

    ENDIF

    * Restore original color setting
    SETCOLOR(old_color)
ENDIF

* Return reversed color string
RETURN new_color
```

SYSHELP

Description:
Displays help and other messages from a database

Syntax:
SYSHELP( )

Returns:
Nothing

File Name:
F_SYSHLP.PRG

Screen Use:
Defines help message by coordinates in the database. Uses bottom line for messages.

Arguments:
None

Typical Use:
To display messages when a hot key is pressed or when called directly by an application

Defaults:
If the global variables *helpfile* and *helpcode* are undefined, they default to *syshelp* and an empty string, respectively.

Error Handling:
An error message appears on the bottom screen line if SYSHELP cannot locate the help database.

Cautions:
Generates a run time error if the condition field in the help database is used and it does not evaluate to a logical value.

Help codes are case sensitive.

If SYSHELP is called only by a hot key, the application must declare it EXTERNAL.

Global Variables:

helpfile – Database containing help messages

helpcode – Ten character code for finding messages

Discussion

Use SYSHELP to display help or other messages. You can call it with a hot key or directly from an application. When called from a hot key, SYSHELP is passed the caller's name, a line number, and the name of the pending GET variable (if any). They are used only if no help message is available. In that case, they appear on the screen along with other design information if the developer presses the caret key (^).

Several Developer's Library functions simulate wait states. They allow you to call hot key functions from them. AEDBAR is one such function. See it and its associated test program T_AEDBAR.PRG for more information.

The structure of the database used by SYSHELP appears below. You should index it on the hlpcode field to an index file with the same name as the database. The index extension defaults to NTX or NDX, depending on whether the application was linked with NDX.OBJ supplied with Clipper.

SYSHELP Database Structure

Field	Type	Length	Description and Use
HLPCODE	C	10	Help code (index) – used to locate specific message groupings
HLPCOND	C	250	Help condition – evaluated to locate specific messages
HLPTOP	N	2	Top row
HLPLEFT	N	2	Left column — Help message
HLPBOTT	N	2	Bottom row — screen coordinates
HLPRGT	N	2	Right column
HLPBOX	L	1	If true, the help message is displayed in a box
HLPBX	C	1	Type of box: S = single, D = double
HLPCLR	L	1	If true, clears screen before displaying the help message
HLPCOLR	C	10	Help message color
HLPMSG	M	10	Displayable help message

Put the name of the database SYSHELP uses in the global variable helpfile. For example, if your application help database is ARHELP.DBF, put the line

```
helpfile = "ARHELP"
```

at the top of your application.

SYSHELP first tests for the existence of the database specified in helpfile and its associated memo and index files. If the file is not open, it opens it (and also closes it before exiting). If it finds the file open, it leaves it open. For maximum response speed, open the help database before calling SYSHELP. If the specified help file is missing, an error message appears and SYSHELP terminates. When opening the help database, use the alias DL_SYSHELP as in

```
USE yourhelp ALIAS DL_SYSHELP NEW
```

Some Developer's Library functions call SYSHELP through the variable apphelp. To use SYSHELP to display messages with them, put the line

```
apphelp = "SYSHELP"
```

at the beginning of your application. You can also replace SYSHELP with your own function by placing its name in apphelp.

SYSHELP searches the help database for the help code set by your application. When it locates a record containing the code, it checks its condition field. If the field is empty, the message is displayed. Otherwise, SYSHELP assumes other records have the same help code. It then checks each one's condition field until one evaluates true and its message is displayed. If no records evaluate true, a message appears on the bottom screen line. Thus, SYSHELP uses the help code field to quickly locate a group of messages, and the condition field to select a specific record for display. Because the database is indexed on the help code, SYSHELP can find messages quickly, even in a large file. It uses the coordinate, color, and boxing information in the record to display the message.

You can use either the help code or condition field alone to locate messages. If the code is empty, SYSHELP checks the condition field of each record until one evaluates true. However, with a large database, this can be slow. In many cases, simply specifying different help codes is the fastest approach. SYSHELP is flexible, so use it in the way that works best for you.

The hlpcolr field is used to set the message color. You can put the name of a variable in it, or specify the color as a literal string. If hlpcolr is empty, the value of the global variable colhelp1 is used.

For SYSHELP to function correctly, records with the same help code should have a condition entry. The condition field MUST always evaluate to a logical value or a run time error occurs. To force SYSHELP to skip a record, set the condition field to false.

All messages from SYSHELP (except the actual help) appear on the bottom screen line. When creating the help database, you can add a system record with maximum row and column coordinates in the fields hlpbott and hlprgt, respectively. If no such record exists, the maximum coordinates default to the values returned by MAXROW and MAXCOL. If a system record is used, its hlpcode field must contain the code "~~HG_SYS~~", excluding quotation marks. Values in other fields in this record are ignored. SYSHELP uses the information to center messages.

Coding Examples

You normally call SYSHELP from function key F1 to display help messages. To activate F1 as a hot key for it and use the database ARHELP, place the following lines near the top of your application.

```
#include "inkey.ch"
PUBLIC helpfile := "ARHELP"
PUBLIC helpcode := ""
SET KEY K_F1 TO SYSHELP
```

As the application executes, it must load the helpcode variable with codes specifying the desired help for a particular area. SYSHELP is called whenever the user presses F1. If it finds a record matching the code or condition, it displays the corresponding message.

Alternately, you can call SYSHELP directly to display messages from the help database. To do this, place a unique help code in the database, and load the variable helpcode with a matching value. The message can be anything from one line to a full-screen display.

The example below displays the memo field for records containing the helpcode values SCREEN_1 and SCREEN_2. The help database is ARSYSTEM.

```
helpfile = 'arsystem'      // Message database name
helpcode = 'screen_1'      // Code for desired record
SYSHELP()                  // Display screen_1 message
     .
     . After some processing
     .
helpcode = 'screen_2'      // Code for desired record
SYSHELP()                  // Display screen_2 message
```

```
MEMVAR colhelp, colwindow, helpcode, helpfile, hitanykey

*******************************************************************
FUNCTION SYSHELP (callproc, linenum, inputvar, keypress)
*******************************************************************
*
* Displays help or other messages from a database
* Copyright(c) 1991 -- James Occhiogrosso - Holbrook, NY
*
* Three arguments are passed if SYSHELP is called from a hot key.
* If called though a special Developer's Library function,
* keypress is also passed.  All arguments can be used in the
* help condition statement.

#include "setcurs.ch"

LOCAL help_row, help_col,                                          ;
      old_area := SELECT(),                                        ;
      old_col := COL(),                                            ;
      old_color := SETCOLOR(),                                     ;
      old_cursor := SETCURSOR(SC_NONE),                            ;
      old_help := IF(TYPE('helpcode')!= 'C' .OR. LASTKEY() = -1,;
                  '', TRIM(UPPER(helpcode))),                      ;
      old_row := ROW(),                                            ;
      old_screen := SCRNSAVE(0, 0, MAXROW(), MAXCOL()),            ;
      open_flag := .F.

STATIC help__on := .F.

* Prevent recursive entry
IF help__on
   * Help already active
   RETURN .F.
ELSE
   * Initialize help variable
   help__on = .T.
ENDIF

* Set defaults for undefined variables
IF TYPE('helpfile') != 'C'
   PRIVATE helpfile := 'SYSHELP'
ENDIF
IF TYPE('helpcode') != 'C'
   PRIVATE helpcode := ''
ENDIF

IF VALTYPE(keypress) != 'N'
   * Call may not be from a Developer's Library function.
   * Initialize keypress to prevent run time error.
   keypress = 0
ENDIF

* Check for direct call. If fewer than 3 arguments, SYSHELP was
* called directly. Initialize arguments to prevent error.
IF PCOUNT() < 3
```

```
        callproc = ''
        linenum  = 0
        inputvar = ''
ENDIF

* Select helpfile or open it if necessary. Note that help
* is addressed only by its alias dl_syshelp.  The help
* database can have any name.

IF SELECT('dl_syshelp') = 0

    IF FILE((helpfile) + '.DBF') .AND. FILE((helpfile) + '.DBT');
          .AND. FILE((helpfile) + INDEXEXT())

        * Help file exists, open it and set flag
        USE &helpfile ALIAS dl_syshelp INDEX ((helpfile)) NEW
        open_flag := .T.
    ELSE
        * Help file not found
        old_screen = SCRNSAVE(MAXROW(), 0, MAXROW(), MAXCOL())
        CENTERON(MAXROW(),'Helpfile not available. ' + hitanykey)
        ERRORBEEP()
        INKEY(0)
        SCRNREST(old_screen)
        RETURN .F.
    ENDIF

ELSE
    * Help file already open, select it
    SELECT dl_syshelp
ENDIF

* Set up maximum row and column for SYSHELP messages. Look for
* special system record with maximum screen coordinates. If not
* found, default to entire screen.

SEEK '~~HG_SYS~~'
IF .NOT. FOUND()
    help_row = MAXROW()
    help_col = MAXCOL()
ELSE
    help_row = dl_syshelp->hlpbott
    help_col = dl_syshelp->hlprgt
ENDIF

* Locate message
GO TOP
IF .NOT. EMPTY(helpcode)
    SEEK helpcode

    IF FOUND() .AND. TRIM(helpcode) == TRIM(dl_syshelp->hlpcode)

        * Display message if condition empty or true
        IF EMPTY(dl_syshelp->hlpcond)
           HELPMSG(help_row, help_col)
```

```
            ELSEIF CHKCOND(helpcode)
                HELPMSG(help_row, help_col)
            ELSE
                * Otherwise, no help is available
                NOHELP(callproc, linenum, inputvar, helpcode, ;
                    help_row, help_col)
            ENDIF
        ELSE
            * Help code not in file, display message
            NOHELP(callproc, linenum, inputvar, helpcode, ;
                help_row, help_col)
        ENDIF
    ELSE
        * No helpcode passed, evaluate condition field only

        IF CHKCOND(helpcode) .AND. EMPTY(dl_syshelp->hlpcode)
            * We found one, display it
            HELPMSG(help_row, help_col)
        ELSE
            * No help available
            NOHELP(callproc, linenum, inputvar, helpcode, ;
                help_row, help_col)
        ENDIF
    ENDIF

    * Restore entry conditions and return

    IF open_flag
        * We opened help file, close it
        USE
    ENDIF

    * Restore everything and return
    SCRNREST(old_screen)
    SELECT(old_area)
    SETCOLOR(old_color)
    helpcode := old_help
    SETCURSOR(old_cursor)
    DEVPOS(old_row, old_col)
    help_on := .F.
    RETURN NIL

    *******************************************************************
    STATIC FUNCTION NOHELP (callproc, linenum, inputvar, helpcode, ;
                            help_row, help_col)
    *******************************************************************
    * Display no help available message

    LOCAL keypress, old_screen

    * Clear message row and display error message
    ERRORBEEP()
    @ help_row, 0 CLEAR TO help_row, help_col
    SETCOLOR(colwindow)
    @ help_row, INT((help_col - 52) / 2) SAY ;
```

```
                ' No help available. ' + hitanykey

keypress = INKEY(0)

* The code below is for development. If the "^" key (key 94)
* is pressed when no help is available, calling conditions
* appear in a window.

IF keypress = 94 .AND. TYPE('callproc') = 'C'

   old_screen = SCRNSAVE(10, 17, 15, 60)
   @ 10, 17, 15, 59 BOX ' ┌|┘─└| '
   @ 11, 20 SAY ' Calling Procedure ...... '+ callproc
   @ 12, 20 SAY ' Line Number ............ '+ LTRIM(STR(linenum))
   @ 13, 20 SAY ' Input Variable ......... '+ inputvar
   @ 14, 20 SAY ' Help Code .............. '+ helpcode

   @ help_row, 0 SAY PADC('Test key pressed!' +  ;
                    hitanykey, help_col)
   INKEY(0)
   SCRNREST(old_screen)

ENDIF

RETURN NIL


*****************************************************************
STATIC FUNCTION CHKCOND (helpcode)
*****************************************************************

* Check condition field of help file. If it is false or
* empty, return false. Otherwise, return true.

LOCAL checkit

DO WHILE TRIM(helpcode) == TRIM(dl_syshelp->hlpcode) .AND. !EOF()

   IF EMPTY(dl_syshelp->hlpcond)
      * No condition specified
      SKIP
   ELSE
      checkit = UPPER(dl_syshelp->hlpcond)
      IF &checkit
         * Condition evaluates true
         RETURN(.T.)
      ENDIF
      SKIP
   ENDIF

ENDDO

RETURN .F.
```

```
*******************************************************************
STATIC FUNCTION HELPMSG (help_row, help_col)
*******************************************************************

* Display help message at specified position

LOCAL boxdef, mhlpcolr := dl_syshelp->hlpcolr

@ help_row, 0 CLEAR TO help_row, help_col

SETCOLOR(colwindow)
@ help_row, INT((help_col - 52) / 2) SAY ;
      ' Use up/down, PgUp/PgDn to view. Press Esc to EXIT. '

* Set help color. If no entry, default to colhelp1
IF .NOT. EMPTY(dl_syshelp->hlpcolr)
    SETCOLOR(&mhlpcolr)
ELSE
    SETCOLOR(colhelp1)
ENDIF

IF dl_syshelp->hlpclr
    @ 0, 0 CLEAR TO help_row - 1, help_col
ENDIF

IF dl_syshelp->hlpbox

   * Load selected box type
   boxdef = IF(dl_syshelp->hlpbx = 'S', '┌─┬┐│┘─└', '╔═╦╗║╝═╚')

   * Draw box at defined position
   @ dl_syshelp->hlptop, dl_syshelp->hlpleft, ;
     dl_syshelp->hlpbott, dl_syshelp->hlprgt BOX boxdef

   * And display message inside box

   MEMOEDIT(dl_syshelp->hlpmsg, dl_syshelp->hlptop+1,   ;
            dl_syshelp->hlpleft+2, dl_syshelp->hlpbott-1, ;
            dl_syshelp->hlprgt-2, .F.)

ELSE
   * Display message without boxing

   MEMOEDIT(dl_syshelp->hlpmsg, dl_syshelp->hlptop,     ;
            dl_syshelp->hlpleft, dl_syshelp->hlpbott,    ;
            dl_syshelp->hlprgt, .F.)

ENDIF

RETURN NIL
```

SYSSAVE

Description:
Backs up or restores data files from Clipper

Syntax:
SYSSAVE(<nMode>, <cDiskDriveLetter>, <aFileNames>, [<nMessageRow>])

Returns:
Zero if the operation succeeds, or a number indicating error type (see the table below)

File Name:
F_SYSSAV.PRG

Screen Use:
Entire screen or a single message line

Arguments:
<nMode> – Number from 1 to 4 specifying the desired operation as follows:

1. Full-screen message – backup
2. Full-screen message – restore
3. Single-line operation – backup
4. Single-line operation – restore

<cDiskDriveLetter> – Single character for backup/restore drive

<aFileNames> – Array containing names of the files to back up (modes 1 and 3 only)

[<nMessageRow>] – Optional row number for operating and error messages

Typical Use:
To back up and restore data files to and from floppy or other drives in a Clipper application

Defaults:
Message row defaults to the bottom screen line if not passed

Error Handling:
Has extensive error trapping. See discussion below.

Cautions:
Inhibit hot key procedures that may allocate memory while using SYSSAVE.

Does not validate the passed drive letter. If you are unsure of the disk or drive status, use LASTDRIVE, DISKTEST, or both before calling SYSSAVE.

Close all files before copying.

Discussion

SYSSAVE is a general-purpose file backup and restore utility. It completely controls the critical tasks of saving or restoring data files without leaving your Clipper application. Descriptive messages identify errors and instruct the user when to insert or change disks. SYSSAVE displays the name of each file as it is copied. If it is aborted prematurely by the operator or by an unrecoverable error, it returns an error number (see the code table at the end of the function description).

To back up a group of files, first load an array with the file names. Then call SYSSAVE with the mode set to 1 or 3, a drive letter, the array name, and an optional message row.

Restore operations are even simpler. To restore a group of files, call SYSSAVE with the mode set to 2 or 4 and a drive letter. The array of file names is not mandatory. To specify a message line without one, pass a null for the array.

Thus, with just a few lines of code, you can provide a complete backup and restore process for your application.

SYSSAVE avoids the shortcomings of the DOS BACKUP and RESTORE commands. Although it works similarly, it has powerful features the DOS versions lack.

For example, the backup process has the following key features:

> It copies files without alteration. Copies are *byte by byte*. Unless a file is split across multiple disks, it can be used directly as is.
>
> It creates a numbered identifying file on each backup disk. The file contains date, time, and file name information in ASCII format. By reading these files, you can recover information about the backup in case a disk is misplaced.
>
> SYSSAVE supports backup or restore operations for disks of any size. It allows up to 99 disks. It copies files until the disk is nearly full (see below). It can use any valid DOS drive.
>
> SYSSAVE handles problems such as write protected or unformatted disks without requiring an abort. For example, it allows an operator to format or replace an unformatted disk detected during backup. The operation then continues. Furthermore, if a backup disk cannot be erased completely due to read-only files, system files, or multiple directories, a warning message appears and the program stops. The operator can then change disks or proceed using the current disk.

The restore process has the following key feature:

> It reads the identifying file from the first backup disk and saves its identifying code string. It then checks later disks for proper sequencing and set identification. This protects against the operator inserting a disk out of sequence or from another backup set.

Several functions in the Developer's Library are linked automatically when you use SYSSAVE. Some are assembly language support functions that do extensive low-level error trapping. They make the backup or restore operation as reliable and simple as possible. SYSSAVE accounts for the possibility of an operator inserting unformatted, write-protected, or system disks in a drive, and it permits easy recovery from these and other errors.

All operating and error messages appear on a single line. The line number is passed to SYSSAVE in <nMessageRow>. It defaults to the bottom screen line.

A full-screen message option is available for both backup and restore operations. Use it in situations where the software gets only occasional use, or where there is rapid personnel turnover. It displays a full-screen explanation of the process before running the function. The single line used for operating and error messages (<nMessageRow>) remains the same.

Theory of Operation

SYSSAVE does buffered copying of files in both backup and restore modes. To achieve maximum speed, it allocates as much memory as possible for the copy buffer. To avoid running out of memory, do not allow other procedures to change the allocation while SYSSAVE is in progress.

During a backup operation, SYSSAVE copies each file named in the passed array byte-by-byte to the specified disk drive. It adds the name to an identifying file (see below) on the target disk. During a restore operation, SYSSAVE reads and verifies the identifying file. It restores only the files named in it. Thus the target disk can contain other files or directories.

Unless memory is severely limited, SYSSAVE can usually back up or restore a set of files (from your Clipper application) just as fast as the DOS COPY command.

SYSSAVE does not alter files during copying except to split large ones over multiple disks. When a file is split, it is simply closed on the first disk and continued in the next byte on the next disk. If necessary, you can reassemble split files manually using the DOS COPY command with the /B switch. Before doing this, you must give each part of the file a different name. The syntax to reconstruct a split file using COPY is

```
COPY /B part1 + part2 + part3 filename
```

SYSSAVE creates an identifying file on each target disk during backup. The file is named BACKUPnn.DAT, where "nn" is the disk's sequential number. It is created in the disk's current directory. SYSSAVE erases all files in the directory before copying the specified ones. Although SYSSAVE is usually used with floppy disks, this feature allows it to be used with other storage systems. Since it reads and writes only to the current directory on the target drive, you simply change to the desired directory before calling it. You can do this using the command RUN CD \newdirectory. After SYSSAVE executes, you can return to the original directory.

The structure of the BACKUPnn.DAT file is as follows:

```
bytes 1 - 8:   ....... Backup date in format mm/dd/yy
byte  9:       .......... Space
bytes 10 - 17: ..... Backup time in format hh:mm:ss
bytes 18 on:   ....... List of file names
```

While copying data files during backup, SYSSAVE adds each one's name to the BACKUPnn.DAT file. It precedes the name with a space and, if the entire file is on the current disk, terminates it with an exclamation point. If the file is not entirely on the current disk, SYSSAVE terminates its name with a plus symbol. The last byte of the file is a Ctrl Z (ASCII 26) character.

Assuming that database files FILE1, FILE2, and FILE3 fit on a disk, SYSSAVE writes a typical BACKUP1.DAT file as:

```
08/20/90 11:50:25 FILE1.DBF! FILE2.DBF! FILE3.DBF!
```

If you add another database (FILE4) to the backup that causes it to require another disk, the BACKUP1.DAT file on the first disk would contain:

```
08/20/90 11:50:25 FILE1.DBF! FILE2.DBF! FILE3.DBF!
FILE4.DBF+
```

And the BACKUP2.DAT file on the second disk would contain:

```
08/20/90 11:50:25 FILE4.DBF!
```

Note that the date and time information is the same for all disks in the series regardless of how long backup takes. The sequence repeats as needed for up to 99 backup disks. SYSSAVE writes files to each one until it is nearly full. It leaves 2K of free space in case the user wants to add a short documentation file. SYSSAVE continually tests available space on the disk while copying, so it can work with disks of any size.

A plus sign at the end of a disk's identifying file indicates that another one follows. Thus, the file shows whether a disk is the last one in a series. This is useful if the number of backup disks is uncertain, or if sets are combined inadvertently.

During a restore, SYSSAVE checks each disk for correct backup number and series date and time. It thus guarantees both sequence and set validity. To succeed, a restore must start with the first disk and continue sequentially through the entire set without error.

Error Handling

SYSSAVE returns the numeric code indicated by the table below when an error occurs. With the exception of operator controllable items (disk drive or disk problems), it does not try to correct errors. All errors cause the program to halt and display a message.

If the operator does not (or cannot) correct the problem, the function returns with an error code. By testing the returned value, the caller can determine how to proceed.

SYSSAVE Return Codes

Code	Meaning
−1	Error in passed parameters
0	No error
1	Insufficient memory to run function
2	Cannot open source or target file
3	Error reading source file date/time
4	Unable to create target file
5	Error in array of file names
6	Unable to write to target file
7	Error writing backup ID file
8	Error reading source file data
9	Error writing target file data
10	Error closing target file
11	FORMAT cannot be run
12	Aborted by operator after startup

Coding Examples

The example below displays a menu of choices. Item 6 allows the operator to back up and restore data files. All other options are inactive. The backup routine has an additional option of current or history files. I extracted this example from an application; its source code is in the disk file T_SYSSAV.PRG .

```
*******************************************************************
* Test program for SYSSAVE function -  FILE T_SYSSAV.PRG
*******************************************************************

* Copyright(c) 1991 -- James Occhiogrosso

LOCAL choice := error_flag := file_types := mode: = 1
LOCAL clippath := '', filelist := {}

INITGLOBAL()
SETCOLOR(colstd)

SET MESSAGE TO 24

DO WHILE choice > 0 .AND. choice != 7
   CLEAR
   @  3,34 SAY  "   MAIN MENU   "
   @  4,34 SAY  " ───────────── "

   * Menu below is for demonstration purposes only
   * Only option 6 (backup/restore) is functional

   @  1,10 TO 20,70 DOUBLE
   @  6,27 PROMPT " 1. File Maintenance         "           ;
          MESSAGE PADC("Maintenance for all system data files")
   @  7,27 PROMPT " 2. System Reports           "           ;
          MESSAGE PADC("Menu of system reports")
   @  8,27 PROMPT " 3. Utilities Menu           "           ;
          MESSAGE PADC("System setup and housekeeping utilities")
   @  9,27 PROMPT " 4. Daily Report Series      "           ;
          MESSAGE PADC("Special daily reports and procedures")
   @ 10,27 PROMPT " 5. End of Month Closing     "           ;
          MESSAGE PADC("Month end posting and report series")
   @ 11,27 PROMPT " 6. Data Backup or Restore   "           ;
          MESSAGE PADC("Data file backup/restore to/from A:")
   @ 14,27 PROMPT " Esc --  EXIT SYSTEM         "           ;
          MESSAGE PADC("Return to DOS")

   * Display instructions and get operator's choice
   SETCOLOR(colwindow)
   @ 17,20 SAY " Select an option by moving the cursor,  "
   @ 18,20 SAY " .. or pressing the appropriate number.  "
   SETCOLOR(colstd)

   MENU TO choice

   DO CASE

   // CASE  choice = ??
   //       Other choices here

      CASE choice = 6
```

```
* Set Clipper's path same as DOS path in case FORMAT is
* needed. Assume that FORMAT.COM is on the DOS path.

clippath = GETE("PATH")
SET PATH TO &clippath

* Display available options

@ 22, 16 SAY 'Select Operation: '
@ 22, 36 PROMPT ' Backup files    '
@ 22, 52 PROMPT ' Restore files   '

mode = 1
MENU TO mode

IF mode = 1
    * More options for backup only
    @ 22, 16 SAY 'Select file group: '
    @ 22, 36 PROMPT ' Current files    '
    @ 22, 52 PROMPT ' History files    '
    file_types = 1
    MENU TO file_types

    * Create array of files for backup. Any file type
    * can be placed in the array, including compressed
    * or archived files. The TEMPn.TXT files below are
    * samples only. In this example, file names are
    * hard coded in the array. You can also load the
    * array with the Clipper DIRECTORY function.

    IF file_types = 1
        ASIZE(filelist, 6)
        filelist[1] = "TEMP1.TXT"
        filelist[2] = "TEMP2.TXT"
        filelist[3] = "TEMP3.TXT"
        filelist[4] = "TEMP4.TXT"
        filelist[5] = "TEMP5.TXT"
        filelist[6] = "TEMP6.TXT"
    ELSEIF file_types = 2
        ASIZE(filelist, 2)
        filelist[1] = "TEMP7.TXT"
        filelist[2] = "TEMP8.TXT"
    ELSE
        LOOP
    ENDIF
ELSEIF mode = 0
    LOOP
ENDIF

* Call SYSSAVE to perform selected operation.
* For this example, we are using single-line mode,
* and we have hard-coded the backup drive as A.
```

```
            error_flag = SYSSAVE(mode + 2, "A", filelist)

            IF error_flag != 0
               * Error occurred, display its number
               ?? CHR(7)
               CENTERON(24, IF(mode = 1, 'Backup', 'Restore') + ;
                        ' operation failed with error number '+ ;
                        LTRIM(STR(error_flag)) )

               INKEY(0)
            ENDIF


      OTHERWISE
         IF choice != 0 .AND. choice != 7
            ERRORBEEP()
            CENTERON(24, 'Option not installed. ' + hitanykey)
            INKEY(0)
         ENDIF
      ENDCASE
ENDDO

CLEAR
RETURN
```

```
*******************************************************************
FUNCTION SYSSAVE
*******************************************************************
* Back up and restore data files from Clipper
* Copyright(c) 1991 -- James Occhiogrosso

#include "box.ch"
#include "inkey.ch"
#include "set.ch"
#include "setcurs.ch"
#define drive_num   ASC(drive) - 64
#define K_f 102
#define K_F 70

LOCAL old_cursor := SETCURSOR(SC_NONE), old_screen := '', ;
      old_dateset := SET(_SET_DATEFORMAT)

PARAMETERS mode, drive, filelist, msg_line

* Initialize all variables

PRIVATE initsize := needed := ret_value := remaining ;
        := total := shandle := size := thandle := 0

PRIVATE backfile := backtext := backupid := buffer := ;
        disktext := sourcetime := source := target := ''
PRIVATE diskno := 1, sourcedate

* Test critical passed arguments
IF PCOUNT() < 2 .OR. TYPE('mode') != 'N' ;
              .OR. TYPE('drive') != 'C'
    * Wrong parameters passed, return error
    RETURN -1
ENDIF

IF mode < 1 .OR. mode > 4
    * Check mode passed. If not between 1 and 4, return error
    RETURN -1
ENDIF

IF (mode = 1 .OR. mode = 3) .AND. TYPE('filelist') != 'A'
    * Both backup modes require a filelist array
    RETURN -1
ENDIF

* Set up default message line if not passed
IF msg_line = NIL
    msg_line = MAXROW()
ENDIF

* Save screen area
IF mode < 3
    * Full screen mode
    IF MEMORY(1) <= 8
        * Insufficient memory to run in full-screen mode
```

```
            ?? CHR(7)
            CENTERON(msg_line, 'Insufficient memory to run. ' + ;
                              hitanykey)
            INKEY(0)
            RETURN (1)
        ELSE
            old_screen = SCRNSAVE(0, 0, msg_line, MAXCOL())
        ENDIF
    ELSE
        * Single line screen mode
        old_screen = SCRNSAVE(msg_line, 0, msg_line, MAXCOL())
    ENDIF

    * Strip all but first character of drive passed
    drive = UPPER(LEFT(drive,1)) + ':'

    backfile = drive + "BACKUP" + LTRIM(STR(diskno)) + ".DAT"

    IF mode = 1 .OR. mode = 2         && Full screen modes
        CLEAR
        @ 3, 0
        TEXT
            This function uses the DOS FORMAT program if it detects
            an unformatted disk during a BACKUP operation.

            FORMAT.COM must be present in the directory or on the
            DOS path, or the process will abort. Label and number
            all disks during BACKUP according to screen instruc-
            tions. Improperly numbering a disk may cause serious
            problems!

            When restoring, be sure to load the numbered disks in
            the sequence shown in the screen instructions.

        ENDTEXT
        IF mode = 1
          SETCOLOR(colbarhi)
          @ 18, 7, 20, 72 BOX B_SINGLE + SPACE(1)
          @ 19, 9 SAY 'CAUTION: Files in current directory on drive ';
                    + drive + ' will be erased.'
          SETCOLOR(colstd)
        ENDIF
    ENDIF

    * Allocate copy buffer 1/4 of available free memory
    initsize = (MEMORY(1) * 1024)/ 4

    * Return if initial buffer size less than 2K
    IF initsize <= 2048
        ?? CHR(7)
        CENTERON(msg_line, 'Insufficient memory to run. ' + ;
                          hitanykey)
        INKEY(0)
        RETURN(1)
    ENDIF
```

```
* Initialize copy buffer size
size = initsize
buffer = SPACE(size)

IF mode = 1 .OR. mode = 3

    * If this is a backup operation, check files in passed array
    * by checking size. FILESIZE returns -1 on any file error.

    num_files = LEN(filelist)
    FOR cntr = 1 to num_files
        curr_file <= FILESIZE(filelist[cntr])
        IF curr_file = 0
            CENTERON(msg_line, 'Error reading file ' + ;
                     filelist[cntr] + '. ' + hitanykey)
            INKEY(0)
            RETURN(5)
        ENDIF
        needed = needed + curr_file
    NEXT
    * Advise operator of disk space needed for backup operation
    SETCURSOR(SC_INSERT)
    CENTERON(msg_line, 'Backup will need approximately ' + ;
                     LTRIM(STR(INT((needed/1024) + 2))) + ;
                     'K of disk space.  Proceed? Y/N     ')
ELSE
    CENTERON(msg_line, 'Proceed with restore operation? Y/N    ')
ENDIF

@ msg_line, COL() -4 SAY ''
IF .NOT. OPCONFIRM()
    * Operator aborted
    SCRNREST(old_screen)
    SETCURSOR(old_cursor)
    RETURN(0)
ENDIF

* Ask operator to insert a disk
SETCURSOR(SC_NONE)
DO INSERTDISK
IF LASTKEY() = K_ESC
    SCRNREST(old_screen)
    SETCURSOR(old_cursor)
    RETURN(0)
ENDIF

* Perform selected operation
IF mode = 1 .OR. mode = 3
    DO BACKUP
ELSE
    DO RESTORE
ENDIF

* Restore everything and return
SCRNREST(old_screen)
```

```
SETCURSOR(old_cursor)
SET(_SET_DATEFORMAT, old_dateset)
RETURN(ret_value)


******************************************************************
STATIC PROCEDURE BACKUP
******************************************************************

* Back up files to selected drive

LOCAL counter := 1, disk_free := 0

* Check out and clear disk
DO NEWDISK

IF LASTKEY() = K_ESC
    * Abort if Esc terminated any operation
    ret_value = 12

    RETURN
ENDIF

SET CENTURY OFF
backupid = DTOC(DATE()) + ' ' + TIME() + ' '
backtext = backupid

DO WHILE counter <= LEN(filelist)

    * Get file to back up and create target file name
    source = LTRIM(UPPER(filelist[counter]))
    target = UPPER(drive) + source

    * Open files
    IF .NOT. OPENSOURCE() .OR. .NOT. OPENTARGET()
        ret_value = 2
        RETURN
    ENDIF

    CENTERON(msg_line, 'Backing up file '+ source +' to drive ' ;
             + drive + ' - Disk No. ' + LTRIM(STR(diskno)))

    DO WHILE (remaining > 0)

        * Check disk space remaining
        disk_free = DISKSPACE(drive_num)

        IF disk_free <= 2048
            * Reset everything and get new disk
            size := initsize
            buffer := ''
            buffer := SPACE(size)

            * Close partial target file and date it
            FCLOSE(thandle)
```

```
      IF EMPTY(FILEDATE(target,sourcedate)) .OR. ;
            EMPTY(FILETIME(target,sourcetime))

          * Empty return is error in writing date or time
          CENTERON(msg_line, ;
             'Error writing file date or time to ' + target)
          ?? CHR(7)
          ret_value = 6
          RETURN
      ENDIF

      * Add + to target file name if copy incomplete

      backfile = drive +"BACKUP"+ LTRIM(STR(diskno))+".DAT"
      backtext = backtext + SUBSTR(target,3) + '+ '
      IF .NOT. MEMOWRIT(backfile,backtext)
          CENTERON(msg_line, ;
             'Error writing backup identification file')
          ?? CHR(7)
          ret_value = 7
          RETURN
      ENDIF
      * Prepare next disk
      backtext = backupid
      diskno++
      DO INSERTDISK
      DO NEWDISK
      IF LASTKEY() = K_ESC
          * Abort if Esc terminated any operation
          ret_value = 12
          RETURN
      ENDIF

      * Create target file on new disk
      thandle = FCREATE(target)
      IF FERROR() > 0
          CENTERON(msg_line, ;
             'Fatal error! Cannot create file '+ target)
          ?? CHR(7)
          ret_value = 6
          RETURN
      ENDIF
      * Redisplay current backup file/disk information
      CENTERON(msg_line, ;
          'Backing up file ' + source + ' to drive ' ;
          + drive + ' - Disk No. ' + LTRIM(STR(diskno)))

  ELSE
      * Reset buffer size
      IF disk_free - 2048 > initsize
          size = initsize
      ELSE
          size = disk_free - 2048
      ENDIF
      buffer := ''
```

Clipper Developer's Library

```
                buffer := SPACE(size)
            ENDIF

            IF .NOT. COPYBUFFER()
                RETURN
            ENDIF
        ENDDO

        * Done! Close files
        IF .NOT. CLOSEFILES()
            RETURN
        ENDIF

        * Add ! to target if complete

        backfile = drive + "BACKUP" + LTRIM(STR(diskno)) + ".DAT"
        backtext = backtext + SUBSTR(target,3) + '! '

        IF .NOT. MEMOWRIT(backfile,backtext)
            CENTERON(msg_line, 'Error writing backup data file')
            ?? CHR(7)
            ret_value = 7
            RETURN
        ENDIF

        * Set up for next file in array
        counter++

ENDDO WHILE counter <= LEN(filelist)
RETURN


****************************************************************
STATIC PROCEDURE RESTORE
****************************************************************

* Restore backed up files

LOCAL splitfile := .F.
diskno = 1

* Verify correct restore disk
IF .NOT. CHECKNEXT()
    RETURN
ENDIF

DO WHILE LEN(backtext) > 0
    IF .NOT. splitfile

        * Get source and target file names
        IF AT("!", backtext) > 0
            target = SUBSTR(backtext, 1, AT("!", backtext) -1 )
        ELSEIF AT("+", backtext) > 0
            target = SUBSTR(backtext, 1, AT("+", backtext) -1 )
        ENDIF
```

```
            source = drive + target

            * Open files
            IF .NOT. OPENSOURCE() .OR. .NOT. OPENTARGET()
                EXIT
            ENDIF
ENDIF

* Strip file name from list
backtext = SUBSTR(backtext,LEN(target)+1)
CENTERON(msg_line, ;
    'Restoring file ' + source + ' to hard disk.')

* If marker is "!", copy is a complete file
IF ASC(backtext) = 33
    splitfile = .F.
    DO WHILE remaining > 0
        IF .NOT. COPYBUFFER()
            EXIT
        ENDIF
    ENDDO
    * Strip file marker and space
    backtext = SUBSTR(backtext,3)

* If marker is "+", copy is a split file

ELSEIF ASC(backtext) = 43
    * Copy first disk unconditionally
    IF .NOT. splitfile
        DO WHILE remaining > 0
            IF .NOT. COPYBUFFER()
                EXIT
            ENDIF
        ENDDO
    ENDIF
    diskno++
    splitfile = .T.

    * Close source file on old disk
    FCLOSE(shandle)
    DO INSERTDISK

    * Reinitialize memory variables for next disk
    IF CHECKNEXT()

        * Reopen source file on new disk
        IF .NOT. OPENSOURCE()
            EXIT
        ENDIF

        * Continue copying source
        DO WHILE remaining > 0
            CENTERON(msg_line, 'Restoring file ' + source + ;
                ' to hard disk.')
            IF .NOT. COPYBUFFER()
```

```
                    EXIT
                ENDIF
            ENDDO
        ELSE
            * Operator terminated with Esc
            ret_value = 12
            EXIT
        ENDIF
    ENDIF

    IF .NOT. splitfile .OR. (splitfile .AND. ;
            SUBSTR(backtext,LEN(target)+1,1) = '!')

        * Copy complete. Close and date target
        IF .NOT. CLOSEFILES()
            RETURN
        ENDIF
    ENDIF
ENDDO
@ msg_line, 0
RETURN


*******************************************************************
STATIC PROCEDURE NEWDISK
*******************************************************************
* Check disk drive status and space

LOCAL cnt := delcnt := errorcode := keypress := 0, delfiles := {}

* Activate interrupt 24 handler
SETINT24(.T.)

DO WHILE .T.
    SETCOLOR(colhelp1)

    * Check for disk error
    FCLOSE(FCREATE(backfile))
    errorcode = GETINT24()

    IF errorcode = 1 .OR. errorcode = 3
        IF errorcode = 1
            CENTERON(msg_line, 'Disk in drive ' + drive + ;
                    ' is write protected. ' + hitanykey)
        ELSE
            CENTERON(msg_line, ;
                'Drive ' + drive + ' not ready. '+ hitanykey)
        ENDIF
        * Wait for operator to correct problem or abort
        ?? CHR(7)
        IF INKEY(0) != K_ESC
            LOOP
        ELSE
            ret_value = 12
            EXIT
```

```
        ENDIF
    ENDIF

    IF errorcode = 13
        CENTERON(msg_line, ;
            'Disk is unformatted. Press F to format it, ' + ;
                                  'or any key to try again.')
        ?? CHR(7)
        keypress = INKEY(0)
        IF keypress = K_ESC
            * Operator aborted
            ret_value = 12
            EXIT
        ELSEIF keypress = K_F .OR. keypress = K_f
            IF FILE("FORMAT.COM") .OR. FILE("FORMAT.EXE") .OR. ;
                   FILE("FORMAT.BAT") .AND. .NOT. EMPTY(drive)
                SAVE SCREEN
                CLEAR

                @ 1,0 SAY 'Running DOS format. ' + ;
                          'Follow screen instructions'
                ?
                ?
                RUN FORMAT &drive
                RESTORE SCREEN
            ELSE
                * DOS FORMAT file missing
                CENTERON(msg_line, ;
                    'FORMAT program not on DOS path. ' + ;
                    'Cannot proceed.')
                ?? CHR(7)
                PAUSE(2)
                * Force return to main menu on exit
                KEYBOARD CHR(K_ESC)
                ret_value = 11
                EXIT
            ENDIF
        ELSE
            * Operator pressed a key. Restart for disk change
            LOOP
        ENDIF

    ELSEIF errorcode > 0
        CENTERON(msg_line, ;
            'Unknown error -- Press any key to abort')
        ?? CHR(7)
        INKEY(0)
        ret_val = ABORTED

    ELSE
        * No errors. Delete files in root directory
        CENTERON(msg_line, ;
            'Erasing files on disk in drive ' + drive)
        delcnt = ADIR(drive + "*.*")
        IF delcnt > 0
```

```
            ASIZE(delfiles,delcnt)
            ADIR(drive + "*.*", delfiles)
            FOR cnt = 1 to delcnt
                * Erase all files except COMMAND.COM
                IF delfiles[cnt] != 'COMMAND.COM'
                    FERASE(drive + delfiles[cnt])
                ENDIF
            NEXT
        ENDIF

        * Check whether all files were erased
        IF DISKSIZE(drive_num) != DISKSPACE(drive_num)
            ?? CHR(7)
            SETCURSOR(SC_INSERT)
            CENTERON(msg_line, ;
                'All files on disk were not erased! ' + ;
                'Do you want to change disks?     ')

            * Position cursor and wait for operator

            SETPOS (ROW(), COL()-2)
            IF OPCONFIRM()
                SETCURSOR(SC_NONE)
                CENTERON(msg_line,'Insert new disk. '+ hitanykey)
                INKEY(0)
                LOOP
            ELSE
                SETCURSOR(SC_NONE)
                CENTERON(msg_line, ;
                         hitanykey + ' (or Esc to abort)' )
                INKEY(0)
            ENDIF

        ENDIF
        EXIT
    ENDIF

ENDDO

SETINT24(.F.)
SETCOLOR(colstd)
@ msg_line, 0
RETURN


*****************************************************************
STATIC FUNCTION CHECKNEXT
*****************************************************************

* Test and initialize parameters for next restore disk

LOCAL errorcode := 0

* Activate interrupt 24 handler
SETINT24(.T.)
```

```
DO WHILE .T.
    * Check for disk error
    DISKSPACE(drive_num)
    errorcode = GETINT24()
    IF errorcode > 0
        CENTERON(msg_line, ;
            'Drive ' + drive + ' not ready. ' + hitanykey)
        ?? CHR(7)
        IF INKEY(0) != K_ESC
            LOOP
        ELSE
            * Operator aborted
            ret_value = 12
            RETURN(.F.)
        ENDIF
    ENDIF
    EXIT
ENDDO
* Clear INT24 handler
SETINT24(.F.)

* Verify disk number
backfile = drive + "BACKUP" + LTRIM(STR(diskno)) + ".DAT"
DO WHILE .NOT. FILE(backfile)
    CENTERON(msg_line, ;
        'Incorrect disk ID or disk is not a backup disk. ' + ;
                        hitanykey)
    INKEY(0)
    DO INSERTDISK
    IF LASTKEY() = K_ESC
        ret_value = 12
        RETURN(.F.)
    ENDIF
ENDDO

* Read disk's backup identification file
disktext = MEMOREAD(backfile)
IF diskno = 1
    backupid = SUBSTR(disktext, 1, 17)
ELSE
    * If not disk 1, verify it
    DO WHILE .NOT. backupid == SUBSTR(disktext, 1, 17) .OR. ;
            .NOT. target == SUBSTR(disktext, 19, LEN(target))
        CENTERON(msg_line, 'Disk ID invalid! - ' + hitanykey + ;
                ' (Esc to exit)')
        ?? CHR(7)
        IF INKEY(0) = K_ESC
            ret_value = 12
            RETURN(.F.)
        ENDIF
    ENDDO
ENDIF
@ msg_line, 0
backtext = SUBSTR(disktext, 19)
RETURN(.T.)
```

```
*******************************************************************
STATIC FUNCTION OPENSOURCE
*******************************************************************

* Open source file

* Get date and time of source files
sourcedate = FILEDATE(source)
sourcetime = FILETIME(source)

* Verify that everything is readable
IF EMPTY(sourcedate) .OR. EMPTY(sourcetime)
    ?? CHR(7)
    CENTERON(msg_line, ;
        'Error verifying ' + source + 'file. ' + hitanykey)
    ret_value = 3
    INKEY(0)
    RETURN(.F.)
ENDIF
shandle = FOPEN(source)
* Open all files and check for errors
IF FERROR() > 0
    * Source error
    CENTERON(msg_line, 'Fatal error! Cannot open file ' ;
            + source + ' ' + hitanykey)
    ?? CHR(7)
    INKEY(0)
    ret_value = 2
    RETURN(.F.)
ENDIF

* Get total source file size
total = FSEEK(shandle, 0, 2)
remaining = total

* Reset file pointer to BOF
FSEEK(shandle, 0)
RETURN(.T.)


*******************************************************************
STATIC FUNCTION OPENTARGET
*******************************************************************

* Open target file

thandle = FCREATE(target)
IF FERROR() > 0
    * Target error
    CENTERON(msg_line, 'Fatal error! Cannot create file ' ;
            + target + ' ' + hitanykey)
    ?? CHR(7)
    ret_value = 4
    INKEY(0)
    RETURN(.F.)
```

```
ENDIF
RETURN(.T.)


******************************************************************
STATIC FUNCTION CLOSEFILES
******************************************************************

* Close source and target files - redate target

FCLOSE(thandle)
FCLOSE(shandle)
* Write date and time to target file before closing
IF EMPTY(FILEDATE(target,sourcedate)) .OR. ;
   EMPTY(FILETIME(target,sourcetime))
     * Error occurred in writing date or time
     CENTERON(msg_line, ;
        'Error writing file date '+ target + ' ' + hitanykey)
     INKEY(0)
     ret_value = 10
     RETURN(.F.)
ENDIF

@ msg_line,0
RETURN(.T.)


******************************************************************
STATIC FUNCTION COPYBUFFER
******************************************************************

* Write buffer area to target disk

size = LEN(buffer)
IF (remaining < size)
    * Set size to remaining bytes in file
    size = remaining
ENDIF

* Read "size" bytes into buffer and check number read
IF FREAD(shandle, @buffer, size) != size
    ?? CHR(7)
    CENTERON(msg_line, ;
       "Fatal error reading " + source + ' ' + hitanykey)
    INKEY(0)
    ret_value = 8
    RETURN(.F.)
ENDIF

* Write "size" bytes to target and check number written
IF FWRITE(thandle, buffer, size) != size
    ?? CHR(7)
    CENTERON(msg_line,  ;
       "Fatal error writing " + target + ' ' + hitanykey)
    INKEY(0)
```

Clipper Developer's Library

```
      ret_value = 9
      RETURN(.F.)
ENDIF

* Compute remaining bytes in file
remaining = remaining - size
RETURN(.T.)


******************************************************************
STATIC PROCEDURE INSERTDISK
******************************************************************

* Display message and wait for operator to insert a disk

CENTERON(msg_line, ;
        'Insert backup disk # ' + LTRIM(STR(diskno)) + ;
        ' in drive ' + drive + '. ' + hitanykey)
DONEBEEP()
INKEY(0)
@ msg_line, 0
RETURN
```

SYSVERSION

Description:
Determines if an application has changed by comparing its date and time to a stored value

Syntax:
SYSVERSION(<cAppExeFile>, <cVersionFile>)

Returns:
True if the first file was created before the date and time string in the second file; false otherwise

File Name:
F_SYSVER.PRG

Screen Use:
None

Arguments:
<cAppExeFile> – Name and optional extension of the file whose date and time stamp will be compared to the stored date/time string. Usually the application EXE file.

<cVersionFile> – Name and optional extension of a version control file containing a date and time string

Typical Use:
To revise database, index, and other files in an application to conform to a new program version

Defaults:
Assumes EXE or DAT, respectively, if <cAppExeFile> or <cVersionFile> lacks an extension.

If <cVersionFile> does not exist, it is created and SYSVERSION returns false.

Error Handling:
Since SYSVERSION is usually critical to application integrity, it returns to DOS with a message if an error prevents version updating.

Cautions:
For correct operation, system date and time must be set.

See Also:
MAKEDBF, MAKENDX

Discussion

Use SYSVERSION to determine if the currently executing program has been updated. Call it at the beginning of your application.

Typically, one uses SYSVERSION to read the DOS date and time of the main application EXE file and compare them to a string stored in a version control file. If the two do not match, SYSVERSION returns false. The application can then recreate or update databases or indexes, or perform other tasks required for a new version.

By calling SYSVERSION near the top of your main application, and using MAKEDBF and MAKENDX, you can be certain that all necessary changes are made each time an update occurs.

When used for the first time in a new application, SYSVERSION creates the version control file and returns false.

Coding Examples

In the example below, the application uses the executable file ar.exe, a version update control file arvers.dat, and a data dictionary file arsystem.def.

SYSVERSION compares the DOS date/time stamp of ar.exe with the date/time string in arvers.dat. If ar.exe is newer, indicating that the program has been updated, SYSVERSION writes the new date and time to arvers.dat, and returns false. On the other hand, if ar.exe is older, SYSVERSION simply returns true.

If SYSVERSION returns false, the Developer's Library functions MAKEDBF and MAKENDX update the database and index files with the latest changes.

```
* Check for correct version
IF .NOT. SYSVERSION("ar.exe", "arvers.dat")

     * Automatically create (or recreate) application database
     * and index files using data dictionary file arsystem.def

     MAKEDBF("arsystem.def")

ENDIF
```

Note that the example specifies all file extensions for clarity. This is necessary only if you deviate from the defaults.

```
************************************************************
FUNCTION SYSVERSION (app_exe, app_dat)
************************************************************

* Compare date and time on a file to that stored in another file

* Copyright(c) 1991 -- James Occhiogrosso

* Caution: Since SYSVERSION is critical to application
* integrity, it returns to DOS with an error message on any
* error that prevents proper version updating.

* app_exe is typically the application EXE file
* app_dat is typically the version control file

LOCAL dat_size := FILESIZE(appt_dat), new_vers := '', old_vers := ''

IF PCOUNT() != 2
    * Critical error - return to DOS
    ?? CHR(7)
    ? 'SYSVERSION error - Both parameters are required.'
    QUIT
ENDIF

* Check file extensions. If not passed, use defaults.

IF AT(".", app_exe) = 0
    * Assume first file is application EXE file
    app_exe = TRIM(app_exe) + '.EXE'
ENDIF

IF AT(".", app_dat) = 0
    * Assume second file is a DAT file
    app_dat = TRIM(app_dat) + '.DAT'
ENDIF

* Verify existence of application file

IF .NOT. FILE(app_exe)
    * Critical error - return to DOS
    ?? CHR(7)
    ? 'SYSVERSION error -- Incorrect DOS file name passed - ' ;
              + UPPER(app_exe)

    QUIT
ENDIF

* Check control file size. Allow 15 bytes (the correct length)
* or -1 (file does not exist). This prevents accidentally
* overwriting an important file if the version control file
* name is passed incorrectly.

IF dat_size = 15 .OR. dat_size = -1

    * Size of control file is correct or file does not exist
```

```
      * Read and format DOS date and time from first file
      new_vers = DTOS(FILEDATE(app_exe)) + ;
                 STRTRAN(FILETIME(app_exe),':')

      * Read version control file's date/time string
      old_vers = MEMOREAD(app_dat)

      * If new version, update version control file
      * Compare new version string to old version string
      IF EMPTY(old_vers) .OR. new_vers > old_vers
           * New version. Update version control file
           MEMOWRIT(app_dat, new_vers)
           RETURN(.F.)
      ELSE
           * Otherwise, version strings match
           RETURN(.T.)
      ENDIF

ELSE
      * Size of control file is incorrect. Do not rewrite it.
      * Programmer probably specified wrong name.
      ?? CHR(7)
      ? 'SYSVERSION error - Control file ' + UPPER(app_dat) + ;
        ' - incorrect size'
      QUIT
ENDIF
```

TEMPFILE

Description:
Creates a unique temporary file on the selected disk drive

Syntax:
TEMPFILE([<cExtension>], [<cPathName>])

Returns:
Name of the file created, or a null string if one cannot be created using the passed arguments

File Name:
F_TEMPFI.PRG

Screen Use:
None

Arguments:
[<cExtension>] – Three character file extension

[<cPathName>] – DOS drive or path string

Note: To pass a drive or path string ([<cPathName>]) without a file extension, pass a null string or a comma for <cExtension>.

Typical Use:
To generate a unique temporary file with a known name to avoid conflict in a network or other environment

Defaults:
Both parameters are optional. If <cExtension> is not passed, it defaults to TMP. If <cPathName> is not passed, the temporary file is created on the default drive in the current directory.

Error Handling:
Returns a null string if it cannot create the temporary file for read/write access.

Cautions:
Returns a null string for all errors. To obtain more detailed error information, use the DOSERROR or FERROR function in Clipper, or the Developer's Library critical error (INT24) handler.

See Also:
DOSERROR, FERROR, GETINT24, SETINT24

Discussion

TEMPFILE creates a unique file name in the format TEMPnnnn.EXT, where nnnn is a number from 0001 to 9999. TEMPFILE supports full drive and path names.

If TEMPFILE executes successfully, the new file is truncated to zero bytes and closed. It is then available for later operations. The user should erase temporary files when they are no longer needed.

Coding Examples

```
* Create a temporary file with no extension on drive A in
* the \TEXT directory

TEMPFILE("", "A:\TEXT\")

* Create a temporary file with extension DOC on drive A in
* the \TEXT directory

TEMPFILE("DOC", "A:\TEXT\")

* Create a temporary DBF file in the current directory

TEMPFILE("DBF")

* Create a temporary file with a TMP extension on the
* default drive in the current directory

TEMPFILE()
```

```
****************************************************************
FUNCTION TEMPFILE (extension, path)
****************************************************************

* Creates a unique temporary file name on the selected disk
* Copyright(c) 1991 -- James Occhiogrosso

LOCAL temp_ext, file_name, counter, handle

file_name = ''

* If path not passed, default to current drive and directory
IF path = NIL
    path = ''

* If path passed without a trailing backslash ("\"), add it
ELSEIF SUBSTR(path, -1, 1) != '\'
    path = path + '\'
ENDIF

IF extension = NIL
    * Default to TMP if extension not passed
    extension = 'TMP'
ELSE
    * Trim extension to DOS maximum of 3 characters
    extension = SUBSTR(UPPER(extension),1,3)
ENDIF

FOR counter = 1 TO 9999

    * Create unique file name in format TEMPnnnn.EXT
    IF EMPTY(extension)
        file_name = path + 'TEMP' + PADL(counter, 4, '0') + '.'
    ELSE
        file_name = path + 'TEMP' + PADL(counter, 4, '0') + ;
                    '.' + extension
    ENDIF
    * See if file name just created already exists
    IF .NOT. FILE(file_name)
        EXIT
    ENDIF
NEXT

IF counter >= 9999
    * Cannot find a unique name, return null string
    file_name = ''

ELSE
    * Unique file name, create and close file
    handle = FCREATE(file_name)
    file_name = IF (FCLOSE(handle), file_name, '')

ENDIF

RETURN(file_name)
```

VRULER

Description:
Displays a vertical ruler line

Syntax:
Normally called by pressing the Alt-V key combination

Returns:
Nothing

File Name:
F_VRULER.PRG

Screen Use:
One vertical column

Arguments:
None

Typical Use:
To determine vertical positions or measurements from an application

Cautions:
If VRULER is called using a SET KEY statement, you must declare it EXTERNAL in your application.

See Also:
DEVELOP, GRID, HRULER

Discussion

You generally use VRULER only during development. It draws a calibrated vertical ruler line at the center of the screen. To facilitate measurements, you can move the ruler horizontally using the left and right arrow keys. To leave

VRULER, press the Esc key. Pressing Alt-H while inside VRULER calls HRULER. Thus, vertical and horizontal ruler lines can appear simultaneously (see HRULER for more information).

VRULER can be called recursively. Pressing Alt-V while inside it causes another vertical ruler line to appear. Thus, you can display as many lines as you need. One line is removed and the screen below it restored each time Esc is pressed.

Coding Examples

```
* Include standard inkey header file supplied with Clipper
#include "inkey.ch"

* Declare VRULER external to force linking
EXTERNAL VRULER

* Set up the Alt-V key combination for VRULER
SET KEY K_ALT_V TO VRULER
```

You can use the DEVELOP function at the top of your application program to set up the Alt-V key combination and link VRULER. DEVELOP also links other utility functions (see it for more information).

```
****************************************************************
FUNCTION VRULER
****************************************************************

* Display a calibrated vertical ruler line

* Copyright(c) 1991 - James Occhiogrosso

#include "inkey.ch"
#include "setcurs.ch"

MEMVAR colbarhi
LOCAL counter := 1, keypress := 0, old_color, old_cursor,   ;
      old_col := COL(), old_row := ROW(), old_screen,       ;
      v_col := INT(MAXCOL()/2), v_row := 0, v_ruler := ''

* Save entry conditions
old_cursor = SETCURSOR(SC_NONE)
old_color  = SETCOLOR(colbarhi)
old_screen = SCRNSAVE(0, v_col, MAXROW(), v_col)


* Display vertical ruler
@ 0, v_col SAY 'B'
@ MAXROW(), v_col SAY 'A'
FOR counter = 1 TO (MAXROW() - 1)
    * Display double horizontal marks on each 5th row
    @ counter, v_col SAY IF(counter % 5 = 0, '╪', '┼')
NEXT

* Save ruler screen area
v_ruler = SAVESCREEN(0, v_col, 24, v_col)

DO WHILE keypress != K_ESC
    keypress = INKEY(0)
    SCRNREST(old_screen)

    * Adjust row and column for each arrow key pressed
    IF keypress = K_RIGHT
        v_col = IF(v_col < MAXROW(), v_col+1, MAXROW())
        old_screen = SCRNSAVE(0, v_col, MAXCOL(), v_col)

    ELSEIF keypress = K_LEFT
        v_col = IF(v_col > 0, v_col-1, 0)
        old_screen = SCRNSAVE(0, v_col, MAXCOL(), v_col)

    ENDIF

    * Display ruler in new position
    RESTSCREEN(0, v_col, 24, v_col, v_ruler)

    IF keypress = K_ALT_H
        * Display horizontal ruler line
        DO hruler
    ENDIF
```

```
   IF keypress = K_ALT_V
      * Display another vertical ruler
      DO vruler
   ENDIF

ENDDO

SCRNREST(old_screen)
SETPOS(old_row, old_col)
SETCOLOR(old_color)
SETCURSOR(old_cursor)
RETURN NIL
```

Appendix A

Introduction to Library Concepts

What Is a Library?

When you compile or assemble a program, the compiler (or assembler) generates an *object file*. It has an OBJ extension and is linked with your application using a utility called a linker. Each object file contains machine language instructions and symbolic information that enables the linker to do its job.

A library is simply a collection of object files created by a library manager. The manager adds, deletes, and replaces files, and maintains the library in the proper format. Thus the library is a special object file, consisting of other such files called modules. The library manager also adds an index that the linker uses to find modules quickly and combine them with your application. Library files use the extension LIB by convention.

All discussions that follow describe LIB.EXE, the library manager that comes with Microsoft languages. Other managers are similar.

Why Use a Library?

Many beginners put their UDFs into a single program file and link it with each application. However, as the number of UDFs and applications increases, this method becomes impractical, if not impossible. The reason is that it links all functions in the file with each application, even if it does not use them!

Linking unused modules unnecessarily increases the application's size and memory requirements. Since memory is usually at a premium, placing all functions in a single file is not viable. The large file is also difficult to maintain. Of course, you can divide functions into different files, but then common ones must be copied (and maintained) in each place.

Here is where a library becomes invaluable! If you place your UDFs in a library file, the linker will link only the modules explicitly used in your application and those they depend on. In other words, you get only what you need!

Thus, you can put many modules in the library without worrying about its overall size. Different applications can use the same library, with each linking only the functions it actually uses.

Another benefit occurs when you revise a module. After testing it, update the library. Applications using the function will be updated the next time they are linked. Thus, using a single library for many applications simplifies maintenance considerably.

With Version 5, most disadvantages of using libraries with Clipper became history. Their benefits make it highly impractical for a serious developer not to use them.

Object Modules and Object Files

Usually, when building a library, you put each function in its own program file and compile it separately. Each object file contains the code for a single function. However, complete isolation is not mandatory. An object file can contain several related functions. Each file is called an object module. It is the smallest unit that can be linked to your program. When your application uses any function in it, the entire module is linked. This makes sense only if all its functions are always used together or are interdependent. Otherwise, the unused ones waste space and should be compiled separately.

Another reason to combine functions is that they must share variable information. A major new feature of Version 5 is static variables. One defined outside a function has a file-wide scope. That is, it retains its value for use by all functions in the program file. Several modules in the Developer's Library contain multiple functions that share variables.

For example, the functions in F_SCRNS.PRG use a static array and counter to manipulate screens. Only they can access the static variables. In other words, the values can be used by any function in the file, but are hidden from all others. For this to work, the functions must be linked as a single object module. For more about static variables, see Rick Spence's *Clipper Programming Guide*, 2nd ed., (San Marcos, CA: Microtrend Books, 1991).

Symbols and Linking

A symbol is the name of an element in your program. It can be a function, procedure, or variable. Unless you specifically declare a function or procedure as "static", Clipper treats it as a public symbol. It is then accessible to the entire application. Other languages require that you explicitly declare it public for this to hold.

Complex modules often requires support functions. Before Version 5, they were public symbols visible to the entire application. Now, however, if you declare them static, their visibility is limited to the file that contains them. Several functions in the Developer's Library use this feature. MAKEDBF is an example.

When you compile a program file with Clipper, it generates an object file containing the names of the public symbols it uses. The linker creates a table with an entry for each one. When one is found in a library, the module declaring it is linked. If that module declares other public symbols that the linker has not yet seen, it adds them to the table and the process continues. This is called resolving the symbols.

When all symbols referenced in the program have been located and linked to the application, the process is complete. If the linker cannot resolve a symbol, an error message appears. Some linkers abort without producing an EXE file in such cases. Others still generate the EXE file, but a run time error occurs when the program tries to use a missing symbol.

All symbols inside explicitly specified program files are resolved immediately. For others, the linker searches all listed libraries. When it finds the symbol, it links the object module that declares it. Identical symbols declared in other libraries are ignored. The linker usually warns about duplicate symbols. You can use the warnings to resolve naming conflicts when using multiple libraries.

When resolving symbols, some linkers consider the order in which libraries are specified. Others, by default, search all libraries, regardless of order. Some linkers report an unresolved symbol if a symbol declared in library 3 uses one from library 2. Again, depending on the linker, you may be able to correct the problem by reordering the libraries or using a special command. The order of the libraries may also affect linking speed. A little experimentation and careful reading of your linker manual (usually an excellent cure for insomnia) may be well worth the time invested. When determining the order of libraries, remember that the first symbol found is the one used. This may not be what you want if functions in two libraries have the same name.

Be sure the linker is aware of all symbols. Otherwise, a run time error will occur when the program tries to use an undefined one. Symbols will be undefined if they are passed to another function as a parameter or defined in a macro. If possible, avoid these practices. If you cannot, be sure to declare all such symbols as external in your application.

For example, the Developer's Library MEMOCTRL function controls the Clipper MEMOEDIT function. It is passed as a parameter to MEMOEDIT. Unless your application declares MEMOCTRL external, it will not be linked. In that case, MEMOEDIT detects that the defined UDF is not linked and no run time error occurs. However, the application will not perform as expected. In most other cases a run time error occurs.

Creating and Managing a Library

The library manager LIB.EXE, or its equivalent, places individually compiled object files in a library file. You use LIB either interactively (by answering prompts) or with an auto response file. For libraries containing more than a few files, an auto response file is more convenient. It eliminates the need to enter the name of each individual module.

To use LIB interactively, just enter

    LIB

It will prompt you for the name of the library to modify, the module operations, a list file name, and the name of your new library.

You can also enter

```
        LIB oldlibrary operations, listfile, newlibrary
```
where

`oldlibrary`	name of the library to be updated
`operations`	module add, replace, and delete operation(s)
`listfile`	optional list file name
`newlibrary`	optional new library name

If you do not specify a new library name, LIB renames the old one with an extension of BAK, and creates a new library using the old name. You can create a list file without updating the library by leaving the operations prompt empty.

Operation commands have the following general format:

−modulename	delete module
+modulename	add module
−+modulename	replace module
*modulename	copy module to a file without removing it from the library
−*modulename	copy module to a file and remove it from the library

For example, to add the file F_NEWFUN to DEVELOP.LIB without creating a list file or renaming the library, enter

```
        LIB DEVELOP +F_NEWFUN;
```

Similarly, to delete F_NEWFUN, enter

```
        LIB DEVELOP -F_NEWFUN;
```

And, to update F_NEWFUN, enter

```
        LIB DEVELOP -+F_NEWFUN;
```

The semicolon at the end of the line tells LIB to use defaults for all remaining prompts.

More complete information on the use of LIB is in the documentation for any Microsoft language.

Auto Response Files

To add or modify just a few functions, the interactive method is satisfactory. However, when creating and maintaining a library containing many functions, manually entering file names on the command line or in response to prompts each time is tedious. A better approach is an auto response file. It is simply a text file (much like a DOS batch file) containing responses to LIB's prompts. The prompts and the responses are displayed as LIB runs. At the very least, the auto response file contains the library name and a list of all modules to be added or replaced. It can have any extension.

For example, an auto response file to add F_NEWFUN to DEVELOP.LIB is

```
DEVELOP +F_NEWFUN;
```

Again, the semicolon terminates the remaining operations.

To add, change, or replace multiple modules, simply list them and the associated operations in the auto response file. For instance, the example below adds FUNC1, deletes FUNC2, and updates FUNC3 in NEWAPP.LIB.

```
NEWAPP +FUNC1 -FUNC2 -+FUNC3;
```

Spaces between operations on a line are optional. The response file can also take the form

```
NEWAPP
+FUNC1&
-FUNC2&
-+FUNC3;
```

The ampersand character continues command operations onto the next line.

When using an auto response file, you call LIB from the command line with

```
LIB @filename
```

The @ indicates an auto response file.

Library Management

Completely recreating a large library each time you make a change is time consuming. By using a batch file and a MAKE utility (with an associated description file), you can update the library only if new modules are added or old ones revised. Thus, the time needed to regenerate the library is reduced substantially. The description file provides default rules for compiling or assembling new or modified modules. See RMAKE in the Clipper manual for more information on a MAKE utility.

The Developer's Library comes with the batch file MAKELIB and a description file DEVELOP.RMK. They work with LIB and RMAKE to update the library. DEVELOP.RMK contains a list of all library modules. You can use it and MAKELIB.BAT to create your own library management system.

MAKELIB calls RMAKE to check the date and time stamp of each program listed in DEVELOP.RMK. New or modified modules are recompiled (or reassembled). When all modules have been processed, a response file is created and LIB is called to regenerate the library. For more details, see Appendix B.

Thus, library management reduces mostly to maintaining the description file (DEVELOP.RMK). You add new modules by simply adding their names to the list. Each time you use MAKELIB, it updates the library with all new or changed modules. The only manual operation is deleting a module. To do so, use LIB in the command or interactive mode. This is acceptable, since deletions are as infrequent as cleaning out files or desk drawers.

Summary

Libraries of User Defined Functions are easy to create with available utilities. Library management can be almost totally automated. A library can contain as many modules as desired, and only ones actually used in an application are linked. Library use greatly simplifies maintenance of multiple applications. See Appendix B for detailed instructions on how to modify Developer's Library functions or add new ones.

Appendix B

Customizing the Developer's Library

Overview

This appendix contains instructions and tools needed to recreate the Developer's Library for those who want to change or augment it. Several utilities are necessary. Some are included here, others are included with Clipper, and still others require you to buy products such as Microsoft's Macro Assembler (MASM) or Borland's Turbo Assembler.

Below are the utilities and files needed, along with their sources. Before trying to regenerate the Developer's Library, make sure you have all of them.

Provided in the Developer's Library:

DEVELOP.MAC	Assembly language macros
DEVELOP.RMK	Make description file for DEVELOP.LIB
DL_KEYS.CH	Developer's Library special keys header
MAKELIB.BAT	Batch file for recreating libraries

The source code for the above files is on the companion disk. It also appears at the end of this appendix. A complete list of files supplied with the Developer's Library is in Appendix C.

Provided with Clipper:

BOX.CH	Box definitions header
CLIPPER.EXE	Clipper compiler
FILEIO.CH	Low-level file functions header
INKEY.CH	Inkey values header
RMAKE.EXE	Program maintenance utility
SET.CH	Set values header
SETCURS.CH	Cursor shapes header
STD.CH	Clipper's standard header

To regenerate the Developer's Library, you will also need a library manager. The discussions in this section use the syntax for the one provided with Microsoft languages (LIB.EXE). Others use similar conventions.

To modify or add functions written entirely in Clipper, the library manager is the only other utility needed.

To modify or add assembly language functions, you will also need Microsoft's Macro Assembler Version 5.1 or later or Borland's Turbo Assembler.

File Naming Conventions

Most functions in the Developer's Library are in their own individual program files. In a few cases, I have grouped ones that are normally used together. A list of files containing multiple functions is in the make description file DEVELOP.RMK.

All files written in Clipper have PRG extensions. Ones containing library functions have the prefix "F_", followed by the first six characters of the function name (where applicable). Test and sample programs follow the same convention except that they use the prefix "T_".

Assembly language functions are in files with ASM extensions. Their names are the actual function names truncated to eight characters. Appendix C contains cross reference tables of all functions and file names.

Where to Place Files

The library program files can go in any directory. I use one named DEVELOP. Since the library has many files, you should not put unrelated ones in its directory.

See the READ.ME file on the disk for instructions on installing the library and its source files.

DEVELOP.LIB is placed in the default directory \CLIPPER5\LIB. If you put it elsewhere, you must change MAKELIB.BAT to refer to the new directory. All other Developer's Library files are placed in \DEVELOP.

MAKELIB also assumes that CLIPPER.EXE, LIB.EXE, RMAKE.EXE, your assembler, and all other utilities are on the DOS path. All object files for the library are created in the current directory.

Theory of Operation

The batch file MAKELIB.BAT initiates and controls creation (or recreation) of the Developer's Library. It can also be used with other libraries. It assumes that Clipper has been installed with the default directory configuration. If not, you may have to relocate Developer's Library files and set environment variables accordingly.

You pass MAKELIB the name of the library to maintain on the command line:

```
MAKELIB Libname
```

It then calls RMAKE (supplied with Clipper). A description file with the library name and an RMK extension defines the handling of each source program. For the Developer's Library, the description file is DEVELOP.RMK. It contains inference and dependency rules for all functions. Source file extensions determine the compiler or assembler needed to recreate the object file.

RMAKE checks each file listed in DEVELOP.RMK to see if it is up to date. If its OBJ file does not exist or is older than its source file, the source program is recompiled or reassembled. New object files are produced for all modified source files. Clipper is used to regenerate files with PRG extensions, and the assembler for those with ASM extensions. The name of each newly created object file is added to a temporary list in LIB_LIST.TXT.

If an error occurs, the process aborts, and a message indicates the error type and the name of the offending file. You must then correct the source file and restart MAKELIB.

If all necessary object files are created without error, control returns to MAKELIB. An auto response file named LIB_RESP.TXT is generated from the temporary list of files (LIB_LIST.TXT) in the format required by the library manager.

LIB.EXE is then called to update the library. If it succeeds, the new library is written to \CLIPPER5\LIB and the temporary files are erased.

You can also use MAKELIB to maintain other libraries or create subsets. Each library must have its own make description file (similar to DEVELOP.RMK), containing the names of the files to be included.

Note that MAKELIB assumes that the library file DEVELOP.LIB is in the directory \CLIPPER5\LIB. If it cannot find DEVELOP.LIB, MAKELIB deletes all object files in the current directory. This forces the entire library to be regenerated according to the descriptions in DEVELOP.RMK. The new library is placed by default in \CLIPPER5\LIB. To use another directory, change MAKELIB.BAT (see the instructions in the source file).

Recreating the Library

If Clipper is installed in its default configuration, and the Developer's Library files are installed as shown above, you can test your configuration by entering

    MAKELIB DEVELOP

If all utilities and Developer's Library files are placed correctly, MAKELIB will abort and the message

    Aborted! Library is current

will appear. It indicates that all files are current, and the library need not be recreated. To test your configuration further, enter

    ERASE F_AEDBAR.OBJ

followed by

    MAKELIB DEVELOP

to restart the process.

This time, the source program for the AEDBAR function (F_AEDBAR.PRG) is recompiled, and the Developer's Library is updated. Since only one module is involved. the process takes just a few seconds. A new copy of the Developer's Library is generated in \CLIPPER5\LIB. MAKELIB displays it using a standard DIR command to indicate that the operation succeeded.

Error Handling

MAKELIB aborts immediately with a message if an error occurs during compilation or assembly. After correcting the error, you must restart it. The library file is not created or updated until all necessary object files are compiled or assembled successfully.

When an error occurs, the name of the file that caused it is displayed. The library manager response file is not created, and the temporary file list is not updated. Thus, the list contains the names of all new object files up to but not including the one that caused the error. This ensures that the library is updated with all changes or additions even if the process is aborted several times by errors.

After the error is corrected, MAKELIB is started again. Files that have already been compiled are not recompiled. If no new errors occur, MAKELIB creates the library and erases the temporary files.

For this to work, LIB_LIST.TXT must not be erased manually. If you inadvertently do so before the library is successfully created, recompiled modules are not updated. To recover, you must delete DEVELOP.LIB and start over. MAKELIB will then recreate the entire library. Although this may take some time, it ensures that the library is current. Under normal conditions, MAKELIB controls the process completely and requires no operator interaction except correction of source code errors in new or modified files.

Changing the Developer's Library

You should test modified or new functions before including them in the library. Testing is much easier outside a library than inside it.

The best approach is to copy the source file containing the function to your working directory. After modifying it, recompile it and link it to your application directly. To do this, specify the modified function as an object file during linking. It will take precedence over the one in the library. Note that your working directory should not be the one containing the library source code.

For example, suppose you want to modify the PICKIT function and your normal link line is

```
RTLINK FI appname LIB DEVELOP
```

Copy F_PICKIT.PRG to your working directory. After modifying and recompiling it, link it directly by changing the link line to

```
RTLINK FI appname, f_pickit LIB DEVELOP
```

You can then change PICKIT without changing the library or affecting the original source code. If you decide to abandon the changes, you need only restore the original link line.

To keep the changes, move the revised program file to the library directory and update the library by entering

```
MAKELIB DEVELOP
```

To link the revised function to your application, restore the link line to its original form and relink.

You can add new functions similarly. Write them and link them directly to your application as described above. When they are working as desired, move them to the library directory, add them to the dependency list in DEVELOP.RMK, and regenerate the library.

Use the switches shown in DEVELOP.RMK when compiling library functions.

Overlaying the Library

This section is included for users of third-party linkers that allow overlaying of non-Clipper code. It does not apply if you are using the RTLink linker provided with Clipper.

The Developer's Library contains both assembly language and Clipper functions. If you link with BLINKER or WARPLINK, you can overlay nearly all of it. Doing this reduces memory usage significantly.

All functions in the Developer's Library can be overlaid dynamically except those in the file INT24.ASM. It contains the functions GETINT24, INT24, and SETINT24 that handle critical DOS errors. Since the application does not know when an error might occur, the INT24 module must be in memory at all times and cannot be overlaid. It must always be in the root section of the EXE file.

To overlay the Developer's Library, you must delete the INT24 object module from it. Do this using LIB.EXE in the interactive mode with the following commands:

```
CD \CLIPPER5\LIB
LIB DEVELOP
-INT24;
```

After removing INT24, follow the instructions in the linker manual to overlay the rest of the Developer's Library. To use the INT24 function set in an application, specify it to the linker as a file outside all overlay areas.

```
; *************************************************************
; DEVELOP.MAC
; *************************************************************
;
; Assembly language macros for the Developer's Library.
;
; Copyright(c) 1991 -- James Occhiogrosso
;
;
; To use this file, include it by placing the directive
;
;       INCLUDE DEVELOP.MAC
;
; at the top of your assembly language source file.
;
;
; ---------------------------------------------------------------
PUSH_REGS MACRO         ; Save Clipper stack/return address
; ---------------------------------------------------------------
          PUSH      BP
          MOV       BP,SP
          PUSH      DS
          PUSH      ES
          PUSH      SI
          PUSH      DI
          ENDM

; ---------------------------------------------------------------
POP_REGS MACRO          ; Restore Clipper stack/return address
; ---------------------------------------------------------------
          POP       DI
          POP       SI
          POP       ES
          POP       DS
          POP       BP
          ENDM

; ---------------------------------------------------------------
RET_LOGIC MACRO         ; Returns a logic value
; ---------------------------------------------------------------
          PUSH      AX              ; Put return value on stack
          CALL      __RETL          ; Call - return logic function
          ADD       SP, 2           ; Clean up stack
          RET                       ; Actual return
          ENDM

; ---------------------------------------------------------------
RET_LONG MACRO          ; Returns a LONG integer value
; ---------------------------------------------------------------
          PUSH      DX              ; Put return value on stack
          PUSH      AX              ;   as DX:AX (32 bit) long number
          CALL      __RETNL         ; Call - return long number function
          ADD       SP, 4           ; Clean up stack
          RET                       ; Actual return
          ENDM
```

```
; ----------------------------------------------------------------
RET_NONE MACRO              ; Returns to Clipper with no value passed
; ----------------------------------------------------------------
        CALL    __RET       ; Call - return nothing function
        RET                 ; Actual return
        ENDM

; ----------------------------------------------------------------
RET_INT MACRO               ; Returns a numeric integer
; ----------------------------------------------------------------
        PUSH    AX          ; Place value on stack
        CALL    __RETNI     ; Call - return integer function
        ADD     SP,2        ; Clean up stack
        RET
        ENDM

; ----------------------------------------------------------------
RET_DATE MACRO REG1, REG2   ; Returns a date string
; ----------------------------------------------------------------
        PUSH    REG1        ; Place segment address on stack
        PUSH    REG2        ; Place offset address on stack
        CALL    __RETDS     ; Call - return date function
        ADD     SP,4        ; Clean up stack
        RET
        ENDM

; ----------------------------------------------------------------
RET_STRING MACRO REG1, REG2 ; Returns a character string
; ----------------------------------------------------------------
        PUSH    REG1        ; Place segment address on stack
        PUSH    REG2        ; Place offset address on stack
        CALL    __RETC      ; Call - return character function
        ADD     SP,4        ; Clean up stack
        RET
        ENDM

; ----------------------------------------------------------------
P_COUNT MACRO               ; Returns number of passed parameters in AX
; ----------------------------------------------------------------
        MOV     AX, 0       ; Request number of parameters
        PUSH    AX          ; Place value on stack
        CALL    __PARINFO   ; Call - parameter info function
        ADD     SP, 2       ; Clean up stack
        ENDM

; ----------------------------------------------------------------
P_TYPE MACRO par_num        ; Get value for parameter type to AX
; ----------------------------------------------------------------
        MOV     AX, par_num ; Request parameter information
        PUSH    AX          ; Place value on stack
        CALL    __PARINFO   ; Return it in AX
        ADD     SP, 2       ; Clean up stack
        ENDM
```

```
;   ------------------------------------------------------------
GET_PARNI MACRO par_num    ; Place numeric integer parameter in AX
;   ------------------------------------------------------------
        MOV     AX, par_num     ; Parameter number
        PUSH    AX              ; Place value on stack
        CALL    __PARNI         ; Return its value in AX
        ADD     SP, 2           ; Clean up stack
        ENDM

;   ------------------------------------------------------------
GET_PARL MACRO par_num     ; Place logical value in AX (1 or 0)
;   ------------------------------------------------------------
        MOV     AX, par_num     ; Parameter number
        PUSH    AX              ; Place value on stack
        CALL    __PARL          ; Return its value in AX
        ADD     SP, 2           ; Clean up stack
        ENDM

;   ------------------------------------------------------------
GET_PARC MACRO par_num     ; Place string pointer in DX:AX
;   ------------------------------------------------------------
        MOV     AX, par_num     ; Parameter number
        PUSH    AX              ; Place value on stack
        CALL    __PARC          ; Return pointer in DX:AX
        ADD     SP, 2           ; Clean up stack
        ENDM

;   ------------------------------------------------------------
GET_PARDS MACRO par_num    ; Place date pointer in DX:AX (YYYYMMDD)
;   ------------------------------------------------------------
        MOV     AX, par_num     ; Parameter number
        PUSH    AX              ; Place value on stack
        CALL    __PARDS         ; Return pointer in DX:AX
        ADD     SP, 2           ; Clean up stack
        ENDM
```

```
// ----------------------------------------------------------------
// DEVELOP.RMK
// ----------------------------------------------------------------
//
// Description file used with MAKELIB.BAT and RMAKE.EXE
// to regenerate the Developer's Library
//
// Copyright(c) 1991 -- James Occhiogrosso
//
// Syntax:
// -------
// MAKELIB develop
//
// Discussion:
// -----------
// DEVELOP.RMK is called by MAKELIB.BAT to compile source files
// for the Developer's Library.  On any error, it aborts without
// altering the library.
//
// The following files contain multiple functions:
//
// File Name         Contains Functions
//
// DIAL.ASM          DIAL, DIALCLR
// F_MVARS.PRG       CLRVARS, EQUVARS, FREEVARS, INITVARS, REPLVARS
// INT24.ASM         GETINT24, INT24, SETINT24,
// F_SHADOW.PRG      CLRSHADOW, SHADOW,
// F_SCRNS.PRG       SCRNCLR, SCRNLOAD, SCRNPOP, SCRNPUSH, SCRNWRIT
// F_GETS.PRG        RESTGETS, SAVEGETS,
//
// Clipper inference rule

.PRG.OBJ:
    CLIPPER $* /a /m /n /q /v
    ECHO -+$*& > LIB_LIST.TXT

// Assembly language inference rule
.ASM.OBJ:
    ECHO Assembling $*.ASM
    MASM $*;
    ECHO -+$*& > LIB_LIST.TXT

// Compile F_MVARS.PRG without automatic variable declaration
F_MVARS.OBJ : F_MVARS.PRG
    CLIPPER F_MVARS /m /n /q /v
    ECHO -+$*& > LIB_LIST.TXT

// Developer's Library - Clipper module dependencies
F_ADDREC.OBJ    :   F_ADDREC.PRG
F_AEDBAR.OBJ    :   F_AEDBAR.PRG
F_AEDMSG.OBJ    :   F_AEDMSG.PRG
F_ALLTRU.OBJ    :   F_ALLTRU.PRG
F_ARREAD.OBJ    :   F_ARREAD.PRG
F_ARREST.OBJ    :   F_ARREST.PRG
F_ARSAVE.OBJ    :   F_ARSAVE.PRG
```

```
F_ARTYPE.OBJ   :   F_ARTYPE.PRG
F_ARVIEW.OBJ   :   F_ARVIEW.PRG
F_ARWRIT.OBJ   :   F_ARWRIT.PRG
F_BACKCH.OBJ   :   F_BACKCH.PRG
F_CAPFIR.OBJ   :   F_CAPFIR.PRG
F_CHKSTA.OBJ   :   F_CHKSTA.PRG
F_CHKZIP.OBJ   :   F_CHKZIP.PRG
F_CENTON.OBJ   :   F_CENTON.PRG
F_CHKKEY.OBJ   :   F_CHKKEY.PRG
F_COMPUT.OBJ   :   F_COMPUT.PRG
F_CSRINS.OBJ   :   F_CSRINS.PRG
F_DAYNUM.OBJ   :   F_DAYNUM.PRG
F_DBVIEW.OBJ   :   F_DBVIEW.PRG
F_DBNAME.OBJ   :   F_DBNAME.PRG
F_DECODE.OBJ   :   F_DECODE.PRG
F_DELREC.OBJ   :   F_DELREC.PRG
F_DEVEL.OBJ    :   F_DEVEL.PRG
F_DONBEP.OBJ   :   F_DONBEP.PRG
F_DSKTST.OBJ   :   F_DSKTST.PRG
F_DTOF.OBJ     :   F_DTOF.PRG
F_DTOL.OBJ     :   F_DTOL.PRG
F_ENCODE.OBJ   :   F_ENCODE.PRG
F_ERRBEP.OBJ   :   F_ERRBEP.PRG
F_FISIZE.OBJ   :   F_FISIZE.PRG
F_FITOUC.OBJ   :   F_FITOUC.PRG
F_FREADL.OBJ   :   F_FREADL.PRG
F_GETS.OBJ     :   F_GETS.PRG
F_GRCHAR.OBJ   :   F_GRCHAR.PRG
F_GRID.OBJ     :   F_GRID.PRG
F_HRULER.OBJ   :   F_HRULER.PRG
F_INITGL.OBJ   :   F_INITGL.PRG
F_ISLAST.OBJ   :   F_ISLAST.PRG
F_ISMEMO.OBJ   :   F_ISMEMO.PRG
F_KEYCOD.OBJ   :   F_KEYCOD.PRG
F_LASTDA.OBJ   :   F_LASTDA.PRG
F_MAKEDB.OBJ   :   F_MAKEDB.PRG
F_MAKEND.OBJ   :   F_MAKEND.PRG
F_MAKEID.OBJ   :   F_MAKEID.PRG
F_MMOCTL.OBJ   :   F_MMOCTL.PRG
F_MMOGET.OBJ   :   F_MMOGET.PRG
F_MMOFND.OBJ   :   F_MMOFND.PRG
F_MMOVEW.OBJ   :   F_MMOVEW.PRG
F_MMOPAC.OBJ   :   F_MMOPAC.PRG
F_MVARS.OBJ    :   F_MVARS.PRG
F_NDXCNT.OBJ   :   F_NDXCNT.PRG
F_NDXKEY.OBJ   :   F_NDXKEY.PRG
F_NDXVEW.OBJ   :   F_NDXVEW.PRG
F_NODUPL.OBJ   :   F_NODUPL.PRG
F_OPCONF.OBJ   :   F_OPCONF.PRG
F_PARSE.OBJ    :   F_PARSE.PRG
F_PASSWD.OBJ   :   F_PASSWD.PRG
F_PAUSE.OBJ    :   F_PAUSE.PRG
F_PICKIT.OBJ   :   F_PICKIT.PRG
F_PRNCHK.OBJ   :   F_PRNCHK.PRG
F_PRNDAT.OBJ   :   F_PRNDAT.PRG
```

```
F_PRNTIM.OBJ    :    F_PRNTIM.PRG
F_READAB.OBJ    :    F_READAB.PRG
F_READTX.OBJ    :    F_READTX.PRG
F_REQDAT.OBJ    :    F_REQDAT.PRG
F_SCNKEY.OBJ    :    F_SCNKEY.PRG
F_SCRNAT.OBJ    :    F_SCRNAT.PRG
F_SCRNS.OBJ     :    F_SCRNS.PRG
F_SCRRES.OBJ    :    F_SCRRES.PRG
F_SCRSAV.OBJ    :    F_SCRSAV.PRG
F_SELVAL.OBJ    :    F_SELVAL.PRG
F_SHADOW.OBJ    :    F_SHADOW.PRG
F_SIGNON.OBJ    :    F_SIGNON.PRG
F_STATE.OBJ     :    F_STATE.PRG
F_STREXP.OBJ    :    F_STREXP.PRG
F_SWAPCO.OBJ    :    F_SWAPCO.PRG
F_SYSHLP.OBJ    :    F_SYSHLP.PRG
F_SYSSAV.OBJ    :    F_SYSSAV.PRG
F_SYSVER.OBJ    :    F_SYSVER.PRG
F_TEMPFI.OBJ    :    F_TEMPFI.PRG
F_VRULER.OBJ    :    F_VRULER.PRG

// Developer's Library - Assembly module dependencies

DEFDRIVE.OBJ    :    DEFDRIVE.ASM
DIAL.OBJ        :    DIAL.ASM
DISKSIZE.OBJ    :    DISKSIZE.ASM
FILEDATE.OBJ    :    FILEDATE.ASM
FILETIME.OBJ    :    FILETIME.ASM
FULLKEY.OBJ     :    FULLKEY.ASM
INT24.OBJ       :    INT24.ASM
LASTDRIV.OBJ    :    LASTDRIV.ASM
```

```
*******************************************************************
* Developer's Library keys include file   ------------ DL_KEYS.CH
*******************************************************************
*
#define K_ZERO          48
#define K_ONE           49
#define K_TWO           50
#define K_THREE         51
#define K_FOUR          52
#define K_FIVE          53
#define K_SIX           54
#define K_SEVEN         55
#define K_EIGHT         56
#define K_NINE          57

#define K_STAR          42
#define K_PLUS          43
#define K_MINUS         45
#define K_PERIOD        46

#define K_CTRL_UP       397
#define K_CTRL_DOWN     401
#define K_CTRL_ENTER    10

#define K_SPACE         32
```

```
:***************************************************************
: MAKELIB.BAT
:***************************************************************
:
: Batch file used to create or update a library
:
: Copyright(c) 1991 -- James Occhiogrosso
:
: Syntax:
: -------
: MAKELIB Makefile
:
: "Makefile" is an RMAKE utility description file for the library
: you want to create or update. It must have the same name as
: the library and an extension of RMK.  Enter it without any
: extension.
:
: Notes:
: ------
: MAKELIB assumes the target library is in the default directory
: \CLIPPER5\LIB. To change this, change all references to it in
: the code below to the desired directory.
:
: If you are using a DOS version prior to 3.30, remove the "@"
: symbol in the ECHO line below.

@ECHO OFF
IF %1!==! GOTO SYNTAX
IF NOT EXIST %1.RMK GOTO MAKFILE

: Delete old library response file if present

IF EXIST LIB_RESP.TXT DEL LIB_RESP.TXT

: Check for existence of library file

IF EXIST \CLIPPER5\LIB\%1.LIB GOTO MAKEIT
ECHO ^G
ECHO Library file \CLIPPER5\LIB\%1.LIB does not exist.
ECHO Press Ctrl-C to abort, or any key to create the library.
ECHO .
PAUSE NUL
DEL *.OBJ

:MAKEIT

: Compile all changed PRG and ASM files

ECHO .
ECHO . CREATING \CLIPPER5\LIB\%1.LIB
ECHO .
RMAKE %1.RMK
ECHO .

: Abort on any error or if a file list was not created
```

```
IF ERRORLEVEL=1 GOTO ERROR
IF NOT EXIST LIB_LIST.TXT GOTO CURRENT

: Otherwise, create response file

ECHO \CLIPPER5\LIB\%1.LIB  LIB_RESP.TXT
IF NOT EXIST \CLIPPER5\LIB\%1.LIB ECHO Y > LIB_RESP.TXT
TYPE LIB_LIST.TXT > LIB_RESP.TXT
ECHO ;: > LIB_RESP.TXT

: And generate library

LIB @LIB_RESP.TXT
DIR \CLIPPER5\LIB\%1.LIB
:
: If you have a RAM disk, you should copy the library to it
: to speed linking. The COPY below assumes drive E is a
: RAM disk. Remove or change it if your RAM disk is different
: or you are not using one.

COPY \CLIPPER5\LIB\%1.LIB E:   NUL

: Delete all temporary files and exit
:
IF EXIST LIB_LIST.TXT DEL LIB_LIST.TXT
IF EXIST LIB_RESP.TXT DEL LIB_RESP.TXT
IF EXIST \CLIPPER5\LIB\%1.BAK DEL \CLIPPER5\LIB\%1.BAK
GOTO END

: ---------------------------------------------------------------
: MAKELIB --- Error messages
: ---------------------------------------------------------------
:
:ERROR

ECHO   Aborted! Error with above file
GOTO END


:SYNTAX

ECHO   Aborted!   Correct SYNTAX is ..... MAKELIB libname
ECHO              Do not enter extension. Default is LIB
GOTO END

:CURRENT
:
ECHO   Aborted!   Library is current.
GOTO END

:MAKFILE
:
ECHO   Aborted!   %1.RMK file missing.
GOTO END
```

```
:END
:
: Sound bell and quit

ECHO ^G
ECHO .
```

Appendix C

File and Function Tables

Assembly language modules are marked with asterisks and have an ASM extension. All others are Clipper modules with a PRG extension.

Table C-1. Functions, File Names, and References

Function	File Name	Referenced by
ADDRECORD	F_ADDREC	
AEDBAR	F_AEDBAR	
AEDMSG	F_AEDMSG	AEDBAR, CHKSTATE, CHKZIP, DBVIEW, MEMOCTRL, MEMOGET, NODUPL, READABORT, REQDDATA
ALLTRUE	F_ALLTRU	
ARREAD	F_ARREAD	
ARRESTORE	F_ARREST	SCRNLOAD
ARSAVE	F_ARSAVE	SCRNWRIT
ARTYPE	F_ARTYPE	ARWRITE, PICKIT
ARVIEW	F_ARVIEW	DEVELOP
ARWRITE	F_ARWRIT	
BACKCHAR	F_BACKCH	
CAPFIRST	F_CAPFIR	

Appendix C

Function	File Name	Referenced by
CENTERON	F_CENTON	MEMOCTRL, PRNCHECK, READABORT, SELVALUE, SIGNON, SYSHELP, SYSSAVE
CHKKEY	F_CHKKEY	
CHKSTATE	F_CHKSTA	
CHKZIP	F_CHKZIP	
CLRSHADOW	F_SHADOW	
CLRVARS	F_MVARS	SELVALUE
COMPUTE	F_COMPUT	
CSRINSERT	F_CSRINS	MEMOCTRL, MEMOVIEW
DAYNUM	F_DAYNUM	
DBNAMES	F_DBNAME	
DBVIEW	F_DBVIEW	
DECODE	F_DECODE	PASSWORD
* DEFDRIVE	DEFDRIVE	
DELRECORD	F_DELREC	
DEVELOP	F_DEVEL	
* DIAL	DIAL	
* DIALCLR	DIAL	
* DISKSIZE	DISKSIZE	SYSSAVE
DISKTEST	F_DSKTST	
DONEBEEP	F_DONBEP	SYSSAVE
DTOF	F_DTOF	
DTOL	F_DTOL	
ENCODE	F_ENCODE	
EQUVARS	F_MVARS	
ERRORBEEP	F_ERRBEP	CHKSTATE, CHKZIP, DBVIEW, NODUPL, OPCONFIRM, REQDDATA, SYSHELP
* FILEDATE	FILEDATE	SYSSAVE, SYSVERSION
FILESIZE	F_FISIZE	SYSSAVE, SYSVERSION
* FILETIME	FILETIME	SYSSAVE, SYSVERSION

Clipper Developer's Library

Function	File Name	Referenced by
FILETOUCH	F_FITOUC	
FREADLINE	F_FREADL	ARREAD, DBNAMES, MAKEDBF, MAKENDX, READTEXT
FREEVARS	F_MVARS	
* FULLKEY	FULLKEY	SCANKEY
* GETINT24	INT24	DISKTEST, SYSSAVE
GRAPHCHAR	F_GRCHAR	
GRID	F_GRID	DEVELOP
HRULER	F_HRULER	DEVELOP, VRULER
INITGLOBAL	F_INITGL	
INITVARS	F_MVARS	
* INT24	INT24	
ISLASTDAY	F_ISLAST	
ISMEMO	F_ISMEMO	DBNAMES, MAKEDBF
KEYCODE	F_KEYCOD	DEVELOP
LASTDAY	F_LASTDA	DAYNUM, DTOL, ISLAST
* LASTDRIVE	LASTDRIV	
MAKEDBF	F_MAKEDB	
MAKEID	F_MAKEID	
MAKENDX	F_MAKEND	MAKEDBF
MEMOCTRL	F_MMOCTL	MEMOVIEW
MEMOFIND	F_MMOFND	
MEMOGET	F_MMOGET	
MEMOPACK	F_MMOPAC	MAKEDBF
MEMOVIEW	F_MMOVEW	MEMOGET
NDXCOUNT	F_NDXCNT	ADDRECORD
NDXKEY	F_NDXKEY	NDXVIEW
NDXVIEW	F_NDXVEW	DEVELOP
NODUPL	F_NODUPL	
OPCONFIRM	F_OPCONF	MEMOCTRL, NODUPL, READABORT, SYSSAVE

Function	File Name	Referenced by
PARSE	F_PARSE	CAPFIRST, DBNAMES, MAKEDBF, MAKENDX, MEMOFIND
PASSWORD	F_PASSWD	
PAUSE	F_PAUSE	PRNCHECK, SIGNON, SYSSAVE
PICKIT	F_PICKIT	
PRNCHECK	F_PRNCHK	
PRNTDATE	F_PRNDAT	
PRNTTIME	F_PRNTIM	
READABORT	F_READAB	
READTEXT	F_READTX	
REPLVARS	F_MVARS	
REQDDATA	F_REQDAT	MAKEID
RESTGETS	F_GETS	
SAVEGETS	F_GETS	
SCANKEY	F_SCNKEY	KEYCODE
SCRNATTR	F_SCRNAT	
SCRNCLR	F_SCRNS	
SCRNLOAD	F_SCRNS	
SCRNPOP	F_SCRNS	
SCRNPUSH	F_SCRNS	
SCRNREST	F_SCRRES	ARVIEW, GRAPHCHAR, GRID, HRULER, MEMOCTRL, MEMOVIEW, NDXVIEW, PICKIT, PRNCHECK, READABORT, READTEXT, SCRNPOP, SHADOW, SYSHELP, SYSSAVE, VRULER
SCRNSAVE	F_SCRSAV	ARVIEW, GRAPHCHAR, GRID, HRULER, MEMOCTRL, MEMOVIEW, NDXVIEW, PICKIT, PRNCHECK, READABORT, READTEXT, SCRNPUSH, SHADOW, SYSHELP, SYSSAVE, VRULER
SCRNWRIT	F_SCRNS	
SELVALUE	F_SELVAL	
* SETINT24	INT24	DISKTEST, SYSSAVE

Clipper Developer's Library

Function	File Name	Referenced by
SHADOW	F_SHADOW	
SIGNON	F_SIGNON	
STATENAME	F_STATE	
STREXPAND	F_STREXP	
SWAPCOLOR	F_SWAPCO	MAKEID, PASSWORD, SELVALUE
SYSHELP	F_SYSHLP	
SYSSAVE	F_SYSSAV	
SYSVERSION	F_SYSVER	
TEMPFILE	F_TEMPFI	DISKTEST, MEMOPACK, SELVALUE
VRULER	F_VRULER	DEVELOP, HRULER

* Indicates assembly language module

Table C-2. File Names and Public Functions

File Name	Public Functions	Also Links Library Functions
* DEFDRIVE	DEFDRIVE	
* DIAL	DIAL, DIALCLR	
* DISKSIZE	DISKSIZE	
F_ADDREC	ADDRECORD	NDXCOUNT
F_AEDBAR	AEDBAR	
F_AEDMSG	AEDMSG	
F_ALLTRU	ALLTRUE	
F_ARREAD	ARREAD	FREADLINE
F_ARREST	ARRESTORE	
F_ARSAVE	ARSAVE	
F_ARTYPE	ARTYPE	
F_ARVIEW	ARVIEW	SCRNREST, SCRNSAVE
F_ARWRIT	ARWRITE	ARTYPE
F_BACKCH	BACKCHAR	
F_CAPFIR	CAPFIRST	PARSE
F_CENTON	CENTERON	

File Name	Public Functions	Also Links Library Functions
F_CHKKEY	CHKKEY	
F_CHKSTA	CHKSTATE	AEDMSG, ERRORBEEP
F_CHKZIP	CHKZIP	AEDMSG, ERRORBEEP
F_COMPUT	COMPUTE	
F_CSRINS	CSRINSERT	
F_DAYNUM	DAYNUM	LASTDAY
F_DBNAME	DBNAMES	FREADLINE, ISMEMO, PARSE
F_DBVIEW	DBVIEW	AEDMSG, ERRORBEEP
F_DECODE	DECODE	
F_DELREC	DELRECORD	
F_DEVEL	DEVELOP	ARVIEW, GRID, HRULER, KEYCODE, NDXVIEW, VRULER
F_DONBEP	DONEBEEP	
F_DSKTST	DISKTEST	GETINT24, SETINT24, TEMPFILE
F_DTOF	DTOF	DTOL, LASTDAY
F_ENCODE	ENCODE	
F_ERRBEP	ERRORBEEP	
F_FISIZE	FILESIZE	
F_FITOUC	FILETOUCH	
F_FREADL	FREADLINE	
F_GETS	RESTGETS, SAVEGETS	
F_GRCHAR	GRAPHCHAR	SCRNREST, SCRNSAVE
F_GRID	GRID	SCRNREST, SCRNSAVE
F_HRULER	HRULER	SCRNREST, SCRNSAVE, VRULER
F_INITGL	INITGLOBAL	
F_ISLAST	ISLASTDAY	LASTDAY
F_ISMEMO	ISMEMO	
F_KEYCOD	KEYCODE	SCANKEY
F_LASTDA	LASTDAY	

Clipper Developer's Library

File Name	Public Functions	Also Links Library Functions
F_MAKEDB	MAKEDBF	FREADLINE, ISMEMO, MAKENDX, MEMOPACK, PARSE
F_MAKEID	MAKEID	REQDDATA, SWAPCOLOR
F_MAKEND	MAKENDX	FREADLINE, PARSE
F_MMOCTL	MEMOCTRL	AEDMSG, CENTERON, CSRINSERT, LASTKEY, OPCONFIRM, SCRNREST, SCRNSAVE
F_MMOFND	MEMOFIND	PARSE
F_MMOGET	MEMOGET	AEDMSG, MEMOVIEW
F_MMOPAC	MEMOPACK	TEMPFILE
F_MMOVEW	MEMOVIEW	CSRINSERT, MEMOCTRL, SCRNREST, SCRNSAVE
F_MVARS	CLRVARS, EQUVARS, FREEVARS, INITVARS, REPLVARS	
F_NDXCNT	NDXCOUNT	
F_NDXKEY	NDXKEY	
F_NDXVEW	NDXVIEW	NDXKEY, SCRNREST, SCRNSAVE
F_NODUPL	NODUPL	AEDMSG, ERRORBEEP, OPCONFIRM
F_OPCONF	OPCONFIRM	ERRORBEEP
F_PARSE	PARSE	
F_PASSWD	PASSWORD	DECODE, SWAPCOLOR
F_PAUSE	PAUSE	
F_PICKIT	PICKIT	ARTYPE, SCRNREST, SCRNSAVE
F_PRNCHK	PRNCHECK	PAUSE, SCRNREST, SCRNSAVE
F_PRNDAT	PRNTDATE	
F_PRNTIM	PRNTTIME	
F_READAB	READABORT	AEDMSG, CENTERON, OPCONFIRM, SCRNREST, SCRNSAVE
F_READTX	READTEXT	FREADLINE, SCRNREST, SCRNSAVE
F_REQDAT	REQDDATA	ERRORBEEP
F_SCNKEY	SCANKEY	FULLKEY

Appendix C

File Name	Public Functions	Also Links Library Functions
F_SCRNAT	SCRNATTR	
F_SCRNS	SCRNCLR, SCRNLOAD, SCRNPOP, SCRNPUSH, SCRNWRIT	ARRESTORE, ARSAVE, SCRNREST, SCRNSAVE
F_SCRRES	SCRNREST	
F_SCRSAV	SCRNSAVE	
F_SELVAL	SELVALUE	
F_SHADOW	CLRSHADOW, SHADOW	SCRNREST, SCRNSAVE
F_SIGNON	SIGNON	CENTERON, PAUSE
F_STATE	STATENAME	
F_STREXP	STREXPAND	
F_SWAPCO	SWAPCOLOR	
F_SYSHLP	SYSHELP	CENTERON, ERRORBEEP, SCRNREST, SCRNSAVE
F_SYSSAV	SYSSAVE	CENTERON, DISKSIZE, DISKSPACE, DONEBEEP, FILEDATE, FILESIZE, FILETIME, GETINT24, OPCONFIRM, PAUSE, SCRNREST, SCRNSAVE, SETINT24
F_SYSVER	SYSVERSION	FILEDATE, FILESIZE, FILETIME
F_TEMPFI	TEMPFILE	
F_VRULER	VRULER	HRULER, SCRNREST, SCRNSAVE
* FILEDATE	FILEDATE	
* FILETIME	FILETIME	
* FULLKEY	FULLKEY	
* INT24	GETINT24, INT24	
	SETINT24	
* LASTDRIV	LASTDRIVE	

* Indicates assembly language module

Clipper Developer's Library

Table C-3. Files Provided with the Developer's Library

Library and general information (3 files)

DEVELOP.LIB	Developer's Library
READ.ME	Last minute information MUST READ THIS
ZIPS.DBF	Zip code database

Demonstration programs and databases (23 files)

CUSTOMER.DBF	ORDERS.DBF	T_DIAL.PRG	T_MMOGET.PRG
CUSTOMER.NTX	ORDERS.NTX	T_DISKS.PRG	T_SCRNS.PRG
ITFILE.DBF	T_AEDBAR.PRG	T_FILES.PRG	T_SELVAL.PRG
ITFILE.DBT	T_CHKKEY.PRG	T_GETS.PRG	T_SYSSAV.PRG
ITFILE1.NTX	T_COMPUT.PRG	T_MAKEND.PRG	TESTDICT.DAT
ITFILE2.NTX	T_DBVIEW.PRG	T_MMOFND.PRG	

Clipper source programs (82 files)

F_ADDREC.PRG	F_DECODE.PRG	F_MAKEDB.PRG	F_PRNTIM.PRG
F_AEDBAR.PRG	F_DELREC.PRG	F_MAKEID.PRG	F_READAB.PRG
F_AEDMSG.PRG	F_DEVEL.PRG	F_MAKEND.PRG	F_READTX.PRG
F_ALLTRU.PRG	F_DONBEP.PRG	F_MMOCTL.PRG	F_REQDAT.PRG
F_ARREAD.PRG	F_DSKTST.PRG	F_MMOFND.PRG	F_SCNKEY.PRG
F_ARREST.PRG	F_DTOF.PRG	F_MMOGET.PRG	F_SCRNAT.PRG
F_ARSAVE.PRG	F_DTOL.PRG	F_MMOPAC.PRG	F_SCRNS.PRG
F_ARTYPE.PRG	F_ENCODE.PRG	F_MMOVEW.PRG	F_SCRRES.PRG
F_ARVIEW.PRG	F_ERRBEP.PRG	F_MVARS.PRG	F_SCRSAV.PRG
F_ARWRIT.PRG	F_FISIZE.PRG	F_NDXCNT.PRG	F_SELVAL.PRG
F_BACKCH.PRG	F_FITOUC.PRG	F_NDXKEY.PRG	F_SHADOW.PRG
F_CAPFIR.PRG	F_FREADL.PRG	F_NDXVEW.PRG	F_SIGNON.PRG
F_CENTON.PRG	F_GETS.PRG	F_NODUPL.PRG	F_STATE.PRG
F_CHKKEY.PRG	F_GRCHAR.PRG	F_OPCONF.PRG	F_STREXP.PRG
F_CHKSTA.PRG	F_GRID.PRG	F_PARSE.PRG	F_SWAPCO.PRG

Clipper source programs (82 files)

F_CHKZIP.PRG	F_HRULER.PRG	F_PASSWD.PRG	F_SYSHLP.PRG
F_COMPUT.PRG	F_INITGL.PRG	F_PAUSE.PRG	F_SYSSAV.PRG
F_CSRINS.PRG	F_ISLAST.PRG	F_PICKIT.PRG	F_SYSVER.PRG
F_DAYNUM.PRG	F_ISMEMO.PRG	F_PRNCHK.PRG	F_TEMPFI.PRG
F_DBNAME.PRG	F_KEYCOD.PRG	F_PRNDAT.PRG	F_VRULER.PRG
F_DBVIEW.PRG	F_LASTDA.PRG		

Assembly language source programs (8 files)

DEFDRIVE.ASM	DIAL.ASM	DISKSIZE.ASM	FILEDATE.ASM
FILETIME.ASM	FULLKEY.ASM	INT24.ASM	LASTDRIV.ASM

Library regeneration (4 files)

DEVELOP.MAC	DL_KEYS.CH	DEVELOP.RMK	MAKELIB.BAT

NOTE: Object files (OBJ) are also provided for all library functions.

Bibliography

Angemeyer, J. and K. Jaeger. *MS-DOS Developer's Guide*, 2nd ed. Indianapolis, IN: Sams, 1990.

Dettmann, T. *DOS Programmer's Reference*, 2nd ed. Carmel, IN: Que, 1990.

Simrin, S. *MS-DOS Bible*. Indianapolis, IN: Sams, 1990.

Somerson, P. *PC-DOS Power Tools*, 2nd ed. New York: Bantam, 1990.

Spence, R. *Clipper Programming Guide*, 3rd ed. San Marcos, CA: Microtrend Books, 1992.

Wyatt, A. *Using Assembly Language*, 2nd ed. Carmel, IN: Que, 1990.

Trademarks

Blinker	Blink
Clipper	Nantucket
dBASE	Ashton-Tate
DOS	Microsoft
LIB	Microsoft
Lotus	Lotus Development
Macro Assembler	Microsoft
MASM	Microsoft
MS-DOS	Microsoft
Norton Guides	Symantec
PC	IBM
PKzip	PKWARE
Plink	Phoenix Technologies
RTLink	PocketSoft
Turbo Assembler	Borland International
Warplink	Hyperkinetics

Index by General Category

Application Management

AEDBAR	Single-line data entry menu bar and message window	7
DBNAMES	Extracts database names from data dictionary	109
DEFDRIVE	Determines current default drive	123
GETINT24	Gets error code from critical error handler	211
INITGLOBAL	Initializes application global memory variables	235
LASTDRIVE	Determines highest-lettered valid DOS drive	259
MAKEDBF	Creates database files from text file definitions	263
MAKENDX	Creates index files from text file definitions	285
NDXCOUNT	Determines number of active indexes for a database	327
PICKIT	Creates array of selections from list of choices	365
READTEXT	Reads text file of any size	387
RESTGETS	Restores most recently saved set of GETs for nested READs	403
SAVEGETS	Saves current set of GETs for nested READs	405
SELVALUE	Creates temporary indexed file of selected records for reports	451
SETINT24	Sets internal critical error (INT24) handler on or off	467
SIGNON	Creates application sign-on screen	477
SYSHELP	Displays help or other messages from a database	493
SYSSAVE	Complete backup and restore function	503
SYSVERSION	Detects new version of application	527
TEMPFILE	Creates unique temporary file	533

Array Manipulation

ARREAD	Reads lines of a text file into an array	31

577

Index by General Category

Array Manipulation

ARRESTORE	Restores an array from a disk file	35
ARSAVE	Saves an array in a disk file	39
ARTYPE	Determines whether all elements of an array are the same type	43
ARVIEW	Displays an array	47
ARWRITE	Saves elements of an array as lines in a text file	51

Database Operations

ADDRECORD	Adds a record by recycling	1
CLRVARS	Clears field variables created by INITVARS	91
DBVIEW	Provides key processing for a popup DBEDIT view	115
DELRECORD	Deletes a record and marks it for recycling	127
EQUVARS	Loads field variables from fields in current record	171
FREEVARS	Releases field variables created by INITVARS	203
INITVARS	Creates memory variables for fields in current database	239
NDXKEY	Determines key value from an index file	331
NDXVIEW	Displays key values of all indexes in a directory	335
REPLVARS	Replaces fields in current record from field variables	395

Data Conversion

DECODE	Decodes a string previously encoded by ENCODE	121
ENCODE	Encodes a string	167
STATENAME	Converts a two-letter abbreviation into a full state name	482
STREXPAND	Expands a string with spaces	485

Data Entry and Validation

AEDMSG	Displays window messages for AEDBAR	21
ALLTRUE	Permits any function to be used in a WHEN or VALID	27
CAPFIRST	Capitalizes first letter of each word in a string	59
CHKKEY	Confirms and optionally displays key data in a file	69
CHKSTATE	Validates state code abbreviations	75
CHKZIP	Validates Zip Code range for two-letter state abbreviation	79
COMPUTE	Displays computed values on screen during a READ	95
GRAPHCHAR	Allows easy entry of graphics characters as data	215

Data Entry and Validation

MAKEID	Creates six character ID code from a name	279
NODUPL	Checks current file for duplicate key values	341
OPCONFIRM	Gets operator Y/N response	347
PASSWORD	Gets and verifies password	355
READABORT	Tests for Esc and confirms before aborting a READ	383
REQDDATA	Forces data entry in a required field	399

Date and Time Manipulation

DAYNUM	Determines number of days from start of year	105
DTOF	Determines first day of month	159
DTOL	Determines last day of month	163
ISLASTDAY	Indicates whether a date is the last day of a month	243
LASTDAY	Determines the day number for the last day of a month	255
PRNTDATE	Converts date to a printable string	375
PRNTTIME	Returns time as AM/PM string for printing	379

Development Utilities

DEVELOP	Forces linking of development functions	131
GRID	Displays a calibrated grid on screen	227
HRULER	Displays a calibrated horizontal ruler	231
KEYCODE	Displays scan code and ASCII value for a key	251
VRULER	Displays a calibrated vertical ruler	537

Environment Control

DISKSIZE	Determines formatted size of a disk	145
DISKTEST	Tests a disk and its drive for readiness	151
PAUSE	Pauses for a specified time	361

File Operations

FILEDATE	Gets or sets date on a DOS file	179
FILESIZE	Determines size of a DOS file	185
FILETIME	Gets or sets time on a DOS file	189
FILETOUCH	Sets date/time stamp on a DOS file to system date/time	195
FREADLINE	Reads next lline from a text file	199

580 Index by General Category

Keyboard Control

CSRINSERT	Changes cursor shape from Insert key	101
FULLKEY	Returns a unique number for any key pressed	207
SCANKEY	Determines the scan and ASCII values for any key	411

Memo Handling

ISMEMO	Determines whether a database contains memo fields	247
MEMOCTRL	Generic control function for MEMOVIEW and MEMOEDIT	295
MEMOFIND	Finds text in a memo field	303
MEMOGET	Gets memo field in a READ using a trigger field	309
MEMOPACK	Packs database memo file	315
MEMOVIEW	Generic view/edit function for memos	321

Miscellaneous

DIAL	Dials a telephone number	133
DIALCLR	Disconnects modem after a successful DIAL	143
DONEBEEP	Produces a two-tone beep as a completion indicator	155
ERRORBEEP	Sounds a mildly unpleasant tone for errors	175
PARSE	Extracts a delimited word from a string	351
PRNCHECK	Checks the printer and waits if it is not ready	371

Screen Manipulation

BACKCHAR	Fills screen area with a background character	55
CENTERON	Centers text on selected line in selected color	65
CLRSHADOW	Clears a shadow around a box	87
SCRNATTR	Gets or sets screen attributes at specified coordinates	415
SCRNCLR	Clears screen stack	421
SCRNLOAD	Loads screen stack from a disk file	427
SCRNPOP	Pops a screen from the screen stack	431
SCRNPUSH	Pushes a screen onto the screen stack	435
SCRNREST	Restores a screen area with coordinates from a variable	439
SCRNSAVE	Saves a screen area with coordinates to a variable	443
SCRNWRIT	Saves screen stack in a disk file	447
SHADOW	Displays a shadow around a box	473

Screen Manipulation

SWAPCOLOR   Reverses standard and enhanced colors in a color string . . . 489

Index by Keyword

Accessories	GRID (displays ruler grid)	227
	HRULER (displays horizontal ruler)	231
	VRULER (displays vertical ruler)	537
Addresses	CHKSTATE (verifies state abbreviations)	75
	CHKZIP (verifies Zip Codes)	79
	STATENAME (determines state name)	481
Animation	SIGNON (displays sign-on screen)	477
Arrays	ARREAD (reads text file into array)	31
	ARRESTORE (restores an array from disk)	35
	ARSAVE (saves array in text file)	39
	ARTYPE (tests type of array elements)	43
	ARVIEW (viewing an array)	47
	ARWRITE (saves array in text file)	51
	PICKIT (allows selection from an array)	365
Attributes	SCRNATTR (gets/sets screen attributes)	415
Background	BACKCHAR (fills a screen area)	55
Backup	SYSSAVE (backs up and restores data files)	503
Blank entry	REQDDATA (warns about required entry)	399
Calendar	DAYNUM (day number from start of year)	105
	DTOF (determines first day of month)	159
	DTOL (determines last day of month)	163
	ISLASTDAY (recognizes last day of month)	243
	LASTDAY (determines last day of month)	255
Capitalization	CAPFIRST (capitalizes first letters)	59
Centering	CENTERON (displays centered message)	65
Clear	CLRVARS (clears field variables)	91
	SCRNCLR (clears screen stack)	421
Color	SWAPCOLOR (reverses colors)	489

583

Index by Keyword

Communications	DIAL (dials a telephone number)	133
	DIALCLR (disconnects modem)	143
Computations	COMPUTE (displays computational result)	95
Count	NDXCOUNT (counts active indexes)	327
Conversion	PRNTDATE (converts date to string)	375
	PRNTIME (converts time string)	379
	STATENAME (determines state name)	481
Create	MAKEDBF (creates databases from dictionary)	263
	MAKENDX (creates indexes from dictionary)	285
Cursor	CSRINSERT (controls cursor size)	101
Data dictionary	DBNAMES (extracts names from dictionary)	109
	MAKEDBF (creates databases from dictionary)	263
	MAKENDX (creates indexes from dictionary)	285
Data entry	GRAPHCHAR (enter graphics symbols)	215
Date	DAYNUM (day number from start of year)	105
	DTOF (determines first day of month)	159
	DTOL (determines last day of month)	163
	FILEDATE (gets/sets file date)	179
	FILETOUCH (updates date/time stamp)	195
	PRNTDATE (converts date to string)	375
Days	DAYNUM (day number from start of year)	105
	DTOF (determines first day of month)	159
	DTOL (determines last day of month)	163
	ISLASTDAY (recognizes last day of month)	243
	LASTDAY (determines last day of month)	255
Decryption	DECODE (decrypts character string)	121
Delay	PAUSE (pauses unconditionally)	361
Deletion	DELRECORD (deletes recyclable record)	127
Desk accessories	GRID (displays ruler grid)	227
	HRULER (displays horizontal ruler)	231
	VRULER (displays vertical ruler)	537
Development	ARVIEW (viewing an array)	47
	DBNAMES (extracts names from dictionary)	109
	DEVELOP (links development functions)	131
	FILETOUCH (updates file date/time stamp)	195
	KEYCODE (determines ASCII and scan values)	251
	SYSVERSION (checks if application changed)	527
Disk drives	DEFDRIVE (determines default disk drive)	123
	DISKSIZE (determines formatted capacity)	145
	DISKTEST (tests disk drive)	151

Clipper Developer's Library 585

	GETINT24 (returns internal error code)	211
	LASTDRIVE (determines highest drive letter)	259
Display	READTEXT (displays text files)	387
Duplicates	NODUPL (tests for duplicate keys)	341
Editing	MEMOVIEW (view and edit memos)	321
Encryption	DECODE (decrypts character string)	121
	ENCODE (encrypts character string)	167
Environment	DEFDRIVE (determines default disk drive)	123
	DISKSIZE (determines formatted capacity)	145
	LASTDRIVE (determines highest drive letter)	259
	SETINT24 (critical interrupt handler)	467
Error handling	ARTYPE (tests type of array elements)	43
	ERRORBEEP (produces error tone)	175
	GETINT24 (returns internal error code)	211
	REQDDATA (warns about required entry)	399
	SETINT24 (critical interrupt handler)	467
Expressions	COMPUTE (displays computational result)	95
Files	ARREAD (reads text file into array)	31
	ARRESTORE (restores an array from disk)	35
	ARSAVE (saves an array on disk)	39
	ARWRITE (saves array in text file)	51
	CHKKEY (locates key data in file)	69
	FILEDATE (gets/sets file date)	179
	FILESIZE (determines size of file)	185
	FILETIME (gets/sets file time)	189
	FILETOUCH (updates date/time stamp)	195
	FREADLINE (reads lines from text file)	199
	MEMOPACK (compacts DBT file)	315
	READTEXT (displays text files)	387
	SYSSAVE (backs up and restores data files)	504
	TEMPFILE (creates unique temporary file)	533
Free	FREEVARS (releases field variables)	203
Gather	REPLVARS (replaces fields from variables)	395
Global	INITGLOBAL (creates global variables)	235
Graphics	GRAPHCHAR (enter graphics symbols)	215
Grid	GRID (displays ruler grid)	227
Help	SYSHELP (displays help)	493
Identification code	MAKEID (creates ID code from string)	279

Index by Keyword

Indexes	NDXCOUNT (counts active indexes)	327
	NDXKEY (reads key expression)	331
	NDXVIEW (displays key expression)	335
Input/output	DISKTEST (tests disk drive)	151
	FREADLINE (reads lines from file)	199
	FULLKEY (determines ASCII and scan values)	207
	KEYCODE (determines ASCII and scan values)	251
	OPCONFIRM (waits for yes/no response)	347
	PRNCHECK (tests printer)	371
	SCANKEY (determines ASCII and scan values)	411
Interrupts	GETINT24 (returns error code)	211
	SETINT24 (critical interrupt handler)	467
Keyboard	FULLKEY (determines ASCII and scan values)	207
	GRAPHCHAR (enter graphics symbols)	215
	KEYCODE (determines ASCII and scan values)	251
	SCANKEY (determines ASCII and scan values)	411
Keys	CHKKEY (locates key data in file)	69
	MAKEID (creates ID code from string)	279
	NDXKEY (reads key expression)	331
	NDXVIEW (displays key expression)	335
	NODUPL (tests for duplicate keys)	341
Lines	FREADLINE (reads lines from file)	199
Lists	PICKIT (allows selection from an array)	365
Logical value	ALLTRUE (returns logic true)	27
	OPCONFIRM (waits for yes/no response)	347
Low-level functions	GETINT24 (returns error code)	211
	SETINT24 (critical interrupt handler)	467
Mailing lists	CHKSTATE (verifies state abbreviations)	75
	CHKZIP (verifies Zip Codes)	79
	STATENAME (determines state name)	481
Memo field	ISMEMO (tests database for memo fields)	247
	MEMOCTRL (generic control function)	295
	MEMOFIND (finds text in memo)	303
	MEMOGET (controls memo entry)	309
	MEMOPACK (compacts DBT file)	315
	MEMOVIEW (view and edit memos)	321
Memory variables	CLRVARS (clears field variables)	91
	EQUVARS (loads field variables)	171
	FREEVARS (releases field variables)	203
	INITGLOBAL (creates global variables)	235
	INITVARS (creates public variables)	239
	REPLVARS (replaces fields from variables)	395

Menus	AEDBAR (provides a menu bar)	7
	BACKCHAR (fills a screen area)	55
Messages	AEDMSG (displays a message)	21
	CENTERON (displays a centered message)	65
	DBVIEW (operator messages for DBEDIT)	115
	SYSHELP (displays help)	493
Modem	DIAL (dials a telephone number)	133
	DIALCLR (disconnects modem)	143
Month	DTOF (determines first day of month)	159
	ISLASTDAY (recognizes last day of month)	243
	LASTDAY (determines last day of month)	255
Opening screen	SIGNON (displays sign-on screen)	477
Operator interaction	AEDBAR (provides a menu bar)	7
	AEDMSG (displays a message)	21
	CENTERON (displays a centered message)	65
	DBVIEW (provides database views)	115
	DONEBEEP (produces two-tone sound)	155
	ERRORBEEP (produces error tone)	175
	MEMOCTRL (generic control function)	295
	OPCONFIRM (waits for yes/no response)	347
	PICKIT (allows selection from an array)	365
	READABORT (aborts a READ)	383
	REQDDATA (warns about required entry)	399
	RESTGETS (restores GETs from stack)	403
	SAVEGETS (saves current GETs on stack)	405
	SYSHELP (displays help)	493
Password	PASSWORD (checks password)	355
Pause	PAUSE (pauses unconditionally)	361
Pick list	PICKIT (allows selection from an array)	365
Printer	PRNCHECK (tests printer)	371
Read	READABORT (aborts a read)	383
Records	ADDRECORD (recycles a record)	1
	DELRECORD (deletes recyclable record)	127
Recycling	ADDRECORD (recycles a record)	1
	DELRECORD (deletes recyclable record)	127
Reports	DTOF (determines first day of month)	159
	DTOL (determines last day of month)	163
	SELVALUE (enter selection values)	451
Required entry	REQDDATA (warns about required entry)	399

Restore	ARRESTORE (restores array from disk)	35
	RESTGETS (restores GETs from stack)	403
	SCRNREST (restores a screen)	439
	SYSSAVE (backs up and restores data files)	503
Ruler	GRID (displays ruler grid)	227
	HRULER (displays horizontal ruler)	231
	VRULER (displays vertical ruler)	537
Save	ARSAVE (saves array on disk)	39
	SAVEGETS (saves current GETs on stack)	405
	SCRNSAVE (saves screen in memory variable)	443
	SCRNWRIT (saves screen stack on disk)	447
	SYSSAVE (backs up and restores data files)	503
Scatter	EQUVARS (loads memory variables)	171
Screens	BACKCHAR (fills a screen area)	55
	CLRSHADOW (removes shadow)	87
	CSRINSERT (controls cursor size)	101
	SCRNATTR (gets/sets screen attributes)	415
	SCRNCLR (clears screen stack)	421
	SCRNLOAD (loads screen stack from disk)	427
	SCRNPOP (restores screen from stack)	431
	SCRNPUSH (pushes screen onto stack)	435
	SCRNREST (restores screen)	439
	SCRNSAVE (saves screen in memory variable)	443
	SCRNWRIT (saves screen stack on disk)	447
	SHADOW (displays shadow)	473
	SWAPCOLOR (reverses colors)	489
Screen stack	RESTGETS (restores GETs from stack)	403
	SCRNCLR (clears screen stack)	421
	SCRNLOAD (loads screen stack from disk)	427
	SCRNPOP (restores screen from stack)	431
	SCRNPUSH (pushes screen onto stack)	435
	SCRNWRIT (saves screen stack on disk)	447
Search	CHKKEY (locates key data in file)	69
	MEMOFIND (finds text in memo field)	303
Security	DECODE (decrypts character string)	121
	ENCODE (encrypts character string)	167
	PASSWORD (checks password)	355
Selection	PICKIT (allows selection from an array)	365
	SELVALUE (enter selection values)	451
Serial port	DIAL (dials a telephone number)	133
	DIALCLR (disconnects modem)	143
Shadows	CLRSHADOW (removes shadow)	87
	SHADOW (displays shadow)	473

Sign-on	SIGNON (displays sign-on screen)	477
Size	DISKSIZE (determines size of disk)	145
	FILESIZE (determines size of file)	185
Sounds	DONEBEEP (produces two-tone sound)	155
	ERRORBEEP (produces error tone)	175
Startup	DBNAMES (extracts names from dictionary)	109
	MAKEDBF (creates databases from dictionary)	263
	MAKENDX (creates indexes from dictionary)	285
	SIGNON (displays sign-on screen)	477
	SYSVERSION (checks if application changed)	527
State abbreviations	CHKSTATE (verifies state codes)	75
	CHKZIP (verifies Zip Codes)	79
	STATENAME (determines state name)	481
String	CAPFIRST (capitalizes first letters)	59
	DECODE (decrypts character string)	121
	ENCODE (encrypts character string)	167
	MAKEID (creates ID code from string)	279
	PARSE (extracts word from string)	351
	PASSWORD (compares string to password)	355
	PRNTDATE (converts date to string)	375
	STREXPAND (expands string with spaces)	485
System date/time	FILETOUCH (updates date/time stamp)	195
Telephone	DIAL (dials a telephone number)	133
	DIALCLR (disconnects modem)	143
Temporary files	TEMPFILE (creates unique temporary file)	533
Testing	ARTYPE (tests type of array elements)	433
	DISKTEST (tests disk drive)	151
	PRNCHECK (tests printer)	371
Text files	ARREAD (reads text file into array)	31
	ARWRITE (saves array in text file)	51
	FREADLINE (reads lines from text file)	199
	READTEXT (displays text files)	387
Time	FILETIME (gets/sets file time)	189
	FILETOUCH (updates date/time stamp)	195
	PRNTTIME (converts time string)	379
True	ALLTRUE (returns logic true)	27
Type	ARTYPE (tests type of array elements)	43
Validation	ALLTRUE (returns logic true)	27
	ARTYPE (tests type of array elements)	43
	CHKKEY (locates key data in file)	69
	CHKSTATE (verifies state codes)	75

	CHKZIP (verifies Zip Codes)	79
	COMPUTE (displays computational result)	95
	DBVIEW (display items via DBEDIT)	115
	DISKTEST (tests disk drive)	151
	NODUPL (tests for duplicate keys)	341
	REQDDATA (warns about required entry)	399
Variables	CLRVARS (clears field variables)	91
	EQUVARS (loads field variables)	171
	FREEVARS (releases field variables)	203
	INITGLOBAL (creates global variables)	235
	INITVARS (creates public variables)	239
	REPLVARS (replaces fields from variables)	395
Version control	SYSVERSION (checks if application changed)	527
Viewing	ARVIEW (viewing an array)	47
	DBVIEW (provides database views)	115
	MEMOVIEW (view and edit memos)	321
	NDXVIEW (displays key expression)	335
	READTEXT (displays text files)	387
Wait	PAUSE (pauses unconditionally)	361
Windows	BACKCHAR (fills a screen area)	55
Words	CAPFIRST (capitalizes first letters)	59
	PARSE (extracts word from string)	351
Yes/no response	OPCONFIRM (waits for yes/no response)	347
Zip Codes	CHKZIP (verifies Zip Codes)	79

Reader Comments
Clipper Developer's Library, 2nd Edition

This book has been edited, the material reviewed, and the programs tested and checked for accuracy, but bugs find their way into books as well as software. Please take a few minutes to tell us if you have found any errors, and give us your general comments regarding the quality of this book. Your time and attention will help us improve this and future products.

Did you find any mistakes? _____
_____
_____

Is this book complete? (If not, what should be added?) _____
_____
_____

What do you like about this book? _____
_____
_____

What do you not like about this book? _____
_____
_____

What other books would you like to see developed? _____
_____
_____

Other comments: _____
_____
_____

To be notified about new editions of this and other books of interest, please include your name and address, and mail to:

Name _____
Address _____
City/State/Zip _____

Microtrend® Books
Slawson Communications, Inc.
165 Vallecitos de Oro
San Marcos, CA 92069-1436

The Data Based Advisor® Series
Lance A. Leventhal, Ph.D., Series Director

Clipper Programming Guide, 3rd Edition

by Rick Spence

Nantucket's Clipper compiler for dBASE programs has become one of the most popular productivity tools in the database world. This Third Edition of Rick Spence's best-seller covers the new Version 5.01 of Clipper. It includes extensive new material on linking, scoping, preprocessors, multi-dimensional arrays, color management, screen capture, word processing, data dictionaries, primary and foreign keys, referential integrity, and multiple linked relationships. It also has expanded coverage of error handling, help systems, pulldown menus, message and dialog systems, and C data structures. Even more on Clipper internals, direct file access, networking, and C programming. Contains many examples drawn from actual applications and extensive discussions of all aspects of programming.

Special features of the book are:

- ❑ Timely coverage, deals with all features of Version 5.01.
- ❑ Explains how to use Clipper on local area networks.
- ❑ Detailed examples showing the use of C with Clipper.
- ❑ Description of advanced query techniques involving multiple databases and multiple relations.
- ❑ Extensive set of utilities for viewing all types of Clipper files.

Rick Spence is currently an independent consultant specializing in database applications and Unix systems. He was a member of the Nantucket development team and a co-developer of Clipper. He is the author of the monthly "Hardcore Clipper" column in Data Based Advisor and an expert columnist in Reference (Clipper) magazine.

7 x 9, 700 pages, trade paperback, ISBN: 0-915391-68-6, $29.95
Order #MT68

Available from your favorite book or computer store, or use the order form at end of book, or telephone 1 (800) SLAWSON.

Slawson Communications • 165 Vallecitos de Oro • San Marcos, CA 92069-1436

The *Data Based Advisor*® Series
Lance A. Leventhal, Ph.D., Series Director

Designing User Interfaces

by James E. Powell

User interfaces are often the key to the success or failure of software. Today's users demand software that is easy to learn, intuitive, and efficient. Experienced program designer James E. Powell provides a thorough, common-sense approach to creating effective user interfaces. Drawing from real-world applications, he asks readers to apply design techniques and compare their results with recommended solutions. The book covers user interface fundamentals, analyzing user needs, visual design, data entry, error handling, menus, help, graphics, output, installation, tutorials, user manuals and documentation, creativity, legal issues, and future directions.

Special features of the book are:

- Example programs using the popular FoxPro database manager.
- Many practical examples and sample problems drawn from actual applications.
- Extensive discussions of seldom described topics, such as error handling, data entry design, help design, installation design, tutorial design, and considerations for handicapped users.
- Emphasis on a friendly interface with gentle tone and non-antagonistic approach.
- Descriptions of methods for creating interfaces for both beginners and experienced users.
- Thorough coverage of visual design, windowing, menus, graphical interfaces, and output design.

About the Author:

James E. Powell is a program designer with over 15 years of practical experience. He is also a contributing Editor to Puget Sound Computer User.

7 x 9, 448 pages, trade paperback, ISBN: 0-915391-40-6, $27.95, **Order # MT40**

Available from your favorite book or computer store, use the order form at the end of this book, or telephone 1 (800) SLAWSON.

Slawson Communications • 165 Vallecitos de Oro • San Marcos, CA 92069-1436

From the Lance A. Leventhal Microtrend™ Series,

A complete, one-stop reference guide to all aspects of IBM PC and PS/2 graphics.

IBM PC and PS/2 Graphics Handbook

Ed Teja and Laura Johnson

This single source will answer all your questions about what the standards are, what works with what, what features languages and operating systems offer, how to upgrade systems, what to buy for specific applications and requirements, and how to make programs run on a variety of computers. The book contains many easily referenced tables and charts for quick access and rapid comparisons of systems, hardware, programs, and standards.

Special features of the book are:

- ❑ Covers adapters, monitors, printers, standards, file formats, languages, and applications packages.

- ❑ Includes summaries, a resource list, a glossary, an acronym list, and an annotated bibliography.

- ❑ Focuses on widely used hardware and software for word processing, business graphics, presentation graphics, CAD/CAM/CAE, and desktop publishing.

- ❑ Emphasizes current and emerging standards, such as VGA, 8514/A, Multisync monitors, GKS, IGES, TIFF, Borland Graphics Interface, Microsoft Windows, and Presentation Manager.

- ❑ Describes how to identify the graphics adapter on a system and how to convert between different screen and printer aspect ratios.

Ed Teja and Laura Johnson have been writing professionally about computers and electronics since 1976. A former computer and peripherals editor for *EDN* magazine, Teja has written articles for more than 35 magazines and has published three books.

7 x 9, 480 pages, trade paperback, index ISBN 0-915391-35-X $24.95
Order number MT 35

Available from your favorite book or computer store, use the order form at the end of the book, or telephone 1 (800) SLAWSON.

Slawson Communications • 165 Vallecitos de Oro • San Marcos, CA 92069-1436

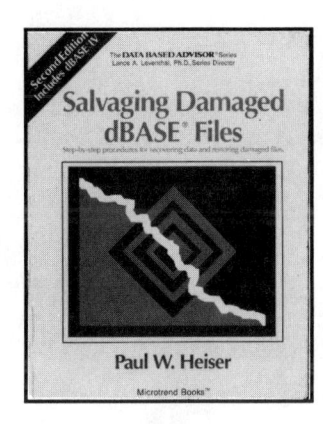

"Paul Heiser is the Peter Norton of the dBASE world, and the author of its bible."—**PC World Magazine.**

"Heiser's book is invaluable, it belongs in every dBASE office next to the first aid kit and fire extinguisher."–**Adam Green, noted author and leading dBASE authority.**

The *Data Based Advisor®* Series
Lance A. Leventhal, Ph.D., Series Director

Salvaging Damaged dBASE Files, 2nd Edition

Includes dBASE IV

by Paul W. Heiser
Foreword by David Kalman

In this new, totally revised edition, file expert Paul W. Heiser describes what can happen to your files and how to undo the damage. Heiser covers dBASE IV and describes how to use DEBUG, Norton Utilities, IBM's Disk Repair, Westlake Data's DiskMinder, Mace Software's dBFix, and his own dSALVAGE and dSALVAGE Professional.

Thousands have bought *Salvaging Damaged dBASE Files* and benefited from its many hints, tips, and tricks. Now you can overcome such problems as spurious data (including non-printing characters), extra end-of-file markers, nulls, damaged or destroyed file headers, displacement, damaged file allocation tables, and cross-linking. You can recover all or most of your data after power loss, improper disk handling, or file or format mix-ups. Heiser provides systematic procedures with step-by-step descriptions that even a beginner can follow. If you're a dBASE user whose business or professional activities depend on database information, this book is for you. Don't wait until disaster happens.

Paul W. Heiser is a well-known database authority and the author of several previous dBASE books. He has been working with dBASE products for many years in a variety of applications. His company also provides specialized software for file recovery. His dSALVAGE program received *PC World* magazine's "Best Buy" award.

7 x 9, 320 pages, trade paperback, ISBN 0-915391-33-3 $24.95
Order # MT33

Available from your favorite book or computer store, use the order form at the end of the book, or telephone 1(800) SLAWSON.

Slawson Communications • 165 Vallecitos de Oro • San Marcos, CA 92069-1436

Order Form

Thank you for purchasing this Microtrend® book. To order additional copies of this book or any of our other titles, please complete the form below, or call **1-800-SLAWSON**.

Name _____

Address _____

City/State/Zip _____

Country _____

Qty	Code #	Title	Price Each		Total
	MT68	Clipper Programming Guide, 3rd Edition	$29	95	
	MT40	Designing User Interfaces	$27	95	
	MT35	IBM PC and PS/2 Graphics Handbook	$24	95	
	MT33	Salvaging Damaged dBase Files, 2nd Edition	$24	95	

U.S. Shipping
Books are shipped UPS except when a post office box is given as delivery address.

Subtotal	
Sales Tax: CA residents add 7.75%	
Shipping Charge: $3.50 per book	
TOTAL	

Form of Payment
☐ Visa   ☐ MasterCard   ☐ Check

Card#: |_|_|_|_|_|_|_|_|_|_|_|_|_|_|_|_|

Expiration date: _____

Signature: _____ Date _____

Mail your order to:

Microtrend® Books
Slawson Communications, Inc.
165 Vallecitos de Oro
San Marcos, CA 92069-1436
619/744-2299